"In a manner analogous to the Father, Son, and Holy Spirit—who are eternally new and surprising to one another within the Holy Trinity—*New Trinitarian Ontologies* reflects the ever-renewing surprise and gift of self-creation within all reality. More than just another theological or philosophical book, this volume brings together metaphysics, ecology, and poetics within the eschatological horizon, illuminating how all things participate in the unfolding mystery of divine life."

—EDUARD FIEDLER, PALACKÝ UNIVERSITY OLOMOUC

"*New Trinitarian Ontologies* is a sumptuous feast of trinitarian speculation which includes many of the foremost Christian thinkers writing today. It is further a clarion call to return to the sources of trinitarian thought after Klaus Hemmerle's 1976 manifesto that calls on Christian thinkers to turn towards the 'distinctively Christian' triune event of love. This volume is a turning towards the newness of trinitarian love as the only viable way for Christian thinking to advance into the uncertain future."

—PHILIP JOHN PAUL GONZALES, ASSOCIATE PROFESSOR OF PHILOSOPHY, ST. MARY'S SEMINARY AND UNIVERSITY, BALTIMORE

"This superb collection of essays edited by John Milbank, Ryan Haecker, JD Lyonhart is after the various deaths triumphantly announced, such as the death of God, the death of Metaphysics, the death of the sign, and moves forward on Piero Coda's call for a new beginning of Trinitarian thought framed in term of the Word which in John's Gospel is associated with the true 'beginning.' The collection is lent authority by the major names in the volume, John Milbank, of course, but also William Desmond, Emmanuel Falque, Graham Ward, Catherine Pickstock, Judith Wolfe, among others. Yet, the real authority of the volume lies more broadly and more deeply in the essays in which the less well-known authors, across the different loci of metaphysics, eschatology, ecology, and aesthetics, perform at the level of their better-known colleagues. It is rare to have a collection in which each essay proves indispensable."

—CYRIL O'REGAN, HUSKING CHAIR OF THEOLOGY, UNIVERSITY OF NOTRE DAME

"As the long-dominant materialist worldview breaks down, there is a widespread search in the secular world for alternatives, including the recent revival of panpsychism, pantheism and idealism. Thank goodness for this new exploration of Trinitarian ontologies, which has so much to offer. The rich compilation in this volume is a very helpful starting point for those who are rediscovering and re-imagining Trinitarian traditions."

—RUPERT SHELDRAKE, AUTHOR OF *THE SCIENCE DELUSION*

New Trinitarian Ontologies

VOLUME I

VERITAS
Series Introduction

"... the truth will set you free" (John 8:32)

In much contemporary discourse, Pilate's question has been taken to mark the absolute boundary of human thought. Beyond this boundary, it is often suggested, is an intellectual hinterland into which we must not venture. This terrain is an agnosticism of thought: because truth cannot be possessed, it must not be spoken. Thus, it is argued that the defenders of "truth" in our day are often traffickers in ideology, merchants of counterfeits, or anti-liberal. They are, because it is somewhat taken for granted that Nietzsche's word is final: truth is the domain of tyranny.

Is this indeed the case, or might another vision of truth offer itself? The ancient Greeks named the love of wisdom as *philia*, or friendship. The one who would become wise, they argued, would be a "friend of truth." For both philosophy and theology might be conceived as schools in the friendship of truth, as a kind of relation. For like friendship, truth is as much discovered as it is made. If truth is then so elusive, if its domain is *terra incognita*, perhaps this is because it arrives to us—unannounced—as gift, as a person, and not some thing.

The aim of the Veritas book series is to publish incisive and original current scholarly work that inhabits "the between" and "the beyond" of theology and philosophy. These volumes will all share a common aspiration to transcend the institutional divorce in which these two disciplines often find themselves, and to engage questions of pressing concern to both philosophers and theologians in such a way as to reinvigorate both disciplines with a kind of interdisciplinary desire, often so absent in contemporary academe. In a word, these volumes represent collective efforts in the befriending of truth, doing so beyond the simulacra of pretend tolerance, the violent, yet insipid reasoning of liberalism that asks with Pilate, "What is truth?"—expecting a consensus of non-commitment; one that encourages the commodification of the mind, now sedated by the civil service of career, ministered by the frightened patrons of position.

The series will therefore consist of two wings: (1) original monographs; and (2) essay collections on a range of topics in theology and philosophy. The latter will principally be the products of the annual conferences of the Centre of Theology and Philosophy (www.theologyphilosophycentre.co.uk).

Conor Cunningham and Joseph Terry, *Veritas Series Editors*

Available from Cascade Books

Anthony D. Baker	*Diagonal Advance: Perfection in Christian Theology*
D. C. Schindler	*The Perfection of Freedom: Schiller, Schelling, and Hegel between the Ancients and the Moderns*
Rustin Brian	*Covering Up Luther: How Barth's Christology Challenged the* Deus Absconditus *that Haunts Modernity*
Timothy Stanley	*Protestant Metaphysics After Karl Barth and Martin Heidegger*
Christopher Ben Simpson	*The Truth Is the Way: Kierkegaard's* Theologia Viatorum
Richard H. Bell	*Wagner's Parsifal: An Appreciation in the Light of His Theological Journey*
Antonio Lopez	*Gift and the Unity of Being*
Toyohiko Kagawa	*Cosmic Purpose*, translated and introduced by Thomas John Hastings
Nigel Zimmerman	*Facing the Other: John Paul II, Levinas, and the Body*
Conor Sweeney	*Sacramental Presence after Heidegger: Onto-theology, Sacraments, and the Mother's Smile*
John Behr et al. (eds.)	*The Role of Death in Life: A Multidisciplinary Examination of the Relation between Life and Death*
Eric Austin Lee et al. (eds.)	*The Resounding Soul: Reflection on the Metaphysics and Vivacity of the Human Person*
Orion Edgar	*Things Seen and Unseen: The Logic of Incarnation in Merleau-Ponty's Metaphysics of Flesh*
Duncan B. Reyburn	*Seeing Things as They Are: G. K. Chesterton and the Drama of Meaning*
Lyndon Shakespeare	*Being the Body of Christ in the Age of Management*
Michael V. Di Fuccia	*Owen Barfield: Philosophy, Poetry, and Theology*
John McNerney	*Wealth of Persons: Economics with a Human Face*
Norm Klassen	*The Fellowship of the Beatific Vision: Chaucer on Overcoming Tyranny and Becoming Ourselves*
Donald Wallenfang	*Human and Divine Being: A Study of the Theological Anthropology of Edith Stein*
Sotiris Mitralexis	*Ever-Moving Repose: A Contemporary Reading of Maximus the Confessor's Theory of Time*
Sotiris Mitralexis et al. (eds.)	*Maximus the Confessor as a European Philosopher*
Kevin Corrigan	*Love, Friendship, Beauty, and the Good: Plato, Aristotle, and the Later Tradition*
Andrew Brower Latz	*The Social Philosophy of Gillian Rose*
D. C. Schindler	*Love and the Postmodern Predicament: Rediscovering the Real in Beauty, Goodness, and Truth*

1. Note: Nathan Kerr, *Christ, History, and Apocalyptic*, although volume 3 of the original SCM Veritas series, is available from Cascade as part of the Theopolitical Visions series.

Stephen Kampowski	*Embracing Our Finitude: Exercises in a Christian Anthropology between Dependence and Gratitude*
William Desmond	*The Gift of Beauty and the Passion of Being: On the Threshold between the Aesthetic and the Religious*
Charles Péguy	*Notes on Bergson and Descartes*
David Alcalde	*Cosmology without God: The Problematic Theology Inherent in Modern Cosmology*
Benson P. Fraser	*Hide and Seek: The Sacred Art of Indirect Communication*
Philip John Paul Gonzales	*Exorcising Philosophical Modernity: Cyril O'Regan and Christian Discourse after Modernity*
Caitlin Smith Gilson	*Subordinated Ethics: Natural Law and Moral Miscellany in Aquinas and Dostoyevsky*
Michael Dominic Taylor	*The Foundations of Nature: Metaphysics of Gift for an Integral Ecological Ethic*
David W. Opderbeck	*The End of the Law? Law, Theology, and Neuroscience*
Caitlin Smith Gilson	*As It Is in Heaven: Some Christian Questions on the Nature of Paradise*
Andrew T. J. Kaethler	*The Eschatological Person: Alexander Schemann and Joseph Ratzinger in Dialogue*
Emmanuel Falque	*By Way of Obstacles: A Pathway through a Work*
Paul Tyson (ed.)	*Astonishment in Science: Engagements with William Desmond*
Darren Dyk	*Will & Love: Shakespeare and the Motion of the Soul*
Matthew Vest	*Ethics Lost in Modernity: Reflections on Wittgenstein and Bioethics*
Hanna Lucas	*Sensing the Sacred: Recovering a Mystagogical Vision of Knowledge and Salvation*
Philip Gonzales et al. (eds.)	*Finitude's Wounded Praise: Responses to Jean-Louis Crétien*
Martin Koci et al. (eds.)	*God and Phenomenology: Thinking with Jean-Yves Lacoste*
Steven E. Knepper (ed.)	*A Heart of Flesh: William Desmond and the Bible*
James Madden	*Thinking About Thinking: Mind and Meaning in the Era of Techno-Nihilism*
Tyler Dalton McNabb	*An Analytic Theology of Evangelism: A Classical Theist's Approach*
Duncan Reyburn	*The Roots of the World: The Remarkable Prescience of G. K. Chesterton*
Pablo Irizar et al. (eds.)	*To Die of Not Writing: Doing Philosophy of Religion with Emmanuel Falque*
Rachel M. Coleman	*Matter as an Image of the Good: Ferdinand Ulrich's Metaphysics of Creation*
Christine Stephenson	*Remembering Augustine: The Symphonic Forms and Fundamental Affordances of Memory in His Theology of Memoria*

New Trinitarian Ontologies

VOLUME I

JOHN MILBANK, RYAN HAECKER,
& JD LYONHART, editors

CASCADE *Books* · Eugene, Oregon

NEW TRINITARIAN ONTOLOGIES, VOLUME I

Copyright © 2025 Wipf and Stock Publishers. All rights reserved. Except for brief quotations in critical publications or reviews, no part of this book may be reproduced in any manner without prior written permission from the publisher. Write: Permissions, Wipf and Stock Publishers, 199 W. 8th Ave., Suite 3, Eugene, OR 97401.

Cascade Books
An Imprint of Wipf and Stock Publishers
199 W. 8th Ave., Suite 3
Eugene, OR 97401

www.wipfandstock.com

PAPERBACK ISBN: 978-1-6667-6811-4
HARDCOVER ISBN: 978-1-6667-6812-1
EBOOK ISBN: 978-1-6667-6813-8

Cataloguing-in-Publication data:

Names: Milbank, John [editor]. | Haecker, Ryan [editor]. | Lyonhart, J.D. [editor]

Title: New Trinitarian ontologies, volume I / edited by John Milbank, Ryan Haecker, & JD Lyonhart.

Description: Eugene, OR: Cascade Books, 2025 | Series: Veritas | Includes bibliographical references and index.

Identifiers: ISBN 978-1-6667-6811-4 (paperback) | ISBN 978-1-6667-6812-1 (hardcover) | ISBN 978-1-6667-6813-8 (ebook)

Subjects: LCSH: Trinity—Philosophy. | Philosophical theology. | Christianity—Philosophy. | Metaphysics. | Philosophy and religion.

Classification: BT40 M553 2025 (paperback) | BT40 (ebook)

11/07/25

Contents

Permissions ix

Abbreviations xi

Introduction: Prolegomenon to Trinitarian Ontology, by *Ryan Haecker* 1

Part One—Trinitarian Ontologies

1. For a Trinitarian Ontology: A Manifesto, by *Piero Coda* 21
2. A Relational Approach to Trinitarian Ontology, by *Giulio Maspero* 33
3. Time, Motion, and Mystery: The Narrative Metaphysics of the Trinity, by *John Milbank* 57

Part Two—Metaphysics and Phenomenology

4. Being, Identity, and Ecstasy: An Essay in Trinitarian Metaphysics, by *John R. Betz* 73
5. Trinitarian Kenosis and the Limits of Phenomenology, by *Emmanuel Falque* 92
6. Counting to Four: Metaxology and the Trinity, by *William Desmond* 107
7. Metacritique and the Dynamics of Retrieval: Radical Orthodoxy, Sergii Bulgakov, and the Task for Trinitarian Ontology, by *Aaron Khokhar* 125

Part Three—Ecology and Liturgy

8 Entangled Unthinkably: Toward a Trinitarian Ecology,
   by *Simone Kotva* 187

9 Participation in the Divine Heart: On Faith and Trinitarian
   Knowing, by *Katherine Apostolacus* 193

Part Four—Eschatology and Revelation

10 Eschatological Being, by *Judith Wolfe* 203

11 Martin Heidegger's Poetics and the End of Ontotheology:
    The "Passing By" of the "Ultimate God," by *Emily Stewart Long* 209

12 From Tragic Ontology to Trinitarian Revelation: The Reconciliation
    with Being in Balthasar's Reading of Nietzsche, by *Paul Raimond
    Daniels* 224

Part Five—Poetics of Reconciliation

13 Christ and the Destabilization of Time, by *Graham Ward* 245

14 Repetition and Re-Presentation: Reaching Eternity Through Beauty,
    by *Isabelle Moulin* 256

15 "The Harmonious Silence of Heaven": Silence, Analogy, and the
    Incarnate Christ in the Music of Olivier Messiaen and Arvo Pärt,
    by *Joel Clarkson* 275

16 God He Sees in Mirrors: "Nabokov's Trinity" Revisited,
    by *Erik Eklund* 287

17 Rivalry, Sacrifice, and the Trinity: Baptism and Inspiration
    in Florentine Tradition, by *Catherine Pickstock* 303

General Bibliography 319

Index 345

Permissions

Permission is gratefully acknowledged:

From Faber and Faber to reproduce selections from "Burnt Norton," by T. S. Eliot, in *Collected Poems 1909–1962* (London: Faber and Faber Limited, 1963).

From HarperCollins to reproduce selections from "Burnt Norton," from *Collected Poems 1909–1962* by T. S. Eliot. Copyright (c) 1963 by T. S. Eliot. Used by permission of HarperCollins Publishers.

To reproduce excerpts from *PALE FIRE* by Vladimir Nabokov, copyright © 1962, copyright renewed 1990 by the Estate of Vladimir Nabokov. Used by permission of Vintage Books, an imprint of the Knopf Doubleday Publishing Group, a division of Penguin Random House LLC. All rights reserved.

To reproduce excerpt(s) from THINK, WRITE, SPEAK: UNCOLLECTED ESSAYS, REVIEWS, INTERVIEWS, AND LETTERS TO THE EDITOR by Vladimir Nabokov, edited by Brian Boyd and Anastasia Tolstoy, compilation copyright © 2019 by The Vladimir Nabokov Literary Foundation. Used by permission of Alfred A. Knopf, an imprint of the Knopf Doubleday Publishing Group, a division of Penguin Random House LLC. All rights reserved.

Biblical Ascriptions

Emphasis added to Scripture quotations.

Scripture quotations marked ESV are from the ESV® Bible (The Holy Bible, English Standard Version®), © 2001 by Crossway, a publishing ministry of Good News Publishers. Used by permission. All rights reserved.

Scripture quotations marked KJV are from the King James or Authorized Version.

Scripture quotations marked NRSV are from the New Revised Standard Version, copyright @ 1989, Division of Christian Education of the National Council of the Churches of Christ in the United States in the United States of America. Used by permission. All rights reserved.

Scripture quotations marked NRSVUE are from the New Revised Standard Version, Updated Edition, copyright © 2021 National Council of Churches of Christ in the United States of America. Used by permission. All rights reserved worldwide.

Abbreviations

1 Apol.	*Apologia i*
2 Apol.	*Apologia ii*
AT	*Annales Theologici*
Cat.	*Categoriae*
Comm.	*Commentarii*
Comm. Tim.	*In Platonis Timaeum commentaria*
Dial.	*Dialogus cum Tryphone*
EO	*Either/Or.* By Søren Kierkegaard. Edited and translated by Howard V. Hong and Edna H. Hong. 2 vols. Kierkegaard's Writings. Princeton, NJ: Princeton University Press, 1987
Ep.	*Epistula*
Eth. nic.	*Ethica nicomachea*
JAAR	*Journal of the American Academy of Religion*
KSA	*Sämtliche Werke: Kritische Studienausgabe in 15 Bänden.* By Friedrich Nietzsche. Edited by Giorgio Colli and Mazzino Montinari. 2nd ed. 15 vols. Berlin: De Gruyter, 1988
Metaph.	*Metaphysica*
NPNF2	*Nicene and Post-Nicene Fathers*, Series 2
NTS	*New Testament Studies*
PC	"Philosophical Crumbs." In *"Repetition" and "Philosophical Crumbs,"* by Søren Kierkegaard, 83–174. Translated by M. G. Piety. Notes by M. G. Piety and Edward F. Mooney. Oxford World's Classics. Oxford: Oxford University Press, 2009

Phys.	*Physica*
Resp.	*Respublica*
R&T	*Religion and Theology*
RevScRel	*Revue des sciences religieuses*
RP	"Repetition." In *"Repetition" and "Philosophical Crumbs,"* by Søren Kierkegaard, 1–82. Translated by M. G. Piety. Notes by M. G. Piety and Edward F. Mooney. Oxford World's Classics. Oxford: Oxford University Press, 2009
RThom	*Revue thomiste*
SC	Sources chrétiennes. Paris: Cerf, 1943–
ScrTh	*Scripta Theologica*
Sent.	*Sententiae ad intelligibilia ducentes*
StPatr	Studia Patristica
Tim.	*Timaeus*
TR	*Time Regained*. By Marcel Proust. Translated by C. K. Scott Moncrieff et al. Revised by D. J. Enright. Vol. 6 of In Search of Lost Time. London: Folio Society, 1992
Trin.	*De Trinitate*
VC	*Vigiliae christianae*
VCSupp	Vigiliae Christianae Supplements

Introduction

Prolegomenon to Trinitarian Ontology

Ryan Haecker

Philosophers once asked the simplest questions of being to investigate the greatest questions of theology. The study of being in metaphysics had been pursued as a preparation for the study of God. And, among the church fathers, this study of metaphysics was explored in imitation of a God who is both one and three. If all this seems today no longer possible, it is due more to the forgetting of the absolute questions of theology than to any discrediting of the answers. For many centuries now, the Christian belief in the Holy Trinity has been relegated to the margins of philosophical investigation: among the medieval Scholastics, it had first been consigned to a *mysterium fidei*, not of knowledge but only of faith; and among early modern philosophers, it had been relegated to a special topic in the philosophy of religion and religious studies. The basic questions of philosophy have since shifted from those of the ground of being (ontology) to the conditions of knowledge (epistemology) and to the context of speaking (language). In analytic philosophy, skepticism of the meaningfulness of metaphysical statements has given way to efforts to corroborate inherited religious doctrines with coherent theories of logic, language, and pragmatics. And, in Continental philosophy, critiques of ontotheology have given way to critiques of presence, truth as power, and regimes of correlation. In each current, the Trinity has been relegated to either a historical or systematic study—either as a belief of Christians past or as an inscrutable mystery of an ancient faith that it seems can never again become the fruitful subject of philosophical investigation. The original rationale for a faith that is Trinitarian has thus been repeatedly submerged by currents of secular reason. And the vital question of the Trinity has since come to be all but forgotten: for, when it is recalled at all, it is just as often remembered wrongly, more as a dead question of bare historical evidence or pious credulity, and less as an urgent call to ask these questions again for ourselves.

In contemporary philosophy of religion, the question of the existence of God has tended to be asked before that of the essence of God. The Trinity has tended to be regarded as an idiosyncratic Christian form of generic theism. And the numerical problem of three persons in one God has typically been upheld as an insoluble logical paradox. Against these trends, we seek to recall the Christian doctrine of the Trinity from the margins of fashionable contempt to the heart of philosophical speculation—not only as it asks of the existence, but ultimately as it explores the essence of God. For since, as early as Plato and Philo, the absolute principle of God had been held beyond all thought and being, nothing can it seems be known of the God who is simply one. Yet since this idea could not be absolute except as it comes to be known, and has shown itself to be known through the revelatory events of human history, the Christian story—of God become flesh to give the life of his Son for the Spirit of the church—must be more radically assumed into the relational essence of the God who is love. The basic argument for the Christian Trinity can, for this purpose, be speculatively conceived: if we begin by positing the idea of God as both simple and absolute, yet such a pure and simple one cannot stand in any complex relation to the many, then, for God to be absolute, God must unfold from simplicity to complexity, from indistinct unity into the multiplicity of the created world, and reflect from the world into all conceivable relations, such that, in sharing the procession of these relations, God can be shown to be a triadic circuit of three cycling in and from the center as one.

Trinitarian ontology names a new way of thinking of metaphysics in imitation of the Trinity. It intervenes in a crucial debate concerning the foundations of ontology. In contrast to formal and foundationalist ontologies, it assumes the origin of being into the divine essence of three distinct persons in one God. As such, it affirms the Platonic "participation" (*methexis*) of being proceeding in and from the first principles beyond being. It is not simply an ontology of the Trinity, a Trinitarian "ontotheology" or Trinitarian "theontology." It is, to the contrary, an ontology that is immanently shaped by the dynamic relations of the Trinity, such that the relational essence of being is ever spoken in and beyond being. It can, in this hyperbolic style, strategically escape the typical postmodern suspicions of ontotheology, presence, and power, as it assumes the most radical difference of being as "other" into the reciprocating exchange of one to an other of the divine persons. It is "ontological," not in the sense of modern formal ontologies of analytic and Continental philosophies, but rather in the classical sense—first spoken of by Parmenides and Plato—of a question of speaking of "what is," that is, of being as being is spoken of by God. It is "Trinitarian," not in the sense of historical studies or systematic summaries of Christian doctrine, but rather as it answers to the challenge of thinking these dynamic relations as it speaks of being in and from an essential ground that ever may be spoken of as most mysterious and most divine. And it is "new," not in the subtractive sense of the medieval nominalists, the modern idealists, or the nihilistic finality of the *via moderna*, but rather and most radically from the evental surprise of revelation.

Trinitarian ontology can thus be called "new" as it responds to the foremost challenge of modern philosophy. Since the late medieval separation of faith and reason, the Trinity has been repeatedly suspended as an article of religious faith that can be hypothetically approached, but never genuinely known with the certainty of science. With the development of mathematical logic and empirical science, the mysteries of religious faith appear to have been suspended above knowledge. And with the paradoxical collapse of the foundations of mathematical logic, along with any procedurally validated correspondence to the observable world, it seems that not only the veracity of science, but reason itself has been variously arrested as a vehicle for truth. Christian doctrines have since tended to be rendered as little more than silent reservoirs of will in action—less of truth and more of power. Lacking a theological foundation, this latest confidence in science has been overturned, first in a more radical skepticism and finally in a more resolute dogmatism. The suspension of the Trinity has thus been upheld as an incontestable presupposition of both modern and postmodern theory. Yet at this speculative impasse, the theoretical obstacles to Trinitarian speculation may also prove to be not less but arguably even more precarious: for if these modern constructions of ontologies had once been held to have suppressed the truth of theology, then the postmodern deconstructions of ontologies and metamodern investigations of a holy middle can now be witnessed to have cleared the path for us to investigate the highest principles of metaphysics or ontology in imitation of the Christian Trinity.

In a surprising way, this latest speculative advance is as old as the Christian faith. The opening lines of the Gospel of John tell how the "Word" (Logos)

was "with God" and "was God" (John 1:1).[1] In this surprise reversal of prepositions, being is spoken of in and with the Logos, the Logos is spoken of as both other than but from Christ, and Christ the Logos is shown to have become flesh within the world of his own making. At the Last Supper, Jesus shows an immanent sharing of divinity from the Father, through the Son, in the Spirit: "All things that the Father hath are mine" (John 16:15). Paul could thereafter write of how God "emptied himself" (*heauton ekenōsen*) of his simple divinity, made himself a servant, and gave his life in human flesh as an absolute sacrifice of God for us (Phil 2:6–8). And Origen could later reinterpret the divine "I am that I am" of Exod 3:14 as an annunciation, not generically of the divine being, but singularly in the Logos "become flesh" (John 1:14), which speaks in the creation of every ontic act of being, and thereafter in any creative rendering of ontology.[2] Due, however, to the collapse of hierarchical ontologies, Christian theology has lately appeared, for Heidegger as for Derrida, "ontotheological," "logocentric," and, for some, ultimately forgetful of the unspeakable difference of being, as of writing. The Christian Trinity has thus tended to be consigned with theology to an unphilosophical epoch of dogmatic metaphysics.

We can argue, to the contrary, that these currents of secular philosophy have tended to suppress the most originary and divine difference of the Trinity. For, in contrast to Plotinus, Spinoza, and many later anti-Trinitarian alternatives, the God of Christianity is not merely one over many, but more richly, a triadic circuit of divine processual relations, in which this divine difference of God from God, and of the world from God, is that of the ever-greater dissimilarity (*maior dissimilitudo*), from which the world is created ex nihilo as the first gift, and can be more radically assumed into the concrete ground of myth, revelation, and all the sacramental media of the church. The classical Trinitarian and christological controversies can, for this reason, be creatively rendered anew in deliberate response to the latest challenges of philosophy. In each controversy, the first difference of the Son from the Father is suppressed in an eruptive opposition that is no less violently sutured in an identity of the same. And yet, in this Nicene-Cappadocian vision of the Christian orthodoxy, we can also hope to discover a much more radical reaffirmation of the non-identical repetition of difference, which can be christologically pacified only as it leaps over this creative difference of the Logos in any speech of being.

---

1. Throughout this chapter, Scripture quotations are from the KJV.
2. Origen: *On First Principles* 1:75; *Gospel According to John* 1:119; *Homilies* 246–48.

Among the Latin Scholastics, this question of being in metaphysics was later raised to the absolutely higher ground of Christian theology. From Eriugena to Nicholas of Cusa, the constitution of ontology was successively reconceived to proceed in and from the creative nova of the Trinity, its vestigial articulations, and its mimetic repetitions in the analogical hierarchy of being. At the Gothic zenith of the high medieval synthesis, Bonaventure and Aquinas could thus render the study of being in metaphysics as a prolegomenon to the study of sacred doctrine, or *sacra doctrina*, and supremely to the divine essence of God who is three in one. Yet in elevating this creative nova of the Trinity beyond the ambit of being, the late medieval Scholastics can also be argued to have torn the earliest fissures of secular reason: first, in simulating the forms of logic as separate instruments for the critique of Christian doctrine; second, in holding the univocal predication of common being (*ens*) over the being of substances (*entia*); and third, in subsuming the analogical hierarchy of participatory relations under an increasingly flat ontology that ever breaks open before its ineffable source. The never-completed synthesis of classical philosophy and Christian theology can thus be observed to have staged the tragic conflict of modern philosophy.

In successive convulsions from the Protestant Reformation to the secular Enlightenment, the constitution of modern philosophy has been repeatedly shaped by this fateful ontological decision. Among the followers of Leibniz and Wolfe, the word "ontology" was first distinguished from the more general science of "metaphysics" as the rational science of being, and its logical implications. Yet in upholding being as an object that can be progressively approached by the subject, it had framed a subject-object correlation, in which the object always escapes and the subject remains unsatisfied in the effort to grasp its source. In this constitution, God appears to hover beyond all beings, in an ontological difference of being that is set over and against beings, of an inner opposition of being to beings, and of an explosion that threatens to evacuate all Trinitarian relations in every speech of being.

Such a spectral conception of God is, as both Friedrich Nietzsche and Henri de Lubac have acknowledged, the oldest root of modern atheism. For in elevating one supreme Being over many finite relations of being, and in withholding the subject of thinking from the objectivity of all such beings, the idea of God has been cast beyond both thinking and being in a false because unmediated transcendence that is liable to collapse into an equally spurious immanence. The God of ontology could thus be represented by Immanuel Kant as an idol of pure reason, which threatens to evacuate the ground of being into nothing so as to subvert any system of being, or ontology, into a system of nonbeing, or meontology. The suspension of a christological finale in G. W. F. Hegel's *Logic* collapsed the true speculative infinite that produces the finite into a pan-logicist conceptual totality. And Martin Heidegger's *Kehre*, or turn, from a phenomenology to a more poetic leaping of being over the abyss of the nothing, has been recapitulated in both the positive constructions of ontology and the negative deconstructions of meontology, which can ironically be sustained only by appeals to an undisclosed source. Yet, in recasting the principle of being as either a chthonic un-ground or a celestial lure, each can be argued to have colluded in counterfeiting the gift of being in a false simulacrum that could not speak again of God as Trinity, or of ontology as Trinitarian.

Modern ontology has since endeavored to construct a tower of science from the relations of beings to being. It could, at its apogee, strive to reach the heaven of certain reason, and from that summit to direct the order of all things. Yet, in neglecting to secure its most originary foundations, it has since initiated a series of dialectical convulsions that have undermined the edifice and precipitated the evacuation of being into nothing as a precursor of modern nihilism. In Immanuel Kant's critique of ontotheology, the modern idea of God as a substance or supreme being has collapsed into nothing under transcendental analysis. In the utmost polarity of modern philosophy, G. W. F. Hegel had constructed an encyclopedic system of ontology by sublating all alternative concepts in and for the self-mediating circuit of dialectics, and Martin Heidegger had conversely deconstructed every such ontical construction of automated and amnesiac reasoning by questioning so as to discover the ever-differentiated truth of being. F. W. J. Schelling can thereafter be recalled to have split the difference between these two flights of ontological speculation—as both the progenitor of Hegel's philosophy and as the precursor of Heidegger, even as he nevertheless heralds a novel return to the Trinity as the principle of being.

The two main lines of later twentieth-century philosophy have pivoted between this polarity of theological impossibility. Most analytic ontologies have, following Gottlob Frege, presupposed the forms of mathematical logic as an axiomatic foundation; while most Continental ontologies have, following Edmund Husserl, presupposed the content of phenomenal intuition as an appearing foundation. Due to an insatiable desire for cognitive mastery, the more daring leaps of speculative theology have been suppressed under a simulated terrain of finite logic and observation. In this separation of form and content, each had colluded in suspending the principal source for questions of the ground and purpose of any such analysis of logic and phenomena. The foundations of such formal ontologies had, however, long ago been critically subverted by Ludwig Wittgenstein's critique of the social use of logic and Martin Heidegger's critique of the unstable construction of ontology.

W. V. O. Quine and Jacques Derrida have since gestured to the dissolution of all ontological foundations. And Richard Rorty and Alain Badiou have charted new paths beyond the spurious analytic-Continental divide to a new speculative plateau that plays as freely with the forms of reason as with the contents of intuition. A third path between these two modern poles of impossibility has thus opened again from within the unstable fissures of secular reason to take flight and ascend to the empyrean heights of first philosophy.

However, this latest renewal of metaphysical realism has remained arrested by the sterile questioning of the philosophy of religion. Where formerly the existence of God beyond reason could not be questioned, today it more often seems that reason alone cannot begin to establish the existence of God. In this sudden reversal of rationalism into fideism, a more radically immanent metaphysics that threatens to collapse God into the world has strangely recapitulated the nihilistic trajectory of late medieval and early modern theology from Duns Scotus to Baruch Spinoza. The post-Heideggerian "metaphysical turn" has since authorized a dazzling proliferation of new metaphysical projects. In the Deleuzian "new materialism" of Manuel DeLanda, Rosi Braidotti, Bruno Latour, and Catherine Keller, the hyperbolic arcs of mystical theology have been subsumed under a field of more vital and affective matter. And, in the Badiouian "speculative realism" of Iain Hamilton Grant, Quentin Meillassoux, Ray Brassier, and Graham Harman, the idealist correlation of thought to being has been concentrated into an increasingly agonistic pleroma of monadic objects. Yet, in each oscillation, this spiralling penumbra of orthogonal trajectories can also be observed to have successively foreclosed a more essential third way, in which the one is made precisely from the relations of the many, and the gift of being exceeds in charity all conceptual oppositions.

With a leap of wonder, we call for a return to this subterranean current of Trinitarian speculation. No edifice of modern ontology can any longer stand against the Lord of Being itself: for if such ontologies cannot contain but rather and more radically point to God, and if all nature thus tends toward the angelic, then we may once more renew this central investigation into the metaphysics or ontology of the Trinity. In a creative genealogy, Trinitarian ontology draws from the Christian sources of Paul, Origen, Nyssa, Augustine, Pseudo-Dionysius, Maximus, Eriugena, Bonaventure, Anselm, Albert, Aquinas, Eckhart, and Cusa. It calls attention at this moment to a submerged current of Trinitarian speculation as it has been variously articulated in Ficino, Cudworth, Rosmini, Newman, Biran, Ravaisson, Kierkegaard, MacDonald, Solovyev, Bulgakov, Bergson, Weil, Lubac, and Balthasar. It also observes a pivotal caesura: beginning in the radicalization of a weaponized Aristotelian logic in Duns Scotus, William Ockham, and

Jean Buridan; continuing in the spatialized renderings of Ramus, Descartes, Spinoza, and Leibniz; and reaching its forgetful apogee in Kant, Hegel, and Heidegger. Between these two currents, we can also observe a pivotal split between the analytic heirs of Frege and the Continental heirs of Husserl, as this division is increasingly sutured by post-analytic pragmatism, and as it ever suspends theology from ontology. Yet beyond the secular, all such formal ontologies have previously been contested by German metacritiques of the Enlightenment, by French *nouvelle théologie*, and, most recently, by the Nottingham and Cambridge school of Radical Orthodoxy. Trinitarian Ontology shares with Radical Orthodoxy a critical suspicion of liberal, postmodern, death of God, radical, and weak theologies. It elides the autonomy of natural reason and the secular foundations of all formal ontologies. And in its evangelical and traditioned exhortation to return to the ecumenical sources of Christian theology, it continues to champion the progressive spirit of the church as the living water of renewal for all that had been lost, and the fruit of all that may yet be found.

New Trinitarian Ontologies names this third way of speaking of being, spoken as given, of a gift that imitates the triple relationality of the divine hypostases of God as Trinity. The Bishop of Aachen Klaus Hemmerle first recollected, in a 1976 letter to Hans Urs von Balthasar, how the "event-like character" of Christian doctrine may transform the speech of being "from out of the heart of our faith, from the Christ-event [as it is] read in a Trinitarian fashion."[3] The unique claim of the Christian Trinity resides in this its radical relationality: for, in contrast to both Plotinian Platonism and Arian subordinationism, Christian orthodoxy affirms that being (ousia) is a relation that is shared from the Son to the Father, from the Father and the Son with the Spirit, and, by a free gift, in the creation of all substances. In the most general sense, it speaks of these ecstatic relations that may erupt from the *metaxu* "between" beings to connect all substances, things, and persons in pursuit of their originary source and final destiny. In double contrast to Hegel and Heidegger, it speaks of being neither as fully indeterminate nor determinate, but only as it may be shaped and given in its being, to give again and be itself as a gift. It is thus always already shaped as given in the riches of its relations, in a form that can be both dispersed and collected beyond and for any further relations, and, ultimately, as its entire significance proceeds to be shaped in and from the source of its triple relationality. The relational *schesis* thus encompasses and enriches the participatory *mathesis*,

---

3. Hemmerle, *Theses*, 8.

extending in a lateral excess that may ever diagonally return as to its source. And yet, in its more complete and specific sense, it may also speak of this gift of these relations that are shared by God for God, released by the surplus relationality of the Spirit, and, from the sacrifice of the cross, recreated through all the revelatory and creative poetics of the church.

New Trinitarian Ontologies will ask this question of faith before any question of being. It will begin with what seems the simplest and richest of philosophic questions. It will ask the simplest question of "What is being?" as it may yet be answered in faith with the absolute question of "What is God?"; and it will speak, with Aristotle, of what simply "is," so as to speak, with Augustine, of the creative cause of all being. The circuit of these questions may afterwards exceed any naïve belief that it had held from its first beginning. Its surplus is a cipher of its novelty. In the course of these investigations, it will address a diverse range of topics, including: ontology, metaphysics, phenomenology, history, literature, politics, ecology, and poetics. It will gather all these disciplines to be systematically ordered from its principle source. It will thus search both before and after the speculative impasse of modern philosophy. And it will, for this reason, be advanced to undercut the sclerotic oscillation between liberal and conservative theologies, in which the former skeptically challenge while the latter dogmatically recapitulate all inherited doctrinal formulae. It will attempt to navigate between an abject skepticism that would sunder theology from ontology, and any ready-made dogmatism that would regiment all theological answers in advance. It will gesture instead over this speculative impasse to the oldest conversation that echoes from its deepest source; to the dynamic and processual relations of the divine principles; as to the restoration of the Trinity from the margins of fashionable and forgetful incredulity. To restore this third path, we must ask the central question of the Holy Trinity in a new way. We must not merely draw all that is past into the present, but must, more radically, leap over this burdensome forgetfulness of the past to chart a new beginning.

The collection of essays contained in this volume have been written in response to invitations to the September 13–15, 2019, New Trinitarian Ontologies Conference at the University of Cambridge, which was organized by a team of graduate students led by Ryan Haecker, Jonathan Lyonhart, Alex Abecina, Austin Stevenson, Matthew Fell, and Sebastian Milbank. This conference was made possible with the support of the University of Cambridge Faculty of Divinity, the Pontifical University of the Holy Cross Relational Ontologies Research Institute, and the University of Fribourg St. Nicholas Study

Centre for the Eastern Churches, as well as the generous financial assistance of Peterhouse, Emmanuel, St. John's, Queens, Magdalene, and St. Edmund's colleges. This event has since been followed by the March 2020 New Trinitarian Ontologies Symposium in Cambridge, England; the June 2020 New Trinitarian Ontologies panel of the European Academy of Religion in Bologna, Italy; the June 2023 New Trinitarian Ontologies panel of the European Academy of Religion in Münster, Germany; and the June 2023 New Trinitarian Ontologies panel of the European Academy of Religion in St. Andrews, Scotland. Additional papers from these and future events are projected to be published in subsequent volumes and special journal issues. We owe a special debt of gratitude for the advice and assistance of John Milbank, Catherine Pickstock, James Orr, Andrew Davison, Janet Soskice, and Rowan Williams.

The essays that have been collected from these events will be distributed across two volumes: the first volume is addressed to the philosophical question of what is Trinitarian ontology; and the second volume is addressed to the historical question of the story of the Trinity. The first volume of *New Trinitarian Ontologies* is divided into five parts, addressed to the metaphysics of the Trinity; challenges to Trinitarian ontology; and explorations of Trinitarian ontology in art, music, and literature.

In part 1, Piero Coda, Giulio Maspero, and John Milbank present a new introduction to Trinitarian ontology.

Piero Coda opens the volume with a call to rethink the basis, dynamic, and destiny of thought itself. The concept of the Trinity was, as he narrates, shaped by the progressive discovery of the unprecedented and decisive significance of the divine Logos become flesh in Jesus of Nazareth, and as the vital horizon for the interpretation of the mystery of being—both in the expression of the Word and in the reciprocal communication of the Spirit and gift of love. Yet he argues that premodern Trinitarian theology failed to generate that place of experience for the relational and communitarian exercise of thought transfigured by the ontological novelty of the Trinity. The resulting crisis initiated the division of theology and philosophy, culminating in a purely rational science of being. The thesis of Trinitarian ontology is that the mystery of being is understood in the light of the Trinity as theology is exercised together with philosophy and the sciences, reciprocally and each according to their distinct methodology, in a synodal dialogue that becomes the shared place for experiencing and understanding that is reality rooted in the Trinitarian dynamic of agape.

Giulio Maspero describes the ontological picture of Christian theology as a "theology of the gap." In the book of Genesis, Adam could call the Creator "Father." Yet in the Gospels, Jesus calls the Creator "Dad." These scriptural passages present a philosophical challenge: the one and triune

God is a single substance, infinite, and eternal, even as it is one in three persons. Trinitarian ontology is presented as a relational ontology inspired by Cappadocian theology, in which this gap is a relation that involves the coincidence of the substance of each of the divine persons with relation of each to the other. Hence, the "gap" of God from the world does not simply distance man from God, but instead brings him closer because of the radical difference between the eternal and created natures, which enables the reading of their relationship as an eternal relation of gift. Maspero shows how this relational ontology not only reformulates the ontology of the one and triune God, but also reinterprets the ontological basis of the world and its relation in the light of the Trinity.

John Milbank recommends that we read the story of God in the divine essence of the Trinity. Since the most ultimate way to speak of God is in narratival, temporal, and dynamic terms, we must not fall into the error of supposing God to be simply an eternal and static idea. Rather, since he is radically involved in this story, and so intensively narratival so that he could become flesh within the human story of Israel, Mary, Jesus, and the church, the arc of our souls' ascent to God should not be expected to leave the time of narrative behind. The only way, he argues, to conceive of God would thus be "to think of the One as itself generating the 'breakout' of the many and yet of the unity of the many, as only ever indicatively conveying the unity of the unfathomable One beyond its own immanent totality."[4] We can, accordingly, "not possibly understand or experience God as Trinity without rethinking and reliving the entire structure of our everyday reality in a Trinitarian style."[5]

In part 2, John Betz, Emmanuel Falque, William Desmond, and Aaron Khokhar develop new approaches to the metaphysics and phenomenology of the Trinity.

John Betz investigates Trinitarian ontology in terms of three interrelated concepts: being, identity, and ecstasy. He argues that the analogy of being (*analogia entis*) does a far better job safeguarding the mystery of being, and preventing it from collapsing into the kind of univocal conception that prevails in modern nihilism, than does Heidegger's "ontological difference." Where Heidegger refuses to think of the gift in theological terms, a Christian metaphysics can, he contends, go further in faith to see that the mystery of the gift of Being to beings is an analogy of an even more mysterious gift of the Father to the Son. Far from being univocal, being is thoroughly analogical, as it is constituted at its core by the dynamic interplay of essence

---

4. Milbank, "Time, Motion, and Mystery," in this vol., 63. [X-REF]
5. Milbank, "Time, Motion, and Mystery," in this vol., 67. [X-REF]

and existence. The theological difference, and the decisive overcoming of Heidegger's ontological nihilism, consists in this: for Trinitarian ontology, Being is nothing but Love. In short, we are not already what we are, but must become what we are, until that day when what we are will be revealed at the coming of Christ (1 John 1:2–3).

Emmanuel Falque describes Trinitarian ontology as: a "God of power" in the person of the Holy Spirit, against the constant recourse to weakness and powerlessness, even of God himself. Between the "extended body" (Descartes) and the "lived body" (Husserl), he contends that there is a third type of intermediary "spread body," which is the totality of our own corporality that the Savior comes to indwell and to assume. The Eucharist also has the purpose not only of converting our humanity into divinity, but also of transforming our animality into a humanity that shares in the filiation of Christ. It is therefore *before God*, also passing *by the "other,"* that the horizon of finitude takes shape, in the very possibility of separating what the Father has himself joined together since the origin of creation, and every conversion experience must be found again. It is, he argues, only in such a "connection" that the possibility of "separation" is expressed, and in the union that the event of rupture that it is read. Trinitarian ontology here takes its finished form, and it is in searching in our deepest darkness that the Father comes also to reveal himself.

William Desmond asks what are the implications of metaxology for Trinitarian ontology. To secure an ontologically robust otherness, we must count to two. And to count to two, we must first count to four, that is, to the quadratic betweenness of metaxology. In contrast to Hegel's triadic logic, he advances a quadratic logic. Beyond self-determination, he recommends the super-plus communication within the Trinity from the symmetrical giving and receiving of the over-full to the over-full: the Father is the origin and surplus good that is overdetermined; the Son is the expression of the surplus good that is also overdetermined; and Spirit is the communal intermediation or the love that also is overdetermined. This agapeic *metaxu* is being between, betweening, the Father, the Son, and the Spirit, and between the Trinity and the creation. Christ is the eternal *metaxu*, given to time as the divine incarnation of the agapeic *metaxu*, the one Word of the divine between, and double in being both the uncreated and created *metaxu*, the doublet of the immanent and economic Trinity. Trinity could thus be rendered in terms of agapeic betweening, as a doubling and redoubling. The Trinity thus inspires the metaxological betweening of agapeic love. Contra Hegel, however, this divine betweening that gives creation to be is not a symmetrical intermediation between God and the world. Counting to four helps makes sense of the ontological gift of the irreducible otherness and the contingency of given creation.

Aaron Khokhar explores a "full-blooded" metaphysics that is both christological and Trinitarian. Interrogating the "background" structure of various philosophical images of discursivity, he argues that their culmination lies in a pragmatically unified image of concept and intuition that can be held together only by the apocalyptic Christian understanding of our human spirit. Providing a rival "affirmative" reading of supposed closures for thought that may now be reconfigured in a theological fashion, he further contends that presuppositional reductions in philosophy remain incomplete and secure only an illusory autonomy, which surreptitiously depends upon what is refused in theology. Against this unstable ground of rationalist conceptuality, he develops a genealogical analysis that refuses the Hegelian conceit of "presuppositionlessness" by proposing that all assumptions be circularly affirmed in an open challenge of virtual simulation by competing hermeneutical idioms, and guided not only by the coherency of concept but also the valence, relief, and life of intuition. In this process—a metacritical and poetic alternative to Hegel—Khokhar recommends a Desmondian refiguration of the essential meaning of transcendentality, where the dimensions of our discursivity—linguisticality, phenomenality, historicity, and so on—are brought to recognize themselves in a new theological confidence. As in Sergei Bulgakov, the original binding third of the Spirit, which assures love and life for the dyadic cleavage of Father and Son, is presented as both a transcendentally secured metaphysical cornerstone and capstone—whereas this is implicitly rejected by philosophy, blindly read as voiding excess. Such a rejection is revealed as the transcendental procedure of received post-structuralism, which therefore perpetuates a degenerate virtual approximation of Trinitarian difference. In answer, Khokhar argues that only the Christian belief in the philosophical significance of the Trinity can resist the dissolution of the real from the sheer impotence of finite thought, offering instead the promise that a unity of concept and intuition, theory and practice, and form and content may be thought, hoped for, and lived now as they shall be in the perfect love of the life to come.

In part 3, Simone Kotva and Katherine Apostolacus study the hidden traces of the Trinity in the material entanglements of ecology and the divine liturgy.

Simone Kotva explores the ecological implications of Trinitarian ontology. She contends that it is difficult to think, and to really attend to the relationship between the persons of the Trinity, without living and relating differently to the other than human. In the place of the single system there is a cascade of entangled relations. And in place of a single principle, there is Trinitarian life. Every mystical apperception is an ecological exercise in becoming aware of this entanglement, and then acting accordingly. The Trinity is a way of thinking of the God who changes how we think everything else for which God is the tug and pull. What theology thinks of an entangled human-divine world must be worked through by reentering the unthinkable complexity, not only of earthbound life, but also and especially of earthbound life's doctrines and traditions. The Trinity is thus an image of human flesh spiraling ecstatically with nonhuman and more-than-human spirits. It is, accordingly, a tool of spiritual practice for teaching and thinking of divine relations by which it would be possible to touch, indirectly, upon the entanglement between human and nonhuman.

Katherine Apostolacus contends that faith derives its epistemic character from the nature of divine knowledge. It is not an assent to believe in a set of fixed and finite propositions, but rather in the God who is given to us to be understood in and through experiential media. Such knowledge can be acquired only through some degree of participation with the other. To have faith is not merely an assent to a set of propositions, but rather and more corporeally to embody a certain manner of being that overflows beyond oneself, even as it concretely inscribes the intentions of the self into a corporate and spiritual body. To pray the orthodox creeds is both to participate as a corporate whole in the divine being, and to petition for the church to increasingly become like Christ. Knowledge is, she argues, not simply an adequate reflection of reality, nor developed only through imitation of epistemic virtue, but it is also a manner of existing with and for another beyond oneself. Through prayer, through the sacraments, through Scripture, we come to know God as he is revealed to us, as incarnate, and as he exists in and for us in a Trinitarian style.

In part 4, Judith Wolfe, Emily Stewart Long, and Paul Raimond Daniels explore the themes of eschatology, ontotheology, and revelation in response to the Trinity.

Judith Wolfe contends that to try to conceptualize or imagine a radical participation in divine plenitude from within human conditions of experience would result in an existential antinomy. Humans cannot conceptualize or imagine a fulfillment of desire that is not, at the same time, a cessation of life in its essential character of movement and growth. For phenomenologists like Heidegger, this is a reason to bracket the idea of participation or eschatological completion from philosophical thought altogether. She distinguishes, in the twentieth century, two main theological strategies developed for responding to such phenomenological strictures: "diastatic" arguments against the exclusion of God from phenomenological description, which focus on the implications of desire as a basic mode of human intentionality;

and "diathetic" arguments, which focus on the human openness to identity-shaping experiences that come from without their own structures of intentionality. Ontologically, the first conceives God analogically as Being; the second conceives Being univocally, and God as beyond it. The movements of both *ressourcement* and Radical Orthodoxy have primarily adopted the first, the diastatic strategy of overcoming the phenomenological challenge from within. Such a strategy is partly effective. However, a phenomenological critique in turn demands an eschatological dimension to Trinitarian ontology: a theology of participation that takes more seriously the eschatological preliminariness of human knowing and being.

Emily Stewart Long presents a new interpretation of Heidegger's critique of "ontotheology," a term active in his later work that characterized the history of metaphysics as the history of theology. Only emerging as a theme after Heidegger's radical historicization of ontology and his shift away from *Being and Time*, Long argues that Heidegger's encounter with ontotheology is best understood by looking to the role of poetry during *die Kehre* (the turn), a period ranging from the completion of *Being and Time* in 1927 until the early 1940s wherein Friedrich Hölderlin became Heidegger's key interlocutor. Though the status of poetry in Heidegger's philosophy resists brief summary, one can say with certainty that it was with Heidegger's first Hölderlin lecture in 1934–35 that poetry became his select partner in bringing about an end to ontotheology and seeking an "other beginning" of thought, which Heidegger understood in terms of salvation, "the holy," and the role of the divine as they appear specifically in the futural hermeneutic quality of poetry. For Heidegger, poetry has the capacity to shelter the divine, making possible a final turning away from technological modernity characterized by what he calls "the passing by of the ultimate God," a God to be guarded as a mystery. A theology of this kind, in Heidegger's view, would perform the revelatory function of aletheia or "truth" in intimate counterrotation with respect to the preservation, the guarding, of the mystery of Being.

Paul Raimond Daniels examines how Hans Urs von Balthasar reads the aesthetics of Nietzschean tragedy as evacuating Being into a nothingness that ultimately subverts its affirmative powers. Within the ensuing collapse of Being itself, Balthasar identifies a performative theological transfiguration of the tragic: an apophasis of ontological distance by which the subject is restored to a communion with Being and beauty as divine gift. Because Nietzschean subjectivity shapes itself by the denial of God, its character assumes something of the theological negatively. When, in this way, it is itself denied in the nothingness of its self-destruction, we do not rest with *ex nihilo nihil fit* but glimpse an apophasis of a specifically Christian metaphysics. The ontological distances within God himself and between God and humanity, then, comprise the precondition for the possibility of love at all. Our reconciliation with Being is both a stillness and a play; our intuition of beauty as a divine gift renews our wonderment at existence itself, inviting and enfolding us into the mystery of the Trinity and the distance and identity of its persons.

In part 5, Graham Ward, Isabelle Moulin, Joel Clarkson, Erik Eklund, and Catherine Pickstock render the poetics of the Trinity as a call to reconciliation.

Graham Ward develops a christological reading of time, in which the rhythmic movement of time reverberates all the way down through the gospel narrative. The word Jesus uses in the Gospels is not *chronos* (time as duration), but rather *kairos* (the chosen time, the right time, and the critical moment). What *kairos* is, then, is time filled in and through the plenitude of grace. And yet it is a concrete time, a time that is meaningful because it can be received, experienced and lived. *Kairos* is graced time, and time as grace, in whose gift historical time is made meaningful. But kairos is, for us, also mythical time. *Kairos* is not delivery from time and the world, but rather part of an ongoing conversion. Hence, it is time lived to a different beat, as it is transposed by the economy of a divine rhythm. The coming of Christ thus inaugurates "the fulfillment of time," and the cross of Christ is the most profound display of this inauguration. History is *in* the aeonic, the transhistorical, the eschatological, just as Christ is in his creation, and creation is a Trinitarian event *in* God.

Isabelle Moulin explores the concept of repetition as a way for theologians to understand the Trinitarian God. She shows how repetition, which articulates identity and difference, accounts for the reappropriation of time by human creatures through the experience of beauty. Repetition is, she contends, not simply the Hegelian dialectical reconciliation of these two "moments," but rather the Greek sense of "recollection" (*anamnesis*), which considers time upside down. True repetition is a renewal, a difference then, lived within the coexistence of sensation and imagination, present and past. Art is thus the *mise en lumière* of truth through the manifestation of the difference. And the intelligence is the light. For God, this repetition of the Trinitarian relation between identity and difference takes place beyond time in eternity. Art can then be a domain where something that belongs to the divine can be found. Yet it can also be theologically expressed. Repetition is, as Kierkegaard has rightfully demonstrated, a way for created beings to live, in a certain way, the life of God, not simply in its essence, but more decidedly in his Trinitarian dimension.

Joel Clarkson interrogates the christological integration in twentieth-century sacred concert music of actual and analogical silences into music.

He considers two composers, Olivier Messiaen and Arvo Pärt: with his clear-minded representation of christological concepts in musical analogy, Messiaen sought that end through a more distinctly theological and dialectical means; whereas in taking up a musical idiom steeped in the waters of restraint, Pärt oriented his listeners in a more mystical manner that eschewed propositional discourse and pursued a singularity in sound. By the use of birdsong as a metaphor for earthly human experience crossing the threshold of time into eternity, a paradoxical distance is created between the listener's contemplation of the music's representational elements, which requires an understanding of the properties and relationships of that which is being represented; and the possibility of an actual, encountered eternal silence, which would, by nature, exceed the limits of representation. Messiaen and Pärt are efficacious in engendering an inner silence in their listeners, not because either implements a "correct" analogical framework, but rather because they both gesture from their distinct ecclesial postures toward the limitless generosity of the mystery of the incarnation.

Erik Eklund examines the authorial enigmas of Vladimir Nabokov's *Pale Fire* to discover how authorial unity may be conceived of as transcending the dichotomy of identity and difference. The maddening ways in which *Pale Fire* parodies the idea of an original text challenges the fitness of categories like source and copy and origin and variation. Eklund argues that non-identical repetition provides the best conceptual apparatus for analyzing this problematic, as it accounts for the possibility of a true gift by including "not only the return of an equivalent but different gift, but also a non-exact mimesis (but therefore all the more genuinely exact) of the first gesture in unpredictably different circumstances, at unpredictable times and to unpredictably various recipients."[6] Reframing the authorial enigmas of Nabokov's masterpiece around non-identical repetition frees readers from the perceived necessity of assigning authorial primacy among the novel's competing authorial voices, suggesting instead that the two texts of the novel (poem and commentary) are each mirrors of one another, in whose mirrorly confrontation the conventional dichotomy of source and copy or origin and variation falls away into oblivion. This alternative way of reading Nabokov's greatest novel offers a new literary playground for discovering a Trinitarian ontology of non-identical repetition and for considering how one could conceive of the paradox of framing and so of giving intelligible form to the infinite.

Catherine Pickstock explores the theological connections that can be observed on the relief depictions on the doors of the baptistery in Florence.

---

6. Milbank, "Can a Gift," 125.

She illustrates how Trinitarian invocations both sustain a Christian critique of excessive human pride and rivalry, and yet also integrate this with a Christian humanist dimension. The fact of the incarnation and the cross reveal that the triune God is eternally and, not just for us, also the God connected in his inner sanctum of cultic initiation to the cosmic doors of human historical entry. Here the gift of one's identity is the gift of harmony with the identities of others, attained by the blending of differences rather than the monadic imposition of a single point of view. In the constant displacement of the angelic and human dance, every place that is graciously forsaken admits the other to return in a way that is all the more to open one's own place at the next turn of the dance. In our specific finite origin, such a movement of going back to heaven is also our baptismal rebeginning. To walk into this baptismal space of unique personhood in relation with other persons, beyond imitative rivalry, is to walk into the ontological space of the Trinity.

The air of astonishment that had formerly accompanied scientific considerations of the Holy Trinity has, it seems, at last begun to pass away as the world reflects again upon its oldest stories and secret hopes. The failed effort to consolidate the truth of religion with a concordance of secular reason now invites us to investigate the higher question not only of whether, but of who is the God that we should desire. In hindsight, the bifurcated search in epistemology for the categories of cognition, and in ontology for the structures of reality, has continued to be sustained by a tacit reliance upon the hidden ground of theology, myth, and revelation, that pure reason vainly attempts to hollow out. All the arts and sciences stand upon this ground of prior assumptions that is as metaphysical in the beginning as it is more ultimately theological in the end. If the questions of faith come before those of being, then the most originary questions must be those that answer to styles of answering to this hidden call of revelation, destiny, and desire. Yet if, in the cry of its pure impossibility, reason looks back to its source, and recalls the tri-hypostatic principles of metaphysics, then the dynamic relations of the Trinity may still await to be discovered across a variety of disciplines. The chorus that can be heard to emerge from among these essays will carry to ears that can still hear the Orphic song of angelic speculation that many of the most daunting challenges in contemporary philosophy can be answered only by such a renewal of theological speculation into the ways in which the structure of being shares in participation with the God who has shown himself to be three in one.

Ryan Haecker
University of Austin
Holy Trinity Sunday 2024

Part One

Trinitarian Ontologies

1

For a Trinitarian Ontology

A Manifesto[1]

PIERO CODA

The Challenge: Rethinking Thought

EDGAR MORIN WRITES THAT "rethinking thought" is what is urgently needed today. Crucial, unprecedented, unavoidable challenges

---

1. The genesis of this "manifesto" is at the basis of the project for a Dynamic Dictionary of Trinitarian Ontology (DDOT) begun by the group of theologians and philosophers collaborating for some years with Piero Coda in the purview of Trinitarian ontology: Andrea Bellantone (Catholic Institute of Toulouse); Alessandro Clemenzia (Theological Faculty of Central Italy, Florence); Vincenzo Di Pilato (Theological Faculty of Bari); Massimo Donà (Vita-Salute University, Milan); Vito Limone (San Raffaele Vita-Salute University, Milan); Mauro Mantovani (Salesian Pontifical University, Rome); Massimiliano Marianelli (University of Perugia); Giulio Maspero (Pontifical University of the Holy Cross, Rome); Carmelo Meazza (University of Sassari). Commentaries accompany the manifesto in the form of "glossa," to enrich and support the text with reflections, some of which emerged in moments of dialogue during classes on Trinitarian ontology at the Sophia University Institute in Loppiano (Florence, Italy); see the first volume of the DDOT series: Coda et al., *Manifesto*. Of this series, seven more volumes have since been published; see bibliographic references at https://ontologiatrinitaria.org/ddot/.

confront the human family and undermine our common home in various contexts. Structurally iniquitous economic and political paradigms propitiate a *globalization* that is dangerously deficient, especially from the anthropological point of view. *Old and new kinds of poverty* widen the condition of vulnerability among more and more persons, social classes, and entire peoples, on the socioeconomic level as well as the psychological-relational and spiritual level. An *ecological crisis* has also now reached the point of no return, foreshadowing irreparable catastrophes unless there is an immediate, adequate conversion of lifestyle. Even the context of the *technological revolution* presents a challenge as digital, biogenetic, and robotic technology too often lacks a soul and ethical orientation. Meanwhile the *global health crisis* struggles to find a way out, definitively calling for an urgently needed, radical conversion of life.

To effectively and responsibly face these challenges with a realistic impact requires thinking in a creative and rigorous way and in solidarity. But at the root of these challenges there is an urgent need to "rethink thought" itself, and even more so because *"the king is naked"* before them.

A way to think in light of the beauty of truth and in the quest for the good of happiness shared by everyone in harmony with creation appears to be dramatically missing. The new generations sincerely and painfully desire it precisely for this reason. All too often this is for the sake of a rationality that is merely practical and calculating, which brackets out and even consigns to oblivion the conscience's inescapable personal commitment, and the exciting universal vocation to unity in freedom as the encounter and reciprocal gift of diversity in which our identities are enriched.

Kairós: Prophecy of a New Thought

This urgency has become increasingly compelling and provocative in the last two centuries, especially in the 1900s, the "brief century" wounded by the unheard-of brutality that still nails us to the stabbing question: "But how could, and in fact did, that happen?" It has been felt in the social, artistic, scientific, philosophical, and theological sectors as an indignant, determined reaction in response to the frightening tragedies experienced by humanity in the past and still today, especially because of the ascendancy of an anthropologically deficient and even distorted thought.

Generous and unprecedented paths for bearing witness to and promoting a performative understanding of reality have flourished from the most diverse cultural roots and sensibilities in the suffering cry of men and women tormented by such tragedies, leading to: phenomenology, existentialism, personalism, dialogical thought, ethics of otherness, hermeneutics of the truth, the linguistic breakthrough, the anthropology of bodiliness and sexuality, the philosophy of science, technology and ecology, the culture of encounter among the various religions and convictions . . .

Even if these paths initially appear to be different and unconnected, they make it possible to recognize a deeper convergence indicating the *prophecy of a "new thought," rather a true and authentic "cultural revolution" on a wide and collective scale*. As a result of this testimony, the spiritual strain and ethical passion are present and operative in the culture of our time to discover and pursue a way of thought and corresponding action with transparency, trust, determination, and fraternity.

Without eliding their specific and precious originality, what establishes their kinship and keeps them in ideal solidarity is the conscious commitment to recognize again the inexhaustible, luminous, satisfying fruitfulness of the sense of truth, good, unity, and beauty of that B/being, in which "we live and move and have our being" (Acts 17:28).[2] This recognition occurs in the fruitful womb of thought and in the historically effective field of action.

In a few words, it is the experience, understanding, and practice of an *open, integral ontology*, expressing and promoting the living mystery of B/being in its multicolored self-expression, which is ultimately self-giving as gift and as a promise of life, freedom, communion, and joy. As old as thought, and at the same time as new as the *kairós* erupting and inviting us in our time as in every epoch, such an ontology is called to be put into practice and to enable us to recognize, declare, and share *the truth* of B/being with humility and *parrhesia*, as offered to our experience in the rich, plural phenomenological spectrum of its meaning, without preconceptions, reductionisms, and false absolutizations. The gratuitous invitation of such an ontology results in the responsible, creative response of personal and social conscience being able to freely recognize, embrace, and promote the *promise of good* to be shared with everyone.

Diversity is thus allowed to converge in a dialogical relationship of *unity in plurality*, where it is possible to care for one another mutually, striving with tender strength to nurture each other and together, and to nurture the common home. As a result, the projects and days in the journey of life and the multicolored expressions of humanity are able to manifest and irradiate the fascinating *beauty* and *joy* in which B/being communicates itself to us and, in so doing, transfigures us little by little in the clarification of the "Light that never fades." History and the universe are thus enlightened from

---

2. Throughout this chapter, Scripture quotations are from the NRSVue.

beneath and within, because the ultimate, definitive sense of our common destiny is effectively made present as time passes.

Inventio: The Concept of the Trinity in the Fathers of the Church

Thought and action that have reached and dwell in the hospitable region of such an ontology, and its liberating though demanding ethos, call for a *rereading* of the tradition of thought, which has matured through history leading to this point. With its gains and drifts, the indispensable paths undertaken, the unexplored questions and horizons of sense could now prove to be opportune and meaningful today.

Such an endeavor is clearly rich and diverse. It cannot be reduced to any interpretive system that presumes to be exhaustive and definitive. And yet in this perspective, we can see how a *crucial junction* was historically produced in the West, which now resonates with a universal significance. It is the encounter between philosophy from the Greek mold, in which the ancient wisdom (from the East as well) flourished on one hand, and the understanding of revelation on the other hand from the biblical-Christian mold, which comes about in the golden age of the patristic period.

In the discovery and discernment of the truth about B/being, the most theoretically and practically significant outcome from this troubled but fruitful encounter was produced in the *inventio* of the ontologically revealing and regulating concept of *God-Trinity*. It is a concept that is intrinsically *overflowing* by its nature, because it is called to find the measureless measure of its truth again and again from within the ever-greater Reality it is called to express.

The *inventio* of this concept was historically determined from within the thought formed by a Greek philosophical paradigm by taking up the challenge inherent in the progressive discovery of the singular unprecedented theor-ethical significance represented by the eschatological event of God's Word (*Lógos*) becoming flesh in Jesus of Nazareth. Having taken on flesh, being born "of woman" (Gal 4:4), Christ, the Word, testified that he was turned toward "the" God in the beginning (ἀρχή), being God himself (John 1:1), so that everything became what it is in and through him (John 1:3). This testimony was produced in the unfathomable, loving kenosis of the incarnation Christ lived to the point of abandonment on the cross (Phil 2:7; Mark 15:34). This was where and when he was constituted as the alpha and omega in the resurrection, which discloses and recapitulates the new creation (Eph 1:10) in the Father's gift of the Holy Spirit's *claritas* (John 17:22).

For all intents and purposes, the concept of the Trinity was advanced in this way in the history of thought (inclusively, not exclusively; as an invitation, not an imposition) as the *gratuitous, decisive horizon* for the interpretation of the meaning of B/being, stemming from the intersection between the human quest for wisdom (φιλο-σοφία) and the grace of God's Word (Θεο-λογία):—both *with reference to God*, the infinite Being who, coming out of the silence of his abyss, expresses himself in the Word and in the breath of the Spirit as gratuitous, reciprocal reciprocating relationship of freedom and communication where he gives everything in himself and beyond himself as *Agape* (1 John 4:8–16)—Father, Son, Holy Spirit;—and *with reference to creation*, and to the human being as creation's peak and guardian as a finite being capable of the infinite precisely because he or she was wanted and placed in being out of love and called in love to recognize and participate in his or her own way (really, to the point of unspeakable fullness) in the beauty, truth, and goodness of God the Trinity in that unprecedented form of unity in diversity where the finite is transfigured in a Trinitarian way into the infinite, tapping by grace into its original and definitive vocation in this way: "As you, Father, are in me and I am in you, may they also be in us" (John 17:21).

In the interweaving of the interpretive and performative fabric of B/being, the concept of Trinity in the patristic age has therefore favored the realignment of meaning, and in some cases the creation of decisive concepts *ex novo* with reference to God, humanity, and the cosmos: for example, hypostasis, person, relation, love, freedom, generation, spiration, unity, perichoresis, communication, etc. It suffices to mention Irenaeus of Lyons, Hilary of Poitiers, Augustine of Hippo, Gregory of Nyssa, Basil the Great, Gregory of Nazianzus, Dionysius the Areopagite, Maximus Confessor, and John of Damascus, etc.

The Journey: From the Middle Ages to Modernity

The extraordinary promising gain was intuited and proposed in the concept of the Trinity as the measure illuminating the meaning of B/being. In fact, it progressively inspired the subsequent journey of thought in Western culture explicitly and implicitly, in various forms and even with contrasting outcomes. And this was in all the manifold expressions of the fields of thought.

On the basis of the robust resignification of the meaning of B/being produced by patristics, ingenious attempts at synthesis were generated especially in the Middle Ages, interweaving and cross-fertilizing philosophical research stemming from the Greek background (Plato, Aristotle, and Plotinus), which was also transmitted through the mediation of Islamic culture. The experience of Jesus's gospel in the church's journey was discovered and lived *sine glossa* with growing fidelity, in spite of the objective digressions that are always possible. And theological understanding was nourished by the charisms of Benedict of Nursia, Francis of Assisi, and Dominic de Guzmán. Doctors of the great Middle Ages include Anselm of Canterbury, Albert the Great, Thomas Aquinas, Bonaventure of Bagnoregio, and Duns Scotus.

However, the concept of Trinity failed to completely generate that place (*locus*) for the experience and for the relational and communitarian exercise of thought (beginning with the original, paradigmatic relationship between male and female) that corresponds to the Reality it had received and embraced. Such a place would make it possible to experience in existence and to fathom in understanding the ultimate foundations and the practical implications beyond the gains offered by the Greek metaphysical paradigm, even if this latter might have been reshaped by its encounter with the understanding of revelation. In spite of the great Trinitarian theology from these centuries for which we are indebted because of the extraordinary precious gifts of understanding of the faith and the fantastic illumination of reality as in the case of Dante Alighieri's *Divine Comedy*, we must recognize that it failed in fact to imbue all its expressions at the root—the anthropology, and ultimately the exercise of thought itself, which they sought with urgency to be able to express in everything, in the new situation of their being, established by the event of Jesus Christ and interpreted within the parameters of the concept of the Trinity.

This gradually produced a radical *krísis* over the course of modernity. It was expressed in a lacerating and ultimately irresolvable separation whereby philosophy (as reason and freedom) and theology (as faith and tradition) diverged little by little to the point of opposing one another irretrievably. And yet while this occurred, new and promising forms of knowledge (the natural sciences, the humanities, the social sciences) began to emerge. They were fostered by the discovery of the positive ontological significance of creation resulting from God's Word having become flesh. And the forms of thought generated by Oriental religious wisdom were appearing on the scene of the cultural *agorà* that had become a worldwide horizon by then.

At the beginning of the nineteenth century, philosophical thought (Fichte, Schelling, and Hegel, in particular) attempted the generous, powerful undertaking to cross this chasm, opening up the concept of the Trinity, and the incarnation of the divine in the human, through an original, dialectical, and all-pervasive rationality. This attempt was, however, found to be closed within the completely modern perimeter of the immanence of "pure reason," exercised by the "I" (Kant's *Ich denke*) interpreting reality as the subject that could not be transcended as reason. As a consequence, this frustrated the deep-rooted need that was felt to reopen the way of thought to God's truly divine revelation (this was the case, for example, with the later Schelling, Kierkegaard, and then Blondel and Heidegger after that, clearly with different emphases and outcomes). The purpose of this effort was to reach the integral promotion of the human being, effectively recognizing their dignity and individual and social rights, in view of humanity's transcendent origin and destiny.

Accordingly, the failed outcome of this undertaking pushed subsequent philosophy to expunge from itself any reference to God revealed in Christ in order to honor this manifold, changing, and elusive experience of the finite and then wounded "I." But this ended up too often with the abdication of its deepest vocation to freely and tirelessly think about the meaning of B/being.

With the shrewd insight resulting from the implementation of a radical hermeneutic of suspicion (Nietzsche, Marx, Freud) with respect to any presupposition taken as absolute, philosophical thought and the thought of the human and social sciences as well proceeded more or less knowingly into the "dark night" of nihilism—recognized and managed as such, or critically denounced, or suffered with resignation, or removed with a bad conscience—ending up in fact by handing over thought and freedom to the impersonal logic of totalitarianism, technocracy, and post-humanism.

For its part, theology in modernity was tempted by the apologetic reduction of faith, and, in particular, of the regulating concept of the Trinity, to an indisputable, merely confessional religious dogma. This is how the concept of the Trinity was cooped up within the perimeter of categories, from a form of thought marked by an objectifying, reductive metaphysical pre-understanding because its meaning was not transformed in the ontologically decisive crucible of the Cross's no and the yes of the resurrection of the Word made flesh, as it is available by now in the common life of those beautiful free relationships that are the gratuitous fruit of the Holy Spirit's gift "without measure" (John 3:34).

As Karl Rahner showed on one hand, and Hans Urs von Balthasar on the other, with their determined effort to rediscover the living, radiating center of revelation again, theology had lost the radical sense of the illumination and vivification of B/being and behavior irradiating from the Holy

Trinity, in Jesus Christ, through the Holy Spirit. As a result, theology underwent the experience of gradually being cast off the path of thought and becoming sterile on the practical level.

The experience and understanding of the Trinity continued to shine out as a source of light and life with mysticism, from Ignatius of Loyola to Teresa of Avila and John of the Cross in the West, from Sergius of Radonež to Seraphim of Sarov in the East. However, that did not actually effectively impact the growing demand for reform of thought and practice, advancing more and more in the philosophical, theological, and scientific spheres in the 1900s, except for some promising foretaste, especially in the Ignatian tradition, from Gaston Fessard to Henri de Lubac and Erich Przywara.

Who—What—Where: Toward a New Beginning

Today it is possible to discern an original and promising qualitative leap in the way thought and conduct are conceived and practiced, beginning with the living cradle of revelation transmitted by the tradition of faith lived in the koinonia of hearts and minds aroused by Christ in the breath of the Spirit who "guides into all the truth" (John 16:13). It is in dialogue with the precious gains in dialogue with the most acute farsighted philosophy, art, and contemporary science, at all geopolitical latitudes and in all the most diverse cultural and spiritual expressions, developing under the same Spirit's breath, to be "poured out on all people" (Joel 2:28). This is with the critical awareness and the perspective offered by this historical memory, bearing in mind the provocations and issues stemming from the present challenges, beginning with the threefold, but unitary at its root, and the *krísis* of modern thought in the West—in its philosophical, theological, and scientific expressions, indeed in its own radicality.

In this light, the prophecy of the "new thought" in the philosophical sphere on one hand and the renewal of theology in all the Christian denominations (from a Trinitarian standpoint: from Karl Barth to Eberhard Jüngel and Jürgen Moltmann, from Sergius Bulgakov to Karl Rahner and Hans Urs von Balthasar) on the other, throughout the 1900s, are an invitation to broaden horizons beyond the shoals of metaphysical rationalism and religious dogmatism. They knowingly take up the demand for radical purification and free transfiguration incubating in the "dark night" of nihilism.

Just think of the intense virginal mystical testimonies of Therese of Lisieux, Edith Stein, Simone Weil, and Chiara Lubich from the dawn of the twentieth century into the heart of its tragedy, and up to the promises beyond all that. It is not by chance that they were all women; it is almost a foretaste of a new generativity. That is how today's *krísis* can recover its truest meaning: that of an unprecedented promise produced once for all (ἐφάπαξ) in the crucified Christ's cry of why, borne through this *kairós* in the *krísis*.

Starting from this point, our working hypothesis is that philosophy and theology can find the place again for a rebirth and *reconfiguration of ontology*, in which the guiding thought of the Trinity is taken up in its original irradiating meaning, with the *focus* on Christ's cross and resurrection, and examined in the yet-unfathomed promise it contains. This rebirth and reconfiguration would be at the gratuitous and indispensable service of the genuine responsible practice of thought and action equal to the present challenges, because they would be in direct contact with the flowing source of the "good, beautiful news" (Mark 1:15) that "makes everything new" (Rev 21:5).

This is the ambitious project being advanced with simple trust and thoughtful decision: *Trinitarian ontology* as it was first denominated by some authors in the late 1900s, even with different formulations and emphases. The human and intellectual performance of Klaus Hemmerle, an avant-garde thinker between philosophy and theology, gave us inspiration and orientation. But we already find significant foreshadowings of it at the turn of the nineteenth century: in Italy, for example, in Antonio Rosmini's *theosophy* (a lemma containing the crucial element within itself), and in Russia with the "Trinitarian logic" of Pavel Florensky.

In the context of postmodernity, the reference to the Trinity simultaneously expresses a meaning that is subjective, objective, and topological in this ontology, with a Trinitarian inspiration and intentionality. In fact, it both evokes and qualifies the who (the subject), the what (the *res, die Sache*), and the where (the *locus*) for thinking about being as agape. In fact, it is a matter of embracing and thinking B/being in its self-expression as reciprocal, inexhaustible gift of self in the manifold, dramatic concreteness of history and in responsibly taking on the challenge of the "not" of freedom—that "not" whereby one is *not* the other but each one is him- or herself in being gift to the other in the T/third "between" the two, as the ever-new experience of the truth, of good, of unity, of the joy to be freely shared and communicated.

Reference to the "subject" emphasizes that in the Trinitarian ontology, the "I" exercises thought in dialogue with the "you" of God, who is the first one to address himself as "I," and in the "we" of communion with all the other "I's," where the "I" fully and freely becomes *this* "I" and not another. Reference to the *res* emphasizes that the reality forming the object of Trinitarian ontology is B/being, illuminated and thoroughly examined in the Trinitarian grammar characterizing it, and giving rhythm to its dynamic in the relationships between infinity and finitude. Reference to the *locus* emphasizes that the Trinitarian ontology is given and expressed within that space and time that, as such, foster the disclosure of the meaning of B/being in the dialogue "between" those welcoming, thinking, and expressing it.

In short therefore, in the practice of a dialogue pursued as a radical experience of transparency, reciprocity, and openness in and to the truth, Trinitarian ontology is qualified to recognize and express the Trinitarian meaning of B/being in a Trinitarian way, receiving its gift in the shared responsibility of "Trinitizing" it, in the multiplicity of expressions it takes on, and the connections it offers within the range of all types of knowledge (Chiara Lubich). This can occur only within the place inhabited by intersubjective relationships that freely allow themselves to be determined by the form of Trinitarian agape, thus becoming a real christologically given and pneumatologically vivified experience on the journey of participation in the life that is a gift from God. This occurs and becomes what it is by the grace that is ever greater (*magis*) than our heart, which is thereby communicated to us (1 John 3:20).

Thus, in *the context of epistemology*, Trinitarian ontology implies a radical repositioning of the relationship between theology and philosophy, moving from the effective phenomenological giving of the experience of B/being, offering a place for the relationship between the sciences and the diverse forms of wisdom, and favoring the adoption of an integral strong ethos of encounter, sharing, and reciprocal care. In light of the Word becoming flesh to the point of abandonment on the cross, the *theor-ethical* context acquires a renewed hermeneutic of the relationship between infinite Being and finite being in its rich variety and in its historical journey. It is a relationship that becomes an event in the encounter between the God who is Trinity and creation, since they are freely called together in their insurmountable difference and asymmetric reciprocity of self-giving, to the eschatological universal goal of "that God may be all in all" (1 Cor 15:28).

Through a historical hermeneutic, a theor-ethical illumination, and a heuristic identification of the questions and prospects required by a Trinitarian ontology, the project for a *Dynamic Dictionary of Trinitarian Ontology* offers a discreet invitation and an initial entrance to the dialogical practice of this ancient and always-new way of thinking.

The Way: *Weg-Gemeinschaft* with Mary

From the methodological standpoint, the project of the *Dynamic Dictionary of Trinitarian Ontology* is an invitation to practice dialogical thinking lived with a Trinitarian rhythm. It is a matter of being engaged in what

Klaus Hemmerle defined as a *Weg-Gemeinschaft*, a journey in community and a community on a journey. So it is taking up that "marvelous way" (ὁδὸς θαυμαστής) indicated by Plato in Letter 7 as the high road of love for wisdom and which is relived by the one made flesh and crucified, in the account of the disciples of Emmaus (Luke 24:13–35), when the flaming light of the risen Christ ignites the heart burning within the travelers through the dialogue where he himself interprets and communicates what refers to him in all the Scriptures (διερμήνευσεν τὰ περὶ ἑαυτοῦ ἐν πάσαις ταῖς γραφαῖς).

So it is first of all indispensable to reacquire the original meaning of *methodos* as an orientation for research, born and enriched in dialogue stemming from an experience lived together, without expecting to capture anything in an all-encompassing conclusive way, but with the intent of welcoming correlated directions and marks for the journey to focus and communicate in a rigorous, shared way the forms, themes, and questions for the performative understanding of B/being.

In a word, it is a matter of being involved in a method of "something more," which does not exclude or surpass specific exploratory methods with their originating paradigms. Rather, it redirects them beyond their respective findings to the original open horizon fostered by the formation of a Trinitarian ontology. It is the horizon of encounter exceeding the single methodologies and their mere sum. It occurs as a result of a persevering heuristic dialogue without preconceptions. In this way, each is required to become explorer and protagonist in proposing and receiving indications and perspectives to be evaluated and undertaken from time to time in harmonious agreement.

The epistemic assumption propitiated by the method of Trinitarian ontology is that of the truth offered as the inviting horizon for communitarian discernment, which is disclosed in the time and place of a rational dynamic, inasmuch as it is relational. This is precisely because it is finding its constantly oncoming fulfillment in the truth being given as gift.

Access to the truth must be operative in all the stages, and on all the levels of the research, so that the personal and communitarian perspectives qualifying it can be implemented. These characteristic perspectives come about from advancement of and dwelling in the "castle" that is both "interior" and "exterior," which is inhabited by the truth. This implementation of the personal and communitarian perspectives comes about in the reciprocal resonance between their interaction in reciprocal distinction.

Specifically, the cardinal points fostered by this method *to orient* the journey are those establishing and giving rhythm to the experience of thinking as language and communication in that dialogical event where each I is able to exercise itself in the space of we, opened and guided by participation in the shared experience of God's gift in Christ through the Spirit.

More than simply asking "What is it?" *the question* posed is also "How?" (*Wie geht das?*). How does it happen that the truth of B/being gives itself? The *intention* is that of the offer, the reception, and the redundancy of the gift, which becomes rendering thanks to the O/other (*Denken* is *Verdenken*), because "seeing itself happens only in the simultaneity of a giving projection [*Entwurf*] and a receptive understanding—a simultaneity which is no compromise, but is the novelty and unity of seeing."[3] The dialogical relationship (rather, the "tria-logical" relationship) is the one that fosters the exchange of the gifts of understanding of B/being as reciprocating reciprocity in the T/third, an asymmetrical event that penetrates more and more into the inexhaustible abyss of the truth in a spiral movement where all the actors are protagonists.

The temporal existence is what happens beyond what is lived subjectively, closed in itself and almost impossible to transcend, in order to open up to the "between" of the relationship, in the free moment of the *kairós* experienced eschatologically as anticipation and expectancy—in the already and not yet—of the fulfillment that can come from and occurs in only God. In the free offering of self, *the negative* is intersected, starting with the recognition that names it, sharing the limitation, the wound, the defeat, and the conflict, in union with the intersection lived already, once for all (ἐφάπαξ), as overflowing grace of the crucified Christ's abandonment. The *language* is what comes to be woven into the λόγοι πνευματιχοῖ (1 Cor 2:13), which are the words imbued with the Spirit of love by whose breath the word is articulated and shared in giving form to the "evenemential" connotation that expresses the truth received and experienced in a "kiss" of love between dialogue partners, consumed each time again.

This is how the community is formed along the way. It is where the art of freedoms encountering one another is put into practice, with the exchange of one's own works, life, and thought, in the common work where *thinking with one another* is meant to be fulfilled in *thinking in one another*, drawing from the νοῦς Χριστοῦ (1 Cor 2:16) in which thinking is increasingly proleptically consonant with the rhythm of the Trinitarian perichoresis. It occurs in the always-new articulation of *existence* and *thought*, rigorously and creatively pursued, since this is the way to B/be what is lived, thinking it and thinking oneself performatively, in the truth of receiving and sharing the gift that we are.

---

3. "Thesis 32," in Hemmerle, *Theses*, 61–62.

2

A Relational Approach to Trinitarian Ontology

GIULIO MASPERO

Introduction: Do We Need Metaphysics?

THE PRESENT PAPER AIMS at illustrating a concrete form of Trinitarian ontology. Trinitarian ontology is understood not only as an ontology *of the* Trinity, but also as an ontology *from the* Trinity, that is, a consideration of the being of the created world in the light that flows from the Trinitarian revelation.[1] It concerns, specifically, the relational ontology developed by the fathers of the church during the disputes that led in the fourth century to the formulation of the dogma of the Trinity at the Councils of Nicaea and Constantinople.[2] Therefore, we shall have (1) to show in what it consists, (2) to prove that this relational ontology is a Trinitarian ontology, (3) in order then to indicate its strength in the history of theological thought from the Middle Ages to the present day.

---

1. See Coda, "Ontologia trinitaria, che cos'è?"
2. For an analysis of the discussions, see Maspero, *Essere e relazione*.

This question of Trinitarian ontology is not a trivial one. For, particularly in the Reformed sphere, the procedure of the fathers has been seriously criticized on the basis of the principle that it supposedly supplants the language of the Bible with that of pagan Greek philosophy.[3] The dialectical rejection of the metaphysical component in Christian thought had its origins in a response to the over-complicated philosophy, which was signaled by Scholasticism and nominalism.[4]

However, the metaphysical perspective of Trinitarian ontology is that which the fathers of the church had indicated with the expression "common notions." This is the body of basic knowledge shared by people in their common life. In fact, metaphysics is used all the time in everyday life. Think, for example, of a restaurant, when one orders meat rather than fish. If the waiter makes a mistake in bringing the dish, the complaints are always founded on a metaphysical judgment, albeit an elementary one. The same could be said of theology: even if a human being does not study it at the scientific level, the concrete choices that each person makes in his own life indicate the assumption of certain theological positions. If one devotes one's whole life to searching for financial gain, making it the sense of one's proper existence, then money will be considered as one's de facto god, in this case an idol, even if one is not aware of this as a theological choice.

From this perspective, the Bible, and the gospel in particular, stake everything on a metaphysical question. From the moment when Adam is called to name the different animals created by God, without finding anyone to address personally, to Moses's encounter at the burning bush and to the manna in the desert, the whole of the Old Testament is speaking about a metaphysical question. Not by chance, the fundamental question of this kind of knowledge is "What is it?," the precise meaning of *man hu* (Exod 16:15). Israel has to grasp in practice that God is a reality totally different than the world, that is, that he is unique and absolutely transcendent by contrast with the pagan divinities, which were personifications of natural forces.

In the New Testament, the problem is still more acute because Jesus says that he is this God, the one God. In all the Indo-European languages, there are two fundamental roots referring to father: *pater* and *atta*.[5] In English, these are represented by the terms *father* and *dad*. The first implies origin alone and can, therefore, be predicated of different metaphysical realities: Adam could call the Creator this; the Jews could say that God was the

---

3. An example above all is Harnack, *Entstehung des Kirchlichen Dogmas*, ix–x.

4. The theological *ressourcement* of the last century could be connected to work to overcome this dialectical approach. See Renczes, "Patristica."

5. See Benveniste, *Économie, parente, société*, 210–11.

Father of the people; just as today we could say that the founder of a business is its father or that a politician is the father of his country. However, the second, more familiar term implies not only origin but also consanguinity. *Pater* could refer to the tribal chief, to the ancestors, and, in the first place, to the gods. *Atta*, on the other hand, is only one's own father. This reveals that, when Jesus calls the only God, Creator of heaven and earth, his *abba*, he is presenting us with a very serious metaphysical problem—the most serious ever being openly posed. The Cross itself is a consequence of this metaphysical scandal, dictated by the fact that Jesus, who is perfectly man, says that he is God, that is, another *thing*. Thus, the resurrection will be the proof of the need to modify classical metaphysics, bringing alongside the question of "what is" the question of "who is." In fact, Jesus is the same thing as the Father, but is a different *who*, that is, another person. From this perspective, the paschal mystery can be considered as the greatest and most fundamental metaphysical judgment in history. Thus, Scripture itself faces its readers with a philosophical challenge because the one and triune God is a single substance, infinite, and eternal, even as it is one in three persons: three different *whos* who are only a single *thing*.

The Fathers: Mind the Gap

So then, if the metaphysical question is not something superimposed upon Scripture, it is natural that the Trinitarian disputes of the first four centuries were characterized by a strong development of *ontological* thought. With this term, we are not referring to Heidegger and the meaning introduced by his hermeneutics. Nor are we referring to the *metaphysica generalis* of Leibniz and his successors. Rather, we are using it according to its etymology, "the *logos* about being," to distinguish it from Greek metaphysics. The latter can be considered a particular example of ontology, characterized essentially as the study of the reality, which is the causal basis of *ta physika* or nature. In fact, Plato and Aristotle established a second exploration, which is distinct from the first philosophical results of the pre-Socratics as it pushes the study of the first principle beyond the visible cosmos itself to discover the *arché* in the sphere of the intelligible dimension. The Platonic ideas or the Aristotelian forms are the metaphysical principles, in which the visible world is grounded in the invisible one. Plato says that men are plants rooted in heaven, ascribing the metaphysical view to the memory.[6] Aristotle, however, indicates the act by developing this Platonic insight further by conceiving of a hierarchical sequence of movers, which elevates this metaphysical

---

6. Plato, *Tim.* 90.a.

series back toward the absolute and actual purity that is constituted by the Unmoved Mover—the thought of thought.[7]

Thus, in their thought, both Plato and Aristotle elevate thought to the *arché* by proceeding from cause to cause. The Greek term to indicate the latter is, precisely, *logos*. And the possibility of this ascent is identified in a structure that is common to the thought of both the great thinkers, according to whom the first principle and the world are linked by a series of necessary causal connections. These connections are indicated by none other than the term *logos*, in such a way that God and the cosmos constitute a single metaphysical level, structured in a series of descending ontological density, starting out from the perfection of the *arché* itself. Since only the universal can be identified with perfect intelligibility, the principle of individuation is always bound up with an element of imperfection. Thus, in Plato, it is matter, formed in the receptacle or *khôra* by the divine craftsman or demiurge according to the ideal archetype, which introduces the specific identification, whereas, in Aristotle, it is played out in the interaction of the pair act-potency. In each case, this ontology, which embraces both the first principle and the world in a single level, is characterized by finiteness and eternity.

From the biblical perspective, these two metaphysical elements have to be radically overcome, because the Creator of the world is infinite and eternal while the world is finite and temporal. The overcoming of this finite and eternal ontology inspired a long process, begun by Philo and taken forward by the fathers, in interaction with Neo-Pythagoreanism, Stoicism, and Middle- and Neo-Platonism, to arrive at an ontological conception on two levels. Between God and the world, in fact, it was necessary to introduce an authentic metaphysical *gap*, that is, an infinite hiatus to distinguish the unique ontology characterized by infinity and eternity from the ontology of the created world marked radically by a beginning in time and by finitude.[8]

It is precisely this journey that is fundamental in the location of the problem of Trinitarian ontology. In fact, the introduction of two different ontologies for the first principle and for the world inevitably involves the discussion of the relationship between the two. The point is that, in a certain sense, this relationship is already an expression of the conception of the *arché*: if the latter is understood to start out from necessity, it is perfectly consistent that the world is necessarily connected to it, and that it is distinct only through a process of degeneration. In fact, the only form of identity possible is the ideal one and its dialectical negation. If being *sic et simpliciter* is identified with the intelligible, then *tertium non datur*. However, if being

7. Aristotle, *Metaph.* 12.7:1072.a.21–26.
8. See Maspero, "Patristic Trinitarian Ontology."

transcends human knowledge, then there is a third possibility of relation, on the basis of which two realities can be distinct for the same reason that unites them. In fact, the gap further implies that the relationship between the first principle and the world has to be understood in a relational sense, without introducing an opposition between creature and Creator, and so without devaluing the former in order to affirm the latter.

The radical nature of this new ontology is shown precisely by the claim of Jesus to be a single *thing* with the Father, being a different *who* from him. "Dad-hood," in fact, refers to a new form of identity, never known before, because the Son cannot be called *god* as belonging to the same category, as happens for a species. In the case of the absolute first principle, this counts, by definition, as a single element. The tag "god" cannot be attributed to several members according to an identity of a Platonic type, through which an element is identified by its belonging to a category, which is subject to an idea—for example, a particular horse, which is such because it corresponds to the idea of "horseness." In the case of God, too, we cannot apply dialectical identity because the gap prevents us from defining what God is by contrast with something other. In fact, the world is no longer necessarily connected with the first principle and is not forever.

On the other hand, Jesus of Nazareth claims, "Before Abraham was, I am" (John 8:58). In effect, he says that he is the eternal Son of the eternal Father, who himself is not God except in and through the Second Person of the Trinity. He says, "I am in the Father, and the Father is in me" (John 14:10), thus presenting an enormous challenge to classical metaphysics, for which accident and participation were bound up precisely with inhering in another substance, that is, with being *in alio*. But here, the Father himself is *in Filio*, the reason dictating the conclusion that the Son is eternal, that is, he is absolute, as will be said again of the Holy Spirit, who, as Spirit of the Father and of the Son, is *in* them just as the First and Second Persons are *in* him.

This new form of identity was to require the development of a new ontology, which we shall call Trinitarian precisely because it tackles the problem of the relationship between the first principle and the world in the light of the gap introduced by the fathers of the church in their development of the Trinitarian dogma. Very gradually, the fathers arrived at a relational understanding of the identity of the three divine persons, starting out from the scriptural data of their revealed proper names, which speak of relation. In fact, Father, Son, and Spirit-Love refer to one another.

However, that required a process that we could summarize as beginning with Justin, who, as a good philosopher, was well aware of the challenge. His own biography led him to explain the distinction between the Father and the Son in terms of the Logos, taking up the Johannine Prologue.

From eternity, the Father thinks the world in such a way that this thought is his: it is in him, but is distinct from him. Thus, every truth known by anyone before the incarnation can be read again as an expression of the Logos and, so, as part of the Christian heritage.[9] This solution presented two main disadvantages: first, although eternal, the existence of the Son was necessarily bound up with the cosmos because of the identification with the Logos; and second, the full divinity remained exclusively that of the Father who, for this reason, was not called person in that this term indicated limitation and was predicated only of the Son.[10] It could be said that, for Justin, the world does not have its being on account of the Logos but exactly the opposite. The distinction between the divine persons is again expressed through subordination according to the Platonic heritage. It is extremely significant that the intra-Trinitarian distinction between the first principle and the world appear here as superimposed and not as perfectly distinct. In fact, the gap has not been formulated in all its force.

That is why Origen's contribution will be shown to be essential: Origen superseded the apologists' theology of the logos[11] to formulate the clear belonging of the Father, the Son, and the Holy Spirit to a unique ontological level.[12] He affirms, in fact, there is no more and no less, a formula reserved in metaphysics for substantial fullness.[13] The *gap* is expressed here perfectly. Yet, precisely in the context of Origen's Trinitarian theology, there appears with force the need for a further metaphysical development, which would lead to a proper Trinitarian ontology. In fact, Origen sought to distinguish the three divine persons from the creation by attributing to them alone pure spirituality.[14] Both angels and men, on the other hand, were supposed to be characterized by a corporal element, which was all the more subtle the nearer they were to perfection. As will be noted immediately, there was no strong concept of the *physis*, such as was to be developed later by Athanasius in the fourth century. Thus, according to Origen, the Son is God is second grade compared with the Father. Neither he nor the Spirit are identified with the

---

9. Justin, *1 Apol.* 46; *2 Apol.* 1–2.3; 2.6.

10. Justin, *Dial.* 127.

11. See Pazzini: *In principio*; "Interpretazione del Prologo."

12. For a serious and effective criticism of any interpretation of Origen's theology in the line of subordinationism, see Ramelli, "Origen's Anti-Subordinationism."

13. Origen, *On First Principles* 1.3.7.

14. From Origen's perspective, John 4:24 ("God is *pneuma*") was fundamental as it implied the necessity to affirm the pure spirituality of God against the stoic interpretation of *pneuma* as corporeal. See Origen, *Gospel According to John* 13.

divine attributes of the Father; they only participate in them.[15] We could say that Origen was strongly aware of the need to distinguish the ontology of the Trinity from that of the creation. However, his attempts, although ingenious, continue in part to project on to God the metaphysics that had previously been developed by Greek philosophers in the sphere of the categories. In fact, the systematic structure of the first principle demonstrates an ontological inadequacy on the level of the immanent distinction of the three divine persons, which is, again, the result of a metaphysical deficiency. Without there being an actual subordination, the Father, the Son, and the Spirit appear to be situated once more in a decreasing ontological series.

The Arian crisis was to be the precise result of this tension in expression. Both Arius and Eunomius were to appeal to the words of Origen, taking the ontological gradation outside the divine immanence. If the Son is a second-class *god*, then, in the name of the gap demanded by the doctrine of creation, he must be a creature and, therefore, have originated in time. But then there must have been a time when the Second Person was not, and so when God was not Father. Athanasius replied with the introduction of the theology of the "natures," on the basis of which the Trinity is identified with the unique eternal and infinite nature, which is separated by an absolute *gap* from all the other natures created in time and finite. In other words, Athanasius excluded the possibility of grey intermediate areas within the gap itself. The transmission of the perfect divinity within the divine immanence is assured, however, by a perfect proportionality, through which the Son-Logos is in relationship with the Father, precisely as the Spirit is in relationship with the Son-Logos.[16] This already represents the elaboration of a great ontological novelty, which succeeds in answering the Arian arguments precisely by starting out from the proportional function of the logos also in the Pythagorean-Platonic and geometrical tradition. However, this solution was to receive the criticisms of the Pneumatomachians, that is, of that heterodox group who accepted the divinity of the Son, beginning from the fact that he was generated and so of the same nature as the Father, but who also denied the divinity of the Third Person precisely because he was not *Son*. These critics attempted to threaten Trinitarian thought by affirming an *aut-aut*: either the Second Person is not the only begotten, because he has a brother in the Spirit; or else the Father must be the grandfather of the Spirit as the parent of the one who generated the latter. This was a demonstration ad absurdum as both conclusions were manifestly unacceptable.[17]

15. Origen, *Comm.* 2.10, 76, 2–7.
16. Athanasius, *Ep.* 2.10.2.
17. Athanasius, *Ep.* 3.1.3.

This opened the way for Cappadocian thought, which, especially with the two Gregories, was to be able to present a new understanding of ontology in a relational key. The point is bound up precisely with the need to distinguish the divine persons in their immanence only by starting out from their relations of origin.[18] But that required reexamining Aristotle's metaphysics on a capital point: for the Stagirite, relation was not only a simple accident, but the least of these in that, in order to subsist, not only was there need of one substance, but of at least two, so as to exclude the possibility of the substance itself belonging to the relative dimension.[19] Relation was thus conceived as an excrescence of the substance, whose loss could in no way change the substance itself. For the Cappadocians, on the other hand, the proper names of the divine persons speak of relation, introducing a distinction within the unique eternal and infinite substance. The radical novelty of this distinction consisted in the fact that it implied the perfect identity of each of those thus distinguished with the divine attributes, per se unique. The Father, the Son and the Spirit are, therefore, the same thing, God, but the one is not the other because they are distinguished by the relations inherent in their own names.

This novelty was formulated in formally metaphysical terms by Gregory of Nyssa, who found himself tackling the use of *schesis*, i.e., relation, by Eunomius precisely in order to demonstrate the presumed substantial difference of the three divine persons.[20] Thus Basil's brother affirms clearly that the Logos belongs to the relative realm (*ta pros ti*), and that the characteristic that distinguishes each person from the others is the *pôs einai*, that is, its mode of subsistence, the relation through which it possesses, eternally and infinitely, the infinite and eternal being which is God.[21] The *pôs einai* itself is a modification of the Stoic *pôs echein*, which has been taken from the level of having, to which *schesis* also refers etymologically, to that of being. Thus, the fact that the Son is *in* the Father just as the Father is *in* the Son is now being read no longer as a proof for departing from the Aristotelian metaphysics of their substantial difference, but rather as an affirmation of their consubstantiality beginning from a new ontology, in which relation can inhabit the immanence of the divine substance.[22] Thus, first, the Logos and, then, the Spirit will pass from being figures of ontological mediation, which link the different ontological levels of God and the world, to inhabiting and defining

18. Gregory of Nazianzus, *Oratio* 31.9 (*De Spiritu Sancto*).

19. Aristotle, *Eth. nic.* 1096a.21–22.

20. Eunomius, in Gregory of Nyssa, *Contra Eunomium* 1.151.

21. Gregory of Nyssa, *Contra Eunomium* 2.1.386.

22. On the fathers' reading of Aristotelian categories, a very serious and deep research is Edwards, *Aristotle*.

the divine immanence. Gregory Nyssa would have to present the Third Person as the royal power communicated by the Father to the Son in the act of generation, through which the Son is King precisely as the Father is King. Furthermore, the Second Person returns to the first, eternally and perfectly, this power that can also be called Glory.[23] Similarly, Gregory Nazianzen also presents the Spirit *between* the Father and the Son in such a way as to overcome every possible criticism of the Pneumatomachians, who recognized the divinity of the first two divine persons.[24] The Father, the Son, and the Spirit are thus presented in a correlative way to one another in that each of them is identified with the unique eternal and infinite divine substance, being distinguished from the others only on the level of relation.

That what we have here is an authentic ontological novelty can be proved by comparing these statements with the thought of Plotinus and Porphyry, according to whom being generated necessarily implied the metaphysical inferiority of the one generated to the one generating, along with the impossibility that relation could be raised to the level of substance.[25] For them, the first principle must be absolutely without relations.[26] The point at play here is the distinction between ontology and gnoseology. From the patristic point of view, to the contrary, being is not identified with the intelligible but is a mystery of infinite depth. The convertibility of the universals is maintained insofar as the Logos is the absolute knowledge and expression of Being, but as divine person, because now only God can speak about God. Knowledge becomes relation. That goes, too, for the created world, and eminently for man created in the image and likeness of God. Only relation with the one and triune God can reveal the true identity of the creature. Here, Trinitarian ontology appears in all its force: in fact, the re-understanding of the first principle in a relational key leads to a radically novel reading of the world beginning from the new ontological status of relation itself.

Aquinas: Building the Bridge

Thus far, we have shown first that the fathers of the church developed a new ontology for describing the one and triune God by modifying classical metaphysics, in such a way as to attribute to relation a value that was not merely accidental; and second that, from this position, they read again the creation, object of classical philosophical study, in a new light, indicating

23. See Maspero, *Dio trino perché vivo*, 110–13, and references therein.
24. Gregory of Nazianzus, *Oratio* 31.2 (*De Spiritu Sancto*).
25. Porphyry, *Sent.* 13.
26. Porphyry, *Comm. Tim.* 3.32—4.4.

the role of the gap and of apophatism. At this point, there arises the question of the value of such a process: Does it concern a contingent choice bound up with the cultural movements of the period? What has all this to do with subsequent theological development?

Piero Coda has acutely observed that the Trinitarian disputes of the fourth century can be read as discussion on the exegesis of the Johannine Prologue.[27] In fact, what has been seen until now incipiently finds its real root in the Fourth Gospel, which is thus placed at a foundational and so, in some ways also, inescapable level for Christian thought.

If we read the whole of the Johannine Prologue, we can observe its chiastic structure. As in the figure of the Greek letter *chi*, we see that the text can be divided into two large parts, which meet in the affirmation in John 1:12–13 that whoever receives the Logos who was made flesh becomes a son of God. In the first half, the protagonist is the Logos who (a) is in the *arché* (John 1:1–2); (b) is responsible for the creation, which, however, is disturbed by sin (John 1:3–5); (c) is announced by the baptist who bears witness to the light (John 1:6–8); and, (d), finally, comes into the world as the true light (John 1:9–11). The movement here is top down, from the immanence to the economy. In the second half, however, the same journey takes place in reverse by tracing the same steps as the first part in historical and concrete terms to reveal, finally, the identity of the Logos. Thus (d'), the Logos not only comes into the world as light but is made flesh (John 1:14); (c') and the baptist bears witness precisely to this identity (John 1:15) in such a way that (b') the meaning of the creation can be read fully in the new creation, which, in the gift of grace, replaces the Mosaic law (John 1:16–17), concluding with the revelation that the *arché* is the bosom of the Father and the Logos is the only begotten (John 1:18). In this reading, the ten words of the law are placed in parallel with the ten words with which God created the world at the beginning of Genesis; and this operation seems faithful to the intention of the author, who omits the article in the expression *en arché*, as would be better grammatically in Greek, in order to recall the *be rescit* of Gen 1:1. Moreover, the Logos himself recalls the *dabar* with which God created everything.[28]

The fathers took the Johannine text seriously in a metaphysical way, and placed it as the foundation of a new ontology, in which the *arché* sought by the philosophers is revealed in Christ to have an immanence indwelt by the Logos himself. The latter, then, is *in* the first principle in that it is toward him (*pros ton*). This Greek expression can be read as a reformulation of the

---

27. See Coda, *Per una lettura trinitaria*, 85–94.
28. See Maspero, *Uno perché trino*, 33–35.

pros ti, that is the technical term for the relational dimension.[29] The Second Person of the Trinity is pure relation because he is eternal Son of the Father himself, and from eternity dwells in his bosom. Therefore, both the *arché* and the logos of metaphysics must be read again in the light of a conception of relation, which is no longer a mere accident, but instead subsists in the unique, infinite, and absolute divine substance.

This new relational understanding further implies that only the only begotten can reveal God and make him known (lit. "exegete" him) (John 1:18). From this perspective, the theological position of the fathers, characterized by *gap* and apophatism, can be ascribed precisely to the prologue, and, therefore, be considered to have a defining role in Christian epistemologies.[30] One can have access to Being itself, in its depth, only through personal relation with the incarnate Son, because being itself is relation. Apophatism no longer appears as negation, but rather as a positive affirmation of the inexhaustible ontological profundity of God. Thus, the theological approach cannot be considered as contradicting the philosophical one, because the fathers are looking at being *from within*, through a concrete relation without which they could not have access to such depth. Apophatism does not deny the value of reason, but only signals that its limit can also be a threshold, such that where metaphysical thought enters into crisis, new possibilities are thrust open like windows. In fact, in this way, *ratio* is fulfilled in *relation*.[31]

We note that the prologue can be read as a simultaneous reference to both the biblical elements of *be rescit* and *dabar*, as well as to the metaphysical categories of the *arché* and the *logos*—and perhaps even to the ontological reconfiguration of the *pros ti* as the personal *pros ton*.

The question posed here is how all this is found in subsequent theological architecture. By way of example, two points have been chosen from the thought of Thomas Aquinas, which will illustrate how, even in the context of later medieval Scholastic rereadings of Aristotelianism, apophatism is still maintained as an essential epistemological principle of the theologian and, at the same time, indicates the role of the gap. The power of the Thomist construction will be presented precisely in its ability to build a bridge between the divine and created ontologies, respecting the differences between them. From such a viewpoint, it is possible to recognize how, beyond its

---

29. See Aristotle, *Cat.* 1b26—2a1; 6a36–37.

30. From this perspective, the method of the fathers of the church, who *used* the elements of truth present in pagan culture, as also Christian art did, is rooted in John's Prologue itself. The fathers' method is masterfully presented in Gnilka, *Begriff.*

31. This point is very important also for interdisciplinary studies. See Maspero, "Trinitarian Ontology."

Scholastic form and its tendency to dialectic,[32] Thomas's method can be considered authentically relational.

This is the thrust of the observation of Alasdair MacIntyre that the *Summa* has a real narrative structure.[33] Thomas does not simply demonstrate his own position but perceives that it is really necessary to resolve the tensions of the authors who have preceded him. The force of the *sed contra* is precisely to be the conduit that transmits to the reader not only the result, but also the historical process that is required to reach it. That can be considered an element that is intrinsically relational in a methodological way. It is also the basis of the possibility, which characterizes Thomist teaching, of turning out to be useful, even where the conclusions have been superseded by subsequent study. In fact, it is always possible to retrace the theological process in order to understand why at a certain crossroads Thomas followed a different path.

This intrinsic historicity in his theological method also explains why he opposed Anselm and Richard of St. Victor in the Trinitarian sphere. Compared with the monastic theology, wholly aimed at seeking a synthesis between philosophy and theology, in order to offer that single vision of the whole that was the true aspiration of the medieval spirit, Thomas is always careful to distinguish natural and supernatural, not in order to separate them but to recognize their relationship as free relation of gift. Thus, despite the *vestigia Trinitatis* found in the world, it is clear that these can never establish a demonstration of the uni-triune being of God.[34] One arrives at the Trinity only a posteriori, through the history of salvation and the personal encounter with Christ and his Spirit.[35]

This hermeneutical openness and narrative care are found in the actual development of Thomas's thought. For example, a diachronic analysis of the responses to the, at first sight technical, question over the possibility that Logos is a substantial and/or notional name of God, provides us with an extremely significant fact. Gilles Emery has shown that in his *Commentary on the Sentences*, Thomas's response indicates both possibilities: *Verbum* is a name applicable both to the divine substance in itself and to the Second Person of the Trinity.[36] Yet, in the *Summa*, his position has changed radi-

---

32. In fact, modern dialectic can be ascribed to an improper extrapolation of the Scholastic tendency to resolve every question by introducing conceptual distinctions. Gradually, this method returned to an identification between being and thought, the results of which were to be evident in subsequent centuries.

33. MacIntyre, *Three Rival Versions*, 130–35.

34. See Aquinas: *Summa Theologiae*, q. 32, a. 1, ad. 2; *In Boetium*, q. 1, a. 4.

35. To understand the excesses reached by Scholastic thought, see Friedman, *Medieval Trinitarian Thought*.

36. Emery, *Théologie trinitaire*, 217–31. See also Aquinas, *In I Sentiarum*, d. 27, q. 2, a. 2qc., 1 co.

cally: for Thomas there denies that the name *Verbum* can be understood in a substantial sense.[37] That this is not a marginal change of position is demonstrated by the fact that, between 1270 and 1271, the Masters of Theology of Paris assembled to condemn as contrary to the fathers and Augustine the position that considered *Verbum* as also a substantial name.[38] Accordingly, Thomas had already begun to modify his position in the *Summa contra gentiles*, preceding his last period in Paris.

What has this theological question to do with apophatism and the *gap*? Despite the apparent technicality of all this, the point is a very practical one: if *Verbum* were also a substantial name, that would mean to say that the divine substance is expressed not only in itself but also with respect to the creation. The apophatic veil would thus be torn away. On the other hand, if *Verbum* is only a notional name, it is perfectly clear that knowledge of God and of his eternal Fatherhood could come only through the personal dimension, which, for man, is through history and the incarnation. Moreover, the doctrine of the Trinity avoids all risk of affirming that it is the divine substance and not the person of the Father, which generates the Son—a position clarified by the Fourth Lateran Council of 1215 in connection with the polemic between Joachim of Fiore and Peter Lombard. The conclusion that has thus been set out is consistent with other readings, which indicate Thomas's apophatism, for which the divine substance is unknowable.[39]

Thomas welcomed the philosophical heritage of Aristotle, now rediscovered, thanks to the Arabs. Yet he inserts Greek metaphysics into a new ontology on two levels. This insertion allows him to develop his theological architecture in a relational sense. Not only is the indwelling of the divine persons in the human soul the point of convergence for the whole Trinitarian construction in qq. 27–43 of the *I. pars* of the *Summa*, but the finding of new meaning for the metaphysical categories concerning the definition of the person permits him to recognize how precisely the clear distinction between natural and supernatural helps, in the context of patristic ontology, to construct a bridge between the created and the uncreated. This distinction between natural and supernatural has been criticized severely just as, on the Thomist side, voices have been raised against a Trinitarian ontology as a supposed violation of the very spirit of Thomas that implies the question of Trinitarian ontology:[40] for the introduction of the gap between the two ontological levels requires theology to undertake to articulate their relationship.

37. Aquinas, *Summa Theologiae*, pt. 1, q. 34, a. 1c.
38. See Schmaus, *Trinitarischen Lehrdifferenzen*, 613–14n40; Pelster, "Roger Marston," 545.
39. See Pérez de Laborda, "Preesistenza."
40. But William Norris Clarke's research offers a very interesting perspective for

Thomas's redefinition of the concept of person serves to illustrate the point. If one considers the history of the definitions of person,[41] one observes a development that is extremely interesting for the subject in question. The link with Trinitarian ontology is clear precisely because the Christian revelation has made possible for the first time the full perception of this dimension of the *who* compared with the simple *what* of Greek metaphysics. A classic definition is that of Boethius in the sixth century: *rationalis naturae individua substantia*.[42] The person would be "the individual substance of a rational nature." It is evident that this choice has a classical philosophical matrix, which easily suits the definition of man and the angel. If applied to the triune God, however, it presents a serious difficulty because the three divine persons would be three substances. The impossibility of conforming to both the first principle and the creature is alien to the spirit of the Middle Ages, which was always seeking to present the world and its Creator in unitary terms.

The synthesis between philosophy and theology, developed with originality in his abbatial environment, led Richard of St. Victor, in the twelfth century, to propose a new definition of the divine person, no longer based on the concept of substance but on that of existence: *divinae naturae incommunnibilis existentia* (incommunicable existence of the divine nature).[43] If the Father, the Son, and the Holy Spirit cannot be distinguished on the substantial level, it will be necessary to move to the plane of existence in that their *sistere*, i.e., their standing or lying, is distinct from the point of view of relation indicated by the preposition *ex*. The progress is significant because an elaboration has been reached, which allows the more proper description of the being of the triune God.

It is essential to notice, however, that, again, this is not a Trinitarian ontology, but rather only an ontology of the Trinity. This means to say that the result is applicable only to the first principle, but, by definition, it cannot descend to the created level, illuminating our world with the light of the Trinity. For this reason, Thomas was to warn of the need to modify Boethius's definition in such a way as to render it valid in both the ontologies, the eternal and the created. Thus, Thomas defines the person as *subsistens in rationali natura* (the subsistent in a rational nature),[44] that of moving on

---

Trinitarian ontology also on the Thomist side. See Clarke: *One and Many*; *Explorations in Metaphysics*.

41. A masterly presented narrative can be found in Daniélou, "Notion de personne."
42. Boethius, *De duabus naturis* 3.
43. Richard of St. Victor, *De Trinitate* 4.22.
44. Aquinas, *Summa Theologiae*, pt. 1, q. 29, a. 3, in c.

to the level of the subject. Here, however, the latter is defined with the aid of the present participle of the verb "to subsist," which signifies to exist really in oneself and not in another. In this way, Thomas was to obtain the result that the divine person would be defined as *distinctum subsistens in natura divina* (the distinct subsistent in the divine nature).[45]

From the point of view of the relational ontology of the fathers, this constitutes a really fundamental development. For the first time, the *Ipsum Esse Subsistens* is formally identified with three eternal and perfect relations. Furthermore, Thomas comes to affirm that *abstracta relatione in Deo nihil manet* (if relation is taken away, nothing remains in God).[46] Certainly, this conclusion is not extended to the created ontology: Thomas always highlights the difference between it and the Trinity. Yet, the construction of the definition of the person in such a way as to pass vertically between the ontology of the Trinity and that of the creation can be considered a peak and a model of Trinitarian ontology.

In fact, Thomas recognizes that the task of theology is precisely that of elaborating a thought that not only can formulate the mystery of the divine, always preserving its transcendence in order to offer it for adoration, but that can also illuminate the created world and indicate the relation between the two ontologies. Thus, the act of theology can be said to be completed when it succeeds to offer words and expressions that allow one to move from the Trinity to the world and vice versa.

It is true that a study of the relationality of the creature was not developed by Thomas. However, the deep rooting of the creative act in the eternal processions permits the affirmation that the real ratio of the world with its multiplicity is the intra-Trinitarian *relatio*.[47]

Contemporaneity: Rethinking Ontology

This is a theme that contemporary theology has felt the need to elaborate. Antonio Rosmini came to define the person as subsistent relation in general and, therefore, also in the created sphere. In his *Theosophy* (*Teosofia*), the argument starts out from the following affirmation: "When the mind is confronted with two entities together, it sees an entity which cannot be seen in one of them alone by leaving the other entirely apart; then this entity is called relation." At first glance, this approach is gnoseological, but Rosmini explains immediately

---

45. Aquinas, *De Potentia*, q. 9, a. 4.
46. Aquinas, *In I Sentiarum*, d. 26, q. 1, a. 2, in c.
47. "Processiones personarum aeternae sunt causa et ratio totius productionis creaturarum" (Aquinas, *In I Sentiarum*, d. 14, q. 1, a. 1, co).

that the definition does not work only on the conceptual level, "but also exists among things that are real and subsistent."[48] Actually, it is precisely this relation that is the bridge between the ontological and the gnoseological dimensions: for the sentient and what is sensed, as also the intelligent and what is understood, are really to be found in this relation. Thus, he reaches the conclusion enunciated above, applying what was said to his definition of the person as "a substantial individual, in that it contains an active, supreme and incommunicable principle." In fact, if the person cannot think without reference to an active principle, which acts as something intelligent and sentient, although in itself incommunicable, then it finds itself before a reality, in which its subsistence is defined by relationality.[49] In other words, the personal substance is characterized by a relational immanence. Taking up the Thomist expression, one could say, by analogy, that *in homine abstracta relatione nihil manet* (if relation is taken away, nothing remains in the human being).

Regardless of whether or not one agrees with this conclusion, what matters is the fact that modernity has perceived the need to continue the Thomist program on the philosophico-theological level. In fact, the reaction to substantialism produced an existentialism that showed both an anti-Christian face—one thinks of Sartre—and a development that was authentically Christian. It is precisely the latter that was the position of great theologians of the twentieth century, like Balthasar and Daniélou, who showed the Trinitarian roots of the discovery of the value of existence by human thought.

In fact, the dialectic between essence and existence, from which derives also that between being and history, finds its causes precisely in idealism's negation of the ontological gap introduced by the fathers of the church. This real secularization of Trinitarian thought is found especially in Georg Wilhelm Friedrich Hegel. Hegel was preceded by the work of René Descartes, who had enclosed the subject in that interior space, the discovery that had been enabled precisely by Christianity, through its doctrine of creation in the image and likeness. However, the secularization of Trinitarian thought was tragically unveiled by Friedrich Nietzsche, who transformed Hegel's dialectical *Aufhebung* into an absolute and objective concept, before which he placed himself as a free and anarchic antithesis. In its radically and explicitly anti-Christian nature, this stance also precipitated the emergence of the point of utmost negation in the Trinitarian thought of Hegel.[50]

The point is that each form of thought is incapable of recognizing the transcendence of the real at its limits, is condemned to remain trapped

---

48. Rosmini, *Teosofia*, 4:222.
49. Rosmini, *Teosofia*, 4:223.
50. See Sciacca, *Ontologia triadica*, 44.

between identity and dialectic, which, in themselves, are pathologies of conceiving of relation as a mere concept of the mind. In order to have a relation that is real, and not only thought, it is necessary, as for the church fathers, to retain the substantial and the relational dimensions simultaneously. Without substance, in fact, it is not possible to formulate clearly the difference between God and the world, and so also to affirm the transcendence of the Trinity with respect to the created. And yet, in the absence of a real ontological gap, human thought tends to project its own categories on to God, thus falling into the temptation of idolatry. The idol is always an image, and a symbol, which usurps the relational value that is intrinsic to the partial good that constitutes it, and thereby ceases to refer beyond itself.

This is why both Jean Daniélou and Hans Urs von Balthasar were compelled to respond to the challenge posed to Christian thought by hermeneutics. In fact, without a convergence of substance and relation, the work of Martin Heidegger and Hans-Georg Gadamer risks trapping man in the intellectual dimension, where interpretation takes place, but which never succeeds in referring to an ontological beyond, remaining always in the logic of *this side*. These two theologians thus mentioned developed a real ontology of history, which, in its Trinitarian origin, is shaped as a theology of history and not as a mere philosophy of history. In fact, in their volumes devoted to this question, both make explicit their intention to respond to existentialism.[51]

Daniélou gives an epistemological stamp to discourse about the one and triune God by emphasizing that the point of access to knowledge of him can only be the awareness of the radical powerlessness of man and, therefore, total humility.[52] He conceives the history of the divine missions as a prolongation of the intra-Trinitarian relations,[53] in such a way that the spiritual life itself and the goal of the world consist in participating in these relations, immersing oneself in them through the missions. Daniélou speaks explicitly of Trinitarian ontology, recognizing, in the light of the Trinitarian thought of the fathers, and, in particular, of Gregory of Nyssa, that the basis of being is neither matter nor the spirit nor the one, but the communion of the divine persons.[54] Yet it is precisely this acute knowledge of the compenetration of relation and substance in God that makes it possible to read again both matter and spirit, as well as the one from the Trinitarian perspective, assigning them an infinite value.[55] Thus, paradoxically, the gap does not distance

51. Daniélou, *Lord of History*, 8; Balthasar, *Theologie der Geschichte*.
52. Daniélou, *Trinité et mystère*, 43.
53. Daniélou: *God*, 124–25; *Trinité et mystère*, 103.
54. Daniélou, *Trinité et mystère*, 52.
55. Daniélou, *Trinité et mystère*, 16–17.

man from God, but instead brings him closer, because the radical difference between the eternal and created natures, which enables the reading of their relationship as an eternal relation of gift, overcomes any need to protect God through a dialectical abasement of the world in relation to the first principle.

Particularly daring and valuable is the interpretation of Balthasar, who sees the foundation of history in the intra-Trinitarian sonship. The earthly life of Christ is presented as a translation into creaturely terms of the eternal relation, which unites the Father and the Son. Describing the characteristic of the Second Person as the pure receiving wholly and perfectly from the First Person, Balthasar states:

> Precisely this receptivity for everything that comes from God the Father is what for him, in his form of creaturely existence, is called time, and is the basis of temporality. It is that fundamental condition of his Being in which he is constantly open to the reception of the paternal mission. This condition is not in contrast with his eternal Being as Son but rather is its direct and sufficient revelation.[56]

Perfectly consistent with Daniélou's statement, this is a valuable theological way to ascribe history to the immanent relationality of the triune God.[57] Indeed, what is history if not time saturated with relations, which order it and give it structure? What is kairos compared with mere *chronos* if not time transfigured qualitatively by relations? But, if the relational dimension is only and necessarily accidental, and so destined to be swallowed up into nothing, then we can never speak of a theology of history, or of salvation, or, indeed, of the value of human existence. In the final analysis, just as in the world of Greek metaphysics, only the intelligible universal will have value.

On the other hand, the incarnation of the Son happened once for all. The hypostatic union was not dissolved with the ascension of Christ into heaven. Rather, his acts, especially those that make up the paschal mystery,

---

56. "Eben diese Empfänglichkeit für alles, was von Gott dem Vater kommt, ist es, was für ihn in seiner geschöpflichen Existenzform Zeit heisst und Zeitlichkeit begründet. Sie ist jene Grundverfassung seines Seins, in der er je und je offen ist zum Empfang der väterlichen Sendung. Diese Verfassung steht also so wenig in Gegensatz zu seinem ewigen Sein als Sohn, dass sie vielmehr deren direkte and angemessene Offenbarung ist" (Balthasar, *Theologie der Geschichte*, 13).

57. Balthasar's limitation is having also projected sin into the Trinitarian immanence by ascribing it to the distance between the Father and the Son. Although one understands his intention, animated also by an extraordinary contemplative power, the proposal seems unable to escape a dialectic element in clear contradiction to the relational ontology of the fathers.

but all of them, even the hidden life in Nazareth, are a union of time and eternity. The contingency of days has thus been embraced and saturated by the eternity of the perfect God, who was made perfect man. In him, the absolute and the particular are united, as the universal and the concrete come together, according to the beautiful expression of Balthasar himself.[58] Thus, the eternal relation between the Father and the Son in their Love, which is the Spirit, holds together not only the life of Jesus, but, in him, the lives of all people of every time also.

From this point of view, Trinitarian ontology gives rise naturally to an ontology of history, which is able to overcome the limits of the idealist and hermeneutical philosophy of history, thanks to a perspective, which, in the light of the Christian revelation, recognizes the relational texture in creation and human existence along with their eternal echo.

However, what is said for history has as an immediate corollary the development of Trinitarian ontology into a theology of the body. In fact, the latter is nothing else than matter impregnated with relations. But if the relationality placed by God in the world can be recognized as an expression of the relationality immanent in the triune Creator, then the body, too, can be grasped as telling of the personal and existential dimension and so of infinite value.[59] Clearly, as with history, we must avoid all risk of projection from the economy to the immanence.[60] Thought can become, in a certain sense, something else altogether: actually creating idols, images that have lost their relational content inherent in their relational symbolism. However, the body is one and only one, precisely that and not another. Polytheism was bound up with intellectualism more than one thinks. In fact, people are always seeking to escape their own creaturely limits, fascinated by their own desire, which is always stretching out for the infinite. This risk is particularly acute today both because of the technological power of the image and of the financialization, which reduces everything to money that can potentially acquire any aspect in the mind of the consumer. Thus, consumerism can be read theologically as a flight into the ideal of the idol, which is inspired by the mass-media interaction of images and money.

---

58. See Balthasar: *Theologie der Geschichte*, 13–15; *Glory of the Lord*, 1:529.

59. See, for example, the reinterpretation of the human body in Gregory of Nyssa, who describes its erect form and the consequent development of the mouth and of the phonatory organs as a relational reflection of being created in the image of the Word who was made flesh (*De hominis opificio* 8).

60. From this point of view, Rahner's theology has not rendered good service to Trinitarian ontology, especially with regard to certain radical interpretations of the *Umkehrung* in the *Grundaxiom*.

The body and time, on the other hand, always set a difference because they establish a dramatic contact with limitation; and the postmodern fears difference that it seeks constantly to deny. In fact, the secularization of Trinitarian thought, effected by modernity by means of the denial of the ontological gap, has entrapped the subject in the mental opposition between identity and dialectic. In a process that is really pathoplastic, the ego is condemned to solitude, because the only form of relationship with the others is their negation. The psychopathological outcome of the life of Nietzsche himself is a tragic illustration of this point.[61] The postmodern has, thus, reacted by denying differences as possible places of conflict. The solution is ineffective, however, because the differences themselves are inescapable, not only on account of creaturely limitation, but, still more deeply, because Being itself, on the pattern of the Trinity, is interwoven with identity and distinction. Thus, the postmodern challenge to Christian thought can be read as a desperate cry raised in search of a thought that makes it possible to recognize differences as relations.

Trinitarian ontology, understood as a rereading of the being of the world starting from the ontology of the Trinity, is not a simple theological choice but rather can be considered as a real necessity that has been highlighted by the crisis of postmodern thought. It is nothing other than a continuation of the theological work that was begun by the fathers, and which has continued to be carried on by the medieval masters, as well as by the theologians of recent centuries.

The particular form of Trinitarian ontology that is the relational ontology inspired by Cappadocian theology is characterized by the recognition of the ontological gap between God and the world with the consequent apophatism, and by the compenetration of the substantial principle with the relational one.[62] This is the foundation of its twofold power: in fact, (1) this relational ontology can be secularly expressed in terms that do not refer to faith; and, then (2), it can be extended to many different areas of human thought.

We cite only four examples of this:

(1) Ecumenism and interreligious dialogue can be read in the framework proposed, not as concessions or gestures of goodwill on the part of the believer but as real and inescapable demands of the Trinitarian faith. One cannot contemplate the world as a fabric of relations, expressions of the

---

61. See Fornari, *God Torn to Pieces*.

62. From this perspective, this reading of the Cappadocian thought differs from the more dialectical one of John Zizioulas, who seems to present the personal and the substantial dimensions as opposite one to the other. See Zizioulas: *Being as Communion*; *Communion & Otherness*, 33–34.

depth of being itself, beyond the wounds inflicted by sin, without working to translate the differences into places of relation.

(2) Still more, the dialogue with the nonbeliever can no longer be conceived of as the simple attempt at conversion, but must be taken on, primarily, as a reciprocal exchange of gifts, because difference experienced as relation illuminates the very identity of the Christian and enriches it. From here there derives a conception of theology as that which is inseparable from philosophy and the other sciences. Moreover, this perspective illuminates not only the dimension *ad extra* but also that *ad intra*.

Indeed, (3), the foundation of the secular dimension and of laicity can be recognized precisely thanks to relational ontology in that, first, the difference between the sphere of the temple and the profane (from *pro-fanum*) sphere, which "stands before the temple," must be understood in a Trinitarian way as relation. Then, the identity of the ordinary member of the faithful can be presented not as a deficiency in relation to a further perfection but as a full relational identity to which all the other ecclesial identities refer. "Lay," in fact, derives from *laos*. A lay person is none other than a member of the people, a *quisque de populo*, and, as such, is defined only by the relation of divine sonship acquired with baptism to which, as we have seen, the center of the Johannine Prologue refers. Thus, the identity of the lay person becomes, relationally, the raison d'être for the ordained ministry and the consecrated, since these are, in the most different ways, whether active or contemplative, at the service of the people themselves. From the point of view of religious history, it is clear how valuable such a change would have been in the tension that led to the Lutheran Reformation by responding to its legitimate request for purification from clericalism.

Finally, (4), still by way of example, the theology of the body, already mentioned, is called today not only to demonstrate the relational riches of the sexual difference but also to highlight the theological value of the sexual act itself. The Trinitarian theology of the fourth century was completely on the ball in affirming the difference between human and divine generation. The discovery of the value of relation is derived precisely from such work. However, now that sexual pleasure (and not the sexual act) has taken the symbolic place of God in the contemporary world, in that, like an idol, it promises an answer to the desire for the infinite that defines the human heart, it becomes essential to reread again these same acts that are linked to human generation from a relational perspective. The being of the one in the other, which is sought for in sexual union, has its deepest sense precisely in the image of the one and triune God that is the human identity. This is a reflection already set in motion by a thinker beyond all suspicion of yielding to sentiment and lack of rigor, Thomas Aquinas.

Conclusion: Mary's Being and the Trinity

Although perhaps too daring, the journey traced here was inspired by the rethinking of the classical metaphysics employed by the fathers of the church, who had thus formulated a relational ontology characterized by the gap, by apophatism as its reflection on the cognitive level, and by the inclusion of relation as a co-principle of being, along with substance, and yet inseparable from it to the point of identifying its immanence. We have shown how this relational ontology constitutes a real Trinitarian ontology, in that it not only reformulates the ontology of the one and triune God, but also reinterprets the world in the light of this reformulation. From here, through the further example of Thomas, we have tried to indicate how Trinitarian ontology represents an absolutely inescapable and crucial point, as it is able to ascribe the modern crisis and the postmodern reaction precisely to a deficit in Trinitarian and relational thought.

This outcome is particularly clear if one follows the thread that leads from Trinitarian ontology to the ontology of history, as has been shown in the cases of Daniélou and Balthasar, and to the theology of the body. From this perspective, then, it could be useful to conclude by showing how Trinitarian ontology itself demands a further elaboration of a Marian ontology. Indeed, if the ontological development of thinking of the being of the one and triune God has led to the rethinking of the creation in a Trinitarian light, it is natural that, in the first place, this is the case for the Mother of God.

Here, the relational version of Trinitarian ontology, which we have just outlined, shows itself to be particularly fruitful. Historically, the full recognition of the ontological gap between the Trinity and human beings coincides precisely with the first attributions to Mary of her being "immaculate," "ever Virgin," and exceedingly "holy."[63] Indeed, in the new ontological structure, these predicates were no longer equivocal because it was absolutely clear that the maid of Nazareth was a creature, and that her perfections were received in her substance through the special nature and excellence of her relation with Christ.

In fact, in Mary's womb, there entered into time the only begotten who, in eternity, is in the bosom of the Father, according to what is gathered from the Johannine Prologue itself. Here, we get a glimpse of the Mother of God in the expression that indicates the coming to dwell among men of the Logos who was made flesh. This is an expression made up of the Greek verb *skēnoô*, which recalls pitching a tent (John 1:14), just as during the exodus and in the desert the ark, and, so, the presence of God, dwelt in the Hebrew

---

63. See Mateo-Seco, "Mariología de San Gregorio"; Gordillo, "Virginidad trascendente"; Maspero, "Misterio."

camp. Thus, it is possible to recognize a relational correspondence: the fact that the Son is *in* the Father and the Father is *in* the Son is translated into the Son who is made flesh *in* Mary who, in her turn, as a creature, was created *in* the Son who was made flesh in her (Col 1:15–20).

In her, as place, as heart, and as frontier, the processions are prolonged in their missions. In her, thanks to her *yes*, participation in the divine relations becomes possible. In entrusting herself to God, who asks her to be the Mother of the Word made flesh, the receptivity of the Son, who always receives and returns himself to the Father, is the basis of the ontological value of history. The eternal generation finds in Mary its free prolongation as generation in time. The Father and the Son are themselves only in the relation of absolute Love, which unites them in the immanence of the one substance. And, this generation is eternal, in such a way that, as we have seen, the relations are subsistent. Mary, on the other hand, is a creature and, therefore, contingent. However, in the moment in which God asks her to be the Mother of the Word made flesh, she becomes Mother in the same moment and for the same reason for which the Son of God becomes Son of Man. Thus, Jesus's filiation to Mary and the motherhood of Mary in relation to Jesus are relations, which arise together in time between different substances.

The ontological novelty comes in precisely here because the Son of God who becomes Son of Mary is a single thing with the Father, that is, he is eternal. As subsistent relation, his person is immanent in the Trinity, in such a way that this eternal relation is poured out into the historical relation between Mary and Jesus. The relation between Mother and Son is in a certain way embraced by the relation between the Father and the Son, filling it with the divine and eternal life. This is the source of Christian salvation. Clearly, Mary and Jesus remain as separate substances, but their relation is united once for all to the intra-Trinitarian subsistent relations in such a way that the unity and life of God are communicated to human beings. Thus, in Mary, everything is relation, to the point that, in a union without confusion and a distinction without separation, her being a creature and daughter of God flowers in becoming Mother of God, Mother of the Second Divine Person who is subsistent sonship. Thus, she can be described as Mother of relation and Queen of relations.

Essential here is the gap and, therefore, the difference between immanence and economy, between eternity and history. In the eternal generation, the Son receives from the Father, absolutely and perfectly, the infinite divine life, which, precisely as the perfect image of the Father himself, he absolutely and perfectly returns to the latter. There is no loss here, because in God everything is infinite and without limit. On the other hand, as man, Christ again receives everything from the Father and returns it to him, but now the human life is finite in such a way that the paschal mystery reveals precisely the Trinitarian identity of God in the death of the Word made flesh. This radical emptying signifies and expresses in human terms, so *ad finitum*, the relation of the absolute and reciprocal gift of the self of the Father and of the Son, which, in the immanence of God, is given *ad infinitum*. Mary, Mother of the Word who is God, is at the center of this translation of the eternal mutual gift of the divine persons into human terms. In fact, that flesh and that human life have their origin from her, from her *yes*, from her freedom, that is, from her total gift and abandonment to the Father. She receives all and restores all, herself and her Son, that is, her own motherhood. In this, she is perfectly daughter of the Father and perfectly mother of the Son, in that she entrusts the relation that defines her identity, that is, her motherhood, to the Father himself, and, in this way, is ever withdrawing it from the power of death and limitation.

Tradition has perceptively expressed this ontological depth of Mary by calling her Daughter of God the Father, Mother of God the Son; and Spouse of the Holy Spirit.[64] In her, everything is relation to each divine person, not through merit but through grace. Her created being is space, flesh, time, totally "Trinitarianized."[65] In her is transfigured the Third Divine Person, who covered her with his shadow, filling her with grace, in pure relational transparency to the Father, the Son, and the Holy Spirit himself. Perhaps for this reason, the traditional expression of the Trinity could be reformulated as Daughter of God the Father, Mother of God the Son, and Home of the Holy Spirit, where the last term is to be understood in a personal and familial sense. Precisely in this home, the contemporary person under the postmodern condition can learn the value of relations in order to lose the fear of differences by contemplating that woman who, more than any other, had a personal and not an institutional relation with Christ, according also to the very aspirations of the Reformation. Thus, her body and being can be read precisely as an eminent setting for Trinitarian ontology, as a personal, temporal, and corporal space, which makes possible the real adoration of the Most Holy Trinity.

---

64. See Francis of Assisi, "Salutation of Blessed Virgin"; Escrivá, *Way* §496.

65. The deeply theological and mystical expression is typical of Chiara Lubich. See Coda and Tapken, *Trinità e pensare*, 422–23.

3

Time, Motion, and Mystery

The Narrative Metaphysics of the Trinity

John Milbank

THE CONFESSION OF THE Trinity lies at the very core of our faith, yet too often this doctrine is neglected by Christians. Much of the time we speak as if we were straightforward monotheists, with the addition of the doctrine that God became human in order to redeem us from our sins.

But it was specifically the Son of God who is said by Christians to have become incarnate. And so, as we see from the Gospels, the Trinity is involved in the doctrine of the incarnation. Jesus Christ proclaimed himself to be the divine-human Son of a divine Father. What is more, he poured upon his followers and the future church his Holy Spirit, which was equally derived from the Father, and which was spoken of also in personal terms. The revelation that we have of God in Christ therefore includes, as the church eventually realized, after the triumph of the Athanasian "radicals," the revelation of the Trinity. The God who stooped to become born on earth is the God who was already somehow eternally a Son. And the Spirit of love that comes to us from the Father through the Son is not just a gift empowering us, but is also the eternal combined gift of the Father and the Son and their eternally linking and productive love.

It is therefore our basic Christian stories that convey to us, when they are radically interpreted, the strange truth that God is three in one. This truth lies at the core of our faith and is indeed an unsoundable mystery. Yet if our faith means anything at all, it must be possible for us to experience this mystery and to some degree understand what it means.[1] A real mystery is not like a puzzle to which there is one solution: a real mystery is a reality that we can never exhaust and yet which keeps on acting as a source of new truths.

In what ways then, is the Trinity a mystery of this kind? The first clue lies in the fact that it is impossible to remove the manifestation of God as triune from history and from narrative. The Father of Christ is the inherited God of the Jews, albeit now addressed by Jesus in more familiar terms than he had sometimes been in the past—addressed indeed as Abba, Father. He is so addressed not simply because Christ, as a human being, now experiences a more intimate relation to God, though that is true, but because he also and shockingly claims to have been with the Father from the beginning, to be essentially one with him and to be the image, Word, or self-expression of the Father, which the Father has never been without.

Nevertheless, we can know this only because the divine Son has now arrived himself upon earth, has taught to us the primacy of love over the old law, has performed miracles, and has been resurrected from the dead, after suffering a cruel execution at the hands of human legal authority. Jesus did not just tell us that he was the Word of the Father or enter into dialogue with the directly experienced voice of the Father from heaven: he spoke many words, did many deeds, entered into many relationships, which manifested to us, in finite terms, but perfectly, just what the paternal self-expression looks like, its very shape and character.

Similarly, we know of the existence of the Third Person of the Trinity, the Holy Spirit, in God, only because he descended first upon the head of Jesus at his baptism in the Jordan, revealing that he formed the bond between the Son and the Father, and again upon the heads of the disciples at Pentecost, thereby founding the church as God's guaranteed self-presence in that body to the end of time.

It is therefore a series of extraordinary historical events that have disclosed to us the truth of the Trinity. And this has a double implication.

First: We can now all share in Christ's more intimate relationship to the Father, just because we can now be participants in the life of the Trinity, which Christ has newly revealed. The entire purpose of the divine Son's becoming incarnate was to raise us all into the condition of sonship and even, through human mediation, all of the cosmos into this condition, as St. Paul

---

1. Milbank, "Orthodoxy, Knowledge, and Freedom"; Hart, *Experience of God*.

implies. God was humanized in order that human beings might be deified, as many of the Greek church fathers tended to put it.

Thus, although we are only "sons by adoption" according to St. Paul (Eph 1:5), nonetheless we can rise to the position of the Son within the Trinity as enjoying the direct love of the Father without the mediation of any law or barrier, or set of restrictions, since this love is a wholly positive gift and knows no evil that requires preventing.

In relation to the Father, we now have the sense of being born from the very source of reality itself, from that which is absolutely "one and all," as the ancient Stoic philosophers put it, the totality of Being. Insofar as we are now emergent from this reality, the Father, and yet entirely at one with its self-manifestation that always belongs to it, the divine Son, then we become free of all suffering and evil, which is always some sort of passive damage that we undergo, some sort of self-argumentation or social discord, whether inflicted by others or by ourselves. Conjoined to the Father who is everything and the potential for everything, we no longer lack, and so we no longer suffer. Insofar as there is still desire, this is no longer a desire that is a tantalizing wanting, unless that means an immediate satisfaction of desire and an endless further satisfaction.

In this new and mystical way, made one with the Son of God through his incarnation, we come to know something of ultimate reality and so our true selves as not separate from this reality, but expressive of it. Thereby, we do not lose our real character, or personality, but start to see how it is compatible with everyone else and everything else: realized more in tranquil harmony and association rather than in self-assertion and conflict, even if we usually have to sacrifice our merely selfish desires in order to transcend their torture and enter into the light of self-giving love that binds us to other people.

From this sense of true understanding arises a certain feeling of excited tranquility, or bliss: a happiness of sharing and further sharing. This is the experience of the Holy Spirit as inspiration and as the love that links our knowledge to the source of reality. It is the feeling that seals our understanding, and it is also a productive and a creative feeling: an experience of beauty as an intimation of the depths of the Father shown through the manifest shape of the Son and a sense that this beauty can be further realized and further realized inexhaustibly.

If the story of the life of Christ and the coming of the Holy Spirit introduces us to the very interior life of God, so that we no longer relate to him in an exterior way as the God of willed commands, then, in the second place, this circumstance also suggests that in some way the category of story is not alien to God as he is in himself.

God was able to become a story for us here on earth only because, in a profound sense, he is internally a narrative; in a certain fashion, as God, he is his own theogony. So just as we no longer relate to God in a merely external fashion as if God was one actor within our finite tale, now it seems more as if we are actors introduced to play parts within God's own infinite self-narration.

For it is a story indeed that the Father sent his Son, that the Son in human guise withstood temptations and obeyed his Father's will, that he experienced apparent separation from the Father on the cross but was resurrected by the Father, besides in his own power and that of the Spirit, on the third day. It is still an intra-divine story that relates how the resurrected Son then spoke with the disciples, ascended to be with the Father once more, but still manifested himself as resurrected to St. Paul and sent his Spirit to form the church at Pentecost. The life of the church itself continues to be the inner divine drama of the Trinity as we, as sons and daughters of God, both lapse and obey, eventually go to our deaths, and trust to rise again in glory.

If God is in his outwardly emanating radiance a story, a story of continuous bliss interrupted by created evil, but restored in its continuity through the redemption of the created order, then, since the immanent God is one with his glory, this implies that we have to rethink just how God is in himself: how his eternal aseity is nonetheless paradoxically at one with a kind of eternal self-causing, self-generation, and self-coming to be—just as the divine essence is not, for orthodoxy, other than the birth of the Son and the procession of the Spirit from the Father. (Perhaps one can should say here that the embarrassment for orthodoxy is that as soon as one ceases however subtly to marginalize the doctrines of the Trinity and of the incarnation in favor of a more straightforward monotheism, the more truths that hover near what has been taken [perhaps wrongly] as belonging to the dangerous margins of esoteric and theosophic Christianity start to intrude themselves.)

That is the first aspect to any Trinitarian metaphysics. In Greek thought and in the Old Testament itself it had often been implied that there is some sort of secondary and assisting god, whether Word or "Throne" or Wisdom, working to create or working within the creation alongside the more ultimate deity, besides a "Spirit of the Lord" who abides within us. The Old Testament and the intertestamental writings had also spoken of a strange "Son of Man" who was a different sort of human or suprahuman mediating figure. But the wholly novel implication of the New Testament is that the second god is fully the equal of the first, and that the second god is identical with the Son of Man.

Of course, there is really only one God, but it seems that the first and second gods (so to speak) are now identical in essence rather than person, alongside the third god who is the Holy Spirit. It also seems that the second god is from all eternity (since God does not change) conjoined with unfallen and perfect humanity and that it is this which is also disclosed to us through the incarnation of Christ.

This new view of God as in himself his own story, a story of three persons, and their intimate connection with the creation and with humanity, of course required a revolution in human thought.

Monotheism could not be abandoned without succumbing to idolatry. But a new sense of "oneness" arose: it was now more fully seen that the real unity is not at all averse to plurality, to relationality, to reflexivity, and to repetition, and is rather confirmed by these things. If God is most of all love, as revealed by Christ's love for his Father, then it was seen that God is not a sort of monster of infinite lucidity, but rather in himself spontaneously creative out of a dark ground (as so many mystics have put it in the wake of Jacob Boehme),[2] and in himself relational beyond mere self-sufficiency, which is after all just as finite a category as dependency. The Father always gives rise to the Son, and both give further rise to the Spirit, who is, as it were, their child, though from another perspective the Spirit is the divine mother in whose womb the divine Son is born. In either case, we see that God is love because he is not just dyadic relation, which can subside into a narcissism à deux, but also triadic, as it were solid and embodied community—the ground for the community of any number of beings.

In more technical terms we can say that it was now gradually seen (coming to a head with Thierry of Chartres in the twelfth century) that the One is only one because absolute unity alone can be identically repeated—cannot step out of itself because it *can* entirely step out of itself.[3]

And this paradoxical relationality of the absolute is, one can suggest, required, today, if we are to be able to speak of the One-All, of the God who is not just infinite unity, but who also enfolds in his *Logos* every conceivable particularity, which are also manifest, *in* their pure particularity, as the creation outside of God.

In any infinity imaginable by us, as mathematical set theory teaches, what is included in infinite unity, namely the plural all, can break out of that unity as greater than that unity: in ideal reality all the fractions of three, for example, plus the original set of three itself and its possible emptiness, form a subset that is more than three; in natural reality, for example, all the

2. See Boehme, *Essential Writings*.
3. See Milbank, "One in Three."

evolved complexities of a seed exceed its visible oneness while including it and its open potential.

But then it can seem that a chaos of everything is greater than unity, unless we unify that chaos as its own ultimate set, but in consequence the same breakout of chaotic plurality will return. The only way then to conceive of the One as also All is to switch to the dynamism of mathematical "category theory" and to think of the One as itself indicatively generating the "breakout" of the many and yet of the unity of the many as only ever indicatively conveying the unity of the unfathomable One beyond its own immanent totality.[4]

But is this mutual excess of the Father as One and the Son as All over each other, itself, as a dyadic relation, a new mode of self-reflexive and self-sufficient unity? A kind of collapse into mutual narcissism? In that case we are confronted either with the mere unity once more, negating the relationship, or else with a reflexive doubling incompatible with the divine simplicity. This can be avoided, one might suggest, if we understand the formal expression of the Father in the Son as also the indicated mediation to a Third Person, the Holy Spirit, which reflexively returns to the Father by way of a pure relationship to him through the Son. There is then no doubling, because of substantive relationship, but also, because of the mediation, relationship cannot collapse back into a single blur. To put this simply and mathematically: a straight line is an irreducible relationship of points rather than a mere single line or arrow only if one inserts an indicative mid-point between the points at its termini. There can be substantive relation only if there is substantive mediation. No divine dyad is possible, only the divine triunity. Substantive relation is such because it is also substantive mediation, in elaboration of the theological tradition.

The doctrine of the Trinity therefore allows us not to qualify the absolute One, but to rethink it more exactly as also perfect repetition, relation and reflexivity, and as a One that is also plurality and difference, but only in a mediated and tensional fashion.

4. Several Russian sophiologists, who were often also advanced mathematicians, thought somewhat along these lines: see, for example, Lev Karsavin, "On First Principles" (1921–25), translated by Boris Jakim (unpublished manuscript; further bibliographic information unavailable). Karsavin speaks of the potential anarchy and "bad infinite" opened by filial plural expression, unless the eternal Son is eternally "resurrected" by the Spirit. This reworking of Schelling contains no Behmenist implication of conflict in God, but only an indication of the ultimate source of evil in finite Trinitarian perversion, since for always this "resurrection" prevents the "death" of the eternal Son. Nonetheless, it is this "preventive" resurrection that allows the resurrection from death and evil in the course of time. On the paradoxes of sets, see also Milbank, "Number and the Between."

To this we can add a christologically ontological postscript. The All that is uttered in the Son-Logos is an infinite All, but it is also, as Thomas Aquinas tells us, eminently the All of every finite thing that we find in the creation. Since God is the All, he must paradoxically encompass the contingent, the entire possibility of creation, which, as being perfectly inclusive and perfectly generous and non-withholding, God inevitably and yet freely actualizes.

This creation is therefore not-God and yet is also God: a seeming contradiction that can be resolved, as Maximus the Confessor and, much later, Nicolas Malebranche taught, only by realizing that God creates only in order to incarnate himself in the creation. God cannot in himself lack even the gratuity of addition, or the honoring of worship, such that the usual pious appeals to God's sheer gratuity in creating prove impious after all, as Malebranche contended. Instead, God adds to his perfection imperfection, lack, and finite worship only because his plenitude turns out to include those things also.[5] This divine incarnation in everything that begins through one particular human person is at once fully realized and yet also *revealed* in its eternal truth in the events related in the New Testament.

Thus, both as Trinitarian and as eternally creating and eternally incarnate (which he must be if God is simple and unchanging), God is in some sense supra-eminently eventful and temporal, rather than atemporal.

There is, of course, no time in God himself: he is indeed eternal and without alteration. We speak of God in terms of before and after, as when we speak of the Father generating the Son, or of the procession of the Spirit from both, or of God becoming Man, only because we are finite creatures bound to speak in temporal terms.

Nor is God in motion in our sense, again because he is unchanging. And yet it would seem that the generation of the All from the One and the spiritual recognition of their identity (by which God becomes in and through and for himself, to speak in Hegelian categories) involves in some fashion a "becoming." The fact that the doctrine of the Trinity implies that the most ultimate way to speak of God is in just these narrative, temporal, and moving terms appears to imply that we must not fall into the error of supposing the nonetheless changeless God to be static or inert or lacking in dynamism.

---

5. See Chrétien, "Limite de la métaphysique." With a refreshing rigor so often lacking in that prevalent Christian sentimentality which betrays the gospel, the great Oratorian philosopher argued that we cannot be sure that mere finite created humility, however great, is really existentially compatible with the infinite simplicity and grandeur of God.

The doctrine surely forces us to reflect that the atemporal as much as the temporal, and rest as much as motion, are sets of contrasts that we have only from our limited, finite perspective, as taught by Plotinus, Marius Victorinus, and Maximus the Confessor. We imagine the eternal in terms of an everlasting present moment, but a present moment is a moment of the time that we know. And we imagine eternal rest in terms of the kind of rest that we experience—a pause in a long day and relaxation in an armchair at the end of it. But whenever we think about God we have to negate these limited contrasts: God is no more in the present than he is in the past or the future. He is surely more like all three things at once. And God is not more at rest than he is moving: he is rather an unthinkable, unchanging motion or moving stability.

If we think of God in this way, then we can say that God no more purely *is* than he has come to be and will develop in the future. He is the God of the present, but also of our ancestors and of the eschatological finality to come. All of these expressions are inappropriate, but perhaps the first no more than the second two. God is in some fashion what has become, what he is, and what he further becomes all at once.

In this fashion, we can say that he has his own formed "habit," style, or character, even though he has never been without it. Equally, we can say that he is "situated" as much as "situating," if the persons of the Trinity constantly and reciprocally frame and "place" each other.[6] As the nineteenth-century philosopher Vladimir Solovyov first taught, the divine essence is not something static: there is a sense in which the Father, the absolute origin, the ungenerated and so undistinguished essence, generates the recognizable essence as well as generating the Son and causing the Spirit to proceed.[7] This is his essence as the personifying Wisdom or Sophia of which the Scriptures speak. It is the metaphorically female active receptivity in God that alone allows there to be any repetition, relation, or reflexivity. This fourth *r* allows us better to see how the three persons nonetheless share a single "personality," style, or habit that is at once a constant "bringing about" and a hypostatic resulting.

The sophianic essence of God is also and immediately the ground of receptivity in creation that diversifies it, in imitation of the Trinitarian plurality. She is in this respect of course entirely created, and yet we can see here the depth of the paradox noted by the great Muslim philosopher al-Ghazālī: just because God gives everything, including receptive gratitude, God is grateful for himself within himself—indeed self-worshiping, as

6. See Milbank, "Trinitarian Ontology."
7. Solovyov, *Lectures on Divine Humanity.*

Malebranche saw.[8] He is grateful to himself for our gratitude, but in Christian terms we can see how this has a Trinitarian and sophiological ground: the active providing of the receptive medium, which is necessary to any real action as transitive (in Plotinian correction of Aristotle), is truly a reception of the receptive by the active, since a perfect receptivity is nonetheless still mysteriously active and entirely at one with its active source.

Thus, in some remarkable way, the doctrine of the Trinity suggests that God is not after all the simple opposite of all the things that characterize our history and our geography: all the contingent, unusual, scarce, and eventful things that make up our lives. It seems that, in an elevated, unimaginable manner, God is not without relation, as he is a set of pure substantial relations that define the Trinitarian persons: not quite without time as the source and consummation of time; not quite without space as being the coincidence of situating and situated; not quite without receptivity, even though he is the active giving of everything; and not quite without distinctive character, even though this is the style of everything whatsoever.

So, as we might imagine, the appearance of God himself on earth brought about a total revolution in how we think about God, a revolution that is ongoing and whose implications we have still not fully through and never will until the end of time. It seems that the single, simple, and unalterable God is now nonetheless the dramatic God of his own story: of relation, event, receptivity, relational connection, and reflexive self-becoming, as he likewise is of character, habit, time, and staging.

Is this simply a change in how we think about God, or does it have implications for our human lives: individual, social, and natural? It surely does. As we saw at the outset, the whole point of the incarnation was the reverse elevation of human beings into deity, into a condition beyond harm and suffering, a wholly positive state where nothing contradicts our positive actions, because we are at one with the source of all positivity. Many religions, especially those of the East, have shared much of this insight, and their views do not deserve to be misunderstood. However, perhaps more than any other creed (although again this insight is not unknown outside Christianity) our faith insists, like the great Anglican poet of the seventeenth century Thomas Traherne, that our dilation or expansion upwards is also a dilation outwards and not simply an abandonment of our bodily lives here below.[9]

Thus if our God is a narrative God, and so much so that he could join to his eternal story a particular human one—the ongoing story of Israel, Mary, Jesus, and the church—then when we ascend to God we do not

8. Al-Ghazālī, *Names of God*, 101.
9. See Chrétien, "Thomas Traherne."

simply leave time and motion behind, any more than we leave behind our own peculiar habits and character, our own situations, susceptibilities, and sets of relationships, or all that goes to render us human.

Rather, all this will be intensified, more fully realized, but without intercreaturely violence and division, or what the Jewish philosopher Spinoza called the "sad passions" of our melancholia, despair and self-accusation.[10] For nothing affirmative is incompatible with time and motion, character, receptivity, and circumstance, such that the story can spiral back into an eternal and unending dance. As such a final rounding-off dance or roundel, the tale is concluded rather than abandoned. And that includes of course the story of our inevitable undergoing of the consequences of human hostility and addiction to the lure of the negative and self-inhibiting. The resurrected Christ retains his wounds, but the cross was already part of the cosmic dance.

It then follows that we cannot possibly understand or experience God as Trinity without rethinking and reliving the entire structure of our everyday reality. The new metaphysics of God is inevitably a new metaphysical vision of everything. It is for this reason that notions of images of the Trinity in this world are not a sort of optional extra; they are not just "tacked on" to the doctrine of the Trinity. To the contrary, the doctrine of the Trinity consists only in these images: to reenvisage God is to reenvisage our approach to God and so to reenvisage the scene of reality in which alone we approach him.

This was true of the very terms in which we came to know about God as Trinity in the first place, as we have already seen. It was impossible to learn that God was in himself the relational and always positively active love of a Father for a Son without displacing the primacy of the negatively reactive law that assumes that there was primordially an evil to be held at bay. Impossible to learn the same thing without learning also that the God of the Old Testament was always the God of *nature* prior to the law, whose word can be fulfilled only with the natural arrival of the perfect human person who exercises nothing but love: the God-Man himself. Impossible, equally, to learn of the reality of the Holy Spirit without the unveiling and arrival of a new sort of human community that renders the purely social more important than the merely political or economic, in the sense of household: the community of the church: at once *polis*, *oikos*, and *societas*.

Therefore, to worship the hyper-temporal, dynamic, and relational God meant from the outset to conceive of the reality that he created in rather different terms. To long to be united with God was no longer to try to will away or to escape evolution, human history, and circumstance, but

---

10. See Milbank, "Problematizing the Secular."

to enter more deeply into these things. Now, it appears that God is not most imaged by stability as though he were a mere rock, but by love and creativity, which involve ecological and social relating and temporal transformation; the slow formation of habits and their abrupt transformation, the faithful performance of specific social roles in our own peculiar way. That operation and integration of many different gifts of which St. Paul also spoke.

Since human beings are the crown and connection of creation, we can also come to understand the reality of everything in terms of its participation in the Trinity. Everything that exists seems to follow what teachers of creative writing call the "rule of three": all passes from beginning through middle to end, from past to present to future. Everything conscious is composed of memory, understanding, and willed expectation, as Augustine taught. And spatial situation is composed of near, far horizon, and intermediate milieu. Any individual thing is itself composed of mediating links between its inside and its outside, else it would have no boundary and no definition. Everything whatsoever has to identify with something else in order to be something itself at all. We are subjects with predicates linked by a copula, and not just in grammar but also in reality, as Antonio Rosmini and Vladimir Solovyov independently realized in the nineteenth century.[11] Thus, as the great nineteenth-century Catholic Romantic philosopher Franz von Baader put it, interpreting Hegel and Schelling, the middle is always paradoxically prior to the beginning, and this is exactly why love is older than any solitary commencement and self-vaunting, which is always but a fantasy of origination.[12]

In a very simple way then, the recognition that the world was created by a triune God and is everywhere marked with that reality places a new emphasis upon the primacy of *mediation*, on what the philosopher William Desmond calls "the between," rather than on things taken in isolation or merely impersonal processes. And to say mediation, as Baader realized, is to say essentially "love." The revelation of the Trinity is the revelation of the ultimacy of love, and that love is the undergirding truth of this world and not just of its Creator, however much that truth might have been obscured and mired by sin. We fully know only by accepting the other in her darkness or by engendering through obscure desire a new reality, whereas the partial knowledge of exact science is merely a sad clarity that is inherently solipsistic.

And the incredible implication of the Trinity, which we are even now only fully beginning to see, is that even divine omniscience is not, after all, alone clarity of sheer "enlightenment" but, as St. John says, what we can

11. See Milbank: "Trinitarian Ontology"; "Foreword."
12. Baader, *Fermenta Cognitionis*, 1.19.

regard as a "romantic" light shining in the equally necessary darkness, a knowledge that it is infinite in its creative and spontaneous expression out of unconscious depths, and its embrace of the other in their mysterious outward shining, which can never be fully penetrated without obliteration of the other in their otherness. Thus, even the Father, Son, and Spirit are mysteries to each other, even though they are in themselves, and exhaustively, ceaseless reciprocal passage through these alien mysteries, only attaining to infinite knowledge in the unendedness of their perichoretic dance.

However, there is one more thing to contemplate. The more that we see the world in terms of mediation, participating in this mystery of God to himself, the more it seems to evaporate as though it were indeed but a veil of maya, as that notion is usually understood (and probably misunderstood). If time is fundamental, then how can we account for the fact that the past is always over, the future never arrives, and the present never stays with us even for a present moment? Time slips through our fingers faster than salt. And if motion is fundamental, then where is it located, since it is not in any fixed point of past position or position to come, not in any origin or destination? It is as elusive as time. The same thing applies to relation, which is in neither of the spatial poles that are related and yet is nothing without them. If I achieve identity only through relational identification and love, then that seems to suggest contradictorily that I am what I am not.

In general, if things are held together only by a vital mediation of time, motion, material receptivity, relation, and love, then they seem to be held together by an intangible film that evaporates on inspection, and we are tempted to think there exist only isolated things after all. But just what is a thing if a thing also mediates itself, in this case inner with outer? Does my bodily boundary belong to me or not, and if my boundary defines me, is it not the whole of everything else at the edge of which I am situated and into which my definition would then fade?

It seems then, that the more we think of reality in metaphysically Trinitarian terms, the more that reality empties out into a void. There is one indeed negative, but also two positive ways of looking at this situation.

Negatively, we can say with Solovyov that, indeed, in a fallen world, time, space, matter, and individuation do not make sense, because the mystery of the integrated is hidden from us and nature is truly riven by destructive and demonic forces, as we see to be constantly at work. Consequently, time tears apart even the fullest present moment, space divides us even from stable place, motion ensures that we will never arrive, even though we have never left, matter disintegrates even its own foundation, and we can never return to ourselves because we do not know who we are.

But positively we can say first, that the mysteries of mediation are themselves signs that nothing is held together save by participation in God and by divine grace, which always works through time, space, motion, matter, and identity to reunite the plural factors within them, which only now, post the fall, operate in a perverted fashion to tear things apart. This is why we cannot grasp these factors, even though they are most palpably real. They are saved from the nihilistic fate of supposed maya when we realize that all their solidity is lent them by the Triune God, who, though ineffable, is more solid and less ethereal than we could ever imagine.

Second, the mysteries of finite mediation are signs of the Trinitarian mystery *in* their very mystery. As we have just seen, God as love is unfathomable beyond knowledge and not just for us but even in himself (as confirmed by some early Christian teachers, like Gregory of Nyssa and John Scottus Eriugena)—although his abysmal depths give rise to the only possible infinite understanding and infinite bliss. The knowledge and the bliss in the Trinity belong to a mystery of their relational arising from this positively dark ground that gives rise to an eternal paternal fire that shines in the Son beyond any finite light. Thus, it becomes possible to say that the "impossibility" and incomprehensibility of ordinary things and processes in our world are the very marks of their source in the divine Trinitarian mystery. Creatures are just as unfathomable as God at their core, since they are made in his image and especially the human creature. For this reason, our appeal to created images of the Trinity does not clarify its mystery but only deepens it and indicates its pervasive sway. The infinity of love does not abolish the inherent obscurity of love, even within God; rather it is the infinitization of love that alone secures any certainty of truth, thereby ensuring that any human truth must be a participation in this infinity, through endlessly extended loving mediation and the consolidation of this mediation as corporeal community.

For what we cannot transparently know, we can already feel, and it is our feeling in the Spirit that puts the seal on the entire Trinitarian arrival and reality. To be fully conjoined to Being is mysteriously to know it through the lure of tempered desire, and this is to seek to consummate in love our world of time, receptivity, and motion, rather than to abandon it.

Part Two

Metaphysics and Phenomenology

4

Being, Identity, and Ecstasy
An Essay in Trinitarian Metaphysics

JOHN R. BETZ

AS MY TITLE WOULD suggest, my purpose here is to consider the relationship between ontology and Trinitarian theology in terms of three interrelated concepts: being, identity, and ecstasy. At the outset, however, some procedural comments are in order, having to do with the future of Christian metaphysics after Heidegger and his identification of metaphysics tout court with what in the 1950s he famously called "ontotheology."[1]

(Analogical) Metaphysics After Heidegger

First, I do not distinguish here between metaphysics and ontology as many have done since Heidegger, alleging that ontology is concerned purely with the question of being, whereas metaphysics is a mishmash of ontology and etiology, which contaminates ontology from the start, imposing upon it a second-order discourse of cause and effect that is inevitably onto-*theological* in nature and thus unsuited to the pure philosophical investigation of being

---

1. See Heidegger, *Identity and Difference*, 23–41. For a longer engagement, see Betz, "After Heidegger and Marion."

qua being. For it bears repeating that metaphysics, as a matter of historical definition, is none other than what ontology is, namely, the science of being, whether we subsequently understand being in terms of etiology or not.

This is not to say that there is no merit to Heidegger's distinction, and that we ought to go on doing metaphysics just as Aristotle did. On the contrary, we have an obligation to consider Heidegger's critique of metaphysics, as well as the so-called ontological difference between being and beings, lest we miss something that he saw and that the metaphysical tradition has, at times, obscured: namely, that being is a mystery, and like any great work of art is more—and much more wonderful—than an effect of a cause, which (as Heidegger legitimately complained) tends to explain it away. Indeed, in this respect, we too might need to make a "leap from reason," as Heidegger suggests in his ironic play on the Leibnizian "principle of reason" (*Satz vom Grund*), so that we can gain some perspective on the novelty of being—really be surprised by it—before it is classified and filed away, along with everything else, within a system of reasons.[2]

At the same time, however, we have reason to be wary of Heidegger's wholesale critique of metaphysics as "ontotheology," inasmuch as it is motivated by his passionate flight from theology and a corresponding attempt to sever the question of being (the *Seinsfrage*) from the question of God (the *Gottesfrage*), however unthinkable this severance finally is. In other words, the severity of his critique of Aristotle is motivated more than anything by his desire to do philosophy without having to think about God. But, of course, to point out this motivation is not in and of itself a sufficient defense. For it is possible to be motivated and right. But there is also this problem, that Heidegger's wholesale critique of metaphysics as ontotheology obscures the difference between Aristotle's more rational theology, which connects being and divinity as a matter of reason, and the more apophatic theologies, stemming from Plato, most famously, that of Pseudo-Dionysius, for whom God is in some sense beyond even being.

For these reasons alone, we should not be cowed by Heidegger into thinking that metaphysics tout court is something to get over en route to an ostensibly pure ontology, which is supposedly concerned, more so than metaphysics, with the mystery of being. We just need to think more carefully, not least about Thomistic metaphysics, which superficially resembles what Heidegger castigates as "ontotheology." For, rightly understood, the venerable Thomistic "real distinction" between essence (*essentia*) and existence (*exstentia*) is an attempt to do justice to the mystery of being, indeed, to liberate being from any necessity that it might have had in standard Greek

---

2. See Heidegger, *Principle of Reason*.

conceptions of an eternal world. To be sure, one can fail to register the full import of this distinction. For example, one can fail to see that it implies the traditional doctrine of *creatio ex nihilo*.[3] But once this is seen, it means that being is totally unnecessary: that it need not have been and therefore stands out from nothing as a gift.

It is not the case, therefore, that Christian metaphysics is necessarily complicit in the forgetfulness of being, as Heidegger alleges. One simply needs to remember what is implied by the real distinction: that being is nothing but a gift of Being, to which it bears a mysterious analogical relation. One could even argue that the analogy of being—the *analogia entis*—does a far better job safeguarding the mystery of being, and keeping it from collapsing into the kind of univocal conception that defines the modern world, than does Heidegger's "ontological difference." For whereas the latter ostensibly preserves the difference between being and beings, for Heidegger the *being* of beings is, at the end of the day, nothing but the being *of beings*, behind which there is precisely nothing. For all that "there is" is the world and nothing else.

Nor is this inevitability avoided by his emphasis on the "it"—the *es*—in *es gibt*, since there is nothing to "it." To be sure, Heidegger speaks of it as a nothing that "gives," which makes being "happen," and so Heidegger cannot help but talk as if it were a "something" after all—something "like" a Creator. But, of course, Heidegger rejects any notion of a Jewish-Christian Creator. Thus, what gives beings to be is not the fullness of Being, which merely appears to be nothing compared to beings as a result of a kenotic withdrawal into a dazzling darkness that gives beings room to be, but rather that which really is nothing and is dialectically related to beings as the ultimate nothingness of *their* being. At the end of the day, therefore, Heidegger's ontology is marked by a profound irony that was picked up by two other students of Husserl, namely, Hedwig Conrad-Martius and Edith Stein. For as they keenly pointed out, no sooner does Heidegger open the question of being than he willy-nilly closes it. As Stein puts it, speaking of Heidegger's method, citing Conrad-Martius: "It is as if a door, unopened for long ages past and seemingly shut for good, was blown open by a blast of sound judgment, wisdom, and unflagging tenacity—only to be slammed shut at once, bolted and so stoutly barred that it seems impossible to get it open again."[4] Granted, this was said in view of *Being and Time*, and not in view of Heidegger's later work and his so-called *Kehre*, but the point remains. For

3. For some recent discussions of this doctrine, see McFarland, *From Nothing*; Robinette, *Difference Nothing Makes*; Soskice, *Naming God*, 66–82.

4. Such is the irony pointed out by Edith Stein, following Hedwig Conrad-Martius, in her brilliant critique of Heidegger's philosophy, which originally appeared as an appendix in Stein, *Endliches und Ewiges Sein*, 481.

whether in the early Heidegger or the late, whatever openness there is to the mystery of being is a deceptive openness; for we are finally thrown back upon nothing but immanence—and ourselves.

By contrast, the analogy of being, which was first formulated in the Thomistic tradition, and has since been elaborated mutatis mutandis by Erich Przywara,[5] Edith Stein,[6] Hedwig Conrad-Martius,[7] Karl Rahner,[8] and, most recently, Ferdinand Ulrich,[9] genuinely opens things up. Not only does it signal the nonnecessity of being implied by the real distinction (which alerts us to the radical givenness of being in every being); it also and at the same time signals a very real difference between Being and beings, inasmuch as the Being of the one who gives beings to be is, notwithstanding a certain analogy of being, radically different than the being of beings. By comparison, Heidegger's "ontological difference," which is supposed to be so mysterious, is facile and flat. For what we have in the *analogia entis* is not one but two major differences, each of which is analogically related to the other: not just between essence and existence (the real distinction) but a further difference between being as constituted by the real distinction and Being, which is declared *in* this distinction as nevertheless *beyond* it—so far beyond it, in fact, that we have at the end of the day *only* an analogical conception of what it means to be.

This is not to say that we cannot learn something from Heidegger. For one thing, there can be no Christian metaphysics today that has not passed through the fires of his (at times) legitimate criticism—though, again, it applies more to various rationalistic forms of philosophical metaphysics (e.g., to Leibniz), than to any theological metaphysics in the apophatic tradition, from Pseudo-Dionysius to Aquinas to Cusa all the way up to the aforementioned representatives of Christian metaphysics in the twentieth century. Nor can we fail to appreciate what Heidegger, from his own standpoint, attempts to show with regard to the gift of being. But at the end of the day, from the standpoint of any theological ontology, this is precisely where Heidegger leaves us wanting, and perhaps scratching our heads, in trying to speak of a gift, even of a kenosis of being in beings, without a Giver, which is to say, without God.

5. See Przywara, *Analogia Entis*.

6. See Stein, *Finite and Eternal Being*.

7. "The concept of being is neither synonymous, nor homonymous, but analogous. There is not only an *analogia entis*, but an *analogia essendi*" (Conrad-Martinud, *Sein*, 36).

8. Although still somewhat under Heidegger's spell and, at the same time, trying to work out his own fundamental ontology on the basis of a transcendental reading of Aquinas, it is notable that for Rahner the concept of the analogy of being is still nonnegotiable. See Rahner, *Hearer of the Word*, pt. 2, ch. 4.

9. Ulrich, *Homo Abyssus*.

It is precisely here, by contrast, that the Christian metaphysical tradition shows its strength: for not only can it better preserve the mystery of being from collapsing into one or another univocity; it also has more resources at its disposal for understanding and pondering the mystery of being as a *gift*. For where Heidegger stops with the gift of Being to beings, which he refuses to think in theological terms, a Christian metaphysics can go further in faith to see that the mystery of the gift of Being to beings is an analogy of an even more mysterious gift of the Father to the Son—a gift that, nota bene, has no guiding reason behind it that could explain it, since it logically precedes the Logos, and thus appears as nothing but the Father's gift of love.

From Analogical to Trinitarian Metaphysics

Having seen how (analogical) metaphysics opens upward, so to speak, to a Logos higher than our own—a Logos that in light of revelation turns out to be the Logos of the Father—we can now see the path that leads from analogical metaphysics to Trinitarian theology. Before we proceed any further, however, let us be clear that what follows is not a rational demonstration for the Trinity, much less a kind of proof. For even Aquinas's "five ways" are only pointers a posteriori in the direction of what it is reasonable to believe, namely, that the world has a cause, etc. A fortiori, therefore, since we are concerned here with the Trinity, which is far more mysterious than the notion of a first cause, I mean here merely to point to the Trinity along a particular metaphysical path—one that leads from the concept of being to the pairing of essence and existence, and finally from the concept of identity to that of ecstasy. If this metaphysical path should retrospectively look like a demonstration, it is not because it was intended as one. Indeed, to most it may not look like anything of the kind. But, if it does look like something stricter and more than a kind of confirmation of what one was already prepared to believe on the basis of doctrine, then let it simply be said that the thought of being, as we have considered it here, seemed to point toward a Trinitarian understanding of being. So, I begin with the first word in my title.

Step One

As Hegel pointed out, no word is more abstract, indeed poorer, than "being"—so poor, in fact, as to be nothing.[10] At the same time, paradoxically, no

---

10. "Being, pure being—without further determination. . . . It is pure indeterminateness and emptiness. . . . There is nothing to be intuited in it. Being, the

word is richer, for *all* that *is* obviously *is*, such that being, notwithstanding its poverty, or precisely because of it, somehow includes everything. Of course, Christian theology must demur when Hegel says that being is "nothing less and nothing more" than nothing; for God qua Being is certainly more than nothing—however much, from the standpoint of finite beings, he can seem, in comparison, like nothing. Nor, as the late Schelling argued, is God real and determinate only as the "result" of a historical process; rather, for the late Schelling (and any recognizably Christian theology), God is God from the beginning and in need of nothing outside of God to be. And yet, bearing these things in mind, I would argue that Hegel was onto something (or had intuited something of profound significance about Trinitarian theology) given what his logic suggests about the Trinity as an *empty fullness* or a *kenotic plentitude*—a notion to which I will return in due course. For now, however, let us begin with the curious fact, which Hegel keenly perceived, that the concept of being, which seems to be simple and so obvious, not only resists identification, but actually "falls apart" as soon as we begin to think about it.

Take the simple statement "it is." It seems banal, but it turns out to be profoundly mysterious and ambiguous, being susceptible of very different readings, depending upon one's philosophical outlook. For example, if you're an *essentialist*, you will immediately want to know the "what" of either the subject or the predicate that the statement suggests. In plain terms, you will want to know *what* is being said about *what*. If you are an *existentialist*, on the other hand, you will immediately pick up on the statement's existential import and the givenness or even *gratuity* of whatever is said to be—which is something more than what logicians mean by existential quantification. In short, where the essentialist hears *quiddity*, the existentialist hears *novelty*.

But if one is a musical thinker, like Erich Przywara, one will hear the statement stereophonically with two ears, picking up on being's dynamic range. By the same token, one will see the world with two eyes and, hence, with a depth perception that allows one to see the *doubling* of being into essence and existence as the *doubling* of simple transcendence into the complex folds of immanence. In other words, one will see the doubling of being into essence and existence as the analogizing of Being itself, which is

---

indeterminate immediate is in fact nothing. . . . Pure being and pure nothing are therefore the same" (Hegel, *Science of Logic* [trans. Giovanni], 59). "It is itself empty and without content, it disdains all community, all configuration; it reigns awesomely over all, as a blind power, past all understanding or concept. It is without concept because only the concrete can be conceived, while absolute necessity is still abstract, has not yet developed into the concept of purpose or achieved specific determinations" (Hegel, *Lectures*, 2.144).

"in" the analogy as its archetype, but at the same time also "beyond" it as a simple *identity* (as opposed to a complex unity) of essence and existence. Of course, all of this is basically implied by the Thomistic "real distinction" between *essentia* and *existentia*, and by what the late Schelling meant in distinguishing between "what" a thing is (*quid est*) and "that" it is (*quod est*); but sometimes it is worth restating and elaborating things that, however old, remain ever new. So, to summarize our first step, philosophical reflection shows that the concept of being, like the wave-particle duality of light, immediately parses into being and essence, or, more precisely, into essence and existence. Accordingly, the first step of any fundamental ontology, as a *Nachdenken des Seins*, is to follow this movement of Being, which has always already occurred.

But if the first step of any fundamental ontology is to see how being inevitably breaks open into essence and existence, such that the ground on which one stands, which one previously believed to be firm, begins to tremble, and one is taken aback by the abyss that yawns between them, which no amount of thought or human ingenuity can span; if, in short, the first step of any fundamental ontology causes one precisely to *lose* one's footing, then the entire modern epistemological quest for a philosophical foundation, an Archimedean "place to stand"—whether it be sought in Descartes's cogito or in Bacon's *Novum Organum* or in Kant's transcendental idealism or in the attempted mastery of modern analytic philosophy—turns out to be a fundamentally dubious enterprise. For its success requires one either to be blind to this more fundamental ontological problem or (worse) blatantly to disregard it, as if the question of knowledge could be answered definitively apart from the more radical question of being.

To give the most obvious example, simply consider how Descartes begins with the cogito in order to arrive at the certainty of being, as if the question of being were so easily dispatched and its mystery eo ipso resolved. Of course, to be fair to Descartes, he was trying to overcome the most extreme skepticism he himself presupposed; like Augustine in his reply to the academics, he wanted something to be indisputable. It remains the case, however, that his proposed foundation for the sciences could be secured only by abstraction from the question of being's complication into essence and existence—not to mention the analogical complication of being and consciousness (ontology and epistemology), which is the principle a posteriori of any genuine philosophy—namely, by isolating the question of existence from the question of essence and then identifying thought with existence, univocally understood (something either is or it is not). And something similar is true of Kant: like Descartes he begins with the question of knowledge ("What can I know"?) without ever really arriving at the question of being, much less things themselves. In both cases what we have is an impossible flight from ontology to epistemology, from the question of being, which cannot be mastered (however much we may grasp the workings of the physical world), to branches of "knowledge," which for Descartes and Kant are ostensibly "in our power" (*Gewalt*), as Kant put it, thereby illustrating the nature of modern epistemology as a form of mastery—not to say, given the connotations of *Gewalt*, violent domination.[11]

Of course, from any theological standpoint, it is precisely here that we see the *proton pseudos* of modern philosophy from which it was born, or rather miscarried from the start: the old lie that knowledge is within *our* grasp, and that we can therefore forget about God and become "gods" without God. Obviously, Descartes and Kant did not take things quite this far.[12] One could even say that their projects were inevitable responses to the inevitable and legitimate question of what we can know in the face of the perennial possibility of radical skepticism. The fact of the matter, however, is that the door was thereby opened to a philosophical-scientific quest for mastery, which has yielded, on the one hand, such benefits as modern medicine, but, on the other hand, an abundance of evils. The old story is therefore true: as a result of our grasping at divinity, we have come experientially to know both good *and* evil, without always being able clearly to distinguish between them.

But the attempt to master reality by recourse to epistemology is not just morally and theologically problematic; it is also problematic from any purely philosophical standpoint. For, quite simply, the question of being cannot be answered epistemologically: being is neither a genus nor a quantifier, to which both Kant and analytic philosophy have tended to reduce it. It is rather, after any serious philosophical reflection, mysterious, akin to the old question of why there is something rather than nothing, which is irreducible to any essential determination of *what* it is that happens to be.

---

11. Kant, *Critique of Pure Reason*, B871.

12. As the talented young church historian Bob Siegfried (BA, Notre Dame, 2023) described to me, even the Jansenist Arnauld thought highly of Descartes and defended his method against his Roman censors, who put his works on the index of prohibited books. As Arnauld put it, "The Censors at Rome have not cared well for the interests of Religion, since they have placed on their Index the works of M. Descartes, in which he establishes, by means of natural reason, the immortality of the soul more solidly than ever before.... This, in effect, takes away from those who have lost their faith every human means of escaping from their pernicious prejudices against this important truth. Is this not to allow them to swallow the poison while withholding the antidote?" (quoted in Nadler, "Arnauld, Descartes, and Transubstantiation," 239). And, as far as Kant is concerned, without God as a regulative idea of practical reason, his entire project would collapse into the very skepticism he himself was trying to combat.

In short, the question of being, which should evoke a certain reverence as before a mystery, refuses mastery: it eludes whatever essential determinations we would bring to bear upon it, like a wave function that reappears the moment the observer in a double-slit experiment has left the room. If we approach it in terms of essence, the question of existence inexorably springs up; if we approach it univocally in terms of existence, the question of essence inexorably springs up. And so we go back and forth from one aspect of the question of being to the other: from the "what" that consciousness would try to grasp in *whatever* it is that appears (a "what," moreover, that is conceivably susceptible to infinite description, say, a single tree or house, not to mention the nearly abyssal essence of any human being) to the "that" of its appearing, i.e., its simple existing or *standing out* to consciousness. My point, in any event, is that existence no more reduces to essence than being to consciousness. Rather, from the question of being we are thrown back upon the question of consciousness, and from the question of consciousness we are thrown back upon the question of being—without any place to stand. Such, then, following Erich Przywara, is our creaturely status: what standing we have is a standing *coram Deo* within the analogical fold of being and consciousness, and thus between ontology and epistemology.[13]

Now, from a theological standpoint, this conclusion is not a problem, because it points us to the One from whom the difference between being and consciousness derives; in short, it points from philosophy to theology. But it is a serious problem for modern philosophy inasmuch as one would deny this natural reference and attempt to provide a purely rational, nontheological foundation for the sciences. For, as we have seen, being is simply too dynamic to master, however much philosophical muscle we bring to bear on it. Indeed, the more we try to grasp it, the more, like water, it slips through our fingers. Even Hegel failed to master it, however brilliantly he tried to reduce it to logic. For it is not that Being is a moment of indeterminacy, equivalent to nothing, in the dialectical movement of becoming, which can be grasped, because, at the end of the day, it is as transparent as a simple judgment that unites an otherwise empty subject with a determinate predicate. Rather, the becoming that is born of the dialectic between being and nothing, far from being *itself* the Absolute, is a dynamic analogy *of* the Absolute—that is, of the God who, following Pseudo-Dionysius, transcends not only all epistemic affirmations and denials, but even the ontological difference between being and nothing. In short, pace Hegel, what appears to be a dialectic is really an analogy. And the same applies to every other attempt to cram everything into what Charles Taylor calls the "immanent frame" of a modern world—a

---

13. See Przywara, *Analogia Entis* §1, "Meta-Noetics and Meta-Ontics," 119–24.

world that can only pretend that it is complete in itself and in need of no Other. For if we can learn anything from Przywara's analogical metaphysics, it is that such attempts to absolutize immanence simply don't work—no more than in physics we can reduce waves to particles, or vice versa.[14]

This, then, I take to be the first step of *any* philosophical ontology, and not just one that would serve the purposes of a specifically Trinitarian ontology, namely, the analogical opening of being to Being.[15] But before we explain what an analogical metaphysics has to do with Trinitarian ontology, we need to deal with another titan of modern philosophy, namely, Heidegger. As with Hegel, we need not think that the engagement is an entirely negative one. For just as Hegel did Christian theology a favor by making the doctrine of the Trinity worthy of thought—indeed, the heart of thought itself—Heidegger inadvertently did Christian theology a favor by rehabilitating the question of being, and thereby renewing (together with Husserl and Scheler) the conversation between medieval and modern philosophy that Descartes had foreclosed.[16]

Step Two

Now, to say that we can learn something from Heidegger is not to say that Heidegger is finally compatible with Christian theology. Rather, as with Hegel, it is a question of how far one can travel with him: Is he a fellow traveler on the road to Emmaus, or do his *Holzwege* finally lead elsewhere— or perhaps nowhere? Obviously, this question is too complicated to answer here. But given how much Heidegger has dominated discussions of ontology in the twentieth century and captivated otherwise excellent theologians, we have to consider what he has to say, even if we ultimately have to bid him farewell on our way to a properly *Trinitarian* ontology. So, even if Heidegger

---

14. And the same applies, mutatis mutandis, to every univocal ontology from Deleuze to Badiou. To be sure, in the case of Deleuze and Badiou there is a celebration of mathematical infinitude and unmasterable difference, but theirs is a difference from which any difference between the immanent and transcendent has been excluded; thus, rather than opening to mystery, the question of being is a sprawling, planar immanence.

15. For further treatment, see Betz, *Christ the Logos*, 159–98.

16. What is more, increasing the charm factor, like the "Stiftler" Hegel, Heidegger too comes from theology (in his case as a quondam Jesuit novice); he too borrows from Christian sources (Luther, Kierkegaard, et al.); and he too speaks in an unmistakably Christian idiom—from the "fall" of *das Man* to his canonical poets who await, like the Lucan shepherds at night, the kenotic advent of being. All of which presents the theologian with a serious task of disambiguation. See Wolfe, *Heidegger's Eschatology*; Wolfe, *Heidegger and Theology*; O'Regan, *Anatomy of Misremembering*, vol. 2.

is hostile to the Christian faith, let me try to summarize what I think we can learn from him—in the spirit of *ab hoste consilium*.

First, we have to appreciate Heidegger for having resurrected the question of being, and for having done so at a time when it had largely been forgotten, inasmuch as it had been reduced either to Platonic eidology, Aristotelian aetiology, the self-positing of an absolute subject in German idealism, or the banality of Comtean and mutatis mutandis logical positivism. For in all of the above the question of being has, in one way or another, already been explained or—more to Heidegger's point—explained away. In other words, it has never really been thought. At the same time, we have to appreciate Heidegger for having given an existential emphasis to the old Scholastic distinction between the question of being, the *Seinsfrage*, and the question of essence, the *Wesensfrage*—and having thereby saved philosophy, but also indirectly theology, from collapsing into a one-sided essentialism.[17] Moreover, we have to appreciate Heidegger for highlighting the difference not just between being and essence, but also, by extension, between being and form, being and logic, being and definition, being and cause, and, indeed, between being and the whole compass of cause and effect.[18] For is being really thought if, *before it is thought*, it is divided into cause and effect? Or has such thinking not obscured something that modern thinking has missed: namely, the givenness of being in beings, which is neither a cause nor an effect, nor indeed any "thing," being curiously hidden in every thing from every essentializing gaze?[19]

There is, then, something that Christian theology can learn from Heidegger. Indeed, I dare say that no Trinitarian ontology of the future can fail to appreciate some of his insights, however indebted to the Christian

---

17. In this respect, though he would certainly reject the appellation, we might even consider Heidegger a good *Thomist*, inasmuch as Thomistic metaphysics is predicated precisely on the *difference* between essence and existence, and for having helped creative Thomists, like Przywara, to arrive at a clearer conception of existence—for which Przywara, in fact, credits Heidegger in the preface to his *Analogia Entis*.

18. In this connection we might even appreciate Heidegger's parsing of the difference between being and beings as the difference between beings and nothing, i.e., his understanding of the being of beings as no-thing—however much he borrows without acknowledgment from Eckhart and the apophatic tradition. For if being, writ large, is just one more "thing," one more "what," one more being in a universe of beings, then existence reduces to essence once more, to something determinate, and the ontological difference is denied. Indeed, if we equate God with being, but treat being itself as just another thing, we have eo ipso turned God into a creature and willy-nilly succumb to idolatry.

19. There is therefore something to be said for Heidegger's famous avowal that "the rose has no why," and in general for the novelty of aesthetic experience, which suggests time and again that there is more to the world than logic.

tradition they themselves may be, for instance: that there is a difference between Being and beings; that existence is irreducible to essence; that to be is a gift; and that the gift of being in beings always bears some kind of kenotic signature.[20] And in this respect we must be grateful, too, for the work of Ferdinand Ulrich,[21] who, building on Gustav Siewerth, put Heidegger in conversation with Aquinas to produce a remarkable philosophy centered on the kenotic non-subsistence of being in beings, which takes us (ironically with the help of Heidegger) one step further, heralding a Trinitarian understanding of *being as poor, but rich in love*.

But if Heidegger can help us on the way to a Trinitarian ontology, does this mean that he succeeded in thinking the question of being? My own view is that he did not (and not simply because he was militantly opposed to any admixture of theology in philosophy, but on philosophical grounds): first, because what he means by being, even in his late period, is nothing beyond the immanent economy of beings, but simply the event *of beings* coming into their own, which is to say, their corresponding with a given historical destiny; second, because he elevates Being over the other transcendentals, obscuring their final unity;[22] third, and more to the point here, because he pushes back so hard against Platonism that the question of essences and real ideas virtually disappears, and along with it, rather terrifyingly, the whole question of real *ideals* and moral standards.[23] Indeed, any essential dimension to which the human being might be ordered—any *ordo essentiarum aeternarum*—is simply ruled out, which makes Heidegger just as radical an

---

20. An entire dissertation could be written on Hegel and Heidegger as heterodox kenotic philosophers: in that both of them, borrowing christological language, subscribe to the notion of a kenosis of being in beings, but for neither of them is this kenosis a proper gift: in Hegel's case, because the kenosis turns out to be erotic for the sake of an absolute as subject; in Heidegger's case, because the kenosis is not a kenosis on the part of anything or anyone, but is simply the no-thing and phenomenological hiddenness of the being *of beings* in beings.

21. See Ulrich, *Homo Abyssus*.

22. In other words, while it is legitimate for philosophy to begin with the question of being, I do not think it is finally possible to think of Being in abstraction from the other transcendentals. By the same token, most philosophies, like Heidegger's, end up failing precisely to the extent that they emphasize one transcendental at the expense of the others, failing to see their final unity—e.g., in Heidegger's case we have fairly robust concepts of being, truth, and even beauty, but the good is notoriously absent, unless the good can be reduced to "care."

23. This is not to say that in Heidegger the question of essence disappears entirely: it reappears the moment Heidegger attempts to explain the *Sosein* of *Dasein* in terms of various existentials and so forth. But the existential terminology is revealing, because we are not talking about essences but about *existential* possibilities.

anti-Platonist as Nietzsche. In sum, denying from the start both any transcendence and any notion of an objective human essence, Heidegger leaves us with a *doubly truncated ontology* that ironically *forecloses* the very question of being it purports to pose.[24]

What is needed, therefore, *even on philosophical grounds*, is a more *open philosophy* of the kind Przywara attempted to provide, namely, an *analogical philosophy*, which remains open to being's *double valence*, and can therefore resist the temptations that have consistently bedeviled ontology: on the one hand, the Platonic temptation to reduce the question of existence to that of essence; on the other hand, in the case of Nietzsche and Heidegger, the opposing temptation to reduce the question of essence to that of existence. For, simply put, whereas the former would turn existence into an illusory projection of essence "from above," the latter would turn all essences, all values, and all ideals, into an illusory projection of existence "from below." In other words, what is needed, over against these inveterate tendencies to reduction, each of which forecloses the question of being in its own way, is what Przywara tried to articulate on the basis of the Thomistic *analogia entis*, beginning with the interplay of essence and existence as properly basic to any serious philosophy—not in order immediately to arrest the play with a theological demand that the philosopher believe, but precisely in order to leave room for the philosopher freely to infer something more absolute, more divine, that is declared in this interplay but mysteriously transcends it. In short, what is needed is an approach that gives room for philosophy to be philosophy and for theology to be theology, without philosophy denying the possibility of the latter (which, after all, may turn out to be its proper telos), or theology encroaching upon the freedom of the former to think about the mystery of being.

Accordingly, following the lines of Przywara's *Analogia Entis*, such an approach will begin (precisely at the level of immanence) by registering both the curious transcendence of existence with regard to essence *and* the equally curious transcendence of essence with regard to existence. In other words, it will register how (negatively) neither is reducible to the other and

---

24. To be sure, one must account for Heidegger's *Kehre* toward a more objective understanding of being, which leads him to speak of the *Wesen des Seyns* and so forth. For, in the absence of any transcendent order this is indeed his attempt to locate meaning in some kind of "essential" correspondence with Being. But any such correspondence with being in its event, *Sein als Ereignis*, is, again, nothing transcendent, but simply the event of beings *coming into their own*—not simply as corresponding with oneself by being authentically toward death, as in *Sein und Zeit*, but now also as corresponding with one's people's historical destiny, which led him eerily to embrace both death and National Socialism as being's self-revelation.

why, consequently, every historical attempt to reduce one to the other—and to press the mystery of being into an immanent conceptual frame—has failed and will always fail. But the result of this analogical approach is not merely negative. For at the same time one comes to see how, precisely in the midst of their irreducibility *one to another* (allo *pros* allo), essence and existence are intimately related *to one another* (*allo* pros *allo*)—to the point that in everything they intersect with one another in their alterity to one another. In other words, it is this very point of intersection, where these opposites meet without being reducible to one another, that constitutes the formal possibility of anything being any thing at all.

Now, admittedly, all of this can seem quite abstract, as though we are prescinding from the concrete nature of things. And, in truth, this intersection of essence and existence is ordinarily hidden from view. But it is hardly an abstraction once it is seen that all things, from the smallest particle to ourselves to the entire universe, are constituted by it. Indeed, it concretely changes how we see everything, or, rather, how we hear everything. For, following Przywara, we come to see, in the midst of our everyday perception of the sensible world, that the entire cosmos and everything in it vibrates with a "resonant rhythm,"[25] which turns out (upon further reflection) to be the ontological signature of creation. At the same time, it elevates music to an ontological status, indicating that music may be closer to reality—indeed, more nearly what reality is—than we realize, and certainly more revealing of reality than modern philosophy, in its search for an analytic foundation for being and thought, has realized. For being is surely more like music than geometry, or anything that could be grasped *more geometrico*, since here differences, even opposites, simultaneously intersect, as in a fugue. Thus, following Przywara, who for a time served as prefect of music in Feldkirch, to do ontology one has in some sense to be like Bach: to be able to hold complex themes together in a single score, which is yet another clue to the genius of creation.

But, being fugue-like, we can say still more. For the fundamental analogical interplay of essence and existence is only the key, as it were, to a more complex interweaving of "existence in and beyond essence" (on a more existentialist reading of the Thomistic real distinction) and "essence in and beyond existence" (on a more essential reading of the Thomistic real distinction). Now, it is not the place here to elaborate such a metaphysical formula, as we have tried to do elsewhere.[26] For present purposes it suffices

---

25. Przywara, *Analogia Entis*, 314.

26. For a sketch of such an analogical philosophy, which seeks to unite the insights of Przywara and Ulrich, see Betz, *Christ the Logos*, 409–32.

to indicate that being, far from being univocal, which is the banality to which being has been reduced in modernity *and* much of postmodernity, is thoroughly analogical, being constituted at its core by the dynamic and infinitely variable interplay of essence and existence; and, furthermore, that it is like a fugue-like event of interweaving themes, which makes it open to interpretation, and a fortiori inasmuch as neither the question of essence nor the question of existence, much less their analogical unity-in-difference and variable explication in a universe of endless differences, has yet been explained or, from any immanent perspective, even can be explained—no more than an analogy explains its analogate. In other words, we have come to that point in our reflection upon being at which the light of divine transcendence is ready to break through, revealing being to be not only an analogy of Being, but a mysterious *gift of transcendence* (*genetivus subjectivus et objectivus*).

In this way, then, from philosophical metaphysics we come to the threshold of theological ontology. Before crossing it, however, let us briefly review our steps. Beginning with the concept of being we have seen that it mysteriously doubles into essence and existence, and that philosophy's inability to reconcile them is like a crack running through every immanent frame. I then suggested that an honest philosophy will remain standing before the mystery of their crossing, as at a crossroads where the questions of essence and existence, after mysteriously meeting, stretch to infinity. Which leaves us wondering in a Marian mode how in the world—and where in the world—essence and existence might coincide so perfectly as to reveal the meaning of being itself.

Step Three

Now, in some sense, we need look no further because this mysterious coincidence is actually everywhere, since nothing could be said to "be" at all were it not *some kind* of *existence*. But such coincidences of essence and existence nevertheless seem (quite precisely) coincidental. In other words, they appear to be happenings of being that leave us wondering where, if anywhere, essence and existence coincide without falling apart again. In other words, is there any place in the world, any crossing, where essence and existence coincide not just momentarily and analogically, but perfectly and completely in such a way that reveals their actual identity?

Now, for Christians, of course, there *is* such an intersection, such a crossing—one that turns out to be the mysterious point on which the being of the world hangs. For if Christ is the one hypostasis in whom divinity and humanity perfectly coincide, he is also the one in whom essence and existence perfectly coincide. Indeed, not only is Christ the perfect coincidence of a particular human essence and existence (and thus truly *totus homo*); he is also the hypostatic identity of this temporal human coincidence with the eternal identity of essence and existence proper to divinity (and thus truly *totus Deus*). In other words, Christ is at once the perfect man, having existed perfectly according to the essence of his humanity, *and* the divine "I AM," whose essence is to exist. In short, for Przywara (and for Balthasar), Christ *is* in himself the analogy of being, comprising both the fullness of divinity and humanity in himself, being a perfect embodiment of the divine essence and existence in the form of a created essence and existence. In the words of Przywara, which bear reference to the stipulated *maior dissimilitudo* of the Fourth Lateran Council with respect to every similarity however great:

> The form of this unity is itself, in the most mysterious sense of the word, analogy. For the innermost mystery of Christ is that in him deity and humanity are *one* person, but within a difference between the two that not only is not negated but, indeed, necessarily cannot be: thus within a hypostatic union that is neither abrogated nor can be, and as such *is* the analogy of "ever greater dissimilarity" that cannot be negated (*non potest*, according to the council).[27]

Of course, with Mary we might ask, "How can this be?" For if in God essence and existence are identical and in human beings they are precisely *non*identical, and if this difference is what we mean by the analogy of being, which stresses the greater *dissimilarity* between divine and created being, how can they be united in Christ? In other words, the analogy of being would seem to leave us without hope that God and humanity could ever really meet, or that a human being (whose essence is in God) could ever fully exist. For to be human (to be any creature) is precisely to be a *nonidentity* of essence and existence. How, then, can Przywara (and Balthasar, following him) say that Christ, insofar as he is man, is the "concrete analogy" of being or, better, the "hypostatic identity" of the analogy of being?[28] The answer to this difficult question, I submit, is that in Christ, *mirabile dictu*, the Way of being, which is given to us, is *one and the same*. In other words, in Christ we see at once what it means for God to be *and* what it means for human beings to be, so that we can arrive at the meaning of being *either* through his

---

27. "The Scope of Analogy as a Fundamental Catholic Form," in Przywara, *Analogia Entis*, 399; emphasis in original. For further discussion, see "The Metaphysics of Chalcedon," in Betz, *Christ the Logos*, 201–29.

28. See Balthasar, *Spirit and Institution*, 287.

humanity *or* through his divinity. In short, the one is the face of the other. In this light let us now turn to the question of Trinitarian ontology proper and to what Christ reveals about the being of God *in se* as Trinity, from which the meaning of our own being follows.

Step Four

Now, thus far I have spoken of God as an identity of essence and existence. But, of course, to say that God's essence is to exist also comes close to saying that God *has* to exist; in other words, it comes close to reducing God to an *ens necessarium*, i.e., to a necessity of reason, and thus, one could argue, to a conceptual idol. Now I do not think one has to see it this way, but it is nevertheless a legitimate concern. So, if we are not to stop with philosophical metaphysics and rest our gaze on an idol, as Jean-Luc Marion has legitimately warned us about, we must proceed to theological metaphysics, recognizing that this philosophical conception is only a veil before a profounder, Trinitarian mystery. For whereas a philosophical conception of divine identity leads to a notion of necessary existence, what Scripture suggests to us is that God as Being is *semper maior*, and therefore more than necessary.[29] We might infer this initially from the seemingly unnecessary doubling of the "I AM" in Exod 3:14. But it is even more evident from the gospel, which suggests to us that the meaning of existence is, quite literally, to *ex-ist* in the way that the Father *exists* in the Son and the Son exists in the Father. In short, the gospel suggests to us a completely different notion of what it means to exist, namely, to be in and for another. It is, therefore, not that we first know what it means to exist, which we then apply to God. For what we have known of existence all along is merely analogical. It is rather that, as we cross over from philosophical to theological metaphysics, the very meaning of existence is transformed.

By the same token, our conception of God as an identity of essence and existence is also transformed. For far from meaning that God is a necessary being, the mutual existence of the Father in the Son and the Son in the Father in the unity of the Spirit suggests that God's essential identity is nothing other than a triune ecstasy: such that the Father has no existence (no identity) except in the Son, the Son has no existence (no identity) except in the Father, and the Holy Spirit has no existence (no identity) except as the love of the Father and the Son for one another. In other words, the gospel suggests that, *in and of themselves*, the persons of the Trinity *have no identity*

---

29. See Betz, *Christ the Logos*, 173–81.

and are *nothing in* themselves except by dint of that essentially existing love by which they are what they are.

Now, admittedly, this makes the Trinity appear like nothing. Indeed, we would seem to have accepted Heidegger's asseveration that Being *is* nothing—*Sein als Nichts*. The theological difference, however, and the decisive overcoming of Heidegger's ontological nihilism, consists in this: that for Trinitarian ontology, Being is *nothing but Love*. In other words, the apparent nothingness of Being is the nothingness that Love makes of itself for the sake of the Beloved. To venture a Trinitarian formula that perfects the philosophical formula, one might say that the Father is the Eternal Ground of the divine essence, which neither exists nor has any form except in the Son; that the Son is the Eternal Ex-istence of this ground, its Eternal Splendor; and that the Spirit is the Eternal Return of God's existence into God's essence—this being, pace Nietzsche, the *real* eternal return of which Christ's life in the Spirit is the perfect image: a perfect reenactment for our sake of the One Eternal Gift and Thanksgiving.

Granted, I have here made a lot of the etymological sense of existence as a standing outside oneself, but I think it is warranted, and that revelation itself confirms what is mysteriously there under our noses in our everyday word for being. For looked at from every angle of the gospel, the identity of the persons of the Trinity would appear to consist precisely *not* in themselves, but rather *outside* themselves in the triune form of a reciprocal, selfless ecstasy. And so, finally, I come to the meaning of the last two words in my title, "identity" and "ecstasy," in which the meaning of being is fulfilled. For it is not that God is (or has) an identity before or apart from his ecstasy, but rather that he remains in himself, paradoxically, by going beyond himself. In other words, in God, immanence *is* transcendence, essence *is* existence, and identity *is* ecstasy.

So, then, from the perspective opened up by Trinitarian ontology, we have an answer to the question of being and, of more immediate concern, that of our own being as a dynamic relation between essence and existence. For in Christ we can genuinely say that our essence is also to *ex-ist*, which is to say, to exist outside ourselves for the sake of God and neighbor—but with this difference: that whereas God's essence is always already to exist in the triune manner just described, the creature's essence is a *gerundive* existence, which is to say that its existence is given to it as a task to fulfill. In short, we are not already what we are, but must become what we are, until that day when *what* we are will be revealed at the coming of Christ (1 John 1:2–3). Nota bene, this dramatically reverses how we usually think about essence and existence. For while we typically think of given natures as things that happen to exist; here we find out *what* we really are, our essence, only by living in a certain way, according to a certain *tropos*, which only in the end reveals our logos, as Maximus says.

But if Christ is our End, he is also our Way, because he alone is the one in whom Logos and *tropos* are one. In the meantime of the saeculum, therefore, as we await the revelation of the children of God, he shows us how to exist: not statically in oneself, much less curved in upon oneself, which is the definition of sin and contradiction of being, but rather to exist as the word itself etymologically suggests, namely, ecstatically, for God and neighbor. To be sure, one who so loves appears to be nothing: for in a sense, nothing of the individual qua individual remains; in the Spirit of Christ, which is the Spirit of thanksgiving, it has been given back (Gal 2:20). And yet, mysteriously, now like the Triune God, it is in this way that we *really* exist. For, as Christ says, to lose oneself is really to find oneself (Matt 10:39).

5

Trinitarian Kenosis and the Limits of Phenomenology

EMMANUEL FALQUE

WE MUST ACKNOWLEDGE THE long journey undertaken by phenomenology. By its pitfalls a possible renewal of thought is born. This renewal is possible not by abandoning or denigrating the phenomenological method, but rather by its molting or transforming as a result of its own insufficiency. Jacques Derrida, Paul Ricœur, Gilles Deleuze, and Michel Foucault foresaw this. In phenomenology we can neither say nor conclude everything. Its great strength (description) is also its great weakness (systematics). There is no question of playing or replaying here the debate between phenomenology and metaphysics. For each side is paralyzed by its own attack on the other. Eristic quarrels have little meaning, insofar as they are content to oppose their protagonists without truly entering into a *disputatio*, or a "loving struggle," which is equally committed and on a level playing field. There remains, however, a third way, which claims allegiance neither to phenomenology nor to metaphysics, but rather and essentially to philosophy. It consists in interrogating the articulation of concepts, so as to cover a spectrum of thought that is broad enough that nothing is forgotten.

In phenomenology, the lack reveals what we must today investigate, not so much to fight against it as to otherwise orient it.[1]

For my part, in my previous work I identified three pitfalls in phenomenology, to which I would add two that remain to be explored: (1) the *primacy of weakness over strength*; (2) the *hypertrophy of the flesh over the body*; (3) the *a priori of meaning over chaos*—to which are added: (4) the *presupposition of otherness over solitude*; and (5) the *claimed self-evidence of the event over the brute fact of existence*. Whatever may become of these pitfalls, we can raise the question: "What is, or could be, the very structure of the being of the Trinity in regard to these lacks of phenomenology itself?"[2] This question may be surprising from at least three points of view. One may rightly ask: (1) Is the collision, even the collusion, of philosophy and theology not here absolutely superfluous and arbitrary? (2) Can one truly ask a dogma to fill the gaps in phenomenology? (3) If this "backlash" of theology does not pay too high a price for philosophy, is it down to God to resolve problems that humans each on their own cannot solve?

I have been saying for a long time what is also pointed out in the gospel: "Each tree is known by its own fruit" (Luke 6:44 NRSV). What is true for this New Testament passage is also true for this astonishing confrontation between philosophy and theology. What matters, and what I will show here, is not that the *propos* is possible. We "crossed the Rubicon" a long time ago while keeping its boundaries intact. Rather, this *propos* is real, even necessary. For it is fecund, capable of producing thought, and even of clarifying the meaning and structure of the divine in a way both philosophical and Trinitarian "that responds to the needs of our time."[3] This enterprise is also justified by its pioneer—Klaus Hemmerle, who invites us to use this method and, with it, to orient ourselves afresh. The expression "Trinitarian ontology" is in fact a syntagma. For it possesses its author. And even though the Freiburg theologian did not invent the expression, it has become directly connected to him, due to his *Theses for a Trinitarian Ontology*. What is striking about Hemmerle's attempt is precisely this double effort to connect

---

1. An initial attempt at this, which in my view is too reactionary (in its opposition of the two camps), is found in Alliez, *Impossibilité de la phénoménologie*. This work echoes and in some way completes the movement begun by Janicaud, *Phenomenology and the "Theological Turn."*

2. For more on this threefold lack, see ch. 1 of my *Wedding Feast of the Lamb*.

3. "What is needed is that this certain and immutable doctrine, to which the faithful owe obedience, be *studied afresh and reformulated in contemporary terms*" (John XXIII, "Opening Address to Council," s.vv. "A Fresh Approach"; emphasis added). As to the method invoked here, see Falque: "The Tree and Its Fruits," in *God, the Flesh*, 10–11; "Finally Theology," in *Crossing the Rubicon*, 137–54.

philosophy and theology starting from the standpoint of ontology. "*We need an ontology for theology's sake*," so that the latter not be limited to a simple history of religions or ideas, or reduced to an anthropology that would deny what is of God himself in himself, or confuse the testimony of faith (*fides qua*) with the content of faith (*fides quae*). "*But we also need ontology for philosophy's sake*," so that we do not lose the inspiration of philosophy under the weight of the ontic or ignore the deep connection that holds together philosophy and theology in the question of being. We need to let the properly phenomenological or "monstrative" role of philosophy appear, which shows, in the language of the gift, what for theology develops in another form—the Holy Spirit. This explains the conclusion of the Bishop of Aix-la-Chapelle: that this "ontology . . . has to be posited together with theology, so that theology can remain theology, and . . . has to be laid bare in philosophy, so that philosophy can remain philosophy."[4]

It is clear that Klaus Hemmerle has already "crossed the Rubicon," but in another or inverse way. As a theologian, he starts from the riverbank of theology to make philosophy appear in a way that is phenomenological for theology, but without annexing it. Yet as a philosopher, I start from the riverbank of philosophy in order better to return—thinking this time that God, at least the concept of God, transforms the human in his or her own thoughts beyond the confessional attestations that might emerge here or there. The highest goal of a "new Trinitarian ontology" is, in my view, not only held in its a priori "from above" of the divine for the human, and the human for the divine. For in holding this double a priori "from above," it would restate the fifth thesis of the claimed self-evidence of the event over the brute fact of existence. Rather, it is necessary for us to pursue a priori "from below," not only for the human to access to the divine, but also for us to find the way to it from within our pure and simple humanity.[5] Today,

---

4. Hemmerle, *Theses*, 3–4; emphasis in original.

5. See Hemmerle, *Theses*, 6–7. The fifth thesis is titled "The double *a priori* of theology" and states: "But this last *a priori* [of the human for the divine] is divine too, an *a priori* 'from above.'" To be sure, we understand from this that we begin from the principle of Trinitarian kenosis as the author suggests. But for the philosopher this cannot be a starting point but a conclusion. And that is why, for my part, we need an a priori "from below." On this point see Jérôme de Gramont's interpretation of Hemmerle, with which I fully agree: "It is in this way that First Philosophy . . . places us at the crossroads of the most common noun, 'being', and the Proper Noun par excellence, God (Trinity). . . . We have the right to expect that a truly First Philosophy would begin with the name that is highest, most explosive, most glorious (God). . . . [But] beginnings are only beginnings. We rightly see in this tautology the poverty of a first word which must be forgotten when a more serious discourse succeeds it" (Gramont, "Nom le plus commun," 12, 13, 14).

we must find such a way to connect rather than to oppose Hans Urs von Balthasar and Karl Rahner: the *Hearer of the Word*, which begins heuristically (Rahner); and the *objective form of revelation*, which has a didactic exposition (Balthasar).[6] It is precisely at this point that we may be able to advance beyond a quarrel that could forever sterilize thought in its ceaseless repetition.

Hence, the purpose of this interrogation will be to see whether this triple pitfall in phenomenology for "Trinitarian ontology" can give us a depiction of God capable of renewing both philosophy and theology. For philosophy is a conceptuality drawn a priori from a philosophy of revelation of the body, the face, excess; and theology is a Trinitarian conception that grants us a figuration of God characterized in its own right by the thickness of the incarnate, the power to save us, and the descent into our deepest abyss. In French phenomenology there is a sort of "irenicism" or happy comfort in descriptiveness, which has today burst into theology and distanced it from a confrontation with the natural character of death (Rahner) or the divine drama (Balthasar). The porosity of both phenomenology and theology can lead to the decisions of phenomenology being imposed on theology, without, however, considering the "backlash" that theology can produce for philosophy.

Two issues are thus opened up: whether, with the theologian Klaus Hemmerle, to start with theology and eventually modify or interrogate philosophy; or whether, as a philosopher, to begin with a renewed phenomenology, and to use theology and philosophy to deploy a figuration of God capable of saving us, or at least to come and seek us where we could not have imagined. "Would not a phenomenology whose dice have not been fixed have more attention for the atrocious, despairing, unqualifiable, or even only undecidable—where our condition is also woven?" asks Dominique Janicaud in *Phenomenology and the "Theological Turn."* And, in a question that matters as much or even more than any question of boundaries, he also asks, "Does not E. M. Cioran reveal himself, then, to be at least as phenomenological as our authors, in many of his ruthless descriptions of our human condition?"[7]

To juxtapose these lacks in phenomenology with the kenosis of Christ in the Holy Trinity amounts to developing a "new Trinitarian ontology." Such a Trinitarian ontology could be characterized in a myriad of ways. A "God of power" in the person of the Holy Spirit, against the constant recourse to weakness and powerlessness, even of God himself. A "God of

---

6. Rahner, *Hearer of the Word*; Balthasar, *Glory of the Lord*.
7. Janicaud, *Phenomenology and the "Theological Turn,"* 69.

the body" in the person of the Son, against the quasi-Gnosticism, phenomenological and theological, of the experience of the flesh and the forgetting of the organic. A "God of chaos or descent into the abyss" in the person of the Father, against the a priori of the meaningful, which makes salvation wait too long for us to emerge from our darkness without seeing or being satisfied with a "being-with" (*Immanu-El*) which is already ours for the taking, at least so that we might be no longer alone.[8]

Strength in Life (Strength/Weakness)

To wager on strength is to return to the thesis of the death of God and Nietzsche's critique of Christianity's radical transformation of power into weakness. To be sure, the death of God was much discussed at the end of the last century and was seen either as the death of a God who precisely "can die" as in "death of God" theologies (Vahanian), or as the assassination of an idol of God so that the icon can be revealed as in Jean-Luc Marion. The difficulty, however, that Alain Badiou showed in his *Briefings on Existence: A Short Treatise on Transitory Ontology* is that the

> God who can die is not, and cannot be, [the] conceptual God.... It must be Isaac, Abraham and Jacob's God, or the Christ who speaks directly to Pascal in his inner Garden of Gethsemane. The living God is always *somebody's* God.... God is dead means that He is no longer *the living being* who can be encountered when existence breaks the ice of its own transparency.[9]

God does not die simply because we announce his death, or else save his life by declaring the idea of him null and invalid. Such a dispute continues to give existence to the very thing it tries to annihilate. On the contrary, God dies insofar as God is forgotten, erased from memory, and thus no longer disputed. What is at stake in the death of God is no longer the *death of the Son*, such that, by his death, he leaves the Father alive, along with the Holy Spirit. If today the Christian God is dying, or could die again, such a deicide would mean not only the death of the Son, but the *death of the Father* himself, or worse still the *death of the Holy Spirit*, the "reviving force" of the Son

---

8. Many of these traits can be found in the respective stages of my *Triduum philosophique* (*Philosophical Triduum*), of which this essay is a sort of Trinitarian rereading: "power in life" or the person of the Spirit (*Métamorphose de la finitude* [*Metamorphosis of Finitude*]); "life in the body" or the person of the Son (*Passeur de Gethsémani* [*Guide to Gethsemane*]); "descent into the abyss" or the person of the Father (*Noces de l'Agneau* [*Wedding Feast of the Lamb*]).

9. Badiou, *Briefings on Existence*, 23–24; emphasis added.

by which he is raised in order to give himself. "God is dead, God *remains dead*," proclaims Nietzsche's madman in the famous paragraph 125 of *The Gay Science*, pointing out, thereby, that it is not enough that "God dies," but rather that he "remains dead"—erased and forgotten from our memory.[10]

The "power of God" is therefore at stake in the will to annihilate him. The question of salvation appears here less in the *ad extra* threat of a world in which we deplore the presence of nihilism, as *ad intra*, in Christianity giving up any attempt to expound its contents in a "credible" and "powerful" manner, or even to exert itself at all. "You will receive power [*dunamin*] when the Holy Spirit [*tou agiou pneumatos*] has come upon you, and you will be my witnesses," proclaims Christ, announcing the Pentecost on the day of his ascension (Acts 1:8 NRSV); and "you were also raised with him," writes Paul to the Colossians, "through faith in the power of God [*energeias tou theou*] who raised him from the dead" (Col 2:12 NRSV).

Contemporary theology's *omission* of any thought of "power" (*energeia, dunamis*), and Florensky, goes to the very root of phenomenology. It is not that theology necessarily consults phenomenology—far from it—but that on this issue both participate in the same cultural movement, rooted so much (and perhaps rightly) in "fragility" that it forgets what there is also of the bestowed "élan vital" (Bergson, for example). The face (Levinas), the gift (Marion), auto-affection (Henry), fallibility (Ricœur), the word (Chrétien), liturgy (Lacoste), etc., certainly remain syntagmata and experiences worth magnifying. Nonetheless, the welcome of the other, the figuration of benevolent listening, and the wisdom of patiently waiting to be awakened in another age must not suppress the "power of this God" who, in the power of the Holy Spirit, comes to "metamorphose" and revive us. Idioms such as the retreat, *tzimtzum*, the powerlessness of God, and also his suffering have today become widely shared, even in Judaism.[11] Yet these idioms tend to forget everything of the "struggle" in life that makes us, even God himself, alive. We too quickly confuse the "struggle *for* life" and the "struggle *in* life" (the law of the living). "Just as trees in a forest," Kant observes in his 1784 "Idea for a Universal History with a Cosmopolitan Aim," "precisely because each of them seeks to take air and sun from the other, are constrained to look for them *above themselves*, and thereby achieve a *beautiful straight* growth; whereas those in freedom and *separated from one another*, that put forth their branches as they like, grow *stunted, crooked and awry*."[12]

---

10. Nietzsche, *Gay Science* (trans. Kaufman), 181; emphasis added.
11. See Jonas, "Concept of God After Auschwitz."
12. Kant, "Idea for a Universal History," 113; emphasis added.

The most beautiful trees are always, in this sense, the ones that have "struggled." We must distinguish "struggle" (*agôn*) from "war" (*polemos*). There are good fights or struggles—not those that abandon their opposition to each other (conflict or cowardice, even sin), but those that engage each other in the tension of strength against strength that makes them precisely what they are (struggle, equilibrium, trial of the self by the other). "I will not let you go, unless you bless me," says Jacob in his struggle with the angel (Gen 32:26 NRSV). It is as if the athletic act of surpassing each other, even confronting each other, depicted so well by Eugène Delacroix in his 1861 painting *Jacob Wrestling with the Angel*, in the Chapel of the Holy Angels in the Church of Saint-Sulpice in Paris, still had something to teach us today about the "power of a Savior," capable both of indwelling and of metamorphosing us.

The Nietzschean accusation of the paralogism of power in Christianity thus awaits to be fully interrogated. Not that there is any absurdity in thinking about a "power in weakness" of the type St. Paul recognized in his Letter to the Corinthians. For "whenever I am weak, then I am strong" (2 Cor 12:10 NRSV). Rather, the renouncing of "human power" can and must be accompanied by confessing and attesting to the "power of God." Nietzsche's posthumous fragment, in which "you need to learn to stand up *by yourselves* or you will fall,"[13] explicitly announcing the idea of a "sur-resurrection" and an "auto-transformation," is made possible not only by us letting go of power, but by God taking up power. That man is not an "overman" (*Übermensch*) does not discount the possibility that the Christian God is and remains in some way an "over God" of the Holy Spirit, of whom nothing separates the effect from its cause, as humans or disciples might work in them. There is, or there must be, something of the *Dionysian* in Christianity. For otherwise, we risk confusing a human attribute (renouncing power) and a divine attribute (the exercise of the Holy Spirit's power), by which it is given for us not only to act, but also to think, to feel, and to love: "I came that they may *have life*, and have it *abundantly*," declares Christ to the Samaritan woman (John 10:10 NRSV). It is a bursting forth of the Dionysian. "The *Gospel according to St. John* born out of Greek atmosphere, out of the soil of the Dionysian," Nietzsche rightly notes, in a posthumous fragment from 1870 (7/80).[14] As an entirely Greek production, the Gospel According to St. John is the fruit of the same spirit where the mysteries were born.[15]

13. Falque, *Metamorphosis of Finitude*, 49; emphasis added.

14. Nietzsche, *Writings from the Early Notebooks*, 33.

15. For this whole passage, see Falque: *Metamorphosis of Finitude* §13, "The Debate with Nietzsche," 47–53; *Wedding Feast of the Lamb* §35, "The Rapture of the Wedding Feast," 224–27.

There can therefore be no Christology in Christianity, or even any treatment of creation from the fountainhead of the Father, without a *pneumatology* that, if it does not precede it, at least founds it thoroughly. We often wrongly believe that the body produces power, in a "thingification" of beings existing independently of the power that they exert—as if, to speak theologically, the Father and the Son preceded the Holy Spirit as facts, only then to love each other. Yet Genesis, from its beginning and in its New Testament rereading, could not be more clear: "In the beginning . . . the Spirit of God [*pneuma*] was hovering over the face of the waters" (Gen 1:1 ESV). As with Spinoza's *conatus*, and perhaps also Thomas Aquinas's *act of being*, which on this point in no way resembles Aristotle's *pure act*, the "Spirit," the "act," or the "power" gives rise to the body, rather than the other way around, as is commonly thought. The same can be said of the eucharistic consecration and human love, where, as I have elsewhere shown in *The Wedding Feast of the Lamb*, love makes the body rather than the body making love. Like the man and the woman who reach toward each other in their difference, love or the "power of the Spirit" *seeks a body* in the epiclesis, in which the eucharistic species receive the "power of the Holy Spirit" in order to transform the "bread" into "body" and the "wine" into "blood": "Make holy, therefore, these gifts, we pray, by sending down *your Spirit* [power] upon them like the dewfall, so that they may *become for us* [by metamorphosis] the Body and Blood of our Lord Jesus Christ."[16]

Life in the Body (Body/Flesh)

If it is true that "power gives rise to the body" and not only that "the body produces power," we must ask what kind of corporeality we are talking about, especially in the Son who became incarnate. Just as a *primacy of weakness over strength* (or of passivity over activity) pervades phenomenology and theology, so also a sort of *hypertrophy of the flesh over the body* is played out in both, to the point where the incarnate is seen more in the experience of embodiment than in its true organicity.

The classical phenomenological distinction between "flesh" and "body" tends to privilege the body's (*Leib*) "lived mode of being" over its organicity or materiality (*Körper*). To be sure, the cure commonly given to a patient clearly takes into account this dimension of the patient's affectivity, their feeling of pain or their corporeality. But this is perhaps sometimes done to the point of forgetting the aspect in them of a "struggle *in* life," which is their organicity, in which a conflict occurs, and for which it is not enough

---

16. Falque, *Wedding Feast of the Lamb*, 132.

to welcome so as to indwell differently. We sometimes like to advocate a "welcoming of suffering," but this can sometimes mean that we lose sight of its rebellion, the "struggle" contained in its attachment to life, and in its exposure to the other, and to the world from which it cannot distance itself.[17]

Certainly, suffering can sometimes purify, in the Greek model of catharsis shared by a number of saints. But it is still true that physical suffering, at least in its extreme form, does not speak—it howls. It expresses the revulsion of the body more than it symbolizes the welcome of the spirit. "The content of suffering merges with the impossibility of detaching oneself from suffering," Levinas underlines in his *Time and the Other*.[18] Rather than always privileging moral suffering over physical suffering as the human distinctive (Lavelle), we recognize to the contrary that incarnate suffering is "exposure to being," "impossibility of distanciation," and that by which something comes to me that is not of me. "Suffering is the imprint in man of something *other than himself*," Blondel highlights in *Action*, which manifests itself like a "revealing sword."[19] If there is a "bodily physics" of Christ's body and the Eucharist (as Paul Claudel says) it is not because the Word made flesh suffers or suffered more than other condemned people, or that his suffering purified him more, but rather because *in the "other" of suffering in him* he welcomes *the "other" of his Father*, and thereby opens the rift of his body by which the Trinity comes to be manifest. "Then Jesus gave a *loud cry* and breathed his last. And the *curtain of the temple* was torn in two," we read in Mark's account (Mark 15:37-38 NRSV). And the Letter to the Hebrews speaks of "the new and living way that he opened for us through *the curtain* (that is, through *his flesh*)" (Heb 10:20 NRSV).

To develop a "Trinitarian ontology" capable of expressing the fullness of both divinity and corporeality requires that we should not shun corporeality—not only the "experience of the flesh" (*Leib*), which is constantly referred to, but also the "materiality of the body" (*Körper*), which we must not forget. The *contemporary hypertrophy of the flesh over the body* is in fact a reaction of the lived body (Husserl) against the extended body (Descartes), such that we now insist more on the feeling of the flesh (Husserl) than the previous geometricization of the body (Descartes). But between the extended body (Descartes) and the lived body (Husserl), I maintain

---

17. We review this point in Falque: "Ethics of Spread Body"; *Éthique du corps épandu*, esp. 55–65, "L'hyper-matérialité du corps."

18. Levinas, *Time and the Other*, 69.

19. Blondel, *Action*, 351; emphasis added. "We may well accept and foresee fatigue, being fed up with work, the reversals of fortune, the betrayals of life; we still remain always surprised and crushed by them because they strike elsewhere than we had feared, otherwise than we had expected" (305).

there is the "spread body," a third type of body, a sort of intermediary or border region reaching to the "silence of the organs" in the human (Leriche's definition of health),[20] but also desired as a being capable of constituting us and that we cannot not inhabit. "Nothing is 'given' as real except our world of desires and passions," we must recognize with Nietzsche, adding our own hypothesis that the Savior himself is not absent from such a world, "as a kind of *instinctual life* in which all organic functions, together with self-regulation, assimilation, nourishment, excretion, metabolism, are all synthetically bound together—as an *antecedent form* of life."[21]

Therein lies the whole paradox of thinking the incarnation, and perhaps the heart of theology's "backlash" on philosophy.[22] Christ did not become incarnate in an angelic body given only to appear, we affirm with Tertullian against the Gnostics (and Valentin in particular), but in a body "to be born" (*ut nasci*) and "to die" (*ut mori*). He did not only "carry the cross" (*crucem gestare*), but also "carried flesh" (*carnem gestare*). The gnostic *Christos angelos* thesis could be seen as the theological version of the phenomenological flesh, namely the hypertrophy of the lived experience of the body over its organicity. The meaning of "word become flesh" is not first of all that of the lived experience of the body, or an intimate auto-affection of the self by the self in the Son, or even by the Father (Michel Henry), but of a real assumption and transformation of our entire humanity, including its materiality and organicity. "For He [the Son] was looked on as a man, for no other reason whatever than because He existed in the corporeal substance of a man," Tertullian rightly observes in his *On the Flesh of Christ*, "the muscles as clods; of the bones as stones; the mammillary glands as a kind of pebbles. Look upon the close junctions of the nerves as propagations of roots, and the branching courses of the veins as winding rivulets, and the down (which covers us) as moss, and the hair as grass, and the very treasures of marrow within our bones as ores of flesh."[23] Christ's "spread body," not only extended (mechanical) nor only lived (psychic), is plainly here. Like a "spread flesh" on a bed in sleep or anesthesia, or spread on the cross at the hour of Golgotha, it is the *totality* of our own corporality that the Savior comes to indwell and to assume, if not to transform, at least to remain there.

20. "Health is life lived in the silence of the organs" is the definition of health proposed by French surgeon René Leriche in 1936 (Canguilhem, *Normal et pathologique*, 180).

21. Nietzsche, *Beyond Good and Evil* (1973), 48 (§36); emphasis added. The thesis of the "spread body" is now largely developed, but one may find its birthplace in Falque, *Wedding Feast of the Lamb*, 12–15 (§1, "The Residue of the Body").

22. See my *Crossing the Rubicon*.

23. Tertullian of Carthage, "On the Flesh of Christ," 530.

Descent into the Abyss (Meaninglessness/Meaning)

There remains the question of meaning (sense), or rather of non-meaning (non-sense). The role of the Father comes to indwell in it, if not to give it reasonableness—at least so as not to leave us alone. As with the *primacy of weakness over strength* (or of passivity over activity), to which the "power of the Spirit" responded, and as with the *hypertrophy of the flesh over the body* to which the "Son incarnate" responds, now comes the *a priori of meaning over chaos* to which the "Father's will for salvation" corresponds—guiding every soteriology capable of being achieved. Trinitarian ontology here takes its finished form, and it is searching in our deepest darkness that the Father comes also to reveal himself.[24]

There is animality in humankind. Theology's forgetfulness of animality, probably even more than that of philosophy (and especially in contemporary phenomenology, which has had great developments in this area), makes the incarnation no longer meet our whole humanity. We need only to refer to the Franciscan vision of the world that is anticipated in John Scot Eriugena and even Irenaeus to be persuaded that the exclusion of the animal from the area of salvation is not unanimously shared. "Didn't the Word, when assuming humanity, receive *all creation*?" argues the Carolingian theologian in his *Periphyseon*: "If He received *all creation* by receiving human nature, surely He saved *all creation* and will do so for eternity."[25] However, we must be careful. The question is, from my perspective, less that of *animals* than that of the *animality* in us, namely our passions and drives, the sublingual aspects that can never be articulated, and the Father, who, in his will for salvation, cannot not be met in order to indwell it. As Husserl argues in his *Cartesian Meditations*, "Its beginning is the pure—and, so to speak, still dumb—psychological experience, which now must be made to utter its own sense with no adulteration."[26]

This animal part of ourselves, however woven from chaos, the abyss, meaninglessness, or the chasm, designates first of all what the Father comes to seek in us, and what his Son came to assume in his body. As I have shown,[27] the Eucharist also has the purpose not only of converting our humanity into divinity, but also of transforming our animality into humanity by sharing in the filiation of Christ. The Ghent Altarpiece shows this well in

---

24. On this point, see Falque: *Metamorphosis of Finitude*, pt. 2, "Toward a Metamorphosis"; *Wedding Feast of the Lamb*, pt. 1, "Descent into the Abyss."

25. John the Scot, *Periphyseon*, 312 (bk. 5, chs. 25–26, cols. 913B–916D); emphasis added.

26. Husserl, *Cartesian Meditations*, 38–39.

27. Falque, *Wedding Feast of the Lamb*.

the 1432 *Adoration of the Mystic Lamb* by the brothers Hubert and Jan van Eyck. It depicts not only a sacrificial lamb, but above all an "animal," which has its place on the altar and is capable of staring at us. Of course, Christ was never made animal, as was said and condemned by the 692 Council in Trullo. But he could not have indwelt our humanity without also taking on our animality, insofar as we also duly share in the latter. We must, however, be careful not to confuse *animality*, as an aspect of our humanity made of passions and drives that Christ assumes in his body, and *bestiality*, which properly marks an aspect of our sin or our ability to deviate from the level from which we were created. To be sure, God came "for us men" but also and first of all "for our salvation" (by redemption)—and to deny this is to fail to grasp the meaning of "God who alone can save us." Only we humans possess, paradoxically, this unique dimension of perfectibility, which is both that by which we may raise ourselves and that by which we may fall. "Man is neither angel nor beast," Pascal observes, "and it is unfortunately the case that anyone trying to act the angel acts the beast."[28] The crouching beast that desires you in the story of Cain and Abel (Gen 4:7), or the beast with seven heads and ten horns that arises at the end of the Bible (Rev 17:3), does not refer to animals, but, on the contrary, to the human possibility, and only human possibility, to fall below animality into bestiality, both accusing and rejecting precisely those passions and drives in us that God comes to indwell, and refusing for our part to offer, or at least to present ourselves. It is not the *animal* in us that is sinful (the chaos of passions and drives), but rather the *bestial*, namely the refusal of the animal, or rather the act by which one part of me escapes salvation. It is not the animal in us that is sinful only because I want to keep it as it is, and not accept that the Father, in his will to save us, wants to meet us in order to convert it, and even metamorphose to it.[29]

We must therefore distinguish, in the "descent into the abyss," which the Father accomplishes with the Son in the power of the Holy Spirit, the *anguish over finitude*, which belongs to our common humanity at the horizon of death, and *anguish over sin*, which comes from our will to refuse both our "limits" and our "plain and simple humanity." The temptation of sin proceeds paradoxically less in holding us in our limits than in our will to surpass them: less in respect for our created state than in our false identification with him who is uncreated. "The created light of glory received into any created intellect cannot be infinite," writes Thomas Aquinas remarkably in q. 12 of the *Summa Theologiae*.[30] He suggests, here, that the "limit-phenom-

---

28. Pascal, *Pensées*, 215 (L.678/B.358).
29. See Falque, *Noces de l'Agneau* §13, "L'envers de l'ange," 136–47.
30. Aquinas, *Summa Theologiae*, pt. 1a, q. 12, a. 7, resp.

enon" indicates another way, not competing, but rather complementary, to that of the "saturated phenomenon" (Denys, Marion).[31]

It is therefore *before God*, also passing *by the "other,"* that the horizon of sin, and not only of finitude, takes shape, in the very possibility of separating what the Father has himself joined together since the origin of creation, and every conversion experience must be found again. It is only in such a "connection" that the possibility of "separation" is expressed, and in the union that the event of rupture that it is read. So it is for Pascal in his remarkable 1654 memorial—fearing a possible rupture in the union that has only just begun, rather than returning to a moment which for him is already gone: "Joy, joy, joy, tears of joy. I have departed from him: They have forsaken me, the fount of living water (*Delirequerunt me fontem aquae vivae* [Jer 2:13]). My God, will you leave me? Let me not be separated from him forever."[32] My God—"*Will you leave me?*" The word is in the future tense, not the past like Christ at Golgotha ("My God, my God, why have you forsaken me?" [Mark 15:34 NRSV]). Could it be that, at the very moment of union, the possibility of separation appears? Is there not for the believer their very own "anxiety *in* faith" which can take a step toward "anxiety *of* faith"—namely, a possible shattering of what a sacrament came to accomplish, and that nothing ever suffices to guarantee if it is not chosen again every day?

The stakes of salvation are here doubled, in believing more than in not believing—not that it is easier to believe, but, on the contrary, that it is harder, having on the one hand to never leave our *common humanity* (salvation by solidarity), and on the other hand to receive every day this *salvation* to which we are intentionally joined by our salvation and by our redemption. The Father does not protect us from our sins, nor does he prevent us from falling. Rather, he teaches us to see them, not so that we remain in them, but at least to reach, both with him and in ourselves, the conviction that we can be rid of them only at the price of a sufficiently daring "descent into our abyss." "To ask grace to know my sins and rid myself of them," instructs Ignatius Loyola programmatically in the first week of his *Spiritual Exercises*.[33] Not to be enclosed there, but on the contrary to see our common humanity indwelt, and watched over, by the Father come to console us.

To demand a "Trinitarian ontology" at the limits of phenomenology thus requires that we renew both philosophy and theology—philosophy, or rather

---

31. On this point, see my "Saint Thomas."
32. Pascal, "Pascal's Memorial." See also Falque, "Blaise Pascal and Anxiety."
33. Ignatius of Loyola, *Ignatius of Loyola*, 134.

first of all phenomenology, in that the *primacy of weakness over strength*, the *hypertrophy of the flesh over the body*, and the a priori *of meaning over chaos* end with the development of a phenomenality of which only the subject is the measure. It could be today, as a result of the authors who have preceded us, that the demand for passivity or vulnerability forgets what there is of a necessary struggle for survival, especially in sickness; that the continually invoked experience of the flesh skips over organicity, even animality, of which we are also made; and that the constant quest for the rational, especially in intentionality, no longer leaves any space for a chaos that yet remains, like a "beyond meaning" or "extra phenomenal," rather than an "antithesis." Trinitarian ontology thus promises to reinvigorate theology, even the Trinitarian dogma itself: in the person of the Holy Spirit, God makes everything begin by new creation, which the Father uses and the Son receives; in the person of the Son, God took on everything, *including the material body* of which we are made, even to transform it without ever forgetting it; in the person of the Father, God *indwells in us to the very deepest parts of our abyss*, in a metamorphosed finitude to be sure (salvation by solidarity), but also a renewed union or connection (salvation by redemption).

Like Spinoza's *conatus*, God makes the effort "with us" (*Immanu-El*) to persevere, or better to enlarge our own being, but in teaching and inspiring us to "love one another" in the most settled part of each of us: in the breath of his Spirit where he expresses himself as "power" ("I will send you a power"), by the thickness of his Son where he is given as "body" ("this is my body"), and in the Father's will of salvation where he meets us in our "chasm" ("In the beginning, the earth was formless and void").

There is thus no philosophy or theology that does not also participate in *spirituality*. It is only by forgetting this that we have become self-absorbed, failing to see that God has assumed everything in order to transform it. Such is the reminder, beyond ontology, from what we may well call mysticism—and that Klaus Hemmerle had the merit of assuming, regardless of the false divisions between disciplines and exercises that various people have imposed for too long: "The theory of a Trinitarian ontology has, as congruent with it, as its condition and as its consequence, a *corresponding spirituality*. But it is not only I, the individual, who am molded and challenged by this; I am at the same time pointed out towards a new relationship to the Thou, to the We, to society in all its domains. . . . To begin with spirituality, with the sustaining 'brief formula' of faith, from which we can surmise the whole plenitude of what is to be believed, it is 'we have known and believed the love that God hath shown to us' (1 John 4.16)."[34]

34. Hemmerle, *Theses*, 27.

(Translated by Barnabas Aspray)

6

Counting to Four

Metaxology and the Trinity

William Desmond

Opening

THE REFLECTIONS I OFFER here are in the nature of an essay in speculative thought: a venture of figuring. My perplexity: Do we humans need to count to four to be able to count to three? Are there Trinitarian implications to how we answer?

I ask these questions because the metaxological metaphysics I have been elaborating can contribute to elucidating the companionship of ontology and theology. This is not the place to give a fuller account of what a metaxological metaphysics entails, and I refer the reader to a fuller elaboration elsewhere.[1] Enough will be said to give a relevant sense of the fourfold sense of being central to a metaxological metaphysics, namely, the univocal, the equivocal, the dialectical, and the metaxological senses of being. I want to say that, in terms of my opening questions, thinking of the Trinity asks us to count to four in terms of this fourfold sense of being: first, the univocal sense that stresses sameness; second, the equivocal sense that stresses

---

1. See Desmond: *Being and the Between*; *Ethics and the Between*; *God and the Between*.

difference; third, the dialectical sense that stresses sameness mediating difference; fourth, the metaxological sense that stresses the plurivocal intermediation of sameness and difference. If one is univocity, if two is equivocity, if three is dialectic (becoming one again in self-mediating dialectic), then four is metaxology. Since, moreover, this four is beyond the self-mediating one tempting dialectic, then properly to count to two, one has to count to four. Metaxology is not monadic, or dyadic, or triadic; metaxology is quadratic. Does counting to four metaxologically allow plurivocal *betweening*, as one might call it? What are the implications of metaxology for a Trinitarian ontology?

This venture is essayed in terms of our human need to make sense of the Trinity and the claims of Trinitarian ontology. Nevertheless, these reflections are ontological and metaphysical, not devoid of theological significance. I am interested in a metaxological approach to the Trinity, if this indeed is at all possible. Certainly, if one is concerned with "new" ontologies of the Trinity, metaxology has sides that are both new and old. It also has sides that are both ontological and metaphysical. I take ontology to tilt the stress of thinking toward the immanent. I take metaphysics to tilt thought toward the transcendent. The "meta" of metaxological metaphysics is double: it thinks on the threshold of a double tilt, both "in the midst" and also "above and beyond." Both tilts are called for in the *metaxu*.

This suggestion that metaxological metaphysics requires quadratic thinking, requires counting to four, may at first seem to be a very unpromising orientation to say anything about the Trinity, given the triadic face of what is at issue. Metaxology can thus be contrasted with the immanent holism of Hegelian triadic ontology. The stress of strong metaphysical transcendence is hollowed out by Hegel's version of dialectical negativity: metaphysical transcendence as other is overtaken and speculatively over grasped by immanent self-transcendence.[2] This, too, has implications for Trinitarian thinking. Speaking metaxologically, an exploration of radical immanence, our being in the midst of things, is inseparable from direction to radical transcendence, and directions received and undertaken toward that which is over and above immanence.

I am referring here to what in *God and the Between* (ch. 6, especially) I call the hyperboles of being. I name four. These refer to happenings in immanence that cannot be given an entirely immanent determination. Such happenings come to us as hyperbolic. In coming to us, they move us in our being thrown beyond ourselves toward transcendence as other. Our being

---

2. *Begreifen* is *Ubergreifen*, the word Hegel uses, for instance, in the *Encyclopedia* (Hegel, *Science of Logic* [ed. Brinkmann and Dahlstrom], 289).

drawn beyond ourselves is not our drawing of ourselves beyond ourselves. The inviting openness of transcendence as other draws us toward it. Our being in the between cannot be articulated entirely in immanent determinate terms. Metaxology as a wording of the between brings us to the threshold of the "immanent frame" and renews our porosity to what is beyond that frame. For the philosopher, metaxology may begin as a way of mindfulness in the midst of things, but as an exploration of the ways of being in the between, it leads in immanence to the threshold on which hyperbolically we are thrown beyond into mysterious transcendence. The wording of the between we come to think comes ultimately from communication with the Word of the between: the Logos of the *metaxu*.

Whether we count one, or count to two or three or four, we always count in figures. We often hold that figuring things (out) is to make them intelligible and comprehensible. "No one has ever seen God" (John 1:18 ESV). How figure what "dwells in unapproachable light" (1 Tim 6:16 ESV)? There is something about God absolutely superior to our figuring. Can we think still on a metaxological threshold? Is there not a figurative character to hyperbolic thought: figuring what cannot be figured. Figuring what cannot be figured is itself telling. A teller counts, and telling here is counting what we cannot tell. A teller who tells of what cannot be told counts on what cannot be finally counted. What figures, what counts as a figure? What or who can figure the Trinity? Who counts, how count, what counts in this figuring? On what or whom can we finally count?

At the risk of misunderstanding, I am wondering if metaxological fourthness suggests a squaring of the Trinitarian circle. Although I may initially appear to be talking in relatively systematic terms, ontological and metaphysical, I will be working toward the goal of saying something significant bearing on the Trinity and metaxological metaphysics. As companions to the thought, I will call on the witness of Aristotle, Hegel, and Peirce.

Counting One—with a Bow to Aristotle

To call first on the companionship of Aristotle: the least number, properly speaking, is two (*Phys.* 220a27). Why so? Aristotle is not talking about divinity, of course, and the statement occurs in a discussion of time, but one can see the point. One has to have the second by contrast with the first, in order to have the first count as a first. In order to determine unity, one has to have a contrast term to unity for the unity itself to be delimited as one. Clearly, what is at stake here is a kind of determinate unity (that perhaps remains paradoxically indeterminate). It is a serious question as to whether when we speak about divinity, we are talking about a determinate unity in any countable sense. Clearly to make the unity a countable one is to finitize it, and hence not to find the absolute oneness of the divine that is sought.

Many of the issues here are connected with perplexities about the nature of the One of monotheism. We are not figuring in terms of the cardinal numbers, or in terms of the unending series of determinate units. Philosophically, the influence of Parmenides in the ancient world might be cited, or the influence of Spinoza in the modern. It would be misleading to speak of Parmenides or Spinoza as monotheist simply, yet there is a certain metaphysical univocity. The overarching and all-absorbing character of the unity of the One makes its presence felt in their metaphysical thinking. It is an interesting question whether the Parmenidean One allows one even to count to one, if one cannot count to two. Parmenides talks about the many who wonder "double headed" (*dikranoi*) and decries their lostness in illusion.[3] Nevertheless, to state that "the One is one" is already to make a statement that is more than the One. Hence, in an Aristotelian sense, counting to two comes to be needed.

The point may similarly be made in modernity with respect to Spinozism: the pivotal transition between the one Substance and the many is unclear or open to contestation. The shadow of paradigmatic Spinoza hangs over even the Trinitarian thinking of Hegel (this is true of Schelling also): Hegel is a reformed Spinozist insofar as he considers the One not only in relation to substance, but also and essentially in relation to subject. There is much more to be said about Hegel's Trinitarian logic, and I will return to him.

The issue is whether, in counting to three in Hegel's way, Hegel can even allow us to count to one. If the second necessary, pace Aristotle, for counting to one becomes in Hegel *the self-doubling of the one*, in counting to two, Hegel is, in effect, not really counting to three and does not in the end get beyond one. The metaxological thought is: to count to two, we have to be able to count to four, that is, the second has to have an ontologically robust otherness to the first and cannot be just a matter of the self-doubling of the original one. Counting to two entails a *metaxu* between the first and the second that is irreducible to the self-relation of the first. If the second is thus irreducible, the space opens up for a transcendence that is not the same as the immanent self-relation of the first.

3. In *God and the Between*, ch. 3, I have spoken of the difference of ancient and modern ways of univocalizing: Parmenides, Plato, and Plotinus think in an ethos where finesse persists for the permeability between thought and the sacred, while with Descartes, Spinoza, and Leibniz, the figuring of geometry tends to form the univocalizing of God.

Counting to Two: From Firstness to Thirdness—with Bows to Hegel and Peirce

To start a second track of considerations, here I want to invoke the thought of Charles Sanders Peirce. Peirce has an extremely interesting doctrine of the categories, as he calls them, which he describes very economically in the following terms: firstness, secondness, and thirdness. In one sense, Peirce is close to the triadic schema of Hegel. Yet in another sense, there is a significant divergence between Hegel and Peirce, particularly on the question of secondness. These categories are woven into the texture of his entire thought, and while many citations might be adduced, here is how he describes the matter in terms of consciousness:

> Here then, we have indubitably three radically different elements of consciousness, these and no more. And they are evidently connected with the ideas of one-two-three. Immediate feeling is the consciousness of the first; the polar sense is the consciousness of the second; and synthetical consciousness is the consciousness of a third or medium.[4]

Note the comprehensive claim. Among other things, firstness has bearing on a sense of immediacy, which of itself has a certain indeterminacy going with it. Secondness has the sense of difference, the idea of an over-against otherness, which, on the face of it, seems to allow only separation and not mediation. Thirdness restores a continuity, though in an articulated and not just immediate form. One can also hear echoes of something like the logical rhythm governing Hegel's unfolding of the issue: immediacy, difference, and self-mediacy; or indeterminacy, determination, and self-determination.

If indeed his description of thirdness echoes the Hegelian stress on mediation, one might suspect that secretly hidden in his way of thinking is an unacknowledged commitment to something like the Hegelian position. In fact, it seems to me that, in a manner that is not fully developed by him, what he says about secondness opens up the character of thirdness in such a way that does not allow that circular and self-recurring mediation that is so characteristic of the Hegelian way of thinking. Secondness refers us to doubles that in one sense articulate the seamless continuity of firstness, and thus introduce articulation into unity that is inarticulate. Yet there is something about this opening up of difference that has a stronger claim on our consideration than is allowed for within the Hegelian scheme of things. Secondness has the bite of otherness that moves us beyond firstness.

---

4. Peirce, *Philosophical Writings*, 97.

And though it might be mediated by thirdness, there is also something irreducible about the otherness as such, irreducible to the first and, as such, not subsumable into the third. Peirce can, in this way, be observed to have taken up the Aristotelian claim about counting, and in a sense he says that to count to two, we have to be able to move to three. There is, however, also something about the second that qualifies the mediation of the third, in such a way that makes the real sense of otherness both possible and irreducible to the seamless unity of the fluid first.

What I wish to suggest is that Peirce's intuition overlaps with the point of metaxological thinking. For it acknowledges an otherness in the between that cannot be recuperated simply for the immanent completion of thirdness. Further, to do justice to the rich reserve of secondness, Peirce himself ought to have introduced a category of fourthness. He would, in this way, have opened up more lucidly the possibility not just of secondness as not being merely dualistic or dyadic, but of secondness also as ontological communication beyond self-recurring mediation, allowing for a metaxological between itself hospitable to a *plurivocal* sense of intermediation. In this way, this plurivocal sense cannot be counted as one, two, three, and four, but rather opens up a sense of infinitude that is quite other to the Hegelian sense of the infinite.

What Hegel says about the true infinite to shows his stress on his ultimately *singular* sense of absolute process: "The infinite is . . . the self-sublation of [the one-sided] infinite and finite, as a *single* process—this is the *true or genuine infinite*."[5] The self-sublating infinite cannot be rendered by the dualistically defined finite and infinite, but note how Hegel stresses the *singleness* of the process. What counts as true infinity is absolutely self-sublating self-counting. If we count to infinity, we can count nothing greater than (the) One. Not surprisingly, the true infinite and the true whole are the same. There is, for theology, no God beyond the whole. The whole comprehends the Trinity. How can you count beyond one if there is no beyond, hence nothing beyond the One?

Counting to Four: Metaxological Fourthness

Why add the category of fourthness to firstness, secondness, thirdness? In part to respond and adapt Aristotle's claim that two is the least number, properly speaking: to truly count to two, one has to count to four. And in

---

5. Hegel, Hegel's *"Science of Logic,"* 137. "Das Unendliche ist . . . das Sichaufheben dieses Unendlichen wie des Endlichen als *ein* Prozeß—ist das *wahrhafte Unendliche*" (Hegel, *Objektive Logik*, 149; emphasis in original).

part, to grant the important connection of thirdness and mediation, but then the issue is: What kind of mediation, and what of its fidelity to secondness, as well as firstness? Suppose we take a simple case of mediation between two who are themselves self-mediating. Is the mediation between those two just another form of self-mediation? How then do justice to what one might call the *betweening* between these two? Must one say the betweening is an inter-mediation rather than any self-mediation, no matter how inclusive: Is it always at least a double mediation and not just a single, whether univocally qualified or dialectically? Metaxologically speaking, fourthness would mean two twos, two in interplay, each incarnating immanent doubling and intimate self-doubling. Each has a secondness not to be described singularly in terms of thirdness. Each of the two is marked by immanent overdeterminacy, preventing the exhaustive definition of each in terms of any binary opposition, and also in terms of moments of a more inclusive dialectic of the Hegelian sort. Counting to fourthness gives the basis for a secondness, rightly affirmed by Peirce but open to the difficulty of dualistic opposition on the one side, and, on the other side, the difficulty of being included in thirdness by a further process of self-mediation. One might see this metaxological fourthness as confirming the insight of Peirce but not the terms needed to do justice to secondness.

As I have elsewhere shown, Hegel's Trinitarian logic is governed by the triad indeterminacy, determination, self-determination. Overdeterminacy helps us name the fourth to indeterminacy, determination, and self-determination. It is not an indeterminacy lacking determination and self-determination, rather a "too muchness," which exceeds all determination and self-determination. Overdeterminacy allows us to grant the hyperboles of being: happenings in immanence that yet exceed immanent determination or self-determination. Count these as offering some resources for thought to think of what is overdeterminate raised to the infinite power: the superlative mystery of God, who, all things considered, "dwells in unapproachable light."

Overdeterminacy is also surplus to mutual determination of a symmetrical kind. This is sometimes attributed to Hegel's Trinity denominated as "divine intersubjectivity." This is not to be denied, but I would claim that the "inter" of this view is governed by an inclusive logic of self-determination, which, however, is inadequate to divine intermediation, both in its own immanence and between divinity itself and the creation God agapeically gives to be. There is a "too muchness" to the terms in metaxological intermediation, which pluralizes without reducing the happening of intermediation or passing in the *metaxu*. Indeed, if there are mutual intermediations that are asymmetrical, then the mediation one way is not univocally reversible into the same mediation the other way; nor are the diverse mediations subsumable into a single inclusive self-sublation. Just as overdeterminacy is, so to say, an affirmative counterpart to a negative indeterminacy lacking in determination, there are asymmetrical relations of an agapeic sort, which are a counterpart to asymmetrical relations that generate dualistic oppositions between terms, or hierarchal reductions or sublations.

Overdeterminacy as figuring the fourth is also a figuring of the first: the origin that is not indeterminacy, not determinacy, not self-determination. Likewise, in our being "in the midst," there is always the overdeterminacy of given being that can never be entirely overreached or over grasped since it seeds all our reaching out, and all our reaching beyond. Beyond our reaching beyond, it seeds the sense of the hyperboles of being, which direct us to the thought of God beyond the immanent whole. It is not a matter of the dualistic oscillation of indeterminacy and determinacy, equivocity and univocity, and not a matter of the dialectical subsumption of these into one singular holistic process of dialectical self-determination. Overdeterminacy is thus a figure of thought pointing to the divine as a "too muchness" to the highest degree, that is, to the superlative splendor of the divine mystery.

The concept of overdeterminacy can, in this way, affirm the superlative life of divinity as being in its own "unapproachable light," and also affirm creation as being agapeically given to be as other and for itself. We are not governed by the triadic logic of indeterminacy, determinacy, and self-determination but rather by the quadratic logic of overdeterminacy, indeterminacy, determinacy, and self-determination. This quadratic logic of metaxology entirely transforms the concepts of indeterminacy, determination, and self-determination, as it also requires a rethinking of all forms of triadic relation. Quadratic metaxology thus involves a metanoetics of Trinitarian thinking.

Metaxological Fourthness and Trinitarianism

What are some Trinitarian implications to counting to four metaxologically? Starting again from our being in the midst of the immanent between, the matter of fourthness bears on the issue of creation, and indeed the issue of the contingency of creation. We are enabled to acknowledge the divinity in itself "dwelling in unapproachable light" and yet metaxologically communicating the gift of the endowed creation. Creation is a giving to be, but I would distinguish between the coming to be of creation and the becoming of beings within creation. In contrast, many process-oriented ontologies do not make the distinction and assimilate coming to be to becoming. In the process of assimilation, they cover over the difference between the absolute origin and given creation; with the result that the becoming within the given creation is hard also to figure differently to the absolute giving of the origin. In opening up spaces of otherness, metaxology allows plurivocal intermediations prior to and beyond univocal and dialectical mediations. Hence, it avoids the dangers of dualism on the one side, and of the reductions or subsumptions of immanent monism on the other side.

Pace Hegel, creation is not the self-creation of God, but rather upheld in being with its own endowed glory. The issue of the fourth arises for us in the context of an immanent ontology, but it has implications for a metaphysical thinking of transcendence, which is not dualistic, but rather affirms the strongest sense of divine transcendence as other, while also allowing for the original porosity between the divine and creation that speaks to the most intimate immanence of origin in creation. Metaxological fourthness can uphold the distinction in relatedness of the immanent and economic Trinity and do so better than Hegel's rendition. That there is a difficulty here for Hegel has been pointed out by many commentators (Cyril O'Regan, for instance). Hegel's understanding of inclusive self-mediating immanence overreaches and over grasps the difference of the immanent and economic Trinity.[6] As a consequence, it threatens to dissolve the eternal in time. The dissolution of time in eternity might well also be a possible option, but it is not the one evident in the post-Hegelian inheritance, nor indeed in Hegel himself. This we see in another consequence that follows, namely, a historicization of divinity, which is untrue to the trans-political character of the divine community. This being untrue seeds a post-religious politics in which, in Hegel's endorsement of the words of the serpent, we will become

---

6. Given O'Regan's groundbreaking work on Gnosticism, I note a point about counting to two sympathetic to his venture. We can be tempted to think of creation and fall in terms of doubles, such that counting to two can become ensnared in counterfeit doubles. "Satan disguises himself as an angel of light" (2 Cor 11:14 ESV). Gnosticism is often connected with dualism, but one might connect it more subtly with doubles and doubling (see, more fully, Desmond, *God and the Between*, ch. 10). To oppose the *proto pater* to corrupt creation seems like extreme dualism, ranging from the extreme transcendence of the absolute First to the extreme corruption of the second creation of the immanent god. But if we think in terms of doubling(s) rather than dualism, dualism can easily mutate into dialectic: the opposites are two at one, doubling overcome, self-overcome. Counting to one by counting through two to three: three is one. The transition from doubles to doubling to dialectical self-doubling helps makes sense of the mutation of a transcendent dualism of ancient Gnosticism to the modern gnostic grammar of a philosophy like Hegelianism as an immanent holism. Here the opposition of extreme dualism and absolute unity do not meet in the middle; rather the middle is the means by which the process of one turning into the other is effected such that at the end there is no middle. There is no middle to begin with, and in the end no middle: the *metaxu* is over grasped as two sides of the one over grasping.

as gods. This completion of metaphysics mutates into a mutilation of transcendence. A metaphysical blasphemy against the immanent overdeterminacy of creation is twinned with a theological deconsecration of the divine overdeterminacy.

In proposing a *metaxu* with respect to the immanent Trinity, one need not be averse to the idea of an immanent self-mediation, so long as this self-determination in the inner life of the Trinity is qualified by properly communal intermediation, and at the least this immanent life would not be the same as the creation of finite being as other. I will say something more about agapeic betweening. To apply the same univocal or dialectical logic to both is not to do justice to the immanent *metaxu* of the divine life nor to the *metaxu* between the divine life and the endowed creation. What passes between the divine in itself in the Trinitarian *metaxu* of God is not the same, either univocally or dialectically, as what passes between the divine and the creation it gives to be. These spaces of betweening are not allowed the full freedom of metaxological intermediation.

Fourthness allows us to rethink is the mystery of the agapeic relation that is more than the self determination of the absolute. God is agape (1 John 4:8, 16). John does not say God is eros. The intermediations within the divine life are agapeic, the intermediations between the divine and the given creation are agapeic. But the betweenings of the agapeic relation cannot be modeled entirely on a self-returning unity that gives in the name of eternal or temporal return to self. There is a self-revelation and a self-relation. Yet there is also a release of selving from self-relation; only that release is the giving of the good that is for the good of the giving, and the beloved other in receipt or reciprocation. Pure generous giving in the betweening of agapeic relating enables forms of selving and othering that cannot be simply mapped on a logos of self-determining Spirit.

From below looking up, one of the reasons for this has to do with the mystery of the agapeic relation as releasing finite creation to be itself as other. If I mention Hegel again, this is one of the recurrently contested points: contested from the side of a Schellingian "that it is"; and contested, say, from the side of a Marxist materialism of nature. For the self-doubling spirit of Hegel is a self-returning spirit that releases only to end in encircling and enclosing. Is there an embrace of love that encircles and that does not enclose? One might parse encircling as self-circling, as self-serving, but agapeic betweening is not self circling and self-serving. The fourth tilts the release of selving and othering into the between where the pure being of love of giving qua giving occurs. In a way, in this between, talk of self and other reaches a limit. One might say that triadic self-giving can be transformed if the pure passing of one to the other and the other to one, infinitely, is inflected with the overdeterminacy of the agapeic. This is why I have turned the word "between" into the wording verb: wording the between, betweening in and through logos.

Perhaps two triads, or the redoubling of triads, can make the point about irreducibility in absolved relativity even more than two twos. Yet two by two allows us to return to the origin of the word "between": it comes from *betwēonum* (Old English, becoming Middle English *betwene*). I think of the Dutch: *bij-twee*, by two, resounding in the word "between."[7] A between means we could never say, "Never the twain shall meet": the between is the milieu where the twain ever shall meet. If our Trinitarian thought asks a figuration of the "by two" of the between, one might say: if one counts to three twice, and the threes have the doubleness immanently at work in each, then each in dialogue is other to itself in its own immanence, as well as in the space of difference that enables the porosity of communication between giving divinity and given creation. The otherness, the mystery of the overdeterminacy, is beyond any univocal or dialectical immanence, or indeed transcendence. Even the most exalted *coincidentia oppositorum* breaks down in incomprehension at this point of radical otherness.

Agapeic Betweening: From Full to Full to Full

Agape, too, is hidden in the mystery of the unapproachable light. There is the mystery of the agapeic relation that immanently and intimately always and ever calls the endowed creation into a community of love with the giving Godhead. There is mystery, too, to the between in which we dwell: this created *metaxu* is the porous space of a community of love between God and the world.

There are sentences here and there in Hegel that resound with an ambiguous echo of the agapeic, and yet are not woven systematically into the texture of his thought. I refer to discussion elsewhere.[8] By contrast, Peirce does talk about the agapastic.[9] I think it is fair to say that his discussion is primarily future oriented. It is more teleological than archeological, though

---

7. There is also a link to Proto-Germanic **bi-* (be-) and **twihnaz* (two each), corresponding to "be-" and "twain." Twain and twin. *Zwischen* has similar etymological resonances from Old High German in *zuisken*, from Old High German, *zuiski*, from Proto-Indo-European **dwis* (twice, doubly, in two). Connect twain with twee and Dutch *tussen*. "Between" resounds with much reserved.

8. See Desmond, *Hegel's God*, ch. 4, esp. 115–16, in connection with things Hegel says about love (*Lectures*, 418).

9. "Evolutionary Love," in Peirce, *Philosophical Writings*, 361–74.

perhaps more richly suggestive than the erotically qualified teleology of Hegel. Is an ontology of agape possible? Is immanent being as agapeic? Is a metaphysics of agape possible: the immanent hyperbole of the agapeic as a sign of an even more hyperbolic agapeics of the divine per se? I think the fourth has to do with our response.

Hegel's Trinity is rendered in light of a more erotic rather than agapeic figure of the divine. Eros has its own plurivocity, and this is not the place to dwell on that, but the triad indeterminacy, determination, self-determination corresponds to a parallel triad of lack, othering, self-returning. The beginning is empty, the middle determinately surpasses empty indeterminacy, the end is the consummate self-accomplishment of the beginning and return of and to the beginning. The Hegelian trinity must mediate with itself because of a "lack" or indeterminacy in the origin (Father), must determine itself as other (Son), must become itself as absolute totality in the community of the Spirit. Some commentators speak of divine subjectivity, some speak of divine intersubjectivity. We might, however, say there is a community here, but that it is self-communication, which the "communally" self-mediating spirit shows. The logic of a self-completing, self-determining totality governs the whole. And indeed this dynamism from lack to fullness is not completely fulfilled in the immanent *eternal Trinity*, but the latter is itself lacking without its becoming of itself in time through creation, which is spirit's historical self-creation. The Trinitarian God thus becomes *immanent* in a sense more recognizable to us who dwell in history. Yet it also seems that this move from eternity to time is driven by the same erotic logic: eternity is an empty indeterminacy till it determines itself in the particularities of time, and through the appropriation of these determinacies becomes fully itself as self-determining. The modern state of freedom is the spirit as self-accomplishing itself in time.

Agapeic love is ecstatic and communicative like eros, but the communication proceeds from a surplus rather than a lack; from a plenitude rather than from an indeterminacy yet to be made determinate; and in the instance of creation, it proceeds from an overdeterminacy of divine transcendence as other to finite determination. Yet as possibilizing the other being of finitude, it also possibilizes a full release into its own being for itself. Agapeic love releases the other as other and for the sake of its otherness as other, and not alone for mediated purposes of its return to the origin. Agapeic creation: it is a release of the free gift of the being there of the other, and as given otherness gifted with the promise of a community *between* itself and the divine source. This between would not be the self-mediation of the divine, or the creation, but rather an intermediation in good, which is the betweening of the two. Otherness, plurality, community would, in this way, all be qualified differently in this gift of the agapeic origin, and show the promise of free intermediations beyond any form of self-mediation, including the self-mediation of God with God.

Beyond the self-communication from initially lacking indeterminacy, through determinacy, to self-recognition and self-determination, we would have to speak rather of *communication from fullness to fullness to fullness*. The excessive good of the gift of the first is given to the second out of fullness not diminished by being given; and the second, as itself surplus fullness of good, is not less and not more than the first; and the third is the fullness recognized as spirit, itself not less or more in overgoodness, or in agapeic surplus, to the first and the second. We thus have an infinitely communicative good, overflowing from over-fullness to over-fullness to over-fullness: from pluperfection to pluperfection to pluperfection, not from imperfection to perfection. And if we have an agapeic community, it is a symmetrical agape in that there is a mutual recognition, but with respect to surplus good; it is a communicative good as infinite, hence beyond any determinable whole. In a sense, this agapeic community would thus be a divine *philia*, in respect of the symmetrical giving and receiving of the full, of the hyper full. And yet, with respect to finite being, this asymmetry of the surplus good is not at all to be surpassed. This super-plus good would be the God beyond the whole.

In the terms of Trinitarian theology, the view here would not be coincident with Hegel's Trinity. In terms of the Father, Son, and Spirit: the Father is the origin and surplus good that is overdetermined; the Son is the expression of the surplus good that is also overdetermined; and Spirit is the communal intermediation or the love of this secret life of the surplus good that also is overdetermined. No holistic logic of self-completing self-determination could do justice to this excessive communication from full to full to full, or from over-full to over-full to over-full—"God from God, Light from Light, true God from true God" (*Deum de Deo, Lumen de Lumine, Deum verum de Deo vero*).[10] We sing: "Holy, holy, holy." The agapeic God is over whole. The over-full is in the origin, hence there is no lacking indefiniteness needing determinacy and mediating its self-determination. Too much of transcendence in the origin is communicated to the second, itself expressing goodness more than determinate, and, as such, inexhaustible. And, as this living surplus good is broadcast and affirmed in the third that is itself overdeterminate, it, too, is a creative power that possibilizes the determinate and self-determining finite being in the most radical sense: giving it to be in a radical coming to be that is not at all a becoming or self-becoming. What rather comes to be in finitude is itself always other

---

10. Nicene Creed, 1975 ecumenical version, in Wikipedia, "English Versions."

than, and, as such, in excess of all determination and self-determination. We are not speaking hence of the Whole of wholes, but of the over-whole God, hence infinite beyond all wholes. And of course, everything thus said is hyperbolic, but there is a proper sense of hyperbole that is most needed in venturing to speak of this God beyond the whole.

Being agapeic as the betweening of love thus allows for a fourthness that endows created finitude with a trans-dialectical sense beyond Hegel's single process.[11] This is the agapeic *metaxu*: being between, betweening, between the Father, the Son, the Spirit; between the Trinity and the creation, an ontologically endowing betweening. If betweening is a circulation of agapeic love, it is not self-circling, given that it is hard to avoid some figure of circling. I think of the circling of rainbows as imaged by Dante at the end of the *Paradiso*.[12] Circulation as agapeic betweening calls more to mind the sense of a *perichōrēsis* (περιχώρησις), where dancer gives way to dancer, at one and other, leading and being led, in a dancing itself giving way. This is giving way in the double, redoubling sense of giving a way agapeically, and in giving way kenotically in being there as giving a way, by not being there as getting in the way. Agapeic perichoresis is thus betweening in a sense that is beyond erotic self-circling. The *peri* figures the divine dancing (*chorein*) as an agapeic *metaxu*: from full to full to full. If we cannot tell the dancer from the dance, this is not monistic melting or dialectical subsumption, but metaxological dancing in the agapeic between. Divine dancing is betweening in this agapeic sense.

Agapeic Betweening and the Cross of the Fourth

If fourthness allows a Trinitarian figuration of the *metaxu* between the creation and the Creator, any resort to the notions of the economic and immanent Trinity would have to look on the becoming of the good in time not just in historicist terms, but rather in terms of what is superior to history. The above: the right side of history is not in the past, not in the present, not in the future: it is in the superior. I take this view to belong to the Augustinian family: the superiority of the kingdom of God and its agapeic service can never be reduced to any of the supposed immanences of political sovereignty. One need not deny excellences to the latter, but they are excellent because they participate secretly in the superiority of the agapeic good. The wheat and the darnel grow together, and the darnel grows because of the same agapeic love that allows the wheat to grow. But the concrescent growth

11. On the transdialectical, see Desmond, *Voiding of Being*, 126–59.
12. Dante, *Paradiso* 33.115–20.

of the two in time is not to be cut in time. Divine betweening may cut into time, but not be temporalized in any univocally leveling or dialectically elevating way.

The Greek word *eschaton* has also the meaning of "edge" or "cut." This cut reveals in time what is above time. The cut paradoxically is the metaxological *link* of heaven and earth. It crosses time, makes a cross between time and eternity, in time, and above time. What is above comes down, but in an agapeic cutting across time that is not horizontally leveling. The cut of the cross rises up, raises up. I take Hegel's Trinitarianism to level the superiority of agapeic transcendence in a self-elevating immanent unfolding, seeming glorious in vision and ambition, yet offering a counterfeit double of eschatology. It presents the declension rather than the ascension of the superior into a flat, flattening of final time into immanent homogeneity.[13]

Metaxological fourthness means that we do not have to think of paternity (Abba) as the incomplete indeterminacy of the Hegelian origin, but of the agapeic overdeterminacy, which is the generous begetter of all. The doublet of the immanent and economic Trinity could thus be rendered in terms of agapeic betweening, as a doubling and redoubling: God giving in eternity from eternity to eternity the Word begotten before all ages; God giving time, and giving to time, as the coming to birth of the Word in and through Mary; and the coming down of Spirit into life before death that is carried beyond death pneumatologically by the breath of the divine. This breath gives and inspires the porosity of being, given to us in our *passio essendi* and inspiring it, endowing and inspiring a free release into being, itself endowing a second free release of our affirmation of being. This second release is our affirming being in our own being, where the inspired *conatus essendi* can become the endowed endeavor to be, open to the breath of God on creation and the breathing of God beyond creation. What of the Trinitarian *persons*? The point is not to imply there are four persons of the Trinity! Perhaps that would be a squaring of the circle too far. However, metaxological fourthness can, I suggest, help us make sense of certain things, such as the notion of person as itself open to agapeic betweening. The meaning of person is a question for another time, but I am tempted with the idea of *agape personans*, or *Agape sonans, personans*.[14] *Agape personans* is not quite thought thinking itself. Rather it reconfigures the person through a metaxological metanoetics, and transfigures it in terms of a community of love. Thought thinking itself, now *agape*

---

13. For fuller discussion of Hegel, see Desmond, *Hegel's God*.

14. See Desmond, *God and the Between*, ch. 9, on God as personal, impersonal, transpersonal. On *agape personans*, see Desmond, "Wording Time."

personans, becomes creative of what is other, because always already agape first, love first in itself as Trinitarian affirming and then as quadratic giving finite being as other for itself.

In contrast to the optics of *prosopon*, one hears the audio of *personans*: being an audience, in obedience to the aural breathing become wording, becomes sounding, resounding, resonant, musical in *agape personans*. The divine mystery sounds through and resounds in the soul. The metaxological thought of the Trinity is not just psychological in the modern sense. In being personal, *agape personans* is transpersonal, not impersonal. "Trans" and "per": these are very metaxological words—words of communication, of betweening. Hear also *agape personans* as divine breath: opening the porosity, the breath comes through (per) in wording the between, singing it to be, and singing its to be. Think of the living being: breathing into the mud, the kiss of God. We are that breath, here now until we breathe our last: the wind within us, the wind at our back, the second wind of spirit, facing the headwinds of the sins against the spirit. Spirit is this inspiring of the divine community, which is more metaxologically fourth than dialectically third in Hegel's sense. As an agapeic *metaxu*, the Trinity inspires the community of agapeic service and the metaxological betweening of agapeic love.

The notions of community and communion are integral to the thought of the metaxological fourth. There is an intermediation of relationalities within and without, in se, *pro nobis*, transcendence and immanence, and both together. Metaxological fourthness allows us to make some sense of the betweening of a Trinitarian koinonia. Recall the famous Andrej Rublev icon: the three, thought of as the angels who visited Abraham, where each is leaning toward the other, into each other, and yet the circle is squared. This icon is metaxologically quadratic in that there is a fourth space, an open space. In the iconic space the opening for the fourth tells us of the porosity of being, of the created opening of hospitality, the hospitality not hostility of being, and the ever-offered invitation to whomever it may concern to join the table of the feast of divine betweening.

The festivity of agapeic betweening: giving again and again, over and over again. "Again"—this is another word of mystery: triply redoubled "again" within the betweening of the Trinity; redoubled "again," too, after the mode of creation in the betweening between God and the given creation. Interim time is given: here, too, there is something hyperbolically mysterious (overdeterminate) about the again and again of given time. Again and again, being is as given and as good, as agape that is also a good giving. Wording the between again and again for us is creation and re-creation; and even in coming unto death, there is yet a yet again. Once more is always more. Once more is ever more than never more.

The fourth is figured by the cross. An agapeic crossing of the *metaxu* has to do with the fourth. The cross is the agapeic *metaxu* revealing the divine in kenotic fourthness. The humiliated *metaxu* on the cross is glory. In crossing the between of finite creation, the cross offers a divine *metaxu*. There is a sacred betweening in making the sign of the cross: crossing oneself in the name of Father, Son, and Spirit. Crossing with the sign of the Trinity is betweening in the modality of the fourth: the gifted prayer of the human being, in which the porosity of being offers the betweening that is crossed by God. If the cross words the fourth, then the *metaxu* also gives the offer of the agapeic marriage of heaven and earth.[15]

Thinkers about the Trinity speak of procession and mission, the immanent transcending of procession, and the economic transcendence of mission: one within the Trinity; the other in the communication of the agape of the Trinity in giving creation, and to given creation as being recreated in communication with its divine endower. I think of sending, mission as also a wording of the between, and as a betweening through the logos of the *metaxu*. If one thinks of Christ as the eternal *metaxu*, immanent in the divine life itself, Christ is also the saving *metaxu*, intimate in interim time: one and two in three; divine and human and in absolving openness to the fourth. Christ is the eternal *metaxu*, given to time as the divine incarnation of the agapeic *metaxu*, the one Word of the divine between, and double in being both the uncreated and created *metaxu*. As doctrine has it, he is the eternally begotten *metaxu* and temporally born *metaxu*: divine and human, without any reduction of one to the other.

Metaxological fourthness in interim time returns again and again in the *betweonum*, the *bij twee*, by two. One thinks of the original fructifying *betweonum* between Adam and Eve, redoubled in the saving of creation, *betweonum*, by the two by two of the animals in the ark, generative promise renewing the ecology of the *metaxu*. Mary and the child are two who reveal the wording of God as from full to full to full: all full of grace. Our time is interim time, but what falls in the interval of time is not a fruitless between. Procession as agapeic betweening can be created and recreated in mission as when Christ sends out his disciples two by two, that is, as *betweonum*. On the cross by two: the perforated Christ between two thieves, one of them awakening to the criminal innocence of the Holy One. The figure on the cross is redeeming fourthness. This figuring of redeeming fourthness is folly. And after the death and resurrection? Again by two, betweening. I think of

---

15. While eros is not mentioned in the New Testament, erotic love brims with the reserve of espoused *passio* (as in the Song of Songs). On marriage as *metaxu* and the erotics of mystical espousal, see Desmond, *God and the Between*, ch. 13.

the two disciples hurrying away, and then companioned by the figure they come across on the way to Emmaus. Resting on the journey, at the breaking of bread in companionship, the third at the table reopens their porosity, and they suffer a metanoetic awakening to their till-then incognito companion, the risen Christ. The third vanishes, and the resurrected *metaxu* sends them forth and back to the Jerusalem they have fled and the mission of divine betweening.

7

Metacritique and the Dynamics of Retrieval

Radical Orthodoxy, Sergii Bulgakov, and the Task for Trinitarian Ontology

Aaron Khokhar

> And in the end, we shall achieve in time
> The thing they call divine,
> When all the stars will smile for me
> When all is well and well is all for all
> And forever after
> Well, maybe in the meantime wait and see...
>
> —SPACEHOG, *IN THE MEANTIME*

In the southerly direction a village ended at the Immanuel Kant roundabout, a purely urbanistic creation of great aesthetic sobriety—a simple circle of totally grey tarmac which led to nothing, enabled access to no road, and around which no house had been built. A bit further on, a river flowed slowly.

—MICHEL HOUELLEBECQ, *THE MAP AND THE TERRITORY*

Gesang ist Dasein
—RAINER MARIA RILKE, *DIE SONETTE AN ORPHEUS*

Our Situation

DISABUSED OF CERTAIN DECLAIMED closures for even its most basic speculative moves, recent theology, in attending closely to both the *ressourcement* effort and recent medieval-philosophical scholarship, moves gainfully toward a "full-blooded" metaphysics both christological and Trinitarian in character. At the root of the most significant of these retrenchments, the critical-epistemological preoccupation of modern metaphysics, lies the invention at once in method and object of an exclusive order of metaphysically relevant thinking and knowing; at the same time, it is grounded in a revisionary and reactionary image of self, which keeps philosophy questionably held apart from the rest of what we are and who we might become.

For theology, in whose operations is nestled each soft frond of our spirit, this is immediately an intolerable result. Yet, the structure of these secularizing and immanentizing moves is scarcely detectable, since this thesis possesses not merely an ideological capture in various measures across the entirety of the modern outgrowth of an autonomous philosophical discipline but emerges from an intellectual drift internal to theology itself.[1] One may increasingly surmise from the historical consequence of this obfuscation that philosophy makes for man an idol of himself. This idol does not resemble him. For in assuming from a quite occult source images of man and his purpose, it has ceded the controlling vantage to proclaim our relation to the infinite and to the divine.

William Blake, in his annotations on Wordsworth, writes,

> Solomon, when he Married Pharaoh's daughter & became a Convert to Heathen Mythology, Talked exactly in this way of Jehovah as a Very inferior object of Man's Contemplation; he also passed him by unalarm'd & was permitted. Jehovah dropped a tear & follow'd him by his Spirit into the Abstract Void; it is called the Divine Mercy. Satan dwells in it, but Mercy does not dwell in him; he knows not to Forgive.[2]

---

1. See, for instance, Boulnois, *Être et représentation*; Milbank, *Theology and Social Theory*.

2. Blake, *Complete Writings*, 724.

For it was not in pure pursuit of self-knowledge that our asking and thinking core was figured in such a way, but rather after the exigency of science—for certain reasoning, however we might attain it. Much has recently been written on these motivations.[3] In the birth of transcendental cognition, an intellectual satisfaction of knowing in clear and distinct conceptuality now casts off the relative inconstancy and unreliability of life, moreover, requiring in turn a homogeneous reserve of scientifically secure operations thereupon. Apriority in concept becomes the essence of thinking, and the essence of what is there to be thought.

Most notably after Immanuel Kant's *Critique of Pure Reason*, the working assumption that the real reduces to the *coincidence* merely of the forms of intuition and the concepts of understanding that happen to be ours[4] sets the concern of philosophy at once with an elaboration of merely finite knowing alongside the insistence that this remains the whole of (possible) metaphysical investigation as such.[5] This understanding prevails today, whether in phenomenological or (neo-)Kantian structuralist-positivistic form.[6] On the other hand, one could argue that if thought concerns us, then it is the whole of human thought, but this has proven unsustainable: Speculation on the externalizing and alienating truth of thought—now it is hardly human either—continues to be a common theme from the writings of Baruch Spinoza, Maurice Blanchot, Nick Land, and Reza Negarestani's recent *Intelligence and Spirit*.[7]

Yet, in return, it is important for us to note that Friedrich Heinrich Jacobi in his time crucially sought to invoke both David Hume and Gottfried Leibniz against Immanuel Kant, arguing that transcendental critique contrives its revolution in already presupposing the divisions of concept and intuition, that it may later recombine them under the sole propriety of its own speculative license.[8] Moreover, as G. W. F. Hegel arguably only half understood, Jacobi resists Benedict Spinoza in the same way,

---

3. See n6 below; Honnefelder, *Scientia transcendens*; Pfau, *Minding the Modern*; Milbank, "Dissolution of Divine Government."

4. See, for instance, Kant, *Critique of Pure Reason*, B136-9.

5. This is already present in Duns Scotus. See Honnefelder, "Raison et Metaphysique." See also "David Hume," in Jacobi, *Main Philosophical Writings*, 253-338.

6. See Rose, *Hegel Contra Sociology*, 1-51, for a good discussion of the critical neo-Kantian roots of modern sociology. For phenomenology's current anti-metaphysical stance, see Marion, *Givenness & Hermeneutics*; Lacoste, *Appearing of God*; Falque, *Crossing the Rubicon*.

7. Spinoza, *Ethics*, particularly §§2-5; "The Relation," in Blanchot, *Infinite Conversation*, 66-74; Land, *Thirst for Annihilation*, 74-85; Negarestani, *Intelligence and Spirit*.

8. See the work cited in n9 below; Jacobi, *Main Philosophical Writings*, 538-90.

maintaining alongside J. G. Herder that cognition in a genuinely integrated image of discursivity would admit no concepts that might be isolated as sheer formalities from an indivisible "empirical" economy of sense, lest we lose all intuitional basis for the real itself.[9] Indeed, as for George Berkeley, simply because the phenomenally incorporate concrete thinks the universal, one cannot thereby straightforwardly surmise here that an achievement of genuine abstraction really obtains.[10] One would thereby beg the question of transcendental cognition, presupposing not only an ostensibly exclusive access to primordial and singularly metaphysically germane formal unities held under conceptual definition but also the pretension to precision for the implements of philosophical method. Perhaps we ought rather to ask whether metaphysical conceptuality is itself as poetic and "suppositional"— and yet ultimately intractable—as the amnion of the empirical we inhabit; and whether the unity and object of philosophy's referential and constructive powers are resistant to any readily articulable rational precipitate, much like the shadowy fasciae binding and driving the real itself.

At the same time, the results of much recent French and German scholarship on the medieval and antique period, as well as the theological work of William Desmond, Erich Przywara, and Radical Orthodoxy (among many others before and between them) has impressively and convincingly isolated and exposed the construction of the modern intellectual lineage as a significant departure from the antique and high medieval speculative base.[11] Our understanding of both the nature and the sheer distance that retrieval must scale in philosophical and theological scope is owed to these efforts, but their genealogies cannot be rehearsed here. In spite of its genius, this advance has thrown the (non-)possibility of speculative totality and the unity of reason into disarray by reviving it in a way that remains yet to be clarified, for if the remit to evaluate presuppositional structure belongs to neither victor of the modern debate—that is, not to a universal solvent of self-effacing equivocal and fragmenting multiplicity, nor to an ultimate univocity in the dialectically self-identical grasp of conceptuality—is there an immanence or *continuity* in and of philosophical reason remaining? How is it to be thought? Moreover, if it can be thought, how does one now understand the

---

9. "David Hume on Faith" (1787), 253–38; "Concerning the Doctrine of Spinoza" (1789), 339–78; "David Hume on Faith: Preface" (1815), 537–90, all in Jacobi, *Main Philosophical Writings*.

10. Berkeley, *Philosophical Writings*, 53, 74.

11. See nn7, 9 above; Milbank, *Theology and Social Theory*; Przywara, *Analogia Entis*; Pickstock, "Duns Scotus," 545; Honnefelder, "Metaphysics as a Discipline"; Reale, *New Interpretation of Plato*; Milbank, "Knowledge"; Courtine, *Suarez*; Desmond, *Voiding of Being*.

nature of the philosophical power that is to carry out the task of retrieval, given that it appears in the face of presuppositionless philosophy that reason must—in seeming contradiction to the metacritiques of J. G. Herder and J. G. Hamann—somehow presume to "dispose" itself *before* its use?[12]

In the first place, if the possibility to rend concept from intuition in sophistic speech and writing is latent within the very nature of human discursivity (rather than an epochal aberrance), as Plato realized, it turns out that a genuinely "critical" and epistemological age cannot really arrive without the prior subordination of the ontological domain—and thus a decision (often a ruse) concerning the ontological—to a controlling formal domain whose nature it cannot really avow.[13] One ought therefore neither to admit at the genealogical level a historical necessity or thoroughfare to philosophical modernity, nor indeed to posit any plain irreversibility in the face of a remedial task of retrieving the possibility of a unity to the disparate elements of experience and their theoretical relation, which has been covered over and rewritten. It appears that a therapeutic question relating to the "background" structure of various philosophical images of discursivity, concerning foremost the interplay between concept and intuition, preoccupies us as a question of presuppositions and of origin for self and its operations. We shall pass by two notable orienting attempts.

In the *Phenomenology of Spirit*, G. W. F. Hegel evaluates philosophical determinations from out of the "existential" ground of individual and historical consciousness from which they are posited. In this way, the contents of consciousness are preserved as original unities of concept and intuition in the active human possession, transmission and development of truth across time and culture. In turn, as one comes to find in the rest of Hegel's work, if the truth of spirit—for the human being *is* spirit—is to be self-consciously free in ethical community, and one goes on only to recollect the variety of historical life as unsuccessful attempts at achieving and articulating this whole, then in every historical moment that subjectivity unfolds further into its truth, we uncover the command and achievement of the self-differentiation of *conceptual structure* unto itself, as well as the conditions and whole from which it might think itself.[14] Hence, most crucially, since freedom itself is the form and content of absolute knowing—or the true knowledge of what *is*—historical process has itself yielded a proto-genealogical field for virtually simulating the theoretical structures issuing

---

12. See Herder, *Schriften*, 303–640; Hamann, "Metacritique."

13. See the discussion of the "divided line" in Plato, *Resp.* 509d–511e, for instance. This line of thought will be developed in this piece.

14. Hegel, *Phenomenology of Spirit*, "Preface," §§1–77.

from unfree soul in history, now arraigned dialectically as partial vantages on unfolding philosophical truth.[15]

For Martin Heidegger, too, after Wilhelm Dilthey, the priority of an analytic of life over conceptual determination binds the "unified" datum of Dasein, in contrast to the neo-Kantian bias toward an epistemologically expedient scission.[16] This investigation reveals self-knowing in its reverse face as a metaphysically purified hermeneutic circularity of our everyday engagements in and as a part of an ontological order whose proper articulation nevertheless escapes us.[17] Heidegger goes on to recover the neglected preconceptual registers for human phenomenality (temporality, linguisticality, mood, etc.)[18] as essential to knowing how one stands in the unveiling of truth *before* the work of proposition.[19] Here, an occlusion of the most proper questions of metaphysics is shown again to lie first in a mis-recognition from an indigent hermeneutic of self.[20] (David Hume, for instance, may be argued to have supplied very similar argumentation.)[21] Demonstrating that the discursive transcendentality in hermeneutic circularity is at once the condition for speculation, wherein it serves as a presuppositional cluster implicitly latent in all philosophy, Heidegger argues not only that a fundamental displacement of the nature of questioning and knowing has taken place, but that this is a problem of not knowing how to live now that we know neither how to think nor live—and vice versa. Hence, the presuppositional reductions constituting *Destruktion* expose the various yields of our ocular obsession from antiquity to modernity, not merely as defective conceptuality but as deficient practice of self-relation in and within the infinite. This virtual simulation washes out the silt of our various grasps for ontic and positivist capture into the basin of epiphanic *Wesung*,[22] awaiting in a

---

15. Hegel, *Phenomenology of Spirit* §788.
16. Heidegger, *Being and Time* (trans. Stambaugh), 206, §§39, 44; see also n10.
17. Heidegger, *Metaphysical Foundations of Logic*, 188, §11.
18. Heidegger, *Metaphysical Foundations of Logic* §§1–4.
19. Heidegger, *Metaphysical Foundations of Logic* §69.
20. Heidegger, *Essence of Truth*, 54.
21. See Milbank, "Hume Versus Kant."
22. *Wesung*, or "essence-ing," is best explicated in terms of Heidegger's notion of a "release" of beings, or *Gelassenheit*, and is intimately tied to his recommendation of waiting to see beings in a self-articulation that beings themselves proffer when we attune ourselves to remain within in this absent glimmer of Beyng that is entrusted to us. Only in being prepared to renounce the spirit of technological mastery of beings and the metaphysical basis of this impulsion are we ready to "leap" to truly dwell as a radical finitude. See Heidegger, *Contributions to Philosophy* 5.198; and note below.

posture of nigh religiosity for beings to show themselves under the poetic figuration of gods-to-come.[23]

In the foregoing, what is set forth in philosophy and what is lived are intrinsically connected, even as the meaning of living and thinking in history require philosophical determination in the course of being thought and lived. As the anti-Kantian *Metakritiker* crucially argue, after Hume, philosophy returns perpetually to the amnion of pragmatic absorbment as the very point of the origin of thought and therefore remains unavoidably linked to the substance of speculative adventure.[24] In contrast, modernity presents primarily as the reign of formality—retelling not merely the story of metaphysics but revising the story of *self* around the minimally demanding captivation of the lowest common methodological artefacture. We are entranced by our theory, to which we clutch to derive an account of ourselves. Yet, if the answers of metaphysics are somehow in the questions of metaphysics, these are in turn presupposed by what he who asks thinks he can and ought to ask. We can also say that the answers metaphysics will provide depend on what—or who—the questioner thinks he is and what therefore his knowing essentially consists of. Hence, to *reassert* that sense, religiosity, linguisticality, imagination, narrative, feeling, persuasion, myth, ritual, and so on are ontologically disclosive and constitutive would be in effect to recognize speculative inquiry as a call-and-answer with our living and making selves rather than the immediacy of knowing mind alone.

Again, following Hume (for whom human science is the *only* science we might have access to, and who demands an attunement that philosophy commonly refuses), a mutually determining refinement of concept and intuition becomes the pivotal matter of our retrieval, and this centers on the reliance of all philosophy on an *anthropological* key to the methodological horizon as such.[25] Coupled with Platonic insistence that the problem of discursivity lies in excess of a purely historicist "emergence" of conceptuality, one might find much in common with Alain Badiou's *Being and Event*, for example. Here, the genealogical operations of revolution, critique, and return are themselves recognized as theses on the nature of cognition (as Nietzsche and Heidegger realized),[26] deriving from the modes of explicating the various images of ontology alongside the processes of thought that

---

23. See, for instance, Heidegger, *Mindfulness* §123; Heidegger, *Contributions to Philosophy* 7.255; Heidegger, ". . . Poetically Man Dwells . . ."; Heidegger, *Introduction to Philosophy* §§4, 6; Vioulac, *Apocalypse of Truth*, 111n261.

24. See n15 above; Herder, *Philosophical Writings*, 65–166.

25. See Hume, *Treatise of Human Nature*, 5–6, 10.

26. Nietzsche, "On Truth and Lying."

generate them; this, in turn, ensures that the conditions of speculation reflect the necessary "homogeneity" of theory with the determining practical and political processes of inquiring subjectivity.[27] This is important.

For, thinking beyond the individual efforts of Heidegger and Hegel themselves, if indeed the variously conceived residual corrals of transcendental cognition—where concept unilaterally predetermines and supplants the pressures of intuition—warp our self-recognition and thereby spoil the feast of thought, it is important to grasp therein the principle of dissent upon which all philosophy appears to place its mark. For the present reading of general hermeneutic circularity, any real departure from modern transcendental cognition must think the nature of discursivity in refusal of the twin limit concepts of a purely opaque intuitive facticity and a wholly ungrounded theoretical conceptuality. This implies that the sole philosophical recourse consists of deploying at some level a pragmatizing hermeneutic of subjectivity and the activity of thought in order to pull away from the stranglehold of a priori, clear, and distinct knowing in the order of method and its pretension to being most basic and original thought.

It becomes clear here that the consummation of this trend is a pragmatically unified presuppositional image of concept and intuition at the twin levels of determination and reflection, which at the height of premodernity was implicit and held together in the human being as inquirer—for inquiry, too, is practice. Indeed, alongside Plato, we might say that the shape of inquiry inherently implies the transcendence of intellectual forms, since the procedure and yield of philosophy is ultimately a functional outlook on functionality itself; yet, if functionality is all there is, it means that the forms might be read "positively" as the *enablers* of life and thus themselves speculatively indispensable. It is important to note here the difference between transcendental cognition and the necessary transcendentalities that speculation both posits and relies upon. As the American pragmatists realized, if it is only from an ineliminable mediating arena of action that "possible effects" as the real extension of pure metaphysical concepts are determined, then philosophy, too, ultimately remains in a "protentive"[28] and experimentalist "laboratory mind" concerning the theoretical, even as speculation must presuppose nothing that cannot later be affirmed.[29] In contrast, the uninterrogated epistemological urge to attempt a *reconstruction* of

27. "Introduction," in Badiou, *Being and Event*, 1–50.

28. Anticipative or "future-grasping." Borrowed from Husserl, *Phenomenology of the Consciousness*, 54.

29. See John Dewey, "Development of American Pragmatism," in Thayer, *Pragmatism*, 23–42. See also Charles Sanders Peirce, "Definition and Description of Pragmatism," in Thayer, *Pragmatism*, 48–60; Margolis, *Reinventing Pragmatism*.

phenomenality from a mechanics of correlation (a strategy underwritten by the ostensible self-sufficiency and foundational status of conceptuality itself) draws its purpose and operation from a certainty that is encoded as the determinacy of philosophical equipment, and transcendental critique then both presupposes and circularly enforces as the bound of speculative warrant the elements that are assumed to most essentially and properly subtend the human phenomenal frame.

In this way, all philosophy may be read to be already (though implicitly) set in opposition to the dead end of a seemingly original sundering of concept and intuition in philosophical images; how it then goes about demonstrating that this rift is questionable and *derivative* may vary, yet the most sophisticated of these attempts explicitly realize that this recapture simultaneously indicates an unveiling of the primordial motion of thought, the revelation of its origin, and the incorporated recollection of the fullest horizon for our actuality—even if transcendental critique is not outrightly refused. Yet, if the signs here are that the horizon for speculative adventure tends toward the grasp of a truth that straddles concept and intuition in an original *determining* unity of our making and living, the ultimate issue is whether and how this may be achieved without denying metaphysical relevance to any dimension of the human scale wherein questioning begins, especially since this integration and the admitting dimensions (remaining yet to be determined both in content and form) will come to constitute the principle of all philosophy, as Schelling, too, foresaw.[30]

In the next section I shall argue that the ruthless hunt of presuppositional reductions ushers philosophy into a domain necessarily belonging to theology, which shows itself to continue an effort that philosophy arbitrarily truncates for its own purposes of shoring up an illusory autonomy. It is important that very little of this is original. What will be offered over the course of this chapter is not a new hermeneutic of some or other facet of philosophy's subject or object, but a pursuit for a higher logic of combination, which, like for Hegel, just is our actuality, though this remains misrecognized. One may then retrospectively think the philosophical attempts we have adverted to in the foregoing in their philosophical failure, since philosophy does not realize the ultimate significance of this decision.

In the remaining sections of this chapter, I wish to use the thought of Sergii Bulgakov to argue that Trinitarian theology best completes this movement of recognizing actuality in order to think concept and intuition together. Invoking apocalyptic theology and Sophiology, we shall take this further in the final section to examine the significance of this symmetry

---

30. See Schelling, "On the Possibility."

134   PART TWO—METAPHYSICS AND PHENOMENOLOGY

for the understanding of transcendentality as such and some of the basic problems of theology. This will be done both through the speculative organization that the doctrine of the Holy Trinity provides and the crucial methodological reform that a proper appreciation of this adjustment requires. A system plan for the remaining argument is as follows:

1. The isolation of a symmetrical relationship between concept and intuition in images of discursivity.

2. The identification of this discursive transcendentality with the methodological basis of philosophical investigation as the conditions for speculation.

3. The methodological heuristic of symmetrical concept and intuition preserves truly *metacritical* discursivity, refusing to foreclose on the incorporation into the highest organizing principles of metaphysics for the intuitive (poetic, imaginative, corporeal, affective, narratival, etc.) as a more faithful hermeneutic of our existential pragmatic absorbment.

4. The transformation of hermeneutic circularity, which subtends the phenomenal frame, into metaphysical transcendentality *on a metacritical basis*, denying speculative license a foreclosure on critically finite lines.

5. Ontologically, the precariously "external" finite is *internally* determined by the infinite. This appears as poetic, supplementing co-creativity from the side of the finite, and self-transcendentalizing declension from the side of the infinite. There is a paradox intrinsic to finitude that is expressed in the apocalyptic relation.

6. An identification of *metacritical* transcendentality in the apocalyptic as a motion internal to the Absolute appears as a rival image for the organization of the paradox. Now, we may refuse a relation to the infinite in the forced disavowal of our own creation and the subsequent disavowal by the infinite; instead, metacritical reform allows a reformed, Christian post-structuralism, with analogically supervised creation through filiation and an abiding vital innervation.

7. An elaboration of Bulgakov's interpretation of trinitarity as non-declining trihypostaticity in a consubstantial self-declension into sophiological expression. This reconciles the paradox of the apocalyptic in a single "tetrahedral" figure. Having established the metaphysical possibility of figurative transcendentality from a metacritical image of discursivity, the Trinitarian *figura* is shown to be the master

transcendentality for metaphysics as such. Its thus serves as own self-justification, since it most basically operates in its role as such a transcendental ground while simultaneously demonstrating that dyadic categories of ground and un-ground might be remedied with an original binding "third."

8. The Trinitarian reformation of metacritical discursivity allows that theory begins in continuity with human life and is not opposed to our life in the infinite. The wound of an independence in the pride of possessing thought and concept is healed in the example of the man Jesus—in whom the Trinity became incarnate—who lived the perfect life and thus demonstrated and offered for us now the binding of concept and intuition, theory and practice, and form and content in perfect love.

The Dynamics of Retrieval

We have seen that a theological consummation of philosophy reveals its logic of combination for form and content to coincide with the extension of conceptual power to an intuitive content active essentially as a hermeneutic of everyday human life—even if its essential character and constitutive dimensions remain yet to be determined. This is because we all *must* return to the amnion of empirical, existential preoccupation in a way that cannot be "bracketed," as Hegel and Hume (and others) realized, and the ancients again eminently intuited. In return, conceptual power affords the ability to these existential registers to legitimate their own status back from the blunt economizations of rationalist cognition—not now as mere *assertion* but overtly incorporated into argumentative structure as necessary elements for the reconciliation of understanding with our abiding within, and alongside, the Absolute in truth.

It is not mere sentimentality that drives the invocation of the shape and truth of retrieval as "incarnational" and ultimately "redemptive" from the critical bowdlerization of the human and the dynamics of our structural *Umwelt* (of myths, narrative, imagination, action, making, etc.). Rather, any self-delimiting decisions of discourse ostensibly extrinsic from theology may be virtually simulated to deflate theology's pretension to autonomy, demonstrating that the supreme image of each disclosive structural register derives its human propriety from Trinitarian and sophiological action. I have two further points to make here.

First, if philosophy's late arrival as our self-articulation places it squarely within historical and cultural making (at the same time as "making" and its metaphysics requires clarification, thus supplying the element of *self*-recognition), then the "demystificatory" function of a distinct conceptuality for the purposes of metaphysical precision recasts the uninterrogated hermeneutic internality of method precisely to the effect of obscuring from view its own original presuppositions. (This is seen today, similarly to Socrates noting in his day the sophists' desire to consolidate a *professional* seriousness to philosophy.) Hence, particular attention must be paid that alterations and reconfigurations of theoretical structure do not remain in hock to the various partial concessions made to the pragmatic that are not intuitionally tied—that is, which are virtually rehearsable and overcome from a higher vantage of a *more attractive* hermeneutic—even if this yoke is disguised in the more sober terms of plain philosophical exigency. This is most often seen in critiques of philosophies of reflection, which, in an angst over the instability of the reflective concept, suspend the phenomenal in and for its later resumption under the ruse of "higher" conceptual transcendentality apparently demanded by pure reason, whether in the form of dialectics or otherwise. Yet, they only maneuver at the level of holding the speculative transcendental at a further remove, declining to reform discursive transcendentality as such.

Hence, one must be especially vigilant here, since this additional "ideological" obfuscation of not reforming transcendentality is a consequence of an *extrapolative* dimension intrinsic to philosophical images. That is, since there is no thinking without some unifying hermeneutic horizon (since only humans speculate, even if they attribute this impulse to a regulative employment of reason, as for Kant), increasingly sophisticated philosophical images will invariably tend with varying success to apprehend and rearticulate the questions, structure, and aporiae of philosophy in an idiom that their own schemes quite naturally produce and reinforce. This is the basis of a hermeneutic tension between rival philosophical idioms. This is quite evident, for example, with Marx's metaphysics of a historical thoroughfare for social organization through capitalism: relying upon an elision of the initial "subtractive" analysis, Marx and Engels install this propelling logic both forwards and backwards in history from an economic (and thus thoroughly modern) refractive point.[31] Yet, as René Girard notes, the ultimate mystification today is in a supposedly once and for all unmasked nakedness to violence and power; just so, we might argue that the various gradations of formalism in philosophy increasingly abandon the faith in noesis to grind

---

31. "For and Against Marx," in Milbank, *Theology and Social Theory* (2006), 175–205.

the dead letter of dianoia, permitting themselves only the various sumptuary allowances from a meager roll of geometric operations that may now be performed.[32] Nevertheless, general demands of internal consistency will dictate that the decisions that begin with questionable and essentially positivist critical reductions at the level of the *anthropos*, and therefore subscribe to excluding purely formal foundations for speculation at some level, ought either to be defended to their own standard of conceptual certainty or else dismissed, since this presumes far too much about the nature of abstraction and not enough about transcendentality at the far end of abstractive power. They must consequently feign complexity in further straining to justify their partial images as though they possessed an ultimate and original character.

This is where the logic of "counterfeit doubles" in the work of William Desmond comes into sharp relief: one can and must sever "surface" affirmations from their basis in philosophical structure, since the latter—a "real" argumentative conceptual extension—are in fact facilitated by an extrapolative "retranslation" of philosophy (with varying success) held in its presuppositional core.[33] This is particularly common with respect to religious statements apparently held in common despite wildly disparate metaphysical structures underneath, as is often found in theological engagements with Hegel.[34]

This is as much as to say that the propriety of "the human" cannot be justified from any conceptual extension without the prior incorporation of the intrinsic possibility for the suspension and virtual simulation of rival hermeneutic internalities *at the transcendental level* of their presuppositions.[35] They may even mistake the nature of transcendentality in the first place, as we shall see below. If this is the case, we may restate that the escape from modern rationalism and a priori conceptuality attempts an approximation of a stable conceptuality that might better integrate concept and intuition as a self-legitimating task grounded in actuality. Heidegger attempts this in various meditations on the sheer capacity of "logos" in pre-Socratic thought on the "fourfold" of the phenomenal aperture to come.[36]

32. Girard, *Battling to the End*, 41.

33. Desmond, *Hegel's God*. See note below.

34. See the discussions in Desmond, "Hegel's God, Transcendence." See also Stephen Houlgate's response ("Hegel, Desmond") and Desmond's reply ("Response to Stephen Houlgate") in the same issue.

35. "Original Structure," in Przywara, *Analogia Entis*. It is notable (though not very well understood) that the first half of Przywara's *Analogia Entis* proceeds by virtually simulating presuppositional reductions of metaphysical positions rather than deriving them in an immanent and dialectical fashion.

36. See, for instance, the essays in Heidegger, *Early Greek Thinking*; Mitchell, *Fourfold* §9.

A necessary upshot here is that, in retrieval, the power of the concept from a higher vantage cannot be seen in advance. Only when a wider horizon for the truth of spirit—more primordial experience and existential allure, refracted in the life of every formality, alongside (though not necessarily coincident with) tradition and nature—is admitted on an intuitional basis of a more "fitting" self-identification, and we enter into its narrative and experience a perspectival shift; here, the reflective concepts achieves both its transformation and its ultimate explanation, whether in *Daseinsanalytik*, schizoanalysis, or dialectical mystical ascent, and so on. This "derailleur," as it were, from one hermeneutic horizon to another, means not only that (self-)justificatory argument becomes theoretically possible because previous vantages can be virtually simulated at the level of demonstrating their mis-recognition of self, but the exercise of presuppositional reduction also increasingly demonstrates the use of metaphysical ground that only a progressively incorporated intuitive or existential can validate at a rational level. Conversely, no higher vantage can be accessed by those who remain in arguing, for instance, that "constitutive" cognition consists of determining judgments posited devoid of feeling, or that language is a mirror of a more primary representing function of mind. For, in each case, they presuppose from the outset a militant exclusion or ideological division of intuitional impress incumbent on honest conceptual capacity. As a result, they never confront what is undesirable in the order of knowing, and often this obstinacy is managed by dualistically and unstably recycling the remainder into indeterminate and *merely* pragmatic and political domains. (Consider Badiou's Marxism or the recent "analytic Foucault" moment.) It is significant and ought to be noted, moreover, that hermeneutic shift does not emerge from a dialectical pressure latent in the given conceptual internality, for the dialectical form depends on its own critical reductions, which may themselves be virtually simulated at the joints, as we shall see below. For now, as long as we can think rival claims and see that *and how* they perpetuate self-mis-recognition (even the mis-recognition of the norms of arbitration and abstraction we are performing in the space of reasons mapped by virtual simulation) no more can be done in the intellectual domain than to note the obstruction and pass over it, as Hegel realized.[37]

In the second place, if we are offering here a hermeneutic of hermeneutic,[38] plumbing resources to find the fullest mutual unity of concept and intuition as it declines into the workings of discourses such as narratology, politics, semiotics, biology, and so on—can this pragmatic

---

37. Hegel, *Phenomenology of Spirit* §206.
38. Heidegger, *On the Way to Language*, 11.

unity be suspended at any point? The decisive dimension of this question concerns the human unity of concept and intuition in its continuity with the ordering power, which goes on to supervise higher regulative dimensions of theoretical structure. A critical reduction of the noetic from the human would somehow allow investigation to slip out of this linguistic, historical, spiritual inhabitation and surrender to the hard professional reality of the instruments of pure philosophical method and the commensurate motion of straightforward abstraction to pure philosophical structures. Here, this will be refused, and our vigilance must be exhaustive: just as the "surface" complexity of arithmetic or geometric series reduces to an iterative elaboration of linear and polynomial expressions, in philosophical terms, various types of transcendental distributions of content can be shown ultimately to collapse into the identical repetition of a purely conceptual construction, and this would mark a return of transcendental cognition in a critical reduction subtending a philosophical ground in an *asymmetry* of concept and intuition in metaphysical transcendentality. Hence, it would be mistaken here to insist on an immanently self-stable basis for the presuppositional reduction of transcendentalities, since this would be to insist on an internal unity of reason, the cognitive basis of which is not human (and therefore treats the poetic, allusive, and imaginative as sub-metaphysical cognition). This is because a formal basis for the reduction of transcendentalities would take consciousness (at once self-reflexive and yet *mediate* in its most basic reflective capacities) out of isomorphy with intellectual structure. Such an anthropology would posit an image of the soul that, thinking against Proclus and for Plotinus, has *not* descended fully into body.[39] There is no straightforwardly rational decision beyond an "intuitionally tied" horizon of self-recognition, but it would be a mistake to consider that decision may simply be avoided.

In this case, theological critiques of Hegel, Heidegger, and so on ought not merely to attempt at an anti-modern metaphysics while leaving uninterrogated the question of whether the argument is conducted with a reigning transcendental asymmetry of concept and intuition, which are the derivative terms of the secular and modern. Rather, once properly understood in terms sketched in the foregoing, it will be seen that modern philosophy (and the gestating modern maneuvers in antique discursivity) has ceded scant concession to the origin of thought as *human thinking* prior to the deployment of its various hermeneutic internalities. For, if Reid, Hume, Wittgenstein, Nietzsche, and Heidegger, for instance, entreat us in various measures to recognize that the decidedly anti-epistemological, *pragmatic*

---

39. See Milbank, *Beyond Secular Order*, 209.

character of thinking is intrinsically contiguous with speculation (such that *self-knowledge* is maintained as the beginning of wisdom), might we not take another look at the uninterrogated redoubts of transcendental cognition that bolster both the construction of the Hegelian dialectical form, and the critical circle of finite phenomenality and linguisticality in twentieth-century philosophy of language?[40] Do these themselves not yield to further presuppositional reduction once the meaning of transcendentality *as such* is understood, with theology offering more compelling philosophical hermeneutics of spirit and thought and avoiding, moreover, the loss of any theoretical rigor and intricacy that these conceptual frames tout as their sole capacity?

To the contrary, a Christian "radical orthodox" metaphysics is more compelling because it does not seek to institute a critical separation, for instance, between felt phenomenal depth and beatitude from analogical transcendence-immanence in fidelity to existential mystery, doctrinal specification, *and* metaphysical structure—each of which is intimated in the others, crucially.[41] The result is that whatever these "incorporated" elements of thinking may be—the mystical and esoteric, for instance—they are central to the thinking of being and to the thinking of the divine. Outside of the resources of theology in doctrine, it is impossible to properly arrive at this unity without canceling the coherence of concept with the sheerly unstructured potency of intuition. Since, however, one may now also read these omissions as themselves determinations made from a *spiritual* misrecognition on the part of the philosopher, one returns theory to a "practical logic," which is set squarely within the arena of ethical, existential (and psychoanalytical) significance.[42] Let us now reconstruct the philosophical significance of this theological transcendentality.

Trinitarian and Sophiological Metaphysical Structure in Sergii Bulgakov

Sergii Bulgakov's Trinitarian ontology proves its centrality to the fundamental problems of philosophy and thus to the task of theological retrieval.[43] The remainder of this essay shall derive from the justification of human life in divine trinitarity a methodological key for the trend of anti-foundationalism,

40. As an example of this analysis, see Rorty, *Philosophy and the Mirror.*
41. Pickstock, "Duns Scotus," 545.
42. See Žižek, *Sublime Object*, as well as n119 below.
43. This interpretation of Sergii Bulgakov owes a tremendous amount to the work of John Milbank, David Bentley Hart, and Brandon Gallaher. See notes below.

which autonomous and secular philosophy cannot complete. In the final section, the Pauline truth of human spirit will be given further elaboration, showing itself to supervise an alternative post-structuralist transcendental vantage that consummates theory in the apocalyptic and pneumatic reality of the Christian cosmotheandric (*world-God-man*) vision.

Bulgakov is well aware of the deep philosophical significance of three co-equivalent hypostases in the Absolute, gleaning from the doctrinal formulations of Trinitarianism the suspension of triadicity and unicity—a *trihypostaticity*—as the basic speculative schema for an ontological image.[44] Eschewing a *reconstruction* of Trinity from out of previous philosophical sensibilities and materials and instead "drawing out" trihypostaticity's unique synthetic "figure," we may read Bulgakov's unique rejection of the reign of unicity as one that replaces the autarchical One at the ultimacy of metaphysical structure, and thus anticipates by going beyond even the various differential transcendentalities of Gilles Deleuze and Alain Badiou, for instance. Yet, again, it is far ahead of both of them, since Bulgakov does not rule straightforwardly in favor of *multiplicity* as such but trihypostatic difference-in-unity.[45] (Alongside surveys of the meaning of the One as such, like those by the Dominican Reiner Schürmann, Emmanuel Levinas, and, more recently, Graham Priest, who have also realized its instability.)[46] Several crucial points pertain here.

First, it often appears in Bulgakov that a "first beginning" in the history of thought was a precariously pagan reign of unicity from which the incursion of dissenting triadic and analogical argumentation almost immediately begins *because* of the "intuitive" pressure of antique contemplative beatitude (of which Plato is exemplary); and thus, it is in articulating a content that is properly trihypostatic on a dormant scheme of unicity that theology was lulled to a false confidence.[47] The "other beginning" (to continue the Heideggerian parallel) is bringing to self-consciousness how one is to think *properly*, not only beginning with a reappraisal of metaphysical structure but aligning this with the organizing influence of doctrinal figuration, gleaning from the faith the consummation of natural theology. One must note again this reason for Bulgakov's refusal of any *reconstructive* effort of articulating Trinity from any priorly distinct intellectual conceptions of unity, essence,

---

44. Bulgakov: *Wisdom of God*; *Lamb of God*, 19–89; "Epilogue: The Father," in *Comforter*, 359–94.

45. Bulgakov, *Tragedy of Philosophy*, 199–200.

46. Schürmann, "In the Name of the One"; Levinas, "Philosophy and Transcendence," 6; Priest, *One*.

47. Bulgakov, *Lamb of God*, 19–89.

nature, and person both in content and form—as though there were, as John Milbank writes, an "altogether different plane" for the instantiation of each, and thus a compartmentalization intrinsic to God in violation of his simplicity.[48] It is essential then to understand this as the rejection of the artifact of methodological conceptuality in formal distinctions at the very ultimacy of ontology, for this occludes the fact that a rigorously consubstantial *action* of trinitarity requires an inherent facilitation of *consubstantial* action in and through the divine being, Sophia. This ontological dimension of God ("created God," as for Eriugena) lies in this "hypostatizing power" that enables—not extrinsically—the actualizing *termini ad quos* of triune actions achieving creation, incarnation, and salvation in the "tetrahedral Absolute" of the Trinitarian life.[49] Accordingly, Sophia is herself cut "laterally" in the order of being into a triadic ontological structure of the ousia, Sophia, and Shekinah (or glory) of God.[50] A powerful incarnational logic follows from this commitment to sophiological consubstantiality. If the Absolute—the All that thought thinks—is itself beyond mere infinitude and finitude (as for Pseudo-Dionysius), it thus declines into in an absolutely underived unity, while, as Godhead, remaining in "causal exaltation" over creation.[51] We will return to this.

Second, given this trihypostatic foundation, a deeper attention to this presuppositional reduction builds up what consciousness is anew. For Bulgakov, as archetype is to image, so is the divine spirit as absolute trihypostatic subject in its eternal expressiveness (fully three, fully one) to human consciousness, whose triadic structure unfolds in time.[52] Thus, second, in Bulgakov the trihypostatic scheme may be read to influence and overcome the formal-critical principles of phenomenological investigation, for to insist on metaphysics as a logic of sense (i.e., that what is be made manifest) and yet ground critical reductions to a final "significance" for phenomenality is to impossibly argue for a single validity for a conceptual possibility; here, concreteness is desired and is invariably better explicated in the description of a phenomenological "neutrality" of cognitive processes whose formal elements are more basic than the mythical, religious, and linguistic real. With

---

48. Milbank: "One in Three," 50; "Sophia and Theurgy," 49. As might be realized, the question of imputing divisions in the divine simplicity is a question of the "sharpness" of our conceptual divisions, which falls back on the power of abstraction and the meaning of theory in the intellectual life of a creature. We shall attempt to resolve these questions below.

49. Hart, "Masks, Chimaeras, and Portmanteaux."

50. Bulgakov, *Wisdom of God*, 31.

51. Milbank, "One in Three," 56.

52. Bulgakov: *Lamb of God*, 94; *Tragedy of Philosophy*, 123.

the Trinitarian unity fully expressive, Bulgakov develops the nature of human consciousness with the Aristotelian-idealist emphasis on the structure of intelligibility of being and the emergence of phenomenality at the level of judgment (particularly as it variously diverges from the short tract *Judgment and Being* from the Tübingen days of Hegel, Schelling, and Hölderlin).[53] The human phenomenal frame is here subtended by, and constituted in, the triadic action of subject, predicate, and copula.[54]

No (human) subject is ever anything except as predication relays and mediates, and the predicate *reveals* the subject without fully exhausting it throughout the temporal outworking of our lives. Bulgakov highlights two levels of judgment for manifestation, different by form and content: first of "A is B" and then of "I am A"; ultimately, priority is given to the latter formulation: everything is really a form of "I am A," even in the instance of ostensibly observational, "neutral" predication.[55] In each case, the predicate reveals the preserving subject, which remains never-yet-exhausted in this manifestation, with the copula expressing the consummation of their mutual kenotic sacrifice.[56]

Third, it is significant how this is a Trinitarian "phenomeno-ontology": standing in a novel relationship to its own transcendentality as the condition for appearance, each component of this threefold condition for manifestation *as such* is not only linked to the two but (so far as it is possible to talk about "form" of trinity) kenotically reinforces their relationship.[57] In this respect, particularly in Bulgakov's *Philosophy of the Name*, a great many insights—from the linguistic philosophies of William von Humboldt, Hamann, Herder, and Heidegger—incorporate the notion of the revelation of being in the expression of linguistic utterance in a way that at once escapes absolute precision and predetermination, *yet* nevertheless most powerfully constitutes human self-realization. (This follows the "middle-voice" metaphysics of co-creativity—sans Christian virtue—which is often spoken about with respect to Nietzsche.)[58] Thought is thus from its outset linguistic, "interested," and *perspectival*—though we may disagree further on with respect to the precise organization of this plural field.[59]

---

53. Bulgakov, *Philosophy of the Name*, 104; see J. Hölderlin, *Essays and Letters*, 231–33.
54. Bulgakov, *Tragedy of Philosophy*, 17.
55. Bulgakov, *Tragedy of Philosophy*, 15; Heath, "Bulgakov's Linguistic Trinity."
56. Bulgakov, *Philosophy of the Name*, 68.
57. Bulgakov, *Philosophy of the Name*, 199.
58. Kofman, *Nietzsche and Metaphor*; Han-Pile, "Doing Is Everything."
59. See Granier, "Perspectivism and Interpretation."

This can very well be read alongside the Eriugenian claim that man is the *officina omnium*, or the workshop of all things.[60] That is, the realization of the subject in predicate, the world (as theophany, for Eriugena, or the manifestation of God),[61] in phenomenality and articulation, is my realization as subject from out of unknowable depths. For to exist among beings and to witness and judge their truth in the eternal realm is, as Dermot Moran notes, at once man's self-discovery of himself, albeit in material burden and temporal dilation.[62] In this "Platonic access" he remains the "co-inheritor" through the incarnate Christ of divine self-manifestation *as* gift.[63] How is this? In *statu lapsus*, having descended from the (spiritual) concept of man in the mind of God, the actuality of fallen man straddles both the Primordial Causes and their created effects.[64] Eriugena appears here to provide a novel Trinitarian supplementation of the principles of premodern gnoseological transmission (as the uptake and illumination of forms into passive and active intellect by virtue of the finite mind participating in eternal actuality of the divine mind) in furnishing its full ontological presuppositions in establishing the "receptivity" of human phenomenal *site* as the eternal inscriptive and creative fount in advance of real manifestation: all things were made for man. The Eriugenian phenomenal frame is not only "analogously" likened with the actuality of God's creation as the self-knowledge of his essence via its effects; rather, one arrives at a conception of manifestation beyond the terms of disclosure and granting in the face of which our passivity effects relative dispossession (as for Heidegger) and as a complex gnoseological-ontological structure: the activity of co-creative self-knowledge as participation in divine self-disclosure subtends all phenomenality.[65] All understanding is more real and excellent than the things that are understood, says Eriugena. Here, an active creative element is insisted upon, since what makes manifestation and understanding possible is that man is, as we have said, at once eternally featured in the Divine Son, the Logos—and yet existing fallen and descended, taking up the manifestation of the created effects of an eternal possession only dimly figured.[66] Something like the reformed, Christian post-structuralism we shall present below is intimated here: the world, given that it was created for the sake of my soul,

---

60. Eriugena, *Periphyseon*, 5.893C.
61. Eriugena, *Periphyseon*, 1.446D.
62. Moran, "Officina Omnium."
63. Eriugena, *Periphyseon*, 752B, 904A; Wood, *Whole Mystery of Christ*, 141–93.
64. Eriugena, *Periphyseon*, 771A, 854C.
65. Eriugena, *Periphyseon*, 580B, 610c, 764B.
66. Eriugena, *Periphyseon*, 532C, 883B.

appears and thus in some sense only is according to me; in its becoming, even as I become, I emerge through the ramification of jangling impulses; I subsist in their momentum; I am taken beyond myself by my own actions, which nevertheless only ever work to constitute me, just as I am.[67]

Fourth, this "middle voice" or "co-creative" poeticism can be arrived at only by securing a justification for finitude at the same time as further integrating philosophical access into its intuitive coherence; and it is significant, as we shall see, that the aporetics that dimly outline this phenomenon—of *porous* facticity in poetic emergence via human making—awaits an incorporation on the back of explicitly mythic and ritualistic structure, as for Nietzsche most notably.[68] Invoking Plato once more, philosophy is then as much a poetic elaboration of the (co-)poetic itself.[69]

Moreover, the figure of trinitarity also enables a virtual simulation of the looming threat of sheer scissiparity intrinsic to the dyadic relation of the first Trinitarian difference, such as when non-Trinitarian metaphysical images seize upon the opportunity to claim it philosophically obvious that signification is arbitrary and upholding the scission between reflection and determination, or between finite and infinite, or indeed between "saying" and "said," and so on. Crucially, then, in terms of the "content" of the pure archetypal image of Trinity, the "tragedy" of the Son's begetting from the Father may be read as the tragedy of the epistemological and nominalistic anxiety concerning the given—specifically, in terms of the spiritual life from which they are born. And yet, just as the nascent "break" of filiation is eternally overcome in the bond of the Spirit so as to never be a bare moment of apparent forsakenness without love's final victory, the suspicion is from the outset put aright in the "confidence" of the copula for full and true attestation into the clearing of human phenomenality from out of a preceding mystery—call it Beyng, or noumena, etc. This is a particularly masterful move in that it bypasses at the level of an abstract philosophical foreclosure a critical delineation and *reduction* of our amnion in the "natural attitude" of pragmatic absorbment as some or other form of transcendental illusion (i.e., as the forgetting of Being, or a mere "trace" of the eternal refusal of any terminus for polysemic metaphorical referral, etc.). Since the ultimate exigencies of the human existential are grounded in God himself, our life

---

67. Bulgakov, *Philosophy of the Name*, 231. See also Bulgakov, *Spiritual Diary*.

68. Nietzsche, *Birth of Tragedy*; Sallis, "Dionysus"; Shaw, *Theurgy and the Soul*. For Vico, see the discussion concerning the "concrete metaphor" in Milbank, *Word Made Strange*, 123–44.

69. Pickstock, "Late Arrival of Language"; Purslow, *Poesis and the Inner Experience*. See also Heidegger, *Introduction to Philosophy*.

in God is possible since the irreducible Trinitarian schema is a master transcendental for the stable conceptuality of motion and action as such.

The pressure of the "existential" successfully dovetails with this structure because the entire edifice stands in a novel relationship for Bulgakov to its own determining transcendentality as the condition for appearance as such without critical reduction of the everyday to transcendental illusion (or an inescapable error that employs concepts—in this case employs registers of human experience—beyond their proper use). Specific attention then ought to be paid to how bare perspectivalism is transformed by Bulgakov into personalism from out of the structure of the trihypostatic (divine) person upon whom we are modeled. This is because the triadic logic of intrinsically perspectival created being inherited from the *imago Dei* secures the centrality of phenomenality, internality, and affectivity as conditions for a kenotically secured fullness of manifestation, since there is nothing in the Father that is not revealed in the Son.[70] The "excess" (though God remains strictly above the finite predications of "excess" and "lack") of each over the other is the love as attestation of the Father through the Son, and the glory of the Father that both the Son and the Spirit express. Now, precisely because an antinomic root of trihypostaticity satisfies the quest for a stable form of "existential" conceptuality that resists both the hysteria of perpetual deconstruction *and* naked aprioristic conceptual fideism, there is hope here to inaugurate the possibility of refiguring the nature of metaphysics and speculation in a genuinely radical way. This is of great philosophical consequence, and we shall return to this further below.

When Bulgakov utilizes the nature of consciousness to interpret the structure of the everyday in a metacritical fashion to derive the latent supervising intelligibility of the everyday from the form of consciousness as such, he maintains the symmetry of concept and intuition by finding in actuality the common root of both theory and practice. As such, Bulgakov supplants the theoretical deflations of practice that the positivistic suspicion of modernity and postmodernity perpetuates.[71] This "existential" priority of a Christian life of faith, virtue, devotion, charity, and love extends over the ostensible theoretical necessity for a pre-spiritual categorial medium of bare thought, since trihypostaticity is, as we have seen, in both form and content an articulation of a singular, "master" transcendentality of *action*—beyond both the sheer presence of conceptual arraignment *and* the absence in the rupturing negativity parasitic on the failure of metaphysical "presence." The

---

70. Bulgakov, *Comforter*, 381.
71. Louth, "Sergii Bulgakov."

possibility of the idea of the Good, for the kingdom of God to be prefigured in the church, and for virtue and ethical life hang on this crucial reversal.[72]

Sophiology allows Bulgakov to avoid an ungrounded transcendentality for finite being, which would initiate a cascade of pseudo-problems that issue from a formal-conceptual scission between Creator and creation, and thus an autonomous determining logic for nature. Since phenomenal resonance between subject and object is taken seriously here as a discursive modification to the conditions for speculation by allowing the intuitive to graft the beginning of the speculative onto the everyday, we have followed Henri Bergson here in maintaining that any serious beginning of the problem of metaphysics realizes that it is already among the "inside" of things rather than entering via an epistemological "asymptotics," which extrinsically circles around them by assuming pure critical delineations in epistemological garb and misrecognizes them—and itself in them—because of its own urge to cerebrally *reconstruct* its own spirit.[73] Our subjectivity can be thought now not as surd impossibility of caustic remainders locked in frames and tranches of antagonistic difference where a native torsion lurks menacingly to subvert any self-assertion for finitude other than its own nihilation. Rather, subjectivity remains harmonious in its preconceptual "everydayness" with the task and aim of the speculation, and homogeneous in its "natural attitude" with conceptuality both metaphysical and ordinary. The reverse is also true: contemplation is properly a spiritual ascent, and the apocalyptic becoming of the world is my own sanctification and restoration to the fate of the divine purity of created Sophia, which shall meet us in the end.

Now, since both dogma and speculation may be sundered from one another in sheerly positive religiosity and professional philosophy, we must conclude that differentiation between doctrine and metaphysical structure must of course be possible. However, one must decline to render this an *epistemological* division rather than a metaphysical-structural question of the place of each element in a distinct theo-logic of combination.[74] A discursive transcendentality that is necessarily triadic and temporal means that for Bulgakov no necessary moments of a-hypostatic, impersonal, and self-identical thinking can be assumed, neither as mere "beginning" unimplicated in speculative materials prepared from religion, nor as the final consummate realm of philosophy. It may then be said that metaphysics now more truly

---

72. The point has been made that the similar priority of triadicity, albeit with a narrower, more logicistic focus, was outlined by the semiotician American C. S. Peirce, and this in fact bypasses the susceptibility to post-structuralist deconstructions as were performed on binaristic Saussurian semiology. See Barnouw, "Peirce and Derrida."

73. Bergson, *Introduction to Metaphysics*.

74. We shall attend to this in detail below.

begins *in media res*, for it combines (in the Platonic manner of the circularity of soul and city) the collective history and community of metaphysicians and their achievement with the soul-making of each comprehending theologian, who must undertake the self-sacrificial task of Christian life to join them and advance their work. Indeed, it is more accurate to recognize this as a moment of refusing presuppositionlessness itself in favor of acknowledging one's presuppositions with the open challenge of virtual simulation in rival idioms with no prior formal-methodological precedent for this negotiation; it is in this regard that the Trinity holds open a supreme metaphysics, as we shall see in the final section. In this way, the speculative unity of dogma and theoretical structure are contained in the common root of theory and practice as the "anthropological" transcendentality of our discursivity; these are outlined explicitly in the practice of Christian life, and so become the site for the dogmas of the faith to demonstrate both their existential actuality and philosophical potency. After this turn of the mind, or metanoia, the theoretical work of seeking understanding becomes not merely plausible but utterly compelling.

We must further note that the various debates on post-critical differential ontology—in Gilles Deleuze, Alain Badiou, and the speculative realists—may convincingly be recollected alongside and within the realms of (1) art and religion, and (2) mathematics (one thinks of David Hilbert's *Anschauliche Geometrie*).[75] Since these are all exercises in figurative, topographical, and doxographic access, whose substance is grounded in sense and imagination, then the speculative organization and liturgical and "existential" truth in Christian doctrine may be read to eminently provide a stable philosophical conceptuality irreducible to mere method and essentially establishing the subject matter of metaphysical transcendentality in the "human" realm of representation. Throughout, then, one detects here an important opening of permitting intuitional dimensions for philosophical argument, since the elaboration of trinitarity as above—that is, not as the complex of the philosophical idiom of eminent unicity and its derivative conceptuality—invokes no purely positive content to secure its ontological image besides the figure of trihypostaticity and its own ensuing logic as shored up by other doctrinal formulations (see note below), which are in

---

75. Étienne Souriau even reads Spinoza this way. See Souriau, *Different Modes of Existence*; Hilbert and Cohn-Vossen, *Geometry and the Imagination*. One wonders if Alain Badiou would have insisted on such a break from the "poetics" of Heidegger to the mathematical-scientific orientation of his Cantorian ontology given this clear subsumption of the latter into the former in the process of excising transcendental cognition. For a good discussion of this issue, see Milbank, "Materialism and Transcendence."

retrospect now seen to coincide with and perfect the intimations of philosophical search.[76]

Now, we will return to the issue of discursive transcendentality implicit here, in the continuing pursuit of a truth of spirit that theology alone proclaims. Following a desiring dimension to truth that Augustine and Nietzsche both stress, in detaching questioning and its equipment from the ontological order in which its own telic form-content unity is initiated in a *desire* for the truth, which might be honestly admitted to oneself, transcendental cognition appears to be nothing other than a particularly degenerate spiritual wish for the compartmentalization of worshipfulness and ethical demand *away* from the theoretical sanctum.

Hence, we ought to note last that philosophy itself has come to admit a crucial reformulation of the image of determination as such, exchanging the notion that it is the fulfillment of a synthetic schema commissioned under conceptual issue to recognizing in it an abyssal "poetic" subterranean constitution of the real that is singularly exemplified in phenomenality and cognition, standing under the regulation of myth, figure, fiction, and *typos*. Just as, for instance, Maurice Blanchot elaborates on finite transcendentality through the mathematical figure of Riemann surfaces in *The Infinite Conversation*, we ought not to be ashamed to advance the very same in theology's own figural transformations of philosophical structure according to the Trinity.[77] It appears then that the supervision of Christian doctrine eminently points to stable conceptuality—in offering both speculative organization and liturgical "existential" truth—by retrieving philosophical transcendentality in the realm of representation itself. Elaborating further, doctrinal formulations such as Trinity or Christology (below) are here given no unwarranted weight than the function that, say, the figures of Narcissus, Echo, or Oedipus hold for Nietzsche, Klossowski, and Philippe Lacoue-Labarthe.[78]

We might then deploy Thomas's idea of the cognition of the real distinction between essence and existence and metaphysical necessity as a synthetic unity of content in excess of the transcendental imaginative motion under Kantian conceptual circumscription and logical formulation.[79] However, figural transcendentality requires that the entire round of hermeneutic circularity is reformed, and this is uniquely theological, as

76. See Milbank, "Genealogies of Truth."
77. "Interruption," in Blanchot, *Infinite Conversation*, 75–79.
78. Lacoue-Labarthe, *Typography*; Klossowski, *Nietzsche and the Vicious Circle*; Obrigewitsch, "Between Narcissus and Echo."
79. See Pickstock, "Duns Scotus," 545.

the opening sections demonstrated. A recent attempt by Gabriel Catren in his *Pleromatica* to specify a "re-ligative" unifying principle of "finite infinitude" upon which post-critical philosophy might be built revolves around what he terms the "phenoumenal" unity we exemplify as conduits for the manifestation for the infinite.[80] Here, despite isolating the twin series of our phenomenal disorientation 'in between cosmic and quantum scales (and indeed our own most complex 'lateral' economies such as semiconductor engineering and global supply chain logistics') and the fate of theory into general axiomatic liquefaction, Catren ultimately fails to find and elaborate on a stable principle for their *intuitive* interconnection, since our Dasein requires an ultimately figurative transcendentality of spirit and incarnation; we shall see that trinitarity alone can provide a metacritical discursive transcendentality. However, this cannot be justified on the purely philosophical terms to which he clings, and Catren must recourse to a reformed Spinozist scheme.[81] It is exactly in this way that the dogmatically outlined "inside" of the Christian religion provides its own reading of philosophical un-ground, having not just offered a conceptual elaboration of this Trinitarian schema in a novel and powerful philosophical idiom, but admitted alongside it a constitutive metaphysical and intellectual-methodological dimension of figures (such as that of porous, co-creative finitude) as *basic* cognitive and ontological transcendentalities.

The completion of this argument relies on the final section, which shall provide an elaboration of the truth of spirit that Trinitarian theology, after our reading of Bulgakov, intimates.

Metacritical Theodicy as a Clue to General Metaphysical Structure

In the foregoing sections, it has been shown that the dimensions of speculative argumentation that flow from Bulgakov's "topographical" and figurative elaboration of Trinity and Sophiology turn out after all to coincide with an incumbent philosophical correction of the asymmetric concept-intuition relation in speculative transcendentality as such—whether in ontology, phenomenology, linguisticality, and so on. (This is in great contrast to the deadlock of late Scholastic Trinitarian paralogisms.)[82] If is the case, then,

---

80. Catren, *Pleromatica*, 29, 53.

81. Catren, *Pleromatica*, 22.

82. See, for example, Duns Scotus, *Ordinatio* 1, d. 2, p. 2, qq. 1–4; *Ordinatio*, d. 2, qq. 6, 11, in William of Ockham, *Opera Theologiae*, 2:175, 368–69. My special thanks to Professor Richard Cross for his presentation on Trinitarian paralogisms at the "Contradictory Theology and Its History" workshop in Edinburgh, Sept. 2023.

in turn, at the level of a methodological presupposition (which all philosophy, as self-articulation, carries), only Trinitarian metaphysics goes on to resist the dissolution of the real from impotence of finite thought from the superlative vantage of an "Absolute" metaphysics. In this section, it still remains to be shown that only the metaphysical structure of an originally triune Absolute, which *of itself* implies a self-declension into an incarnational reality, can uphold for phenomenal form and content a critically irreducible propriety—at the level of both determination and reflection—in the manner that philosophy hopes for in its repudiation of empty concepts and blind intuition. This final moment of this section will argue that this new "post-structuralism" comes to present the core of Christian orthodoxy and its gospel under Christ by intimating the meaning of theory and philosophy in salvation history. The system-plan for this is as follows:

The basis of this, as adverted to in the previous section, is that transcendentality of the phenomenal—now co-poetic rather than merely representational, as evinced from the side of the finite in the experience of living itself as a creative art. In secular philosophy, finitude is forced to be in the first and last place a function of the fundamentally cryptic and alienating convulsions of noumenality unto itself. The effect here is that the image of man in transcendental cognition elevates as the primal forms of thought rational relations that circumscribe the various elements of the phenomenal frame but refrain from affording these a propriety that intuitive grounding for the human *in its humanity* might supply (a strange theological anthropology, of sorts, is thus given in Heidegger). As such, it is responsible for an ambiguous *reversibility* between infinite and finite identical with nothing other than the purely intellectual substrate (like Avicennian "formalities") in which transcendentality consists. Yet, if concept cannot anchor to anything at the level of our intuition, this invariably dissolves the finite and its thought as an aberration in the inscrutable and utterly sublime motion of the infinite.

The consequence of this latter possibility underlies much of the critical residuum of "postmodern" philosophy of the latter half of the twentieth century. We shall also see below how a more supreme image of *metacritical* post-structural reality is essential to self-recognition in the Christian truth of human spirit. To complete this argument, we have to briefly retrace the origins of "postmodern" image of absolute interruption and uncover this as a surreptitious theological supposition of the ontologically interruptive Absolute.

La discursivité desoeuvrée?
Hermeneutic Circularity in and After Heidegger[83]

Though one thinks of Lucretius, after Deleuze, the subsumption of transcendentality into an ontological image in its clearest modern transformation of hermeneutic circularity into metaphysical transcendentality began when the young Schelling offered against J. G. Fichte robustly metacritical argumentation.[84] If the constitutive noetic syntheses inscribing both the phenomenal aperture and objects of experience are not themselves first supremely and securely knowable from the vantage of transcendental reflection as merely subjective a priori determining positing conditions—since object and subject are united in the activity of conditioning as such—one has thereby invalidated the critical round delineating finitude for itself.[85] Moreover, if the concepts of finitude's reflection are themselves functions of transcendentality of determining activity, Schellingian nature as *Urgrund* (and, later, the Hegelian Concept) is the first inception of a transcendental vantage that supervises the nature of difference and phenomenality that characterize much of late nineteenth- and twentieth-century philosophy, as Andrew Bowie has also argued.[86]

This second, more fundamental consequence of this move in the German idealist case involves the thesis on reflection, since it follows that any constructive power of an "Absolute" vantage of the phenomenal itself is inaugurated on the impossibility of immediate reflective access as such. (Many have therefore remarked that Schelling appears to escape the charge of onto-theological metaphysics.)[87] Consequently, if determination threatens to becomes inaccessible to finite reflection in such a much more extreme manner, the single "ontological" determining transcendental here bypasses any automatic reversion to the supposition of a Kantian noumenal residuum beyond legitimate reflective capacity, since reflection may not now peer into negative limits for the unconditioned Absolute. Presence and absence are then originally and intrinsically united and implied when the mythos of co-creative poetics stably "realizes" through this hypostasis of the infinite and finite. However, this is not the avenue that has been taken in twentieth-century philosophy. This particular rendering of the metaphysical

---

83. For *désouvrement* (unworking), see Blanchot, *Space of Literature*.

84. See the rereading of *De Rerum Natura* in "Lucretius and the Simulacrum," in Deleuze, *Logic of Sense*, 266–79.

85. Schelling, "Presentation of My System."

86. Bowie, *Schelling*.

87. See, for example, Tritten, *Beyond Presence*.

transcendentality quite readily transforms into the various images of "postmodernity," which may be united under a common conception of the transcendental regulation of difference, where theology may crucially intervene.

In this respect, Heidegger arguably ought to be read as a much tamer (albeit still pagan) and unstable figure, since, despite the fact that for him the mediation of all hermeneutic circularity is a master transcendentality, its inadequacy in the "abandonment" of human phenomenal dwelling at the break of our ontotheological wandering merely reflects the unresolved epochal anticipation of a future belonging-together of Dasein and Beyng, refusing (whereas Plato affirms) to make the question of *dianoia* and *noesis* the very center of philosophy. This "incompleteness" of thought in its separation from Beyng is then not identified with the negativity latent in mytholinguistic inscription of drive-conflict (as might be said for Nietzsche)[88] but would somehow override it in an altogether arbitrarily noncognitive fashion—supposedly *without* rupturing hermeneutic circularity from without.[89] Hence, language may name this relation with Beyng held beyond all supposedly "ontological" images of Western metaphysics, yet in holding discursive transcendentality apart from an isomorphy with its governing ontology, Heidegger fails to do justice to discursivity (and thus to the dimension of metaphysical transcendentality, as above) by declining to identify just *how* it is that language nevertheless might go on to respond to that which it is only incidentally but firmly separated from. All that is left is to point out the circumstances of occlusion as the result of certain times, languages, and cultures; this directly feeds the cultural and linguistic chauvinism in Heidegger that later becomes uglier. As Jacques Derrida notes, Heidegger continues to pivot his later developments about a self-recognition bound to his focus on grounding, dwelling, and building (a theopraxis of sorts, we might say)—all of which fall back upon a fundamental posture for Dasein,[90] albeit now bound to languages (and not language as such) and peoples, and thus to

---

88. See Kofman, *Nietzsche and Metaphor*.

89. I'd like to thank Professor Catherine Pickstock for a helpful discussion on this point. See also Heidegger, *Contributions to Philosophy* 5.198: "Beyng needs humans in order to occur essentially, and humans belong to beyng so that they might fulfill their ultimate destining as Da-sein. . . . This *oscillation of needing and belonging* constitutes beyng as event, and our thinking is in the first place obliged to raise the movement of this oscillation into the simplicity of knowledge and to ground it in its truth" (emphasis in original). Heidegger's thought as such is demonstrably fraught with irreconcilable tension, but it achieves, in this refusal to submit to merely philosophical reductions of the paradoxical suspension of Beyng and Da-sein, an admirable prescience of what will be united in Trinitarian metaphysics.

90. Heidegger, *Bremen and Freiburg Lectures*, 17, 46.

soil and to the homeland and the *Volksgeist*.⁹¹ Hence, despite the existentials being together suspended upon the belonging together of Dasein and the granting of Being, the corruptive scission to the cooperation of clearing in modernity and conceptual-metaphysical thinking does not name for Heidegger an absolute *statu lapsus* in the face of which there is either only voiding frustration of in-breaking noumenality to be affirmed or a speculative refiguration, through which one may come to recognize oneself as already redeemed through the Christian gospel (see below); rather, our existential diremption from Beyng appears to be a temporary historical embarrassment of the infinite-finite relation whose overcoming we can and must only expect but never prefigure.⁹²

In the wake of Heidegger (whose nihilism is thus generally overstated), it is in fact Maurice Blanchot, who, even beyond Nietzsche, more singularly and ruthlessly identifies in a single transcendental the abyssal nature of linguisticality and thus the truth of human discursivity with an ontological account. Whereas for Nietzsche, philosophizing retains some measure of mythical-narratival intrigue and fictional dress, Blanchot is the real father of post-structuralist transcendentality.⁹³ What emerges as a result warrants close discussion.

In the first place, Blanchot avoids the prevarication between the ontological and epistemological endemic in the vantage of an "infinite finitude" (as Philippe Lacoue-Labarthe argues against Derrida and Jean-Luc Nancy; see below), where finitude is locked into an endless cascade of frustration for its thought.⁹⁴ Rather, the basis of post-structuralist thought can be properly shown to have been an ontological thesis all along, as it was for Schelling. An austerely "philosophical" creation myth is developed here precisely by following out the reversibility of the infinite-finite relation. Instead of the interstitial "deferral" of philosophical truth—which arguably half clings to the stability of concept (and finitude) in outlining a merely reactive incursion of latent negativity—"unworking" as such begins in Blanchot's work as an apocalyptic relation reconceiving phenomenality as "finite infinitude," where the transcendental is reversed and the finite becomes totally subordinate and a mere effluence of the activity of *self-transcendentalizing* noumenality.⁹⁵

91. Derrida, *Of Spirit*. See also Derrida, *Geschlecht III*; "Heidegger's Affair," in Lacoue-Labarthe, *Heidegger, Art and Politics*, 9–16.

92. See also Heidegger, "Provenance of Art."

93. Crucially, see Blanchot, *Work of Fire*, 287–99.

94. Derrida, "Discussion."

95. "The Narrative Voice (the 'He,' the Neutral)," in Blanchot, *Infinite Conversation*, 379–87.

For Blanchot, "creation" leaves no record and no trace; the world pours out of void in disaster and is scarcely itself before void reclaims it for oblivion, even as it appears illusorily to subsist in its finitude. The unnameable transcendent neither is nor is-not: "Nothing is what there is, *and first of all* nothing beyond."[96] It must be pointed out that this is nothing other than good philosophical consistency applied to the impossibility of reflection as such, since it can act only as an improper and ever-underserving claim on noumenal (non-)self (non-)giving.[97] The creating and "unworking" of affliction and affective incursion are read as the very interruptive flares of in-breaking void moving for an inverted enhypostatic *smothering* of that which never was and belonged to no one, since it could not assert itself and was disavowed at its birth. Yet void *alone* is truly "im-proper" to itself, a formulation once again both forcing and refusing the power of finite reflection to identify the noumenal even with itself (whereas Heidegger had dared to call it "the Same").[98]

Hence Philippe Lacoue-Labarthe writes that this "neutral" transcendence is thus a "condition for the impossibility" of all phenomenal satisfaction, since this impossibility scatters and interrupts all concept; nevertheless, concept and the simultaneous hope for a just response *without* concept is the only response that can and must be offered (as ethicized by Levinas).[99] In Blanchot, against the vitalist gloss of Deleuze (although the latter's work is made consistent by Nick Land by returning to Blanchot's metaphysics by way of Georges Bataille),[100] this unnameable neutrality arrives inexplicably into its finitude as an absolutely alienating force, rendering our own deaths as always to arrive, and at once leaving all internality as already-dead fragmentation.[101]

---

96. Blanchot, *Writing of the Disaster*, 72; emphasis added.

97. "The Great Refusal," in Blanchot, *Infinite Conversation*, 33–48.

98. "Affirmation (Desire, Affliction)," in Blanchot, *Infinite Conversation*, 106–22. For unworking, or *désouvrement*, see Blanchot, *Space of Literature*; Heidegger, *Identity and Difference*. See also Heidegger, *Contributions to Philosophy* 2.52–62. Misrecognized desire for deterritorialized transgression can itself be virtually simulated even in an ostensibly theological mode, as is shown by Apostolacus, "Althaus-Reid's Deleuzian Theology."

99. Lacoue-Labarthe, *Ending and Unending Agony*, 79; Blanchot, *Infinite Conversation*, 202–9; Obrigewitsch, "How Is Translation Possible?" See also the discussion in Milbank, *Word Made Strange*, 178.

100. See "Fanged Noumenon (Passion of the Cyclone)," in Land, *Thirst for Annihilation*, 74–85.

101. Blanchot, *Space of Literature*, 86; L. Hill, *Maurice Blanchot*, 279.

Now, it can be argued that the foregoing was always fated in some variation to be the conclusion when critical reductions of the human are presupposed at the level of method, since it is the outworking of an image of self-recognition that values, in the face of the infinite, *nothing* of itself to begin with. Here, only the "symmetrical" recollective vigilance of concept and intuition can forestall such a conclusion, for only an incorporated "intuitive" can jam the reversibility of rational relations that are installed in the ultimate imbalance of an "Absolute" transcendental metaphysics. This is where the anti-psychologism dominant in analytic philosophy sits very well with thinkers who follow "finite infinitude" post Blanchot, since the "existentials" of hermeneutic circularity in Heidegger are simply surrendered away into the processes of self-determining infinity. Arguably, for Heidegger, to understand the "existential" as *logical* remained an achievement that pulled *away* from the paradigm under Kant, even if Heidegger perhaps imputed back into Kant himself certain affinities with this departure.[102] (This has not arisen as an issue for modern secular "post-Kantian" idealist philosophy bred through early modern German rationalist thought, of course, for it stands buried firmly on Scotist soil.) The sheer impossibility of any discursive transcendental, of which reflection is a function, arises here, and we shall attend to this below. It might be seen now just how close Trinitarian metaphysics of creation and spirit, particularly from Sergii Bulgakov, is to the conclusions of philosophy, if a halfway "neutral" structure may be provisionally drawn between them in the form of "in-breaking, self-transcendentalizing noumenality." This, I contend, is the minimal formal structure of metaphysical transcendentality as such; we shall now operate upon it in its Christian meaning to yield a thoroughly and uniquely theological account.

The Feast of Thought: Apocalypse and Metaxology

The "apocalyptic" has been a relation long overdue to be uncovered; often abandoned for representing an ultimate paradox that institutes the suspension of all reason, it has nevertheless been prefigured as a master transcendental in much of the best and most central philosophical discussion. For instance, as the early and late Merleau-Ponty came to agree, a twin "aspectual" justification of both mechanism and vitalism is necessary (even though the former is just a little less real, for it cannot ground itself; this will become important further on), and this asks of philosophy a wholly new category of combination.[103] Again, as Catherine Pickstock argues, Deleuzian virtuality

---

102. For instance, see Heidegger, *Kant and the Problem*, 119.

103. Difrisco, "Merleau-Ponty's Ontology of Life." Compare Merleau-Ponty's *Structure of Behavior*, 224, with his later *Visible and Invisible*, 200.

rests on a reversal of the prior Bergsonian mistake of not allowing a *metaphysical* status, in the face of creative determination as ecstatic continuity, to the reality of divisible space, time and measure beyond a merely secondary stultification of *élan vital*.[104] It is important here that the inability to provide a symmetry of concept and intuition in the structure of "transcendental time" quickly becomes an improbable and uncompelling philosophical hermeneutic of temporality, since it links the apocalyptic to a disclosure of the pragmatic. It is true that what is—the All and us in it—must already *have been* and forever *shall be* (and both of these all at once), yet it does not call for finitude to dissolve into the "zero-point" of noumenal churning.[105] As we have seen in the case of Blanchot, however, its original transcendentality lies in the (disallowed) ontological relationship between the infinite and the *life* of the finite.

Two explanatory points pertain here. The first concerns Bulgakov's elaboration of the Christian meaning of the apocalyptic in the antinomy between the divine and creaturely Sophia as the truth of participation in the triune life of God. Since, unlike Kant, Bulgakov does not posit any securely held finite apriority as the content of the conditioning schemas identical with transcendental subjectivity as such, the necessity of opposing judgments of the *coincidentia*[106] of unity and triadicity expresses the structural character of created reality as such—not a reassertion of the priority of the theoretical in a contradiction which must be maintained at the level of finite judgment, that, under the (regulative) direction of reason, abortively seeks the impossible unconditioned.[107] Hence, the necessity of opposing judgments is not drawn primarily from an epistemological preoccupation with the regulative limits of the faculties of reason, though this theme will recur for us further on below. Hence, second, when Bulgakov elaborates the Christian meaning of the *apocalyptic* in the antinomy between the lateral cut of the divine Being into the "divine" and "creaturely" Sophia, we shall reinterpret these below as the truth of our present participation in the triune life of God. Bulgakov positions the All of infinity versus the relative independence of finitude—or, what is the same thing, the All in All that God shall be versus the theosis of the finite in glorified bodily resurrection—as an antinomy. Yet, the antinomic is nothing other than apocalyptic transcendentality as it appears at the aperture of finite judgment. Herein we find the truth of participation in the triune life of God that is apocalyptic in

104. Pickstock, *Repetition and Identity*, 53.

105. See "Machinic Desire," in Land, *Fanged Noumena*.

106. Gallaher, "Antinomism, Trinity."

107. Kant, *Critique of Pure Reason*, A308/B364; Bulgakov, *Tragedy of Philosophy*, 159–70.

nature.¹⁰⁸ Accordingly, collapsing both pairs (since God must be All in All from eternity), the paradox of apocalyptic transcendentality for Bulgakov is fundamental cosmic motion through and in which the birth of the new, redeemed world (the divine Sophia) in and through the old (its present creaturely form) occurs.¹⁰⁹ Metacritical antinomy at the foundation of thought reflects nothing other than the Christian reading of the fundamental cosmic motion of grace as Pauline "apocalyptics" of the in-breaking kingdom of heaven—prefigured, present, and yet to come. Here, the Christian truth of spirit reasserts itself in justification of the "human scale" of enfleshed reality to be deified and resurrected. For, if the Absolute is beyond infinite and finite, as Pseudo-Dionysius argues, then God is not at his innermost in a divine emptiness that stands at the indeterminate and rarefied peripheries of his energies but in the man Jesus—and apocalyptically in *us*, since our task is to match Christ's example in liturgical dwelling in and for the expectation of our own divine humanity.¹¹⁰ It is crucial to reiterate here that the Trinitarian persons are not even noumenality for us: a philosophical exposition of fundamental apocalyptic cosmic motion ends with the "tetrahedral" circulation of cosmotheandric perichoretics, where only through the divine ousia in sophiological incorporation does the Trinity "really" operate as self-transcendentalizing noumenality.¹¹¹ Furthermore, an apocalyptic image of "finite infinitude" is theoretically undergirded by and carries an alternative, metacritical, post-structuralist transcendentality, which may grant us the recognition that God abides in us; yet, philosophy fatefully ignores this, prefers instead the draw of trans- and post-humanist implications of the self-finitizing of unnameable noumenality.

The momentous work of William Desmond may be invoked here to bring this issue of the basis of Christian metaphysics and the notion of self-recognition into sharp relief. Like Erich Przywara and Milbank, Desmond's work consists of an intricate "interstitial" motion between systems, epochs, and disciplines. Its unique vantage serves as a meditation on the nature of metaphysics, and it gives us opportunity to uncover some of the very highest determining logic for philosophical transcendentalities.

The central theme of Desmond's work is "the metaxological." What follows is a brief reconstruction of the *ordo disciplinae* of his work. Desmond first analyzes methodological and discursive base of metaphysics into three

---

108. "The Foundational Antinomy of the Christian Philosophy of History" and "On the Kingdom of God," in Bulgakov, *Sophiology of Death*, 1–28.

109. Bulgakov: *Lamb of God*, 329; *Philosophy of the Name*, 148.

110. Milbank, "Sophia and Theurgy," 72.

111. Bulgakov, *Wisdom of God*, 23–53.

distinct, basic registers. These are the univocal (commensuration, typically united in the various historical iterations of the Scotist conceptuality), the equivocal (endless otherness gestured at by both differential ontology and human hermeneutic entanglement), and the dialectical (the mediation between univocity and the scissiparous equivocal held under the combinatorial logic of contradiction and resolution). However, Desmond realizes that a fourth, the metaxological—modeled on the *metaxu*, the between or interstice—is required, since none of the previous three by themselves satisfy in describing what the singularly human experience of philosophizing, thinking mathematically or poetically *is*. It is true enough that the mathematical, for instance, harbors a pretension to completeness, or at least the status of a fundamental discipline; yet in its *practice* involves a "poetic finesse" that is often relegated to either a sentimental "aesthetics" external to its content or a more extrinsic question of mere style. In contrast, it is the practice of metaphysics that, for Desmond, is the consummate form of this unifying "master" reflection, since it operates as the meta-suppositional ground of method for thought itself. For Desmond's *metaxu*, thought's hermeneutic of analogical being is agapeic figuration: astonishment exploding self-certain method anew.

Hence, while initially this may present in its comparative aspect as a thesis on discursive transcendentality and no more, I shall argue that we may analyze Desmond's metaxological intersignification of philosophical modes into two further speculative transcendentalities, the metacritical and the apocalyptic; each has two emphases in the existential and the structural; all four are all imbricated in a round.

First, it is crucial to realize the irresolvable simultaneity of "metaxological intersignification" of metaphysical thought comes as the product of cumulative corrections toward symmetry across the four senses of being. We might see then that the metaxological achieves nothing other than a symmetrical relation of concept and intuition at the identical transcendental level of methodology, discursivity.[112] Why is this correction necessary? These are neither philosophically parsimonious resolutions that might resolve in the direction of hierarchized emergence nor overt critical delineation. However, this "jamming" function of increasingly incorporated intuition for conceptuality as such bears much in common with Aristotle's insistence, for instance, that sensibility bears decisively on the invalidity of any abstraction from categorially instantiated real being to a univocal metaphysical concept (the latter is, of course, precisely what transcendental

---

112. Desmond, *Being and the Between*.

cognition permits).[113] The metaxological returns methodological meditation into the transcendentality of spiritual practice.

Second, symmetry helps us not succumb to transcendental cognition, since here we begin to withhold from the possibility that the ultimacy of thinking can shed its humanity and existential ground—even as there can be no self-ground for the existential and spiritual. We can see now that this is not just anti-foundational simply because it occupies a classificatory, "comparative" remove from philosophy; rather, the anti-foundational transcendentality is unique here precisely because its progressive nature does not dismiss either form or the "closed" nature of formal systems, which are shown to naively insist on ideologically converting their pragmatic unity into a univocal identification with formality as such.

Together, we have a methodological meditation that assumes and reinforces a hermeneutic of Christian pneumatic reality. Desmond writes,

> Metaphysical mind is posthumous in trying to think the worth of being, beyond our present immersion in the process of having lived. The speculative imagination is this: one thinks of oneself, having died, as come back to life, as if from beyond death; one is resurrected to the "once," from beyond one's passage into and through the "never."[114]

As a hermeneutic of mindfulness (recall Heidegger), "metaphysical mind" then aims at a "consubstantial" suspension of each basic mode from monopolizing an evaluative position that might obscure a hunger for searching held together in its genius, virtuosity, and scope. The metaxological crucially holds ajar from the narrow, "idiotic" focus of any single mode of thinking being the essential human possibility of reflecting and pondering on the fact of being endlessly dazzled and perplexed anew.[115] Note that Desmond's strategy here is again to boldly unite disparate (though not necessarily internally fragmentary—we shall address this later) discourses under a *pragmatic* transcendentality, which constitutes their originary form and from which they borrow their coherence: thought is *human* thinking, and the whole of the human at that. The beatitude and spiritual nature of metaphysical thinking is then applied to the problems of philosophy and the objects of its concern. Metaphysics, then, for Desmond is apocalyptic as an experiential moment of recurring wonder and questioning in which we

---

113. Duns Scotus, *Ordinatio* 1, d. 3, q. 2, n26.
114. Desmond, *Being and the Between*, 36.
115. Desmond, *Being and the Between*, 415; Desmond, *Perplexity and Ultimacy*.

articulate and are actualized. This reveals the nature of concept and intuition metacritically in its structural aspect.

The crucial height of Desmond's work, however, comes in the insight linking metaxology to the apocalyptic declension of the plenitude of Being into various modes of structural coherence, consummating the image of discursivity in a way that Plato himself may plausibly be argued to have intended with his "divided line" in the *Republic*.[116] This is nothing other than an elaboration of discursivity as returning to an original noetic creation.

Desmond argues that the *experience* of metaphysics with a completeness of reason is derived from and implies the meaning of metaphysics as a spiritual practice: "One has to do the thinking: not sing invocations to possibility, but work to bring forth the realization of the promise."[117] This promise breaks in like Pauline apocalypse, and creates concept to simultaneously clarify and "structurate" intuition from the outset. Elsewhere, Desmond writes of the postural intonations in metaphysical thinking of the erotic and agapeic:

> Eros articulates the self, and if we grant Socrates' account [in *Symposium*], eros initially lacks what it seeks. But the restlessness of eros in the middle cannot stop short at any finite entity or concern; ultimately it is a restlessness for the ultimate. The pursuit of the ultimate itself testifies to a positive power of being in the self; it cannot be mere lack that drives desire beyond lack; it is the original power of being that constitutes the self as openness to what is other to itself; the dunamis of eros reveals a self-transcending openness to transcendence as other to desire itself.[118]

The clue to the metacritical then is in its apocalyptic *structural* basis. Desmond argues that if our "erotic" recollection of the four modes of being is properly a *spiritual* exercise that must avoid lapsing into the myopia of uncomplemented concept or intuition, this is because finite discourse is first dependent an originary "agapeic" *constructive* donation of the infinite of variously intelligible being. The recognition of pragmatic unities of content and form do not immediately bring us to a transcendental meaning for formality *as such*. Desmond's answer is that this transcendentality is apocalyptic in nature, drawing together ontological and discursive motion. How does the apocalyptic appear in discursivity? It is metacritical. This rehearses anew the fundamental philosophical problem with which Plato was chiefly

---

116. Desmond, *Voiding of Being*, 27.
117. Desmond, *Being and the Between*, 310–11.
118. Desmond, *Being and the Between*, 315.

concerned, of establishing the *Transzensus* of the spiritual-noetic with the material-phenomenal in the face of the looming danger that the dianoetic retrenchments of dialectical speech come entirely unfastened from the Good (which is mediated through sense, ritual, and myth) and erect their own sophistic hermeneutic internality in and for the dead witness of pure writing.[119] This is a pivotal "enfleshment" of the noetic into the dianoetic and discursive analyses of motion, pure mathematics, semiology, phenomenology, historicism, criticism, narratology, etc.—for their own sake. We shall see below in Radical Orthodoxy how this is more explicitly drawn out. For now, Desmond metacritically refuses any straightforwardly "reversible" transcendental supervision of the self-revelation of plenitudinous noumenality into its phenomenal declension by securing the propriety of the human scale (with a discontinuity of reflection and measure coexistent with the sublimity of intuition and action) at the methodological level. Indeed, the spiritual experience of encountering variously pure (relative) formality in art and music, for instance, is testament to the notion that, though form may come apart as sheer ideality, structure as such does not obtain but is nothing without "noumenal" energetic procession of plenitude into ontological and phenomenal reception, even as energy is nothing other than its being structurally manifest in metaxological entanglement and thus metacritically wedded to and incarnate in a "structural" theophanic expression.

This Christian rethinking of "Absolute metaphysics" brings us now to the *incarnational* constitution of the noetic in and for the vessel of the dianoetic (which now has no claim to ultimate autonomy), of grace in nature, spirit in matter, and—recalling the late Geoffrey Hill's writing on poetry and criticism—of speech *and* writing, in and through each other.[120] Yet, the ground of this entire movement is an existential event and has no center for its phenomenality. Here, the structural relations are instituted in and through the motion of spirit, which masters them in its "hylomorphic" pragmatic motion (and not necessarily self-consciously, as in the case of grammar and natural language). We will now further elaborate on the link of discursive, metacritical, apocalyptic transcendentalities with Trinity and the meaning of metaphysical transcendentality as such.

We may now virtually simulate the self-defeating *mise en abyme* typical of post-structuralism. Symmetrical elaboration of the existential without a methodological foreclosure on the natural attitude as transcendental illusion (even if not identified with conceptuality as such) culminates in an image of systematicity identical with creaturely human spirit, since

119. Pickstock, *After Writing*, 3–46.
120. G. Hill, "Poetry as Menace and Atonement."

pragmatic absorbment is continuous with the substance of speculative transcendentalities—homogeneous at the level of cognition, even if rarefied. If this is not the case, then everyday speech is still affirmed as continuous with philosophizing medium, except now the content of regulative transcendentalities themselves are put into question by the formal dynamics. The result is an impossibly unstable structure, which nevertheless achieves the effect of making itself appear all the more hallowed since it presents the impossible figural transcendentality of impossibility, which only declines into various paradoxical images (as in Blanchot's astonishing novel *Thomas the Obscure*) but remains in excess of even these. In the next section, we shall argue that a higher vantage on this dynamic might be recollected as the arbitrary presupposition of metaphysical ultimacy as suspended dyadics, and we shall continue to simulate the structure at a further "purity" of figural transcendentality as such by invoking the Trinity. For now, it suffices to say that if what is existentially united cannot be critically unconnected with structural images that we postulate to philosophically situate the pragmatic (and beyond), then a unified discursive register uniting the "natural attitude" with speculation may transcendentally circumscribe the fount of subjectivity in a relation with the infinite in a manner we have variously seen in the work of both Bulgakov and Blanchot.

Here, the Christian truth of spirit reasserts itself in justification of the "human scale" of enfleshed reality to be deified and resurrected, since, again, if the Absolute is beyond infinite and finite, God is not at his innermost in a divine emptiness that stands at the indeterminate and infinite peripheries of his energies but in the man Jesus and our effort in the wake of his example as the reinstatement of liturgical dwelling in and for the expectation of divine humanity.[121]

The Life of Thought: Metacritique as Master Category

One might rightly here ask whether this image of apocalyptic transcendentality, of plenitude declining into being in spirit as the life of structure, does not coincide with the genealogical and speculative work of John Milbank and Catherine Pickstock. In a succession of genealogical narrations, they move to uncover the "unthought" in all philosophical determination from their own evaluative vantage of a latent metaphysical-theological truth.[122] Famously, for Milbank, postmodernity sits atop indigent modern rationalism,

---

121. Milbank, "Sophia and Theurgy," 71.

122. For instance, see the converging treatment of the vast array of thinkers in Pickstock, *Aspects of Truth*; and Milbank: *Beyond Secular Order*, *Word Made Strange*.

which itself unmasks as degenerate theology—and this *precisely because* this "interstitial" genealogical traversal serves a primary aim of virtually simulating theoretical structure.

We may reinterpret this argument beginning with Pseudo-Dionysius. For the Areopagite, the twin regulative denials for the affirmation of finite opposites for God nevertheless coexist with the procedure of dialectically putting away impurities at the outset of contemplation by "pushing off" (as with Aristotle) the torque of finite instances and judgments.[123] This coincidence of mystical ascent's poetic finesse with the structures of the dianoetic go some way to suggest that Milbank's crucial counter reading of post-structuralist metaphysics, which innovates in recombining concept and intuition, really is a recovery of the apocalyptic logic inherent in the *Mystical Theology* and across the Christian tradition. This is why our questioning erotically gestures toward a divine source we first recognize only because we have been loved and have shown love out of ourselves (just as we begin by dialectically sorting through mixtures we have known), yet in front of him before whose unanalyzable depth in loving we would only tremble, because, without the sophiological transcendentality through which the Trinity must express, it would threaten to devastate the dilution in which human phenomenality is carefully woven and *justifiably* sustained, just as the utterly holy unity of God transcends the boundaries that delimit complex mixtures, yet analogically enables a final dialectical return to the human holiness of the man Jesus.[124]

The common content for infinity and finitude that is expressed in the analogical formal relation of divinity and humanity is legitimate just because they are also held together as a single *internal* sophiological apocalyptic motion in the "tetrahedral" divine life. Hence, the continuity and propriety of analogical ground for human metaphysical and axiological reality depends here on the apocalyptic truth that, since Sophia is self-transcendentalizing noumenality, goodness, for example, is both yet to come *and* already in motion in the origin at the heart of nature.

Consider the consequences of this for the conceptually subtended "reversibility" of predicates propounded by Scotist scientia in the guise of a (seemingly innocuous) semanticist necessity supposedly required for legitimate syllogistic referral to God.[125] Given that an analogy of attribution might be read to derive from what is originally an internal motion of the

---

123. Pseudo-Dionysius, "Mystical Theology." See also Haecker, "Gothic Fireflies."

124. Milbank, "Sacred Triads." See also the brief discussion in Milbank, "One in Three," 65.

125. See n15 above.

Absolute in its sophiological aspect, there is now no straightforward claim in favor of the parsimonious univocal as opposed to a perfidious dyad (this will be crucial below) questionably held together in analogy; we have begun to truly move the significance of the analogical vault beyond a collapse into an exercise in transcendental grammatics and to a more secure ontological basis. This is certainly not original here but has proven difficult to defend, yet now the standard of univocal conceptuality has been removed and the (relatively secondary matter of) predicative access to knowledge has been installed *from the side of the infinite* as self-transcendentalizing noumenality. Rather than the deadlock of any possibility of a predicative vault, what now remains to be answered is the question of our disavowal by the infinite or its abidance alongside us and in us—since in some sense *we* are *it*. This ontological basis goes far beyond the logicistic preoccupation into speculative metaphysics and, accordingly, a more radical reform is at hand here, finally exploding the idea that the demands of formal precision by themselves (whether indeed logical or semantic) turn analogy out. Hence, we do not propose to simply rival the standard of superior predicative security that is claimed in the univocal theorist's ontologization of the semantic (which nonetheless remains suspiciously convertible with the logical).[126] Rather than proposing the recovery of analogy through the figural transcendentality of apocalyptic paradox and yet simultaneously leaving transcendental cognition through a priori concepts intact (which is the source of the entire dispute), we must allow the former to correct and virtually simulate the latter as contingent, theoretically questionable, and undesirable.[127] Notable among these is the issue of formality as consistent self-ground, since this rests on the scheme of unicity's rule. Since the recent work of Graham Priest, among others, Analytic Philosophy has been forced to concede to the dialethic reform of logic, which argues that formality as such is self-referentially self-canceling at its ultimacy (such that certain truths must be simultaneously true and false if the integrity of the formal system is to hold at all), yet it has been unable to divine its proper metaphysical significance, and this dilemma remains for it a peripheral surd aberration. It does not see that the "paraconsistent effect" issues from basic "synthetic" figural metaphysical transcendentality, which rightly subordinates the very meaning of formality to an ontological image, as is being shown here. In elaborating upon the unity of the content of analogical referral to its form through a metacritical identification of cognitive transcendentality with the apocalyptic creation and renewal of creation by Goodness himself, our discussion reveals the

---

126. See Milbank, "Dissolution of Divine Government," 548–49.
127. See the discussion in Pickstock, *Aspects of Truth*, 200.

forgotten gnoseological essence of the Thomist "real distinction": just as the positing of ontological structure is the verbalized imaging of an *in-flowing* declension of God's plenitudinous goodness into the goodness of instance and measure, it resists the propositional logicism that features as the sole and irreducibly basic mode of metaphysical cognition *just because* this very transcendentality concomitantly affirms the metacritical declension of the internally intimated "aesthetic" into the externally logical "conceptual." It will be noted that this is nothing other than the transcendental expressing the discursive relationship of intuition to concept we have been preoccupied with, and which Pseudo-Dionysius saw long ago.

On the one hand, for post-structuralism proper, form carries the immanent germ of its own frustration simply because linguisticality and phenomenality are cynically read and "professionalized" into attempts at a stable circumscription of presence. On the other, the consummation in our theological account adroitly reconciles it at once with an intrinsic dimension of content that experience already divines and Christianity proclaims in its essential elements, just because there is a very specific form of refusal in theology to treat theory either as master controller of cognitive activity or as an end in itself. To be sure, the possibility of self-grounding falls with the intrinsic undecidability of any mere system of structural elements (since there is no transcendental cognition that circularly validates its assumed formal ground), yet now they point through themselves and beyond themselves, transformed in this initial appropriative and disclosive gesture into the unity that they occupy for us, to the in-breaking noumenality—through grace—of the divine Sophia, which is both their original and constitutive principle of telic motion. This reform is presupposed at the "anthropological" level of conditions of speculation, carried forward by the determination of ordinary phenomenality, and met by intuitive corroboration in self-recognition—and driven throughout by desire.

Hence, for Catherine Pickstock's critique of Jacques Derrida, an alternative thematization of form and content functions to correct the "unground" of metaphysical conceptuality by forcing difference to operate upon itself and recognize itself aright in human life and worship.[128] For Pickstock, the quietly profound fact is that sense ordinarily settles in given situations in such a way that a critical reduction to a regulatory mechanics of "missing the mark" cannot account for (since deferral as such is a purely "formal" truth, equally indifferent to what might be offered up, received, and responded to).[129] Something is missing. Indeed, if meaning as such is not merely a single

128. Pickstock, *After Writing*, 3–46.
129. Pickstock, *Aspects of Truth*, 65–6.

transcendental deep (as Rodolphe Gasché also remarks), then the "serpentine" shape of this nonidentical semiotic and hermeneutic referral must point to a more complex, ultimately nonformal principle (i.e., one beyond mere suspension) that subtends this "deep" additive and linking motion of "really existing" metaphoricity, which of course need not be denied.[130]

Something of an apocalyptic coincidence of form and content at the organizing levels of metaphysical transcendentality can be found in a degenerate mode in the much-misunderstood self-supplementing "etymologies" of Martin Heidegger and the "creative misreadings" of Gilles Deleuze.[131] For Heidegger, language itself speaks forth the relationship to Beyng, since sufficient attention to the "content" of lexico-genealogical elaborations (in "clearing," "time-space,"[132] "a-lethia,"[133] etc.) serve to deliver us to the (relatively) "formal" existential transcendentalities of disclosure in the hermeneutic event—and vice versa.[134] Yet this is abandoned prematurely for reasons we shall now examine.

This ultimate original relation of form to content might reveal an alternative image to the ostensibly foregone conclusion that each "structural" domain whose overlapping weaves adorn and constitute our human world—semiotics, narratology, phenomenology, mereology, psychology, economics, bioenergetics, mathematics, and so on—are each indifferently annulled at their formal limits by the "unworking" of void, since they are somehow inscribed without a final "vertical" and purposive coherence between them.

It is on this pattern that Radical Orthodoxy posits a "transcendental pneumatics" for the whole of finitude's rescue. For, if what we are in the singular and as inhabiting plural and universal modes of identification might entirely be lost in spools of noetic maelstrom, then there is no theodicy for the thought and conceptuality we possess, for we ourselves are unsalvageable. Yet, by fleshing out the harmony precisely in the "post-structural" idiom of the perfect life of the perfect man, singular and universal, we are offered a single "re-ology" (from the Latin *res*, or thing). In *Repetition and Identity*, Catherine Pickstock writes,

> Indeed, if one were to regard this integrity of things as irreducible (and modern thought usually does not), then it can only be ascribed to a participation in the creative action of God, allowing

---

130. Gasché, *Tain of the Mirror*; Pickstock, *Repetition and Identity*.
131. Deleuze and Guattari, *Anti-Oedipus*, 6.
132. Heidegger, *Contributions to Philosophy* 5.238–242.
133. Heidegger, *Essence of Truth* §§2, 9.
134. Heidegger, *Contributions to Philosophy* 3.

to things a share in his plenitude of formed existence as a kind of grace of coherent beauty to be accounted for in its own terms.[135]

Hence, what a thing is in amid its structural relations—like the identities of persons and things or the sense of *this* exchange we have just shared—requires argumentation at two levels. We shall first attend to the rescue of the various structural economies under christological and Trinitarian transcendentality as general metaphysical transcendentality, and then the retrieval of the concrete.

Christological Post-Structuralism as a Clue to Trinitarian Transcendentality

We can identify three distinct stages in Milbank's development of metacritique. Taken together, the stages constitute first the reduction of the spiritual and energetic into the granular organization of difference, *technē*, concept, social coding, etc., bracketed from a transcendental schema; later, the human scale is won back in a spiritual reconstitution into the life of love, propriety, poesis, intuition (and so on), which is the exemplar for the cosmotheandric motion that stands under Jesus Christ. The final stage arrives with the extended reading of Eastern Orthodox theology, especially that of Sergii Bulgakov.[136] Here, Milbank can be read to implicitly realize that his earlier modifications of post-structuralist transcendentality require Bulgakov's properly Trinitarian explication of an "Absolute" transcendental metaphysics where the paradox of christological suspension of the human and the divine is a movement wholly internal to what I have called the "tetrahedral Absolute." Jesus then is not the convergence of distinct natures but the closing of a wound. It is this reading of Bulgakov's antinomic apocalypticism that closes the circle that began with "Postmodern Critical Augustinianism" in 1991.[137] Metacritique is complete when one sees the two registers of the divine and human as apocalyptically wedded together in the motion of spirit; in the life of Jesus, this is a Trinitarian unity of concept and intuition in love, showing us as a single movement internal to the sophiological life of God, which we must realize for our own interpellation into personhood.

In *Theology and Social Theory*, Milbank emphasizes a "counter-ontology" regulated by an analogical transcendental in lieu of the postmodern

---

135. Pickstock, *Repetition and Identity*, 12.
136. See Milbank, "Sophia and Theurgy," as an example.
137. Milbank, "Postmodern Critical Augustinianism."

bias for the distribution of agonistic difference.[138] This is a "metanarrative," or transcendentality, for a peaceable, loving harmony of created difference. Hence, for Milbank, metacritique initially overcomes the "postmodern problematic," whose own metanarrative of difference affirms scattering, a refusal of concord in favor of agon. Here, the point of predicative possibility between infinite and finite—such that, answering affirmatively, our goodness, truth, unity might resist cynical dissolution—is not only the final and thus unavoidable moment of philosophical conjecture, but in Christian metaphysics this coincides with a justification of the finite as a finitude of instance and measure dependent on the infinite—without yet losing itself into it, which is what postmodernism ought to recommend if it were to be truly consistent.[139]

As we have seen, the claim to abstract formal truths in a philosophically efficacious manner from experience relies on the circular modern assumption that the very same formality is the essence of cognition. Here it might now be seen how the erection of transcendentalities on incomplete intuition remains blind to the truth of an apocalyptic combinatoric logic for reconciling content to human formality. Such a realization relies on a close, humble attunement and prayerful attention to how we live in among the structures of form. Hence, as has been pointed out, the truth of the frustration of a single and final narratival presentation in human interpretive reality may nevertheless find its ultimate culmination in the restorative remembering as re-narration in the act of forgiveness.[140] (It might here be well noted that, following the typical christological formulations, the two memories of the ever-forgiving, embracing Christ are a worthwhile theme for theological meditation.) This continues into further questions of the ethical and political—as taken up by Emmanuel Levinas and Dionys Mascolo, though without the final and crucial Christian core.[141] Let us reconstruct it from first principles: The first mover of all is the grace of the sophiological self-transcendentalizing noumenality of creation, and the original work of this divine grace is nature. Grace apocalyptically reinfuses and re-uplifts nature beyond its own (mis-)estimation of itself. Just so, the space for structures to show this original and determining grace (which comes also to forgive the effects of mis-recognition and sin) therefore allows theology to supremely recover—as Sabbath is to man—the meaning of difference and

---

138. Milbank, *Theology and Social Theory* (1991), 288–325.
139. Milbank, *Theology and Social Theory* (1991), 314–21.
140. Milbank, "Sophia and Theurgy."
141. See Levinas, *Time and the Other Time*; Mascolo, *Communisme*. See also Blanchot and Mascolo, *Maurice Blanchot*.

formality to life. Such a post-structuralism resumes the practice of life away from the failure of frustrated theory to internally discern its own meaning, seeing the intrinsic content of virtue and pedagogy as the original truth in the formality of power and hierarchy; gift as the truth of economy; life as the truth of mechanism; personality as the truth of mind; and the call and depth of iconicity as the truth of signs and phenomenality. Each of these borrows and expresses a relationality in a dynamics of exchange best and most "purely" expressed in trinitarity; hence, the transcendentality of gift does not just inform "existentially" how we ought to receive the role of fatherhood, for instance; rather, since we are told, for example, that those who are fathers have known him from the beginning (1 John 2:14), existence illuminates speculative structures of Trinity.[142] I shall elaborate on apocalyptic and metacritical epitomes of metaphysical transcendentality and lead them back to trinitarity below, elaborating on the specific example of the truth of post-structural life and difference as the church, Christ's own body.

In the essays in *The Word Made Strange* there is an attempt to arrive at a rival transcendental justification for the analogical truth of Christian spirit in the idiom of postmodernism in order to rescue even this philosophical discourse, which wishes to separate transcendental formal self-frustration indifferent to the content operated on. This is achieved by passing the ideal of Christian life—Jesus—through axiomatic-structural abyss of differential philosophy and demonstrating its consummation and true operation in his image. First, there is a metacritical argument on the cognition of formality: in "A Christological Poetics," a distinct "poetic" cognition modeled on the Vichian "poetic concrete universal" is asserted as the basic substance of metaphysical cognition and turns out a formal mechanics ("metanarrative") of hermeneutic encounter in favor of a transcendental schematics standing under the figure, concentrated from religious and mythical narrative.[143] Second, "The Name of Jesus" continues from the discussion of Anselm and Girard in *Theology and Social Theory*, where Milbank argues that it is Jesus's unique human performance of human structural life that makes his announcement of, and invitation into, the kingdom accessible to us precisely because it is the introduction of new "codes" revealing the truth of all cultural life hereon. However, this particular performance of structures, in supplying their own regulative transcendentality ("metanarrative"), surpasses the determination of an evaluative vantage that would render the "Christic idiom" and its imitation just one more player in a game where philosophy decides the rules of interaction, or just one more

---

142. See also the discussion in Pickstock, *Aspects of Truth*, 69.
143. Milbank, *Word Made Strange*, 123–44.

instance of "structuration" in an abjectly plural field.¹⁴⁴ Rather, Jesus Christ serves to displace the *transcendental* regulation of violent multiplicity, to signify and transmit a beatitude in our lives beyond its concomitant cynical reduction to a mere interpolation between the libidinal folds comprising subjectivity. This transcendentality self-recursively supplies a narrative for the very necessity of an incarnation of (and perfection by) the Absolute into the finitude of structure, codes, and difference in the first place, as William Desmond's work implies.

Accordingly, "The Name of Jesus" initiates an initial dissolution of Jesus Christ into the motion of schematizing codes of Jesus's conduct among the hermeneutic trail left in the Gospels, ready to be recollected under a new transcendental metaphysics of difference that coalesces around a new original refractive point in Jesus's own person.¹⁴⁵ In one place, Milbank notes,

> They [the Gospels] suggest that Jesus is the most comprehensive possible context: not just the space within which all transactions between time and eternity transpire, but also the beginning of all this space, the culmination of this space, the growth of this space and all the goings in and out within this space.¹⁴⁶

To understand this, we must return to Milbank's image in *Theology and Social Theory* of the two "infinities" of superlative axiological realization and possible human temporality (which we shall consider in more detail later on) in which the human participates. We may subject this to the incarnational logic of the Trinitarian relations as with the Areopagite above: Jesus consummates both the horizontal-historical axis and vertical-eminent axis in his own individual "post-structural" performance. In his individual model he *is* the intimation of the bounding containment of the differential field as such; this is the philosophically un-surmisable and un-surveyable unity of all difference, the "body" of Christ.¹⁴⁷ Jesus's life is the form and content of structural domains, united in a single differential transcendental of which it is itself both instance and rule. In this way, a metacritique of post-structuralism reads "actually existing" difference as a function of formality that is not originally "pure" but whose shape is "Christiform," so to say, and no longer first subject to any other secular, professional-philosophical reduction.

---

144. Milbank, *Theology and Social Theory* (2006), 403. Note that "Christic idiom" is added to replace "logos" in the second edition.

145. "The Name of Jesus," in Milbank, *Word Made Strange*, 149.

146. "The Name of Jesus," in Milbank, *Word Made Strange*, 149–50.

147. Milbank: *Theology and Social Theory* (1991), 305; "The Name of Jesus," in *Word Made Strange*, 157.

This theological elevation of the "structural" life of Jesus as the perfect, concrete "poetic" figure for the transcendentality of difference transforms and justifies each of our attempts at the *imitatio Christi* into a network of (nonidentical) global mimetics at the fount of which is his person, the Logos, and his life in the Spirit, as the *figura* that inscribes the transcendentality of formality alongside its proper content. That is, it is not the endless diagonal flights of subversion against organization prescribed by a schizoid mystagogy that would have transgression paradigmatically exemplify the hope for a true non-identical repetition; rather, this is the sole prerogative of a mimetic field in which there is maximal human fulfillment under the Christian idea of the Good, the salvation of all men and their lives in Christ. Indeed, just as one may roll into or away from a fractal image yet never escape the rule of its equation, our own unique spiritual *imitatio* in the differential field is our participation in the kingdom of heaven on earth. Note the paradox as Jesus as a member ("the first harvest," as Paul says [1 Cor 15:20]) of the kingdom that is his own body—the *autobasileia*.[148] Here, if we are serious about abandoning the rule of unicity in favor of Trinity, the most truly "one" anything might be is precisely found in the God who—exactly to be who he is—incarnates into and abides alongside his creation. We might further add that implicit here is the crucial idea that the apocalyptic life of Christ (which is, as for Bulgakov, the original and immaculate motion of the reconciliation of the divine and creaturely Sophia) entails an attitude toward the formality of structure that is at once metacritical in its radicalization of law and structure. This is why, in fact, Milbank implies that Jesus just is the model par excellence for the inhabitation of any human structural system we may care to deconstruct him into.[149] Recall that Jesus does not come to abolish law (Matt 5:17), since this would be to deny a necessary incarnation into structure for its redemption and dissolve the combinatoric core of our apocalyptic and metacritical ontology and life. If Christ changes the very definition of death, however, the eternal fulfillment of concept comes in realizing that it is the mere scaffold for a more originary spiritual motion, as we saw with William Desmond above. Concept—structure and organization—is given anew and must return just as an expression of the enhypostatization of our finite life. Milbank writes, "Thus for reasons belonging to the logic of discourse, it is indeed true that incarnation cannot be by the absorbing of divinity into humanity, but only by the assumption of humanity into divinity."[150]

---

148. Milbank, *Theology and Social Theory* (1991), 396.
149. "The Name of Jesus," in Milbank, *Word Made Strange*, 150, 156.
150. "The Name of Jesus," in Milbank, *Word Made Strange*, 156.

Formality cannot *ground* knowledge and yet it cannot be eradicated, for this would be to merely erase Eden's failure and outrightly reverse the beginning of knowledge rather than to forgive and fulfill our error in the perfect free choice of reconciliation in love. Put another way, in Jesus's self-narrativizing and radical re-narration of the lives of others, his discourses on economic exchange and Jubilee, his function in the fulfillment of the sacrificial logic of Jewish law, etc., it is true that he lived as constituted by nothing other than the differential, abyssal logic of structural matrices; yet, in the way that he exemplified them in his spirit, the Holy Spirit—with forgiveness and grace of exception, the priority of the human over the law—he uncovered their true *metacritical* transcendentality by revealing the original superadditum of spirit, in which all concept and structure flows; this spirit is man raised to god.

In this way, we are all created in the body of Christ the Logos; yet, true membership lies in the spiritual journey of earthly sanctification—of inheriting the proper *rule* of these codes in our own, unique reenactment. Jesus did not come to condemn finitude to itself as impossible self-grounding, but uncovered the path—hidden from the foundation—for the reconciliation of each man and all men with God. The concrete metaphor of his name encodes a "metacritical life" held together by nothing reforming nature other than the ideal of love alone—the binding third. This alone is the consummation of concept and structure only in and through the "divinity" of a perfect life of perfect love. Hence, Jesus provides us with the eminent transcendentality of post-structural difference by serving as its "content-ful" center and circumference. That is, it is to enable life that transcendence became incarnate: it is for the possibility to give gifts that the living economy of sense, of phenomenality and linguisticality was ever knit together as a structural field from the repose of plenitude. Yet, how does this break with the previous "order" of misrecognized nature? If we say that narrative was instituted for the possibility that we may desire and enact forgiveness, this is to imply we must desire most of all the repair of love. Yet, we must ask, what else gives the love of repair other than the experience of breaking? What has been intimated here is that this new logic that "repairs" the break of sin is just the desire that we might love more; yet this is contained in the Trinitarian schema now sophiologically applied to the reconciliation of concept and intuition. We can virtually simulate lesser forms of a rejection (or a *fear*) of this repair in the claims of secular philosophy. We have in the foregoing resolved differential transcendentality into its metacritical consummation in the perfect love of Jesus Christ, and we see that the clue to raising this discussion to a metaphysical command that is explicitly *Trinitarian* lies in a "pure schematics" of the figure of Trinity as master transcendentality.

Trinitarity as Metaphysical Transcendentality

It will now be shown that the major alteration to metaphysics in the post-structuralism proposed by Radical Orthodoxy can be more "purely" demonstrated in the figurative and poetic cognition that is at one with the discursivity of metaphysical cognition. Theoretical transcendentalities find their Trinitarian and metacritical consummation here, since it emerges that the ultimate shortcoming of an autonomous philosophy lies in the poverty of its hermeneutic of our life and, second, the resulting generation and suspension of its dualisms (ground and un-ground chief among them).

Now, it is relatively well known that the circular redefinition of the science of being in adequation with cognitive concepts was begun by Duns Scotus and that it culminates in Kant's *Transcendental Analytic*.[151] This "first-order" transcendental of being held in a priori conceptuality empowers finite reflection according to the illusion of self-sufficient transcendental cognition—and thereby invests a propriety to the finite as bearer of certain knowing. Yet, this cannot stand, as we have seen, since, if the infinite really is All in All, the admitted "reversibility" of rational relations obviously provides nothing to sustain any real counterweight to the finite against the infinite, and the annihilation of concept is concomitant with the nullity of finitude and thus the impotence of (finite) reflection. This is why it is *necessarily* revealed in the "second-order" transcendentality of post-structural thought—from a proper recognition of the emptiness of finitude for itself—that a perpetual suspension of any and all pure theoretical grasp must be in order, and rightly so. Further, in this *mise-en-abyme* suspension there can now be no "first" or "second" image, since this is disallowed in the developing transcendentality of a general mimetics that is nothing other than non-identical repetition, as Philippe Lacoue-Labarthe points out; this, again, cannot be disputed.[152] Not only does a refinement in the logic of systematicity follow the examination of transcendentality as such, this now also coincides with the character of an image of human discursivity, as has been our argument all along. The critiques of Plato in Heidegger, Derrida, Deleuze, and so on are solely predicated on misreading Plato's own vision of an incorporated "second" transcendentality as that merely of the modern "first." There can be no other elaboration of an inadmissible Platonic "presence" and nonmimetic "original" other than on this mistaken basis, even if there is warrant that the text itself, in its ambivalent commitment to unicity,

---

151. Honnefelder, "Raison et Metaphysique"; Gilson, *John Duns Scotus*, 550–52.
152. Lacoue-Labarthe: *Typography*, 49; "Bye Bye Farewell."

is entangled in aporiae it cannot solve.[153] At this point, the reactive destruction immanent to *formality as such* (as the fruit of transcendental cognition in modern conceptuality) is necessary, but further elaboration can be given by theology, which alone understands that the apocalyptic motion of sophiological becoming necessitates the heretofore neglected content of various formalities. Here, crucially, a "third" transcendental level might be further invoked to contest not the *fact* of suspension but to reread its nature. Losing one's life in the futility of philosophical self-definition, one finds oneself again un-derivable and only transcendentally circumscribable as gift. In this manner, the "redemptive" moment of human propriety away from the obliterating self-effacement of a mere "finite infinitude" is in the life that has been won in the incarnation; this returns to (a reconfigured) reflection in gift what finitude does not—and cannot—possess properly to itself but finds at the close of the day that no *quid juris* is required of it.[154]

Hence, no more is there the presupposition of a general transcendental condition that subjects the very category of ground itself to a perpetual suspension by an identically repeating un-ground, which scatters the former into indifferently (un-)related content in an unending refusal of either "vertical" or "horizontal" mutual relation. Instead, the trihypostatic figure of trinitarity incorporates in its schema the philosophical exigency of thinking the abyss but now recognizes it anew: here, the meaning of ground is not self-sufficient but arrives as a flight from "un-ground" (the Father) or a beginning that is nevertheless attested for fully and faithfully in the life of manifestation (Son and Spirit). "Origins" are thus saved from necessarily serving a role of disruption and disavowal. A fundamental elaboration and self-grounding of thought by theology in the "second order" un-ground of gift (and not dispossession or abandonment) takes place. For, to ensure an originally symmetrical unity of concept and intuition—along with many of philosophy's central dualisms—not as reactive "indefinite dyads" of oscillation and conjunction between finitude and infinitude, one must refigure the meaning of transcendentality (and its attitude toward the suspension of philosophy and reflection) according to an *original* binding third in the impossible cleavage of the dyad that might otherwise be blindly read by philosophy in the more edgy and meretriciously esoteric and alluring terms of sheerly indefinable excess.

Following Schelling's retraining of speculation from critical transcendental reflection to necessary but *universally postulatory* transcendentalities,

---

153. See "Difference of Virtue, or Virtue of Difference," in Milbank, *Theology and Social Theory*.

154. Morrison, "Re-Enchantment of the Gift."

it will be noted that this alternative reading is necessarily self-legitimating. Its justification operates by performing apocalyptic and Trinitarian moves upon the categories of ground and un-ground themselves, as we have seen.[155] Hence, here at the very ultimacy of metaphysical structure in *figural* elaboration whose determinacy has no originating conceptual circumscription, the introduction of the third moment that sublates "un-ground" itself into a Trinitarian unity with "ground" cannot be dismissed merely as a (pejoratively) metaphysical resolution away from the seductive precipice of indeterminate excess as such, which equally originally goes behind the two and renders them eternally incomplete. This is because such a resistance cannot really avoid collapsing into an underhanded reinsistence on dyadic relational precarity, and these motivations can themselves be virtually simulated.[156] In this respect, we may follow Erich Przywara in reading Hegelian dialectics (Trinitarian or not) as an attempt to articulate the trihypostaticity in the twin steps of dialectical motion as the oscillating motion between suspension and an impossible resolution of the dyad itself; however, this appears to fall quite clearly back on dyadic thought, just now at a further schematic level of contradiction and sublation as a *second* dyadic relation that we now naïvely assume might remain invulnerable to the very same suspension.[157] As Blanchot (and Derrida later) shows, however, this is utterly untenable.[158] The solution, having proposed the figure of the three as an alternative hermeneutic of suspension, is trihypostaticity as the core of Trinitarian theology must displace every consequence of suspended dyadics, since dyad must be allowed to be recognized as having fallen from an original Trinity. Why? This is just a better hermeneutic of pragmatic life in all possible human temporality, refusing to condemn it as fraudulent transcendental illusion in some or other way. Since we assume no discursive transcendentality capable of confidently declaring such critical limits between the everyday and the properly metaphysical, one can simply desire to choose this simple, radically transformative alternative for its philosophical and spiritual effects. Most crucially, with this reform, the shearing back of a "first" and "second" moment for the mechanics governing mimetic transcendentality to an utterly interchangeable formal dyadicity may be seen as an unacknowledged prior reduction that can be refused; now, with this reversed, metaphysical transcendentality is able to essentially contain the

---

155. Pickstock, *After Writing*, 3–46.

156. See n172 and the discussion at the end.

157. Przywara, *Analogia Entis*, 192.

158. See "The Great Refusal," in Blanchot, *Infinite Conversation*, 33–48. See also Blanchot, *Step Not Beyond*.

"content" of personal differentiation proper to the Trinitarian scheme. Not merely Trinity as bowdlerized schematic but Father, Son, and Spirit are thus admitted in the fullest sense that they may be as philosophical speculative ground. Trinitarity is a self-legitimating round and the final truth of transcendentality, since, as we mentioned at the start, it most basically operates in its role *as* such a transcendental ground while simultaneously demonstrating that the dyad of ground and un-ground find their consummation with the original binding "third" of fidelity, love and life given and sustained from above. This recursivity in the evaulation of act's relation to knowledge is the culmination of 'anti-philosophy' (and this final step eludes Alain Badiou) since theoretical transcendentality (as "ground") fails to be securely knowable as conceptual even as it holds in coherence the other philosophical structures that delineate the (now) porous hermeneutic circularity of finitude, the co-creative conduit for the life of the Absolute. This kind of self-recursive un-grounding action for theoretical activity is why the Trinity proves itself to stand at the very ultimacy of metaphysics; it is the final and perfect *figura* because it is the embrace of the gospel "always already" at the heart of the prodigal self-searching that generates theory and yet remains *inevitable*. Three very final points pertain here.

The End of Thought and the Redemption of Theory

There are several levels at which this final section shall operate. They concern our ability now to better think the meaning of theory at all, which then involves the open challenge of besting its simultaneous existential allure and underpinning philosophical supremacy (as seen in the section on dyadicity and trinitarity above). Finally, we shall finish with the justice now given to the *singular* in our general metaphysical structure.

First, we might see here that theology's own answer to the nature of its philosophical future in among the question of worldly futurity is established by taking the unique and consummate ownership of the dimension of figural transcendentality in Trinitarian structure. As the Trinity further organizes an apocalyptic expression of love as the suture for Eden's rupture, this does not signal the erasure of concept; rather, the voiding hesitancy of knowledge of good and evil, like Peter on the water (Matt 14:29; a "post-structuralist" parable, perhaps), is overcome in the life of love, which forgives and pours itself out anew.[159] If God really is eternally All in All, and the Trinity requires

---

159. This is where the fundamental "post-structuralist" edifice must be praised, for it appears that the innermost radicality of the truths of Christianity, concerning universal salvation and apocatastasis, are intimated in its unyielding metaphysical "monism."

Sophia, the divine being as "created God," it can also be seen here that Milbank's "vectoral" field of genealogical traversal permits the possibility of a genuinely Christian retrieval. The realization of an imperishable invitation to life in Christ against the merely historical narrative of conceptual ascendancy and consummation—contra Heidegger and Hegel, respectively—is necessary then precisely because of the reliance on the Trinitarian truth that God the Holy Spirit, maximally expressive, abides to enliven all possible human temporality for an ultimate purpose only prefigured in this life. Paradoxically (though for good reasons), only when the question of discursive entanglement is raised out of being first a (mythic-)historical matter, one is able to better attend to the question of both history and the anticipation of imminent and eschatological futurity as the matter of a single (Trinitarian) transcendental. Any supervising philosophical elaboration must also contend with the historicity of not only its own genesis but that of its presuppositional transcendentalities. Hence, Milbank suggests that a genuine conception of the historicity of reason—and thus a metaphysics resistant to genealogical and presuppositional overcoming—can be defended only in Christian theology, since the metacritical symmetry of a mutual refinement of concept and intuition continues to be inextricable both *before and after* the revolution of the concept in both of reason and revelation, rather than conceptuality in the infinity of all possible human temporality being grasped as a genealogical narrative on the one-sided "meta-narratival" vantages of either a dialectical motion or a critical genealogy (such as in Nietzsche or Heidegger).[160] Another advance here is that the origin of "existentialized" discursive transcendentality in continuity with speculative conceptuality and historicity allows us to generously position non-Western philosophies at various points across a general field of variously realized poetic-intellectual emergence, all without a relativistic suspension of their various content. (Indeed, they may remain superior in certain regards that we have simply lost, as Herder argued.)[161] Having elevated the key to genealogical hermeneutic as such to a presupposition in human cognition and speculative method as such, theology (as Augustine had already shown) apocalyptically presents both a historical dimension of ever-more perfect human practice in our present cultural receipt of the kingdom of God and as a prophesy of perfect fulfillment in the belonging to come.[162]

---

160. See the discussion in Milbank, "Genealogies of Truth," 708–15.

161. Herder, *Philosophical Writings*, 123.

162. An argument for this is outlined in Milbank, *Theology and Social Theory* (1991), 305–6.

Moreover, second, charges of an overconfident Trinitarian speculation on the eschaton themselves risk calling into question the philosophical (but not dogmatic) status of a triune God after the work of our salvation is complete, since, in suspending the continuity of reason in a separation of a metaphysics of this life from the next, apocalyptic dynamics as ontological truth does not tell of eternity reconciling with time but shrouds it in critical finitude. Rather, we ought to see that what ruptures through the cosmos is not just divine *élan* as such, since this reinforces counterposing dead matter against vitality, with God being for us absolutely unnameable and alienating.[163] Rather, what in-breaks is our true lives in God returned to us in the life of God as the cosmos and the body of Christ—since all moments are apocalyptic, and the creative act holds the union of the creaturely and divine Sophia nearing completion. (Hence, we might say that in the next life everything will have changed, and yet so little may in the end really be different.) The "suspended middle" in Radical Orthodoxy's preoccupation with paradox is then in fact the articulation of a Pauline apocalyptic actualization of infinite plenitude and human "structural" life where each is only for the other—and both for the glory of God, who, as the relation of love, is always greater.[164] Nevertheless, the defective runaway logic of either half alone is ultimately reliant on the continued allure in Edenic fruit that we may break free of the incarnation into life, variety, and knowledge that God secretly withholds. Yet, experience may become wisdom only when it ceases to resent the simplicity of innocence. A resistance to grace on the part of mere experience might be read in the desire that a Hölderlinian "openness" of the tragic—the "unending agony" of finitude—not be transcendentally foreclosed, which is why Bulgakov insists upon the transformation of a suspended dyad into Trinity.[165] This image of perpetual tragic suspension is only a reinsistence on the ageless condemnation of finitude in the sorrow and ultimate repression of a primal innocence lost; the philosophical significance of the Trinitarian relations is also then a principled refusal to decide in favor either of wounded finitude punishing itself or an exalted infinitude so pure it cannot touch us but remains as a negative limit. Yet, just as the lips of Isaiah were anointed with flaming coals by the Holy Spirit, so the shame and grief of our irretrievable innocence is glorified in forgiveness and restitution (Isa 6:1–8). Accordingly, to "unsuspend" the paradox of the Trinity for the purposes of philosophical parsimony is to cleave nature away

---

163. See Alarcón, "Restless Negativity."

164. Pickstock, "Cosmic Poetics," 136.

165. See the very revealing discussion of messianism in Blanchot, *Writing of the Disaster*, 141; Obrigewitsch, "Tragic Agony."

on its own terms, and to unmanageably initiate the beckoning of the postmodern cascades of infinitude as hypernoumenal void, as Nick Land shows us. Hence, the essential paradoxes of Christianity point to the apocalypticism of the divine life that alone is and into which we are invited to share, quite without the possibility of an ultimate refusal.

In the last place, the culminating moment of the metacritical argument lies in the transcendentality of identity as coherence; it has been shown that this problem is nothing other than an elaboration of the consequence of a single Trinitarian-topographical thesis on suspension and motion.[166] This can be taken further. To return to an earlier point, as both Catherine Pickstock and John Milbank have recently noted, after Aquinas and Cusanus, all things—borrowing their being from God—are themselves and yet not: all things dance about their centers, neither merely as proper occupants of their own middles, nor indeed merely as collocated relata arbitrarily districted at their peripheries.[167] Insofar as this is again a retrieval of an original "content-ful" shape for form, this echoes the significance (as mentioned earlier) of the real distinction in Aquinas as a rejection of an infinite extendibility of formality under transcendental cognition for what must be figuratively seen (and hoped) in all creation as a dilution and coincidence in finite being of what is totally united in God.[168] This echoes Nicholas of Cusa's essentially topographical refiguration and sublation of formality into "bending" lines of methodological flight toward a point of real simplicity for which we have only the paradoxical and apocalyptic doctrinal apex of Trinity and Christology as just articulation.[169] Indeed, Nicholas invokes the idea of God not only as pure act (and thereby degenerately construed as mere activating will) but also pure potency to preclude a reconstructive field of real determination under a finite scheme of compossibility, an arrangement that might otherwise cause the cosmos to fall entirely apart.[170] There is here no possibility (contra Hegel) that we might fix our eyes to retrace the immanent route that God takes in his essence to decline into creation (as "not-other") and return again only to himself.[171] In the end then it appears that thought, concept, and the yield of speculation as such really remain as a "lagging strand" to the creation and determination of the real, and it is true that this stands not

---

166. Pickstock, *After Writing*, xv.

167. Pickstock, *Repetition and Identity*, 12.; Milbank, "One in Three," 61.

168. Milbank, "Dissolution of Divine Government," 561.

169. Nicholas of Cusa, "De Docta Ignorantia"; see also Milbank, "One in Three," 53.

170. Nicholas of Cusa, "De Docta Ignorantia," 91.

171. Nicholas of Cusa, "De Visione Dei."

unrelated to the Kantian declamation of an ultimately regulative reason for human cognition, which cannot produce its own objects.[172] However, it is invoked less as a retreat to critical metaphysics but rather metacritically in a "poetic" modification of Hegelian speculative recollection of the concept in Trinitarian metaphysics, as above. Here, phenomenological perspectivalism is at one with its ontological image, since, following Eriugena's own "logic of sense," theophany just is God's mode of being. Catherine Pickstock writes,

> This would give one leave to say that the explanation for things is paradoxically that which is shown forth on their surface edge; the snowdrop holds together in order to be a beautiful snowdrop, in order to show forth "galanthus," and so forth.[173]

Ostensibly "surface" concretions like selves, persons, beings, and words do not then collapse into the unavowable energies of their genesis or the frustrations immanent to the structural field from which they borrow their substance; rather, in the search for a *vinculum substantiale*, *res* as the singular instantiation of form emerges as justified in its finitude entirely from above in the loving, free act of creation. Just so, Essence himself declined into appearance to fashion our psychological depth, giving truth to the glimpse and gasp of ephemeral vignettes in the blurs and mist of memory. In the end, archetype, idea, and form rely on *our* creative realization forwards and backwards in an "existential" elaboration on the basis of a poetic transcendentality that is the life of God himself, even if this is a decisive romantic and Christian reconfiguration of the antique speculative base. Hence, it means little that we remain unable to know things from the inside, given that neither knowing, selves, nor things actually ever possessed their own insides in the first place.

We now complete the transformation of hermeneutic circularity into metaphysical transcendentality in this Christian post-structuralism. The meaning of systematicity lies with the life of human spirit, encoded within the action of human discursive transcendentality. The essential transcendental motion of our spirit is apocalyptic; this is its sophianicity, since our noumenality is the divine Sophia. Divine humanity describes the finality of cosmotheandric perichoretics; "analogy" has thereby resolved into the apocalyptic motion of self-reconciling Sophia, since our infinite desire just *is* the life of God in and with us as it shall be in the end. At the structural level, sophianicity is Trinitarian, since everything sophianic is consubstantial and therefore reflects the open promise of restorative transcendentality

---

172. Kant, *Critique of Pure Reason*, A19/B33, A669/B697–A732/ B704.
173. Pickstock, *Repetition and Identity*, 12.

that the Holy Spirit represents for the resolution of dyadic scissiparity at the concrete root of philosophical and psychological dualisms. This repair is first shown in the life of Jesus Christ, the beginning and end of all creation. Finally, at the phenomenal level, human life is theophanic sophianicity, since we cognize and live in a depth freely given, unmerited—and, in this, never truly more ourselves than in receiving now a taste of the life to come.

If we search in philosophy, as Wilfred Sellars writes, for a genuine "hanging together" of form and content and method and object, we foresee it to unify and come forth in the perfect practice of praise from the human being, the speculative animal, who finally sees the divergent logic of pure writing set aright in a reformation toward the ecstatic completion of speech in worship. Why spend thousands of words parsing and reaffirming basic dogmatic truths through the philosophical convolution? The answer is that both concept and intuition are bound and sanctified in the life of love, and it is a spiritual depth that handles structural elaboration in a virtually theoretical intensive field. For, if discursivity is originally creaturely, then the "depth" of philosophical structure in presuppositional reduction is not a function of the theory resolving itself; rather, self-recognition is its task, and it consists in the activity of issuing preemptory suspensions of the very principles that might initiate "counter readings" by rival philosophical images, since the power of thought that enters into this exchange of persuasion is spiritual. The noetic constitution and scaffolding of metaphysical structure in any resolution of theoretical engagement is then a function of a higher spiritual motion and its purposes. Recall that we have in this piece ventured to articulate Thomas's real distinction three times over, in varying idioms and philosophical constructions. If they nevertheless converge, it is not because we wish to be insensate to the nuance separating them, despite the fact that, as far as this turns again on the hermeneutic question, it becomes a question of theoretical assertions as they feature in schemes of non-identical repetition. Rather, they are held together by our own poetic, intuitive mastery of philosophical mytho-logos in a *spiritual* motion. None are ultimately supreme—including Thomas's own formulations—and yet all become necessary in their own times and in their own particular dialogic situations. Theology's retrieval must keep apace with the depths of philosophical rebellion, even if this is nonetheless itself necessary for a just Irenaean completion of our humanity. All things are for the sake of our wisdom, and we—just as God before us—cross into wasteland and contend with barren formality before we might return, desiring with all our hearts the repair only love might bring. Transcendental time as the transverse axis of *theory* as well as history has Irenaean circumscription. Our hope for the salvation of thought lies with Blake's tearful, forgiving Jehovah, who follows behind last of all to fulfill even the flight of Minerva's owl and close the day and resurrect the next. Solomon's rescue is the return of philosophy apocalyptically within the "representational" realms of religion and art. It is the life of perfect love, the infinite desire for which is brought to self-consciousness only after we break, devastated in realizing that all human self-justification *must* fail, yet, we can only return to live as ourselves. For, turning away from the Trinitarian God is, as we have seen, self-mutilation in intellect and soul. Only in Christ's sacrifice do we receive the gift to see ourselves aright and live assured beyond our wretched, self-sure lot.[174]

Much has been outlined here in very brief terms, and we are only at the quickening of the speculative adventure of our age. However, we might also say that though individual hermeneutics and exhortations will perforce continue to be set forth, the end of philosophy does appear to draw near, since the organization of transcendentality *as such* approaches saturation, and the very barest theoretical formulations of concept have been plumbed and inflict their chaos all around us. We now must dress bone with sinew. The stabilizing conceptuality of a philosophical "outline" is met from one pole by the intuitive ground of pragmatics (a theological anthropology aided by doctrine, sacramentology, liturgiology, and so on) from another, in a round. Increasingly, the ultimacy of metaphysics more completely regulates every addition of "first-order" interpretation as we turn to clarify the meaning of theory as such. For, the resolution of theory in our apocalyptic mode ultimately overturns the methodological symmetry of concept and intuition, and nature and grace, into a posture toward him who is Grace himself, for the Trinity teaches foremost the free and assured worship of him who cannot be seen, and yet he comes to worship in and with us. It is true that the source of wonder and our desire for the infinite cannot run dry, yet this cannot subsidize theoretical exertion indefinitely to the effect again of compartmentalizing human discursivity—as though knowing God were a task in itself quite apart from loving him. Indeed, if we say apocalyptically that love is the life of knowledge, this is because knowledge boasts nothing of itself besides waiting to know—and know more perfectly—according to a more perfect love. In this life we thereby keep vigil for that day when we shall know perfectly just because we shall love perfectly. This is also the story of the concept, which belongs to man alone and is his pride. Hence, again, if we say that intuition is the life of the concept, this is because concept, if it is not to be sophistic, asserts nothing of itself besides awaiting and speaking out the continual breath of intuition. For, lest we forget, the work of our renewal belongs alone to the Spirit.

174. See Milbank, *Word Made Strange*, 141–70.

> Thus saith the Lord God unto these bones; Behold, I will cause breath to enter into you, and ye shall live. And I will lay sinews upon you, and will bring up flesh upon you, and cover you with skin, and put breath in you, and ye shall live; and ye shall know that I am the Lord. (Ezek 37:5–6 KJV)

Part Three

Ecology and Liturgy

8

Entangled Unthinkably
Toward a Trinitarian Ecology

Simone Kotva

THERE IS NO DOUBT that the doctrine of the Trinity has had ecological implications, in its intra-action and economy, of getting along and co-creating, and for as long as there has been discourse about the nature of God. These implications can be discovered alongside Christianity in the trinitarian theologies of Hinduism, the *Chaldean Oracles*, and other religious and philosophical traditions. Naturally, such doctrines are held up as images of relevance for earthbound existence as instances of companionship, of giving and taking, as well as of sorrow, death, violence and rivalry—in short, of life. Millennia before environmentalism began to worry about ways of effectively modeling coexistence between humans and other-than-human creatures and things; the Trinity was there with an image that said it all: human flesh spiraling ecstatically with nonhuman and more-than-human spirits, getting along.[1]

There are good doctrinal reasons to be excavated for claiming the urgency of the Trinity in a time of planetary emergency. Many of those reasons are implicit in the project of this volume, which reclaims the Trinity as

---

1. On entanglement, ecology, and theological doctrine, see Barad, "What Flashes Up."

an ontological concept, in this way indicating that the Trinity is concerned with Being and beings. However, the question about the relevance of the Trinity as an ecological concept, and of ecology as an instance of Trinitarian conceptuality, has to do with method, ways of thinking, and modes of practice and styles of living. When reflecting on the Trinity we have to ask: When do speaking and writing about the Trinity become *thinking* Trinitarianly? How does this icon of coexistence actually help, if at all, when it comes to practicing solidarity across species? And how is the Trinity the lure for beings (if we take the Trinity to be another name for the Being of God as Love)? Moreover, how does the Trinity make itself known in the practices of everyday life? I will contend that it is difficult to think, and, indeed, to really attend to the relationship between the persons of the Trinity, without living and relating differently to the other than human; without, to borrow a slogan from Donna Haraway, finding oneself "making kin" with "otherkind," as well as making babies with Homo sapiens.[2] This contention, however, demands that we first look again at the relationship between ecology and theology more broadly.

God has not always been good news for Gaia.[3] It is not possible to suspend from the conversation the countless instances when thinking about the Trinity has justified apparent renunciation of the world into which truth was incarnated: I have in mind that recurrent tendency, among Christian traditions everywhere, to confine imitation of the divine life to special communities set apart from the commons and in part depending on the latter's service for their sustainability. Where Christianity in the West is concerned, the thesis of Lynn White exposed, long ago, the theological roots of the ecological crisis. Ever since White's thesis appeared, it has become increasingly futile to exonerate Western Christian theology of its eco-crimes, and I will not attempt to do so here. What I will assay, instead, is to reexamine doctrine from the point of view of a damaged planet. From this exercise I will conclude that if theology is still significant today it is because and not in spite of its continued insistence on the ontological entanglement, and on the entanglement of ontology that the Trinity bespeaks. It is this continued insistence—both methodological and historical—that I wish to address.

Catherine Keller in two recent books, *Cloud of the Impossible: Negative Theology and Planetary Entanglement* (2014) and *Political Theology of the Earth: Our Planetary Emergency and the Struggle for a New Public* (2018), proposes that there is a homology between ecological and theological thinking. This homology appears, from the side of theology, in mystical theology

---

2. Haraway, *Staying with the Trouble*, 99–103.
3. Ruether, *Gaia & God*, 188.

and the *via negativa* of Pseudo-Dionysius. Pseudo-Dionysius described the ascent to God as a path of negations. One negates speech, reason, will, and desire in order to draw close to God. To love God, for Keller, is thus to embrace ignorance. It is also to embrace relationality, since relations evade epistemic certainty. In the same way, ecological thinking attempts to recognize and foster entanglement.

Keller intimates that one of the reasons for the ecological relevance of mystical theology is its habit of clinging to God's unthinkability. *Thinkability* has been, perhaps, one of the thorniest problems for ecology. The concept of ecology was coined in the nineteenth century by the zoologist Ernst Haeckel. Haeckel proposed ecology as a discipline for mapping the relations of creatures to their organic and inorganic environments. Later, this notion developed into the popular concept of an "ecosystem." The implication was that life was systematic, that is, predictable. Quite aside from oversimplifying the complexity and chanciness of life, Haeckel's ecology made everything that did not fit into the model seem unthinkable. By contrast, mystical theology loves the unthinkable. Moreover, by refusing thinkability to God, mystical theology refuses thinkability also to that to which God is linked by descending degrees of analogy. If the unthinkability of God is linked by analogy to the unthinkability of things, the logical problem of thinking of God is extended in descending degrees of analogy to all entangled relations. If, alternatively, unthinkability coincides with thinkability, and even this ostensible unthinkableness can be conjoined and thought in and through a higher way of thinking, then this problem can be answered by discovering a mystical way of thinking that which is unthinkable. In place of the single system, there is a cascade of entangled relations. And in place of a single principle, there is Trinitarian life. The task of theologians in the Anthropocene is then to attune theology as best as possible to the unthinkability of God of which the world is the vestige and trace; to feel the non-humanness of God; and to remember the godlikeness of the nonhuman.

As Terran life is being hurtled into a sixth mass-extinction event, one way for theologians to kick back against the forces propelling excessive death would be to perceive creatures differently. The world is tangled with God analogues, meaning it is crowded with other-than-human things and creatures who are treated and viewed as considerably less than divinely nonhuman. This way of thinking, which patristic theology understood as the business of reading *phusis*, nature, as God's book, is as endangered in Western Christianity as the species uprooted by some forms of Christian theology. It was a kind of spiritual exercise, and it is as a spiritual exercise that I will be rethinking both ecology and the Trinity.

Negative theology or apophaticism may be a specialized word unfamiliar to most. Yet the hermeneutic that it recommends is a particular way of looking, and does not, at bottom, require any book learning. Mystical perception, like ecological thinking, is a matter of recognizing the nonhuman, our entanglement with nonhumans, a recognition that for many is effortless, and a kind of "magical thinking." As even toddlers can recognize, it is a matter of reacting. For only when we are able to act on the matter of the relations revealed will it be possible to make that thinking matter for the planetary entanglement at stake in the present epoch.

Every mystical appercection is an ecological exercise in becoming aware of this entanglement, and then acting accordingly. As Timothy Morton has shown, "ecological" is not something one becomes but something one already is: "You are already a symbiotic being entangled with other symbiotic beings."[4] Thinking the unthinkable is difficult in theory, but not in practice. It needs to be practiced as well as theorized. For, if we stop at theory, the whole thing could just seem impossible. The French philosopher and mystic Simone Weil reflects on the importance of practice in relation to thinking the Trinity. She argues that when we treat the Trinity as a doctrine, we "[combine] incompatible assertions [of the Trinity] as if they were compatible." For Weil, the presentation of the Trinity one may find in a catechism encourages a reader not to feel the paradox expressed by the doctrine as paradox. Weil calls this insensitivity to the force of paradox an "illegitimate use of contradiction." The "legitimate use," by contrast, she describes as: "accepting two incompatible truths . . . recognizing them as such, and . . . making of them as it were the two arms of a pair of pincers, an instrument for entering indirectly into contact with the sphere of transcendent truth inaccessible to our intelligence." In other words, Weil does not think that the Trinity is accessible to intelligence, that it is "thinkable." Rather than thinking about the Trinity, Weil proposes that the Trinity be used as a tool for relating to God. The "sense" of the Trinity would then lie not in its doctrinal intelligibility, but in the *sensing* of God that would result from a person picking up the Trinity as a tool and with it "entering directly into contact with the sphere of transcendence."[5]

Those sensations are needed, now more so than ever. Picking up the Trinity as a tool for relating to God, one may see in this usefulness also a way of intensifying ecological relationality. The doctrine of the Trinity would then be a tool for teaching and thinking of divine relations by which it would be possible to touch, indirectly, upon the entanglement between human and

---

4. Morton, *Being Ecological*, 215.
5. Weil, *Oppression and Liberty*, 159.

nonhuman. It would then be a means by which entanglement is felt, and "recognized as such."[6] The Trinity has perhaps often been misunderstood, as if the circuit of its hypostases contained no admixture of affect—as though it were a computer-generated consonance from which overtones and inherent dissonances had been digitally edited out. However, that sort of system thinking has no real purchase on a doctrine that encompasses filicide and reproach, any less than it has on the Terran life that birthed it.

Theology has traditionally understood the Trinity to be strange and unthinkable; a dazzling darkness; yet, too often, that strangeness has been estranged from earthbound life. When it first appeared in the West, however, the imagery of a triune deity was presented as an icon of ecstatic and liminal spaces connected to chthonic—that is, earthy—realms. The statue of the Greek goddess Hekate was placed in homes but also and above all at crossroads, clefts in the road creating three paths. Hence, Hekate was depicted as triple and three personed. Locals would offer to this triune Hekate *katharmata*, "garbage, trash, offscourings of any kind," which were plundered by the poor and homeless, and which seem to have been the origin of her connection to the underworld; to death and decay; but also, and by the same token, to the rebirth of life out of the dirt.[7]

In the influential Chaldean theology that emerges around her triple appearance, she is witness to Persephone's abduction and comforter of Demeter. Yet, she is also the one who descends into the underworld and the mother whose child is lost to death. Together with her role as recipient of kitchen waste, she is the mistress of refuse, comforter of the refused and transformer of earth, the composting psychopomp, to whom nothing is excluded, and to whom, indeed, the excluded matters most of all.[8] There is nothing more familiar than kitchen waste and refuse.

The culture of relating to Hekate in the Hellenistic world developed alongside Christianity. Who knows how much now-forgotten cross-spiritual entanglement it had with "our" notion of the Trinity.[9]

How might one think the "Trinity" according to the unthinkability that the concept compels the perceiver to touch and to get in touch with, albeit indirectly? Evoking a triune earth goddess may initially seem irreverent, but may ultimately make good theological sense. For the Trinity is a

---

6. On the ecological thinking implicit in Weil's mystical theology, see Gabellieri and Kotva, "From Self to World."

7. Smith, "Hekate's Suppers," 58. On Chaldean Hekate, see Johnston, *Hekate Soteira*.

8. Smith, "Hekate's Suppers."

9. On Hekate and Christ, see Anne, "Apocalypse of John."

transformation of perception. It is not one specific story about God, but rather a way of thinking of the God who changes how we think everything else for which God is the tug and pull, especially how one may think and interact with the created matter so often thought not to matter. That sort of transformation needs to shake one up, at least a bit.

Unthinkable entanglement is not accessible only in the wilderness, whether spiritual or physical. A walk down any urban street or visit to the compost heap will deliver it in armfuls. The usefulness of an encounter with other-than-Christian trinities is, it seems, made possible by the fact that the obvious entanglement, similarities, and convergences appear to offer an opportunity to think Trinitarianly again of the history of the Trinity. That history tangles its own stories, and what theology thinks of an entangled human-divine world, must be worked through by reentering the unthinkable complexity, not only of earthbound life, but also and especially of earthbound life's doctrines and traditions.

We can begin to weave together these feelings of Trinitarian ontology. The Trinity historically offers many icons for getting high. Spiritual ascents aside, what is at issue here is "*deepening*, of getting *down* as well as *getting high*."[10] It is okay if being entangled makes one shudder and spin—in fact, it is no bad thing. It is okay if the Trinity makes one laugh, weep, jump up and down in rage—in fact, it is even desirable. So long as those feelings do not fester they are a sign of successful reactivation. This happens when those who think about the Trinity also think Trinitarianly; when those who already are entangled begin to sense their entanglement. The unthinkable is not waiting at the end of things; the unthinkable presses in on us now, erupts in every news flash of species extinction and planetary injustice. "Why do you stand looking up toward heaven?" (Acts 1:11 NRSV). The end is entangled with the present, heaven with earth.

What confident articulations of the unthinkable and unspeakable! Still, to say nothing seemed unfitting. For the nothing that is blank emptiness is not anything, while the nothing that swells with possibility is the place of future living.

---

10. Starhawk, *Dreaming the Dark*, 26; emphasis in original.

9

Participation in the Divine Heart
On Faith and Trinitarian Knowing

Katherine Apostolacus

> And, again entering into Capernaum, after some days it was heard that [Jesus] was in a house. And many gathered, so that there was not even room before the door, and he spoke the word to them. And they come bearing a paralytic to him, carried by four men. And, not being able to reach him on account of the crowd, they took away the roof where was and, having gouged out an opening, they lower the pallet on which the paralytic lay. And Jesus, seeing their faith, says to the paralytic, "Child, your sins are forgiven." (Mark 2:1–5)[1]

THE STANDARD READING OF this gospel story hinges on the following points: Jesus lays claim to the title "Son of Man"; he bears the power to forgive sins and heal; and he tells the paralytic, "Take up your mat and walk!" This is, in the broad scheme of things. Yet in the setup for this christological insight, we are often liable to miss a spiritual insight of faith.

---

1. From David Bentley Hart, *New Testament*; all English quotations in this chapter are from this translation unless otherwise stated. See also Matt 9:1–8; Luke 5:17–26. Mark's Greek in 2:5 reads: Καὶ ἰδὼν ὁ Ἰησοῦς τὴν πίστιν αὐτῶν, λέγει τῷ παραλυτικῷ, Τέκνον, ἀφίενταί σου αἱ ἁμαρτίαι.

In each version of this synoptic story, Jesus sees "their faith" (τὴν πίστιν αὐτῶν) and heals the paralyzed man. "Their" (αὐτῶν) is used multiple times beforehand to refer to the men carrying the paralyzed man, excluding the paralyzed man. The suggestion then seems to be that it was not the paralyzed man, but rather the men who carried the paralyzed man whose faith had been the occasion for the healing. They had believed on the paralyzed man's behalf. It does not seem to matter, in this moment, whether the paralyzed man himself believes. Hence, what we see in this story is an epistemic and ontological phenomenon, which is given theological weight.

If one can believe for another, then faith can exceed that which is held by the subject. Faith is not only *mine for myself*, but also *for the other*. This excess is in keeping with the Trinitarian structure of knowledge. Faith constitutes a mode of knowing analogous to the knowledge of God—a sacrificial knowledge, wherein we ourselves are emptied for the sake of Christ, the church, and the world. To bring this into full view, we must investigate how knowledge is not merely an intellectual assent to fixed propositions, but rather, and more richly, a participation in the thing known according to the mode of the knower.[2]

Knowledge in Trinitarian Form

We know the Trinity only by faith, Aquinas says, and not by natural reason.[3] It is known, as Edith Stein describes, by "a dark knowledge."[4] For faith that abides amid suffering is that which assents to a knowledge that is irreducible to fixed, formal, and propositional logic. Our faith does not, as Feuerbach alleges, produce God. Rather, God produces something in us through faith.[5] Hence, faith derives its epistemic character from the nature of divine knowledge. And, moreover, such knowledge can be acquired only through some degree of participation with the other.

Stein tells us that God knows humanity through a perfect and transcendent empathy. Empathy constitutes knowledge of another. It is how we know another consciousness. However, the persons of the Trinity are not "other consciousness" to one another. Rather, according to the Nicene formulae, they are three distinct persons (hypostases) of one and the same essence (ousia). Hence, the Trinity displays a communion of three persons in one divine essence, which shares one being (homoiousios) and, from

---

2. Aquinas, *Summa Theologiae*, pt. 1, q. 16, art. 1.
3. Aquinas, *Summa Theologiae*, pt. 1, q. 32, art. 1.
4. Stein, *Science of the Cross*, 46.
5. Feuerbach, *Essence of Christianity*, 10–27.

its essence, a radical self-knowledge of one divine Logos. This divine self-knowledge or subjectivity is, moreover, intrinsic to the Trinity. It is not learned from a prior state of ignorance; Aquinas describes how "knowledge is not a quality of God, nor a habit; but substance and pure act."[6] If God's knowledge is united as a pure act, then it follows that the nature of knowledge is that of the *unity of being*. We know, therefore, only insofar as we participate in the being of the thing known. Here, we should recall Aquinas's treatment of knowledge: "The thing known is in the knower according to the mode of the knower."[7] To the same end, Catherine Pickstock writes that "knowledge, for Aquinas, is therefore akin to an ontological event" rather than a merely psychological or epistemological phenomenon.[8] Indeed, "love alone is credible."[9]

For the men carrying the paralyzed man, it is not in their having believed a certain abstract proposition that Jesus heals the paralyzed man, but rather by their action that is concomitant with their faith. Action is thus an external unfolding of finite being across time and space. So, to have faith is not merely an assent to a set of propositions, but rather and more corporeally to embody a certain manner of being that overflows beyond oneself, even as it concretely inscribes the intentions of the self into a corporate and spiritual body. In her book *Epistemic Authority*, Linda Zagzebski provides an account of epistemic exemplars. Epistemic exemplars, she writes, are those we admire, those we "desire to imitate."[10] Admiration is thus an emotion of attraction, which, in its epistemic form, is crucial in "acquiring intellectual virtues, learning the norms of inquiry, and assessing our beliefs."[11] It is what ties trust in my own faculties and emotions with those of another. However, we might suspect that Zagzebski's formulation remains far too beholden to a propositional scaffolding of belief. For although she speaks of epistemic values and the cultivation of epistemic virtues, the product values and virtues are self-contained in a system of logical propositions. The consequences are seen well in her discussion of faith as an epistemic phenomenon. Faith is a trust in God's testimony, she argues. On its face, this is a fine proposition. However, she expounds, after a discussion of revelation, that faith is ultimately about the likelihood that the beliefs I acquire from it will be truth

---

6. Aquinas, *Summa Theologiae*, pt. 1, q. 14, art. 1, ad. 1.
7. Aquinas, *Summa Theologiae*, pt. 1, q. 12, art. 4.
8. Pickstock, *After Writing*, 131.
9. Balthasar, *Love Alone Is Credible*.
10. Zagzebski, *Epistemic Authority*, 89.
11. Zagzebski, *Epistemic Authority*, 90.

conducive, and will satisfy conscientious self-reflection.[12] Furthermore she remarks that "what is handed on (*traditum*)" in tradition "is not limited to a product like a text or the process of making a product like Murano glass, but a way of living in contact with God. That includes having certain beliefs about God, human beings, and the relation between them, as well as characteristic emotions, attitudes, and sacraments that express religious truths in simple external ways in which ordinary people can participate."[13]

As the author of Hebrews relates, "faithfulness is the substance of things hoped for, the evidence of unseen realities" (Heb 11:1). Now, in Zagzebski's formulation, we would be hoping for true beliefs. Yet, I suggest, it would be far better for us to hope in a person, or the life of a world to come wrought by that person. Indeed, as has often been pointed out, faith can be dead, even in spite of believing in all of that which is true. As Anselm writes, "A living faith believes *in* what it to believe in, whereas a dead faith merely believes what it ought to believe."[14] Accordingly, our faith is not an assent to believe in a set of fixed and finite propositions, but rather in the God who is given to us to be understood in and through the experiential media that are expressed by those propositions. Belief—as all intellectual activity—happens when we are compelled by a reality other than ourselves.

Pickstock has recently reinvigorated this notion of intellect, with her notion of *conformation*. In *Aspects of Truth*, she writes that "such conforming is not a theoretical, but an existential matter. Truth is eternal reality, which includes eternity's gift of the finite and the unity of the two. To be in truth is a matter of worship, or of being in the state of prayer."[15] But here, Pickstock makes explicit what is only implicit in Zagzebski's account of knowledge, namely, that the most thorough account of truth (and our participation in it) is metaphysical, and not (at its most basic level) epistemological, for it is the eternal gift of God rather than the mastery of the finite mind. And this, likewise, is how the divine persons constitute in their perichoretic gift to each other one simple substance of truth. *It is simply love.*

We are, then, *ontologically bound* in the Trinity by imitating the Trinity's own knowledge. If faith produces any kind of knowledge, it, too, would require epistemic exemplars. After Christ, the best exemplar should be the great cloud of witnesses. For the saints teach us both how to have faith and how they have faith for us. At this juncture, one might object that belief in the communion and intercession of saints would trivialize the free assent

12. Zagzebski, *Epistemic Authority*, 198–99.
13. Zagzebski, *Epistemic Authority*, 197–98.
14. Anselm, *Monologion*, ch. 78; emphasis in original.
15. Pickstock, *Aspects of Truth*, 281. Stein argues similarly in *Finite and Eternal Being*.

of individual belief. However, we can, on the contrary, argue that it makes individual belief the very basis for corporate belief and collective healing. There is no great cloud of witnesses without an aggregate of individual saints. Rather the lives of the saints are each imitations of Christ. For we can have faith in Christ because Christ has faith in us. This cloud of witnesses thus participates in the heart of God, of faith in God and faith in others. Indeed, the gospel is not only for those who believe. Above all, the gospel is for those who do not yet have faith.

Divine love is an example to us, but it is not only an example. It is the very thing that makes our own littlest loves possible. In this way, God gives, as his own gift to us, our gift of love to him. It is not, therefore, a plain economy of give-and-take but an economy that anticipates, enables, and cherishes the gift to come. So God gives his own gift on behalf of us, which cannot be an excuse not to give ourselves in return (lest we succumb to the *vanity of vanities*), but must compel us to give and thereby receive again the eternal gift of God's love.

The *Credo* and Faith for the Other

Creeds are meant to be prayed as well as recited. Their contents are valuable not only as a set of fixed and finite propositional judgments. And when prayed, they are prayed for more than me, more than an aggregate of individual believers. Indeed, as Sarah Coakley writes, "Only *God* can 'take over' nature; that is not human theology's task. It is the Spirit's interruption that finally enables full human participation in God."[16] Such interruptions often happen in prayer.[17] The prayer of the church is a moment for the Holy Spirit to be made manifest to us. Even our most accusatory, lamentable prayers invite God to dwell with us. We are, in another sense, invited in prayer to recognize the presence of God, who is always already here. And this is true as much in rote prayers as in praying the creed.

To pray the orthodox creeds is both to participate as a corporate whole in the divine being and to petition for the church to increasingly become like Christ. And where, in its weakness of spirit, any one member of the church may be weak in believing, the whole corporate church prays for each of them as well. Hence, during the Mass, we *pray the creeds* rather than simply reciting them. The purpose of the creed is not only for each congregant to affirm their own private belief in a list of propositions. The statements of the creed

---

16. Coakley, *God, Sexuality, and the Self*, 89; emphasis in original.

17. This is the subject of her third chapter, "Praying the Trinity," in Coakley, *God, Sexuality, and the Self*, 100–151.

are doxological, in the sense of a performative declaration of what each and altogether hold to be truth of the Christian faith. It is thus a corporate rather than an atomic act of worship. For praying the creeds takes the truth of the creeds into one's own soul such that they may overflow. This practice is much richer than if a group of people were to sign a petition stating that they assent to this list of propositions. As Pickstock writes,

> The *Credo* fulfills its ancient catechetical function not as an exposition apart from faith, but as a performative *act* of faith—a confession in its truest sense—which perforce *disseminates* its components: this doxological expression of the doctrinal boundaries of belief radiates outwards in a contagion of definitive boundlessness.[18]

This "contagion of definitive boundlessness" is not only the boundlessness of content in a negative or apophatic theological mode. But it is an expression of the boundlessness of grace, and of a grace that makes porous the boundaries of any atomically isolated praying subject. Porosity is, like a thatched roof pulled back, to go above the crowd of sense data and mere propositions—like a friend's faith forming me.

Neither is faith reducible to a rationalistic or intellectualist operation, nor does faith exclude the intellect. Rather it names the movement of the intellect toward what is beyond human grasp through any natural capacity. To this end, William Desmond remarks that "philosophy is not just thought thinking itself but also entails thought thinking what is other to thought. In our philosophical attendance on the intimate universal there is more than the autonomous self-determination of thinking seeking to be consistent and at home with itself. There is the opening of thinking, either through itself or through interruption by what is beyond thought, to what is more than thought itself."[19] Similarly, Edith Stein writes that "the unbounded loving surrender to God and God's return gift, full and enduring union . . . is the highest elevation of the heart attainable, the highest level of prayer. Souls who have attained it are truly the heart of the church, and in them lives Jesus' high priestly love."[20] This very heart "can do nothing but radiate to other hearts the divine love that fills [it] and so participate in the perfection of all into unity in God."[21] Participating in this radiance of God's love is, notably, a passive act, but not only passive. It leads us to rest, which, as Stein

---

18. Pickstock, *After Writing*, 207–8; emphasis in original.
19. Desmond, *Intimate Universal*, 116–17.
20. Stein, *Hidden Life*, 15–16.
21. Stein, *Hidden Life*, 16.

suggests, is the telos of all activity.[22] It is not by our own natural power that we are saved but rather and only by a free gift of God. And yet participation in this gift constitutes, as Pickstock writes, an active "submission to a narrative mode of knowledge which disallows the isolation of empirical or intellectual essences, [and] subordinates that which the worshiper knows and does to that which passes through him, beyond his analytic grasp."[23]

Those who cannot yet, in their heart, pray the creed with us, are blessed nevertheless. The heart of God comes to them before they can go to him. The Father approaches Cain, the Son incarnates, and the Holy Spirit is sent as advocate.

Those whose only dogma is the death of God, the so-called "radical theologians," nevertheless have their haven in the church, despite their philosophical hang-ups. Noëlle Vahanian, for instance, remarks that "eyes wide-open, love is like a letter that never arrives or like a message in a bottle, and sometimes, it is like a big sheriff," which is to say something greater than infinity though confined to the utterance of words.[24] Her "secular theology of language" seeks "the reversal of Platonism" for which "there is no sun to see behind the shadows."[25] But there's little arguing with a broken heart; instead, the heart needs the salve of love, whose absence is the cause of its breaking.

Hence, the church prays the creeds for them, not as an empty credo, but rather because it is the house of God, who is pure actuality, immeasurably merciful, perfectly good, and in all triune. The body of Christ thus helps us in our unbelief.[26] Even when the church fails to believe, Christ in us believes for us. This is his grace. And when the world refuses to believe, the body of Christ believes on its behalf. Like the paralyzed man, Christ himself lowers us through the roof to the Father by the power of the Holy Spirit. This is the slightest taste of life of the world to come, love put to its greatest work, putting "all infinity, all wisdom, all power to work."[27]

Since we pray the creeds on behalf of the other, the church intercedes even on behalf of our enemies. The Trinitarian intervention into epistemology, then, consists in this: knowledge is not only an adequate reflection of reality nor only developed through imitation of epistemic virtue, but it is also a manner of *existing with and for another, beyond oneself*. A knower must exist with the known, must participate in being somehow, in order to

---

22. Stein, *Finite and Eternal Being*, 438.
23. Pickstock, *After Writing*, 208.
24. Vahanian, *Rebellious No*, 134.
25. Vahanian, *Rebellious No*, 77.
26. See Mark 9:24; Luke 17:5.
27. Marion, *Erotic Phenomenon*, 22.

know in any way at all. The knower must, in this way, leap outside herself, allow herself to become porous, like a gouged-out roof. Through prayer, through the sacraments, through Scripture, we come to know God as he is revealed to us, as incarnate, and as he exists in and for us.[28]

---

28. Many thanks are due to my friends and colleagues at Villanova for their willingness to give feedback on drafts of this paper: Jake Given, Dr. Stephen Napier, Ailie Posillico, Mal Robinson, Laura Simpson, and Dr. Jim Wetzel. Thanks also to Dr. Delia Popa and my peers in our Decolonial Phenomenology seminar where early musings of this piece were worked out. I am greatly indebted to Kayla Robbins, whose long-lasting friendship and critical eyes taught me more than the earth's books can admit, and R. Michael Wilcher, through whose tragically brief friendship I gained considerable encouragement. Last, many thanks are due to Ryan Haecker, who organized the conference where the original paper was presented and kindly offered hospitality to me while I lodged in Cambridge. *Nisi amor moreretur, nunquam de occatur inferno resurget.*

Part Four

Eschatology and Revelation

10

Eschatological Being

Judith Wolfe

Phenomenology as a Philosophy of Immanence

THE CRITIQUE OF ONTOLOGY defined twentieth-century philosophy in both the Anglo-American and the European traditions. In Europe, the most generative form of this critique was phenomenology, which sought to be true to what can appear and be known to humans from within their cognitive apparatus—in other words, to be true to humans' structures of intentionality, their ways of relating themselves to others and to objects. In the hands of thinkers like Martin Heidegger, this phenomenological method meant a bracketing of metaphysics (which now appeared formulated from a spurious God's-eye view), and with it, ultimately, a bracketing of any talk about God. Because God was, for Heidegger following Kierkegaard, of an "infinite qualitative difference" from humans, coming to them (if at all) wholly from without, philosophers cannot responsibly speak of him.

This suspicion of metaphysics begins as an epistemological argument; but like Kant, Heidegger underpins it with a logical one. What God may give humans—the gift of grace as a participation in divine plenitude—is not in fact thinkable. To try to think it results in an existential antinomy similar to Kant's antinomies of reason: the very "eschatological unrest" that defines human existence—its dynamics of desire—cannot in fact find "completion" without ceasing to be what it most deeply is: life as movement and striving. This was already noted by Kant and even by Hegel.

Death, here, plays a role that is both existential and logical. It bounds our life existentially: at the very moment when we could say, "Now I am fully myself; I no longer have actions and passions ahead of me that will shape and define who I am," we no longer are. The moment of completion is also the moment of death, of no longer knowing ourselves at all. In this role, death, for Heidegger, also serves as a logical symbol of the impossibility of plenitude.

For Heidegger, as we know, this results in a vision of humanity that is defined by an ethical imperative: the imperative neither to deny the pull of plenitude nor to surrender to its illusion. He gives us, in other words, an ethical inflection of the (Kantian) problem of metaphysics, centering on a morally charged description of "the human" as defined most vitally by the tension between ineluctable finitude and the equally persistent desire to transcend it. The aim of philosophy is here no longer to aspire to a transcendent ideal, but to sustain an "authentic" human existence by refusing to collapse this constitutive tension into either a metaphysical metanarrative or an apathetic denial of its allure.

Diastatic and Diathetic Responses to This Challenge

In the course of the twentieth century, two main theological strategies developed for responding to Heidegger's challenge from within a phenomenological tradition; call them the diastatic and the diathetic. By *diastatic* I mean arguments against the exclusion of God from phenomenological description that focus on the implications of *desire* as a basic mode of human intentionality. By *diathetic*, I mean arguments that focus on the human openness to identity-shaping experiences that come from out with their own structures of intentionality.

First, the diastatic. Catholics such as Henri de Lubac (here following Maurice Blondel), Edith Stein, and Karl Rahner argued that rather than naturally bracketing any speculation about a supernatural origin or end to human existence, phenomenology in fact fails in its core task of describing human intentionality if it ignores the inalienable presence within human self-consciousness of an orientation toward the supernatural. The Catholics parse this inalienable presence in different ways: Stein as the infinite toward which finite human consciousness "breaks open";[1] Rahner as the horizon of

---

1. Stein, *Aufbau der menschlichen Person*, 32.

all human acts of knowing;[2] but most influentially, Lubac (after Blondel) as a "natural desire for the supernatural." Although Blondel stressed that only God could reveal himself as the fulfillment of the God-shaped "blank spaces" naturally felt,[3] these existential "needs"[4] themselves were an inalienable part of human experience, and therefore could not be excluded from an existential phenomenology. Lubac shifts Blondel's terminology of "need" to the more affirmative one of "desire," and argues that the experience of desire is not a mere recognition of lack, but itself already an indication of an identity-defining divine call.

Stein, Rahner, Blondel, and Lubac all trace their responses back to Thomas Aquinas. In other words, the challenge posed by phenomenology spurs them to reread Thomas (as well as Augustine, Bonaventure, and others)[5] in a phenomenological light, seeking in the ancients' discussions of anamnesis and divine illumination veins of experience that would not be ruptured by the phenomenologists' razor.

Second, the diathetic. Instead of trying to accommodate an openness to the transcendent in human structures of intentionality (such as desire), later French philosophers, including Jean-Luc Marion, Emmanuel Levinas, and Jean-Yves Lacoste, reject the frame of "intentionality" altogether, arguing instead that the most important phenomena, even of everyday experience, are those that claim or overwhelm us from outside our own intentional movements. It is precisely those irrupting phenomena—for Levinas the face, for Marion and others the saturated phenomenon—by whose affect we are constituted. For the theologian, this means that we are not in fact making a phenomenologically *exceptional* case for God when we claim that he irrupts into human experience from outside human categories or intentionality: many kinds of phenomena do so. As with the diastatic approach, talk of God is saved from the phenomenological critique by a re-staking of phenomenology's bounds from within.

Theologically, these two strategies can crudely be said to map onto familiar divides between theologies of glory and theologies of the cross: the first assumes a connatural stretching toward God, the second the irruption of a radically other God from beyond our structures of knowing.

---

2. See esp. Rahner, *Spirit in the World*.

3. See Blondel, *Letter on Apologetics*, 160; see also Murphy, "Influence of Maurice Blondel."

4. Blondel, *Letter on Apologetics*, 157–58.

5. These are the three Lubac singles out in the service of the church; see Murphy, "Influence of Maurice Blondel," 74.

Ontologically, the first conceives God (analogically) *as* Being; the second conceives Being univocally, and God as beyond it.

Desire and Participation

The movements of both *ressourcement* and Radical Orthodoxy have primarily adopted the first, diastatic strategy of overcoming the phenomenological challenge from within. This is partly because its language of desire dovetails with a renewed, catholic characterization of God not primarily through appeal to infinite qualitative difference, but through appeal to his indwelling in our innermost depths. In other words, these responses are metaphysically underpinned by the assertion of a participation (whether Neoplatonic or analogical in emphasis) in the Trinitarian ground of being. This participation in plenitude also, as John Milbank has often written, calls for a different logic: a logic of gift and excess.

We see this in many places throughout the writings of Radical Orthodoxy. Catherine Pickstock asserts that the Christian desire for the good "does not lack its object in the ordinary sense of lack, but attains its goal in and through the act of desiring."[6] And, in concurrence with Henri de Lubac, John Milbank writes: "Spiritual beings in their deepest identity are lured to unity with God—even in some sense already possess this unity."[7]

Pickstock sees this participation as proleptically realized in the liturgy. Through acknowledgment of our brokenness and limitation, she thinks, we can yet break through, in this hallowed space, to participation in the heavenly realm, in which time is turned to peace: "The request for peace can only be made authentically from within peace, from within the heavenly realm which we now do not merely impersonate."[8]

The work of reconstructing an ontology of finite reality by participation in the Trinity—whether experientially mediated by desire or the reception of saturated phenomena—is vital. However, it faces temptations that must be countered. These temptations arise, in part, from a dilemma: such an ontology needs to be instantiated to count for anything, and yet is manifestly not instantiated now. Hence, reconstructions of an idealized medieval era in which the participatory ontology the writers sketch was real is so integral to their accounts.

---

6. Pickstock, *After Writing*, 13.

7. Milbank, *Suspended Middle*, 56.

8. Pickstock, *After Writing*, 237–38. For a more extended engagement, see Grant, "Eschatological Critique."

Even in the present, there are, of course, always witnesses to experiences of participation, both in and outside the eucharistic liturgy. And yet, many of these witnesses are deeply fraught. They are vulnerable to disconfirmation ("what I thought was plenitude was really manipulation"), to over narrating ("that God saved me from this illness proved his special love for me," regardless of those who died of it), and re-narrating (ask anyone whose family has fallen apart). Narratives of plenitude are hard to shield from the construction of political utopias or the over valorization of perceived instantiations of Trinitarian participation. More generally, participatory ontology finds it very hard to avoid some form of pantheism.

Desire and Eschatology

Martin Heidegger, for all his own blind spots, has to be taken seriously here. Human temporality and mortality cannot simply be outpaced toward participation in plenitude, whether in knowledge or being. Participatory ontology is too often over-realized eschatology.

The phenomenological critique, therefore, demands an eschatological dimension to Trinitarian ontology: a theology of participation that takes more seriously the eschatological preliminariness of human knowing and being. Attending to a phenomenology of desire is essential to this. Because Heidegger is right: the desire we may feel for God is precisely the desire for something that could not be given in our spatiotemporal existence: it is an existential aporia.

The object of our desire for plenitude, in other words, is impossible to determine from within. This is partly because desire is always mediated by imagination, while the fulfillment of desire is strictly beyond our imagination. We can never fully escape the Feuerbachian and Derridean critique that desire and imagination may simply project its own image.[9] Of course we have knowledge of God in Christ: God is not an entire eschatological unknown. Yet what we see in Christ is not, for the most part, God in glory. Rather, it is a God-man obediently walking a path leading to death, "for the joy that lay before him" (Heb 12:2 NRSV). As George MacDonald says, "The door into life generally opens behind us," and "the only wisdom" for one "haunted with the scent of unseen roses, is work," i.e., the imitation of Christ.[10]

This does not mean that we should give up on desire. Thomas Aquinas, in a remarkable passage in the *Summa Theologiae*, even suggests that such desire may increase a capacity for beatitude:

---

9. See Wolfe, *Theological Imagination*, for a fuller elaboration of this point.
10. MacDonald, *Alec Forbes of Howglen*, 1:220.

> The intellect which has more of the light of glory will see God the more perfectly; and he will have a fuller participation of the light of glory who has more love; because where there is the greater love, there is the more desire; and desire in a certain degree makes the one desiring apt and prepared to receive the object desired. Hence he who possesses the more love, will see God the more perfectly, and will be the more beatified.[11]

However, it is vital to remember that desire is, as I've just said, for something that could not be given in our spatiotemporal existence. This is, I suggest, because our very mode of knowing now is merely an image, a preliminary, to the mode of knowing in which alone we could experience plenitude.

We know all things now partly by self-reflection—by taking into ourselves, as the Aristotelian-Scholastic tradition puts it, the thing known in the mode of the knower. But the New Testament suggests again and again that this "return to self" will be broken. "Now I see in a glass darkly; but then I shall see face to face" (1 Cor 13:12 NRSV).[12] "Beloved, now are we the children of God, and it doth not yet appear what we shall be: but we know that, when he shall appear, we shall be like him; for we shall see him as he is" (1 John 3:2 NRSV; see also Col 3:3–4).

To be created in the image of God, in Christ, means that we cannot fully know or be ourselves until we see him face to face. Contrary to the assumption of a basic and immediate epistemological access to the self that is prerequisite to all other knowledge, or the ability to take into ourselves all things known, St. Paul here projects knowledge (or vision) of *God* as the most direct form of self-knowledge. In the eschaton, he suggests, humans will know themselves not by reflecting on themselves but by beholding God and being beheld by him. This cannot mean a taking of God into ourselves, for he is infinite; it must mean a being taken of ourselves, somehow, into God—an entirely eccentric mode of knowledge of which our entire mode of knowing, here and now, where God is still hidden, is merely an image.

But this means that we can live our being-toward-death as a being toward self-surrender, a surrender that is not merely incidental to our entry into plenitude, but rather and essentially part of it. This is an epistemological inflection of Mark 8:35: "For whoever wishes to save his life will lose it, but whoever loses his life for my sake and the gospel's will save it" (NRSV). Being-toward-death, for the Christian, simply is being-toward-God.

---

11. Aquinas, *Summa Theologiae* 1.12.6.
12. See Wolfe, "Eschatology and Human Knowledge."

11

Martin Heidegger's Poetics and the End of Ontotheology

The "Passing By" of the "Ultimate God"

Emily Stewart Long

When first beginning to think a "new Trinitarian ontology," turning to the work of Martin Heidegger may not at all be the obvious choice. Not a thinker who is traditionally compatible with Christian theology, a clear understanding of Heidegger's reflections on the history of metaphysics and theology is, however, critical to a project of this kind. The following is not meant to provide any Heideggerian analysis of Trinitarian ontology, nor is it meant to provide any appraisal. Rather, it is simply designed to provide an entry point from which some creative insight may be taken.

This essay offers an explication of Heidegger's thinking on "ontotheology," a term active in his later work that characterized the history of metaphysics as the history of theology. Only emerging as a theme after Heidegger's radical historicization of ontology and his shift away from *Being and Time*, Heidegger's encounter with ontotheology is best understood by looking to the role of poetry during *die Kehre* (the turn), a period ranging from the completion of *Being and Time* in 1927 until the early 1940s wherein the poet Friedrich Hölderlin became one of Heidegger's key interlocutors.

Though the status of poetry in Heidegger's philosophy resists brief summary, one can say with certainty that it was with Heidegger's first Hölderlin lectures in 1934–35 that poetry became his select partner in bringing about an end to ontotheology and seeking an "other beginning" of thought, which Heidegger understood in terms of salvation, the mystery of the divine, and the myth of "the holy," as these themes appear specifically in the futural hermeneutic quality of poetry itself. For Heidegger, poetry has the capacity to shelter the divine, making possible a final "turning away" from the age of technological modernity characterized by what he calls the "passing by" of the "ultimate God," a God that is to be guarded as a mystery.

But what does Heidegger mean when he says "ontotheology"? From the Greek *ontos* (ὄντος) and *theologia* (θεολογία, a reasoning about the gods), "ontotheology" indicates a theology for which a god (*theos*, θεός) is held to be at once the supreme Being and the ground of all beings. Any clear explication of this term takes us far beyond the period of the *Kehre*, yet its origin is essentially rooted in Heidegger's thinking from the years after the publication of *Being and Time*. In the wake of his 1927 deconstruction of metaphysics, Heidegger claims to have revealed a historical succession of epochal understandings of Being and argues that all of these "epochs" both have metaphysical foundations and make foundational claims. That is, Heidegger now sees the history of metaphysics as establishing the most basic conceptual parameters for the intelligibility of being in our world by ontologically grounding and theologically legitimating the changing historical meaning of what *is*.[1]

As early as 1951 Heidegger begins to offer reflections on his famous first call for a deconstruction of the metaphysical tradition in *Being and Time* in suggesting that it was an altogether "naïve" assumption that this deconstruction would have allowed him to recover a transhistorically binding fundamental ontology, that is, a vision of Being powerful enough to have been operant in every historical epoch.[2] *Being and Time* was a text that famously marked the beginning of Heidegger's confrontation with metaphysics, yet in this work Heidegger can also be seen as assuming an ahistorically valid understanding of Being, one that resulted in what he calls a kind of "permanent presence."

In the years following the publication of *Being and Time*, Heidegger begins to move away from this metaphysics of "permanent presence" and

1. Thompson, "End of Onto-Theology," 131–32.
2. Heidegger, *Seminare, 1951–1973*, 395.

turns instead to a more radical historicization of ontology, which compels him to investigate past historical understandings of Being to which we no longer have direct phenomenological access. For Heidegger this "turn" (*Kehre*) away from a philosophy of permanent presence toward the historicization of ontology is what he terms *Seinsgeschichte* (the history of Being). In *Seinsgeschichte*, the way in which metaphysics grounds the historical intelligibility of Being in a given epoch reveals that successive historical forms (*Gestalten*) of intelligibility have been submerged in and preserved by the metaphysical tradition itself. In categorizing and disseminating an understanding of what beings are, metaphysics, Heidegger argues, then provides each historical epoch with its ontological "bedrock." When Heidegger makes the claims that metaphysics *grounds* history, he means that metaphysics establishes both the most basic conceptual parameters of understanding and at the same time codes the standards of legitimacy for each successive age. These epochal "constellations of intelligibility," as he calls them, thus work to both ground and mirror a series of historical transformations.[3] In providing this bedrock, this *ground*, metaphysics then supplies intelligibility with a foundational justification of itself. Heidegger characterizes this foundational justification as "theological."[4]

But why and how the history of metaphysics became the history of ontotheology perhaps requires some further explication. In deepening fundamental arguments already laid out in his 1929 essay "What Is Metaphysics?," as well as his *Kant and the Problem of Metaphysics* from that same year, Heidegger's investigation begins to ask after the nature of a central question: *Was ist das Seiende?* (What is a being?) Worked out more explicitly in his extensive lectures on Nietzsche, particularly from 1940, 1941, and 1942, the central problem of metaphysics, Heidegger claims, is its attempt to ask after "the truth of the totality of beings as such."[5] In asking after what a being is, and at the same time thinking metaphysics as the "truth of the totality of beings as such," the central problem of metaphysics, that is, its understanding of *das Sein des Seienden* (the Being of beings), reveals itself as conceptually twofold—ambiguous to the bottom.[6]

Out of this fracture, Heidegger tells us, grow the intertwined histories of ontology and theology.[7] It is only in 1961, however, in "Kant's Thesis

---

3. Thompson, "End of Onto-Theology," 130–31.
4. Heidegger, *Seminare, 1951–1973*, 390–98.
5. Heidegger, *Nietzsches Metaphysik*, 4.
6. Heidegger, *Nietzsches Metaphysik*, 4.
7. Thompson, "End of Onto-Theology," 133.

About Being," that Heidegger gives us any tangible identification of these intertwined histories. He writes,

> If we recollect the history of Western-European thinking once more, then we will encounter the following: The question of Being, as the question of the Being of beings, is double in form. On the one hand, it asks: What is a being in general as a being? In the history of philosophy, reflections which fall within the domain of this question acquire the title ontology. The question "What is a being?" simultaneously asks: Which being is the highest being, and in what sense is it the highest being? This is the question of God and of the divine. We call the domain of this question theology. This duality in the question of the Being of beings can be united under the title onto-theology.[8]

What is important to note here is how the central question of metaphysics has necessarily folded over on itself. Heidegger's claim is that in functioning as ontology, metaphysics searches for the most general ground of beings. As more neatly expressed four years earlier in his famous essay "The Onto-Theo-Logical Constitution of Metaphysics" in *Identity and Difference*, metaphysics *is* ontology when it "thinks of being with an eye for the ground that is common to all beings as such."[9] These two questions, Heidegger tells us, are brought together in that when metaphysics thinks theologically, it "thinks of the totality of being as such . . . with regard to the supreme, all founding being."[10] If, for Heidegger, metaphysics asks after the mode of God's existence, then metaphysics seeks to understand the Being of God and finds itself asking questions about "the divine."[11] Yet in Heidegger's view it is precisely in this way that the *deepest problem* shows itself as "the still unthought unity of the essence of metaphysics."[12]

Given as the final lecture of a seminar on "Hegel's Science of Logic" in February of 1957, Heidegger's now famous *Identity and Difference* emphasizes that metaphysics is specially marked by what he calls an "oblivion" of Being, that is, by the forgetting of the ontological difference.[13] It is in this essay that Heidegger shows how Being has been thought of as the *ground* of beings.[14] In this way Heidegger sees metaphysics as grounding beings in the

8. Heidegger, "Kant's Thesis About Being," 340.
9. Heidegger, *Identity and Difference*, 70.
10. Heidegger, *Identity and Difference*, 70–71.
11. Thompson, "End of Onto-Theology," 137.
12. Heidegger, *Identity and Difference*, 55.
13. Heidegger, *Identity and Difference*, 50–51.
14. Heidegger, *Identity and Difference*, 57.

highest being, God. In this scenario, Being as such, God, and all other beings become tangled up, reciprocally grounding and justifying each other in such a way that their *difference* passes into oblivion, meaning that we could never go back to a point where Being and beings could be thought separately. To truly think the history of metaphysics anew, Heidegger argues, we must turn to face the ontological difference.

Meant in the simplest terms to indicate the difference between Being and beings, in Heidegger's thinking the ontological difference varies from that of classical theism in that it does not indicate any separation or distance between the two or their world as with the Trinitarian distinction. For Heidegger facing the ontological difference essentially compels us to turn toward openness—toward what is concealed. Only in 1964, in an essay entitled "The End of Philosophy and the Task of Thinking," does Heidegger explicitly associate the forgetting of *alētheia* (ἀλήθεια, truth as "disclosure, unconcealment") with the beginning of metaphysics and ontotheology.[15] In this essay he suggests that defining truth in terms of calculability is predicated on overlooking the essential unity of *alētheia* as un-concealment with *lethe* (λήθη, oblivion) as concealment, a central motif in Heidegger's thinking since his 1935 essay "The Origin of the Work of Art."[16]

To return again to the "deepest question," that of the still-unthought unity of the essence of metaphysics, it was in an essay from 1940 entitled "Plato's Doctrine of Truth" that Heidegger began to explore the deeper roots of this fundamental problem. In this essay Heidegger argues that the ontotheological distinction was first brought together implicitly in Plato's doctrine of the forms (*Gestalten*).[17] For Heidegger, the forms explain both the "thatness" and the "whatness" of beings. In his essay, Heidegger points out that within this onto-theological ambiguity, "thatness" for Plato becomes subordinated to "whatness," that is, as he writes, "The form accomplishes presence, namely, the presence of every being as what is." In Heidegger's reading of Plato, Being "has its proper essence in whatness."[18] Hence, for Plato, existence is dependent on its form (*Gestalt*).

Though Aristotle famously objects to Plato's contention that the existence of an idea is independent from the beings that instantiate it, in Heidegger's reading, Aristotle, in fact, "inscribes the onto-theological distinction into the heart of metaphysics" when, in order to explicitly differentiate "whatness" from "thatness," he distinguishes between *prōtē ousia*

---

15. Heidegger, "End of Philosophy," 446.
16. Heidegger, "End of Philosophy," 448.
17. Heidegger, "Plato's Doctrine of Truth," 168.
18. Heidegger, "Plato's Doctrine of Truth," 162.

(πρώτη οὐσία, primary substance) and *deutera ousia* (δευτέρα οὐσία, secondary substance).[19] In "The End of Philosophy and the Task of Thinking," Heidegger makes this problem clear in his reading of Aristotle. For Aristotle, *prōtē ousia* refers to the fact that something is. In keeping with Heidegger's understanding of "presence" as the basic characteristic of Western metaphysics, he characterizes Aristotle's description of *prōtē ousia* as a "persisting of something, which lingers in itself" and a "presence in the eminent and primal sense." On the other hand, the *deutera ousia* describes "*what* something is." Heidegger renders this as "presence in the secondary sense."[20] Thus in Heidegger's reading of Aristotle "to be" at all is to be present.

In his essay, Heidegger's claim that Aristotle is formalizing the onto-theological structure of metaphysics cannot, however, answer the question of the original fracture of ontology and theology. The lost phenomenological explanation of the original onto-theological distinction thus remains the "deepest problem" for Heidegger's understanding of metaphysics as ontotheology. The very possibility of answering it diminishes into the misty origins of Western history, into the mythos (μῦθος). To follow Heidegger's investigation of the history of metaphysics as ontotheology any further, we would have to refashion some vision of humanity's first confrontation with earth and heaven.[21]

Yet, for Heidegger, this is not a total loss. While making such investigations in "Plato's Doctrine of Truth" Heidegger is simultaneously working to elaborate a synchronic inquiry into the multifaceted "clearing" of Being at what he calls the "inception of its history."[22] Of this multifaceted clearing, Heidegger offers: "In the inception of its history, Being clears itself as emerging (*phusis*) [φύσις] and disclosure (*alētheia*). From there it acquires the cast of presence [*Anwesenheit*] and permanence [*Beständigkeit*] in the sense of enduring (*ousia*)."[23] In other words, before Being was interpreted in terms of permanent presence, it was thought and named as emergence and disclosure: *phusis* and *alētheia*. Since, further, *phusis* and *alētheia*, names given by Heraclitus and Parmenides respectively, manage to guard Being's inherent temporal dynamism, Heidegger calls this *phusis-alētheia* pair "the inceptive essence of Being."[24]

19. Thompson, "End of Onto-Theology," 33.
20. Heidegger, "End of Philosophy," 234; emphasis in original.
21. Thompson, "End of Onto-Theology," 163.
22. Heidegger, "End of Philosophy," 428–29.
23. Heidegger, "End of Philosophy," 430.
24. Heidegger, "End of Philosophy," 437.

In Heidegger's account of Parmenides and Heraclitus, Being manifests itself phenomenologically not as a *ground* but rather as simply *showing up*. That is, "Being" is expressed in temporally dynamic, non-foundational terms by the understanding of *phusis* as a "self-blossoming emergence" of phenomenological intelligibility and truth as an active "clearing" inherent in the "disclosure" of *alētheia*.[25] For Heidegger, this pre-Socratic understanding of Being as *phusis* and *alētheia* was "forgotten," became ossified into a "permanent presence" in ousia, assembled under the architectonic of technical forms, and was engulfed by the totalizing presence of metaphysics as such.[26]

Heidegger's hope is that taking on this problem could help us envision alternatives to our metaphysical epoch of "enframing" (*Gestell*) precisely by contesting our increasingly homogenized "age of technologically-leveled world civilization" and by recovering a non-metaphysical understanding of Being.[27] This hope forms the core of Heidegger's later thinking, as in essays like "The Question Concerning Technology," and was essentially inspired by the poetic vision behind his enigmatic call for a "new beginning" of thought in the years of the *Kehre*. The "deepest question" remains a misty one, yet this very quality allows Heidegger's thinking on ontotheology to take on a new, poetic form.

Having given a brief explication of Heidegger's thinking on ontotheology from a variety of works written after the *Kehre*, I want to turn to focus specifically on what many scholars consider the single most important moment in Heidegger's thinking after *Being and Time* during the years of the *Kehre*, specifically, his reading of Friedrich Hölderlin. Pervading Heidegger's thought from his first lectures on Hölderlin in the winter semester of 1934–35 until the end of his life, it was only through Hölderlin that Heidegger came to understand thinking as an essentially poetic task, one wherein art and existence transform into players in a hermeneutic wherein no single element can be viewed without the whole, and the whole not without its elements—a process meant to *enact* the function of *alētheia*.[28] Signaling a "new beginning" to thought, poetry would become Heidegger's most valuable companion in continuing to think Being.

25. Heidegger, *Introduction to Metaphysics*, 14.
26. Thompson, "End of Onto-Theology," 163.
27. Heidegger, "Question Concerning Technology."
28. Heidegger, "Origin of the Work," 201–2; Babich, *Gottes Glück*.

In the autumn of 1934 Heidegger composed a series of lectures on Hölderlin, entitled "Hölderlins Hymnen 'Germanien' und 'Der Rhein.'" The first half of the Hölderlin lecture course focused on gaining a preliminary understanding of "poeticizing" in terms of its essence and linguistic character. Heidegger is clear that this linguistic character is not some universal essence of ideal poeticizing—rather, it is the essence that is poeticized in and through a singular poeticizing. Not imposed from outside or above, as is the case through a philosophical application of concepts of poeticizing, this poetics is rather "cleared" through *Erlebnis* (experience). It is a thoughtful encounter with the "manifestation of Being."[29] This experience, Heidegger argues, comes into Being through logos (λόγος, ground or word) in the power of *Sagen* (saying). Heidegger further explains that "language" is not reducible to a kind of expression that articulates some spiritual meaning; it is not at all what it appears. In this way, thinking and poeticizing begin to take their departure from philosophy and from the history of metaphysics and traditional theology.[30]

In making this "turn" away from philosophy to thinking, Heidegger claims that he can no longer maintain a historical vision of the relation of past to future. In Heidegger's reading of Hölderlin, the relation of past and future essentially collapses, that is, poetry breaks free of philosophy and philosophy falls into the past. In turning to poetry, and to Hölderlin in particular, Heidegger maintains that sight into history and the future could now be achieved only by reference beyond philosophy.[31] For Heidegger, poetry reaches deeper than the philosophy from which it derives. In emphasizing Hölderlin's role, Heidegger points to the link between Being and poetry—and therewith to the future-oriented nature of poetry itself.

One way to grant access to Heidegger's poetics is to stress its distance from modern subjectivist aesthetics.[32] "Poetry," he writes, "... is not an aimless imagining of whimsicalities and not a flight of mere notions and fancies into the realm of the unreal."[33] Instead, poetry functions as an essentially clearing projection, unfolding unconcealment and sending it ahead. Poetry lets the opening of *alētheia* occur in such a way that *alētheia* brings beings to shine out in their Being.

In thinking the role of poetry as related to the problem of ontotheology in Heidegger's thought and his desire to bring about an end to this situation,

29. Schluga, *Heidegger's Crisis*, 6.
30. Schluga, *Heidegger's Crisis*, 6.
31. Rockmore, *On Heidegger's Nazism*, 127.
32. Dallmayr, "Heidegger, Hölderlin, and Politics," 83.
33. Heidegger, "Origin of the Work," 197.

it is critical to turn toward the key problem of myth in Hölderlin's works. Elegantly expressed in Hölderlin's poetry, myth, as Heidegger would later phrase it in his 1951–52 lecture course "What Is Called Thinking," remains "the most thought worthy thing."[34] This vision of myth is what compels Heidegger to draw Hölderlin's poetry beyond philosophy into the realm of thought. What Heidegger means here is to make a return to pre-Socratic thought, specifically to the Heraclitean and Parmenidean thinking of *phusis* and *alētheia*, which function not to ground beings, but rather to guard them in a process of concealment and revelation. But for Heidegger, any proximity between poetry and thinking can be claimed in the right way only if their distinction, their difference, is acknowledged and preserved. It is in this way that, for Heidegger, the decisive myth contained in Hölderlin's poetry—the myth of the "holy"—comes to find an echo in the thinking of Being. For Heidegger: "The thinker evokes Being. The poet names the holy."[35]

We have seen how this approach, which would characterize Heidegger's philosophy for the rest of his life, originated with a certain kind of philosophy of history, what Heidegger calls *Seinsgeschichte*. In searching now for an "other beginning" of thought, Heidegger is in the same move searching for an "other beginning" to history. Ultimately, this search becomes transformed through his focus on Hölderlin, resulting in a reflection on the essence of history and the problem of the beginning.[36] For Heidegger, Hölderlin's poetry is critical precisely because it opens new horizons for the present by placing thinking in the frame of a new myth.[37]

What is the myth of "the holy"? In Hölderlin's poetry, particularly in "Grund zum Empedokles" but also in the title poems of Heidegger's lecture series, "Germania" and "Der Rhein," the myth of the holy emerges in an intimate counterrotation of mourning and readiness, culminating in a "holy mourning but ready distress," by which Heidegger is transfixed.[38] This basic tone, Heidegger thinks, works to establish the "location of our future historical Being" and express it.[39] In this sense Hölderlin's poetry becomes a sacrificial experience in that it establishes Being as the intermediate between earth and the gods.[40] As for Empedocles, sacrificial tragedy works to set free a new world, one in which fate is founded on our experience of the

---

34. Heidegger, "What Is Called Thinking," 371.
35. Grossmann, "Myth of Poetry," 30.
36. Grossmann, "Myth of Poetry," 30.
37. Heidegger, *Hölderlins Hymnen*, 123.
38. Heidegger, *Hölderlins Hymnen*, 103.
39. Heidegger, *Hölderlins Hymnen*, 135.
40. Heidegger, *Hölderlins Hymnen*, 146.

plight of "godforsakenness."[41] In the experience of "mourning," a new divine relationship is established, in which a "genuine time" and a "true history" can be renewed.[42] In this way, Heidegger's reflections on Hölderlin's hymns become a search not for a "pure origin" but instead for a place beyond the origin. If Heidegger's lectures on Nietzsche during the *Kehre* have garnered most of the scholarly attention, it is crucial, at this point, to briefly point out that Heidegger's reading of Nietzsche after 1935 is almost entirely a product of his thinking on Hölderlin.[43] For Heidegger, whereas the antagonism set up by Nietzsche between the Apollonian and the Dionysian still carries the imprint of modern metaphysics, the quality of mourning in Hölderlin's poetry both elevates and transcends this situation and becomes the "herald of the overcoming of all metaphysics"—effecting a new spiritual beginning that cannot be overtaken and has always been projecting.[44]

It is in speaking to Hölderlin's "Germania" that Heidegger indicates the essentially poetic character of "turning" in Hölderlin's work by pointing through him to the fundamental, though buried, event of the modern age: the flight of the gods. "Germania" begins with these lines:

> *Nicht sie, die Seeligen, die erscheinen sind*
> *Die Götterbilder in dem alten Lande,*
> *Sie darf ich ja nicht rufen mehr.*

> Not them, the blessed ones, who once appeared,
> The image of the gods of old lands,
> Them I may no longer call.[45]

Not being able to call out to the gods is not any act of resignation but rather the silence of not being able to call becomes a synonym for the endurance of a deep loss, a profound suffering. In this sense, the time of "Germania" becomes the time of mourning. If we recall, in *Being and Time*, mood (*Stimmung*) constitutes a mode of attunement.[46] In this way, we can understand the serenity of this mourning not only as a phenomenological but moreover as an ontological category. On the occasion of the loss of the gods, this mourning becomes a holy mourning (*heilige Trauer*), yet in the

---

41. Heidegger, *Hölderlins Hymnen*, 149.
42. Heidegger, *Hölderlins Hymnen*, 110.
43. Babich, *Gottes Glück*, 107–45.
44. Heidegger, *Hölderlins Hymne "Andenken,"* 143.
45. "Germania," in F. Hölderlin, *Selected Poems and Fragments*, 188.
46. Heidegger, *Being and Time* (trans. Macquarrie and Robinson), 225–35.

sense of a kind of loss that only strengthens the desire for reunion.⁴⁷ In this way, holy mourning becomes an expectant readiness for the "passing by" of what Heidegger calls *der letzte Gott*.⁴⁸

For Heidegger, we have to recognize that the myth of "the holy" does not occur in poetic representation, but rather "the holy" occurs in poetic *presentation* as *revelation*. The challenge here is that any repetition of these poetic presentations runs the marked risk of transforming these into re-presentations, and when this occurs the holy withdraws and is again concealed.⁴⁹ Mirroring the function of the *phusis-alētheia* pair, poetry works to shelter the holy in essentially clearing projection similar to the counterrotation of mourning and readiness.

It is essential to point out that for Heidegger, asking after Being is far more significant than any kind of decision about the divine, and it is only through the myth of the holy that Heidegger comes to ask after the divine at all. To restate this: for Heidegger, it is only from the truth of Being that the essence of the holy can be thought.⁵⁰ In Heidegger's writings after the *Kehre*, a similarly critical point is that phenomenological thinking becomes openly *meditative* as regards the preserving of mysteries *as* mysteries.⁵¹ For Heidegger, meditative thinking takes place when Dasein is set free for the *groundless mystery of Being*. This meditative mystery as it manifests itself in poetry lets Being be as it is—both revealing and withdrawing from comprehension. For Heidegger, "We never get to know a mystery by unveiling or analyzing it; we only get to know a mystery by carefully guarding the mystery *as* a mystery."⁵²

In Heidegger's later writings, references to "the holy" or "the gods" become prolific but are seldom if ever spelled out in detail. Our only way toward an understanding of the increasingly frequent references to these themes is through a moment almost singularly inspired by Hölderlin. This is Heidegger's thinking on *das Geviert* (the fourfold), a term that first appears in the *Beiträge* (*Contributions*). Appearing only fully in his 1954 essay "Building, Dwelling, Thinking," the "fourfold" refers to the link between "earth" and the "heavens," "divinities" and "mortals." One cannot exist without the others. Written privately between 1936 and 1938, the *Beiträge* in its opacity marks a conscious methodological move on Heidegger's part—an

---

47. Dallmayr, "Heidegger, Hölderlin, and Politics," 90–91.
48. Heidegger, *Hölderlins Hymnen*, 80–82.
49. Eikrem, "Possibility of a Metaphysical Theology," 270.
50. Law, "Negative Theology," 153.
51. Eikrem, "Possibility of a Metaphysical Theology," 270.
52. Heidegger, *Existence and Being*, 279; emphasis in original.

attempt to shatter our attachment to traditional modes of thinking—and signals the transition to *Seinsgeschichte*. Near the end of the *Beiträge* he writes, "Philosophy commits suicide when it makes itself intelligible."[53] For Heidegger, philosophical "intelligibility" drags Being down into categories utterly inappropriate to it. These categories represent for him nothing more than the straitjacket of traditional metaphysics.

In the *Beiträge*, Heidegger articulates his thinking on the history of Western philosophy as a metaphysics of presence, undergirding beings. Already in the second section of the text Heidegger becomes concerned with the translation of the "first beginning" of metaphysics to "another beginning" of thought. For Heidegger, this transition comes to pass in what he calls a *Zuspiel* (passing), which works in the manner of Rainer Maria Rilke's characterization of catching a ball not thrown by oneself, but rather by a partner—a process that essentially creates a world in the hermeneutic sense.[54] It is through this hermeneutics of "passing" that the question of Being is delivered from the first beginning to the next.

This transition to "another beginning" of thought is made in terms of what Heidegger calls a "founding leap," by which he means "to bring something into Being from out of its essential source."[55] In many ways, the central theme of the *Beiträge* is this "founding leap," through which Being is understood not as substance in the metaphysical sense but rather as *Ereignis*. That is, it is an "event." Being becomes *Ereignis* or "event" for Heidegger in relation to the idea of *Wesung* (or presence), the past tense of which, importantly, is *das Gewesene*, which expresses the idea that, although the past has passed into the past, it is nonetheless reverberating into the present and the future. For Heidegger, this leap into the *Ereignis* of Being is taken up by what he calls the "future ones" (*die Zu-künftigen*).[56]

The task of "future ones" is to prepare for the "passing by" (*Vorbeigang*) of *der letzte Gott* (the last or ultimate God) and to make the transition from the first beginning of metaphysics to the next beginning of *Seinsgeschichte*, and with it to what Heidegger calls *seynsgeschichtliches Denken* (the historical thinking of Being). All of this helps to explain what Heidegger means when he writes of *der letzte Gott*. The concept of *der letzte Gott* first shows up relatively late in the *Beiträge*, indicating Heidegger's thinking on the question of the "essencing" or "presencing" (*Wesung/Wesen*) of the Being of

---

53. Heidegger, *Contributions to Philosophy*, 435.

54. Rainer Maria Rilke, in Gadamer, *Truth and Method*, vi; Heidegger, *Contributions to Philosophy*, 53.

55. Heidegger, "Origin of the Work," 202.

56. Law, "Negative Theology," 139–48.

a god.[57] In attempting to recover God's mysteriousness, Heidegger is working to release the idea of God from metaphysics and its treatment of God as some kind of entity, or as an infinite substance. For Heidegger, this means recovering the strangeness of God as "the most profound beginning."[58] With the end of the "first beginning" of metaphysics we can understand that, for Heidegger, the first "passing by" of God has already occurred, and the second "passing by" is yet to come. The task of the "future ones" is to create a realm in which this final "passing by" can occur—not as a farewell, but as a reverberation.

When Heidegger speaks of the "passing by" of *der letzte Gott* he enters into dialogue with Hölderlin when he selects the word *Vorbeigang* to indicate the specific temporal quality of this passing. In his poem "Friedensfier" (Celebration of peace), Hölderlin deals with the temporality of the divine, speaking of a God who touches the dwellings of men only for a moment before moving on:

> *Denn schonend rührt des Maases allzeit kundig*
> *Nur einen Augenblick die Wohnungen der Menschen*
> *Ein Gott an unversehn, und keiner weiß es, wenn?*

> For sparingly, at all times knowing the measure,
> A God for a moment only will touch the dwellings
> Of men, by none foreseen, and no one knows when?[59]

In describing the ephemeral brush of the God's hand in this poem Hölderlin selects the term *Vergänglich* (evanescent).[60]

> *Vergänglich alles Himmlische; aber umsonst nicht*

> That's heavenly fleets on; but not for nothing[61]

As Heidegger points out in the *Beiträge*, this term should not be understood as a "passing away," but rather must be understood as a "passing by." Despite the ephemeral quality of this touch in Hölderlin's poetry, it echoes through time—it "fleets on." In speaking of the "passing by" of *der letzte Gott*, in the *Beiträge*, Heidegger replaces Hölderlin's *Vergänglich* with his own *Vorbeigang*, making clear that this "passing by" does not mean that God has

---

57. Heidegger, *Contributions to Philosophy*, 403.
58. Heidegger, *Contributions to Philosophy*, 404–6.
59. "Friedensfier," in F. Hölderlin, *Selected Poems and Fragments*, 210.
60. "Friedensfier," in F. Hölderlin, *Selected Poems and Fragments*, 208–17.
61. "Friedensfier," in F. Hölderlin, *Selected Poems and Fragments*, 210.

been swallowed up by the past; instead, God has touched time in the moment of his passing.[62] It is in this situation that this God is understood not as *Vergänglich*, or evanescent, but rather in terms of *das Gewesene*: "that which is as having been," indicating the futural hermeneutic quality of Hölderlin's verse. In relation to the intimate counterrotation of mourning and readiness in Hölderlin's poetry, this "passing by" of the God indicates a new spiritual beginning, one that has always been projecting.

What does Heidegger mean when he says *der letzte Gott* (the last God)? To return to the critical importance of the *Kehre*, especially those years between 1934 and 1936 when Heidegger is lecturing on Hölderlin and Nietzsche respectively, many have interpreted *der letzte Gott* in Nietzschean terms, where *letzte* refers to the death of the God of metaphysics, indicating a "final" God in terms of a full withdrawal.[63] What if, however, we translated *letzte* not as "last" but as "ultimate"? In this way, the understanding of *letzte* as "ultimate" denotes the omnipotence and omnipresence of a god.[64] In reading *der letzte Gott* as "the ultimate God," the notion of withdrawal fades away and offers instead a recovery of the Being of God that does not simply fall back into metaphysics but rather breaks loose from it by recourse to the mystery and myth of "the holy." This god would not be the God of metaphysics but rather a poet god, in whom the essentially hermeneutic quality of *das Gewesene* would carry with it the "most profound beginning."[65]

In brief, a "Heideggerian theology" would necessarily be poetic in such a way that this theology would take up the hermeneutic task of the poet. That is to say, a theology of this kind would perform the function of *alētheia* in terms of an intimate counterrotation with respect to the preservation, the guarding, of the mystery of Being. For Heidegger, it is always the task of asking after Being that takes precedence over any decision about the divine or about a god. It is instead the Being of a god, more original than metaphysics and theology, that is essential for him.

Not at all meant to offer any hard-and-fast decisions as to the form of a new Trinitarian ontology, neither is this essay meant to present a Heideggerian perspective on the form that ontology might take. It is rather meant simply to offer a brief explication of Heidegger's thinking on theology and the metaphysical tradition in order to provide the reader with a ground for

62. Law, "Negative Theology," 148.
63. Esposito, "Geschichte des letzten Gottes," 51.
64. Prudhomme, "Passing-By of the Ultimate God," 449–50.
65. Heidegger, *Contributions to Philosophy*, 405–6.

further thinking. As an essay contained in a volume meant to offer new ways of conceiving Trinitarian ontology, it is critical to recall that while Heidegger's thinking may be helpful in reflecting on this ontology, this does not mean that Heidegger is compatible with Christian theology. It is from this very incompatibility, however, that the small spark of something truly new may shine out.

12

From Tragic Ontology to Trinitarian Revelation

The Reconciliation with Being in Balthasar's Reading of Nietzsche

PAUL RAIMOND DANIELS

> An indirect light from Christian revelation falls on every object of philosophy; but in any case, philosophy outside the Christian sphere was something alive only where it was at the same time theology; in the Christian sphere it can remain alive only in a passionate dialogue with the theology of revelation, indeed, in the willingness to allow its own hidden theological implications to be demonstrated by the latter.[1]

HANS URS VON BALTHASAR in part articulates his Trinitarian ontology by narrating the question of Being as it evolved from Greek myth through to Martin Heidegger, framing its key aspects by a thesis in which modernity increasingly misconstrues Being to the degree that it is considered apart from the light of Christian revelation. Within the trilogy, Balthasar pays only passing attention to Friedrich Nietzsche, yet in his early work Nietzsche proved foundational as a foil against which a theological a

---

1. Balthasar, *My Work*, 20.

priori could emerge and reconcile the subject to her relationship with the fundamental beauty of Being under the rubric of a Trinitarian ontology of distance. Revisiting Balthasar's early studies of Nietzsche, then, illustrates a way for us to recover a path by which ontology is restored to its theological significance: where Being gestures toward God.

Balthasar was under no illusion that Nietzsche's tragic eschaton seeks a reconciliation between the subject and Being by its affirmation of worldly immanence as fundamentally beautiful, and that, in doing so, it draws "its entire positive power from the denial of any transcendent meaning to the world."[2] For Balthasar, this tragic ontology leads, paradoxically, to a revelation of Trinitarian distance as both prior to and generative of the subject. This paradoxical transfiguration of tragic ontology into Trinitarian revelation commences with Balthasar's reading of Nietzschean subjectivity as leading to an annihilation of the self precisely in its efforts to affirm Being. He writes,

> One need only pierce through the surface of "tragic nihilism" and trace it to the hinterlands of Nietzsche's soul as it seeks out and fights for God, to hear the deep Christian resonance that his words possess. What in a godless worldview must finally become a tragic postulate, justified only by the aesthetics of the attitude it arises from, has its actual fulfilment in that which is Christian.[3]

In this chapter, I consider both the nature of this "piercing" of Nietzsche's tragic affirmation of Being and its subsequent fulfillment within a Trinitarian aesthetics of distance. This is to explore the ways in which Balthasar reads the aesthetics of Nietzschean tragedy as evacuating Being into a nothingness that ultimately subverts its affirmative powers. This subversion, for Balthasar, is theologically performative, though: it comprises a kind of *via negativa* by which the reciprocity between Dasein and Being is restored to an a priori attitude of wonder. Here, Being is the site of the possibility of divine revelation—of a renewed wonder at Being in which the subject can not only recognize God, but participate in the Trinitarian movement by which Being discloses divine beauty.

Nietzsche's Reconciliation with Being

In an early notebook, Nietzsche makes reference to *Seinsanschauung* (intuition of Being) as the "conferment of breath and life upon all things: [the]

---

2. Hans Urs von Balthasar, in Nietzsche, *Anthologien*, 283. Throughout this chapter, all translations from German citations are my own.

3. Hans Urs von Balthasar, in Nietzsche, *Anthologien*, 110.

reconciliation of the human attitude towards life."[4] This idea of reconciling the human person with Being is somewhat of a golden thread throughout Nietzsche's writings, and properly begins with *The Birth of Tragedy*. Here, a tragic ontology of Dionysian Being both attracts and repels Nietzsche's Greek. The Dionysian is an unbearable experience of terror, the "recognition that everything which comes into being must be prepared for painful destruction,"[5] and it is thus that the "terrors and horrors of existence"[6] overwhelm the subject as the unassailable logic of Being. Confronted with tragic nihilism, her personhood becomes paralyzed, and she "is in danger of longing to deny the will," and thus of renouncing Being itself: her desire is for self-annihilation, "for a world beyond death."[7] Concomitantly, though, the Dionysian also lends an intoxicating ecstasy precisely *in* the dissolution of individuation itself, where the pretence of the subject's ontological differences with existence is surrendered. For here, she is free to indulge in her innermost "lust for being"[8] because she identifies a greater delight in the power of Being as it creates and destroys over and above its destruction of meaning for the individual per se.[9] No longer beholden to the strictures of individuation, she surrenders to the fracas of the Bacchic festival in music, orgy, and violence. The subject thus sublates suffering and joy alike into the greater lust of Being in and for itself, placing herself "in the midst of this superabundance of life, suffering, and delight, in sublime ecstasy, listening to a distant, melancholy singing which tells of the Mothers of Being, whose names are delusion, will, woe."[10]

It is the Apolline aesthetic of representation, though, that completes this reconciliation between Nietzsche's tragic Greek and her Dionysian intuition of Being. The Apolline is the exquisite, ineluctable beauty of the plastic arts, which depict a perfected, radiant image of Being through which the Greek could both confront the Dionysian and affirm it. Working in concert with the Dionysian, the Apolline employs its ability to both disclose *and* conceal Being, and it is thus that the aesthetics of the Greek tragic drama

---

4. "Die Übertragung des Athems und Lebens auf all Dinge: Beilegung des menschlichen Lebensgefühls" (*KSA* 7:543 [23(13)]).

5. Nietzsche, *Birth of Tragedy*, 80.

6. Nietzsche, *Birth of Tragedy*, 23.

7. Nietzsche, *Birth of Tragedy*, 40.

8. Nietzsche, *Birth of Tragedy*, 81.

9. Compare to Nietzsche's adaption of the Heraclitean metaphor of life as a child playing checkers into his own image of a child building and trampling sand castles by the sea shore: Nietzsche, *Philosophy in the Tragic Age*, 62.

10. Nietzsche, *Birth of Tragedy*, 98.

succeeds in the affirmation of life: the frenzy of the tragic chorus and the unjust sufferings of the hero comprise that Dionysian glimpse of Being that drives the subject toward nihilistic self-destruction; but the chorus of satyrs likewise manifests a mythology of Apolline definition, and the hero, in his suffering, attains to a nobility of Olympic stature, and he speaks in the golden tongue of the Homeric epic. The Greek is no "spectator" here, but rather a *participant* in this confluence of Apolline and Dionysiac drives borne out in art: "In this enchanted state the Dionysiac enthusiast sees himself as a satyr, and *as a satyr he in turn sees the god* [Dionysus], i.e. in his transformed state he sees a new vision outside himself which is the Apolline perfection of his state."[11]

Nietzsche later remarked that this early philosophy of tragedy embodied a "hostile silence about Christianity."[12] To be sure, there lay a sharp rebuke within Nietzsche's omission of any reference to Christianity throughout his sweeping narration of post-tragic Socratism through to the modern era of Kant, Schopenhauer, and Wagner. However, this was chiefly a silence owing to the very architecture of the Greek ontology of tragedy insofar as it excluded any possibility of a transcendent, absolute God. The miracle of Nietzsche's tragic Greek was her discernment of a "religion for life: complete immanence."[13] As such, the affirmation of worldliness is not so much a revelation of absolute Being as the absolutization of worldly being itself.

Here, Greek divinity is the product of the personification and aestheticization of nature phenomenologically. Thus, Dionysus was the Greek intuition of the chaotic lust for life seen in the fertility of spring, and here there is no ὑπέρφύσις in the sense of "super nature": Dionysus *is* nature, and is witnessed as such. Dionysian power, then, is a "blissful ecstasy which arises from the innermost ground of man, indeed of nature itself."[14] This suggests a consonance between self and world inasmuch as the Greek allowed herself to identify with nature. It allows a tragic affirmation of existence in which "not only is the bond between human beings renewed by the magic of the Dionysiac, but nature, alienated, inimical, or subjugated, celebrates once more her festival of reconciliation with her lost son, humankind."[15]

The triumph of Nietzsche's early philosophy of tragedy was its conclusion that "only as an *aesthetic phenomenon* is existence [*Dasein*] and the

---

11. Nietzsche, *Birth of Tragedy*, 44; emphasis in original.
12. Nietzsche, *Birth of Tragedy*, 9.
13. *KSA* 7:72.
14. Nietzsche, *Birth of Tragedy*, 17.
15. Nietzsche, *Birth of Tragedy*, 18.

world eternally *justified*."[16] Yet if this justification is sustained by an aesthetic act of immanentizing absolutization, Balthasar asks, could we not therefore also assert that the "formula of one's existence [*des Daseins*] itself [is] tragically torn in its fundamental constitution"?[17] And, if so, what then of the subjectivity of Dasein if she is both the creator and recipient of the tragic aesthetic? Balthasar leverages these questions into a persistent criticism of Nietzsche's philosophy, in which the bifurcation of the subject herself leads to her self-annihilation—and thus the self-subversion of life affirmation. However, within the ensuing collapse of Being itself, Balthasar identifies a performative theological transfiguration of the tragic: an apophasis of ontological distance by which the subject is restored to a communion with Being, beauty, and divine gift.

The Greek absolutization of Being into the Olympians spoke of a "triumphant existence [*Dasein*], where everything that exists has been deified,"[18] and insofar as this formed the basis for tragic affirmation, the Greek had need to both surrender her subjectivity *and* maintain an aesthetic self-awareness of that surrender. On the one hand, her reconciliation with Being lay in her ecstatic coalescence with Dionysian Being as absolutized unity. On the other hand, though, this identification with Being is sustained only to the degree that her projection of the Apolline aesthetic maintains an authentic *widening* of distance between herself and Being—possible for the Greek imagination owing to the capacity for the Apolline to simultaneously conceal and disclose Dionysian truth. This bifurcation of subjectivity, then, comprises the dual surrender and capture of subjectivity through aesthetics: the dissolution of individuation concurrent to the subject's self-awareness of her own subjectivity precisely as Being itself torn apart (thus the importance of Dionysus as the dismembered god).[19]

The nature of this bifurcation within tragic subjectivity presents an unsustainable conflict, and this, in turn, necessitates the aesthetic apotheosis of the subject herself as a means of containing it. Her tragic ecstasy now has an ambiguous "supernature" about it: "There now sounds out from within man something supernatural [*Uebernatürliches*]: he feels himself to be a god, he himself moves in such ecstasy and sublimity as once he saw the gods move in his dreams."[20] This affirmation of absolutized, immanent Being requires,

---

16. Nietzsche, *Birth of Tragedy*, 33; emphasis in original.
17. Hans Urs von Balthasar, in Nietzsche, *Anthologien*, 106.
18. Nietzsche, *Birth of Tragedy*, 22.
19. Nietzsche, *Birth of Tragedy*, 52.
20. Nietzsche, *Birth of Tragedy*, 18. *Uebernatürliches* from *KSA* 1:30.

FROM TRAGIC ONTOLOGY TO TRINITARIAN REVELATION

in turn, the absolutization of the subject—not in the sense of metaphysical transcendence, but as the axiological center upon which Being is affirmed.

For Balthasar, Nietzsche's model of tragic subjectivity thus entails the devolvement of Being into a subjective play of mirrors that, ultimately, risks tragic nihilism instead of tragic affirmation:

> All objectivity is only an expression of subjectivity and all form only the outflow of formless life, where everything Apollonian only remains so as the mirroring of the Dionysian, and where all transcendence, and that which it could redeem, is only understood as a process within an eternally enclosed immanence.[21]

Because Nietzsche's Greeks interpret the world through the drives of the Apollonian and Dionysian, Balthasar asserts that their axiological predication of existence cannot be premised upon an intuition of the value of Being in and for itself. Instead, "Dionysian" and "Apollonian" refer to a *process* by which the tragic Greek translates her inchoate intuition of life creatively into art—an externalization that then reflects back to her the content of her creative will as an affective aesthetic of existence. Nietzsche calls this a "transfiguring mirror"[22] and a "sphere of beauty in which [the Greeks] saw their mirror images, the Olympians."[23] The Greek affirmation of existence, then, is a play of mirrors: the tragic world is the "self-mirroring of Dionysiac man,"[24] who is himself intuited as musical dissonance; tragic myth then appropriates the genius of Homer to take that mirror image and reflect it again off a second mirror of Olympic greatness (the aesthetic exaltation of the tragic Greek herself). This double reflection is then held up as an affirmation of existence, as the unity of joy and suffering in Being.

Balthasar's contention is that this aesthetic double reflection of the subject back onto herself fails to constitute an authentic encounter with and affirmation of Being. Instead, we have an axiological echo chamber in the vein of Kantian beauty as an entirely mental play of the faculties.[25] By this double mirroring of the subject, the imaging of Being appears to recursively multiply and extend into an infinite distance: however, it is a false distance by which the subject herself then attains to that infinitude. The combination

---

21. Hans Urs von Balthasar, in Nietzsche, *Anthologien*, 110.
22. Nietzsche, *Birth of Tragedy*, 24.
23. Nietzsche, *Birth of Tragedy*, 25.
24. Nietzsche, *Birth of Tragedy*, 42.
25. A point Balthasar takes up in detail within his genealogy of philosophical aesthetics in the fifth volume of *The Glory of the Lord*, where he writes that Kant's "'critical Idealism' no longer permits space for an experience of worldly Being as an epiphany of God's glory" (5:483).

of an infinity of mythological depth with the immediacy of Dionysian irruption thus yields the self-apotheosis of the Greek, in which, Balthasar writes, "the finite and infinite are one, and but moments of identicality."[26]

Nietzsche, at times, comes dangerously close to recognizing this contradiction within subjectivity itself, as when he comments that "the Greek artist in particular had an obscure feeling that he and these gods where mutually dependent."[27] This "mutual dependence" betrays the fact that those same gods do not so much house the secret of Being as comprise the aesthetic mirroring of the subject herself. This false distance belies, then, an ultimate *groundlessness* to Nietzsche's reconciliation with Being, precipitating the risk of nihilism: of the evacuation of the *Grund* of Being into an *Abgrund*—an abyss, a nothingness.

This is why Nietzsche's prediction of a new tragic age brought about through the Wagnerian *Gesamtkunstwerk* and the rebirth of German myth was bound to fail.[28] Nietzsche had supposed that, with the self-destruction of Socratic optimism with Schopenhauer, the tragic aesthetics of the Greeks could be transplanted into modernity. For, while Nietzsche had premised the success of Greek tragic drama as dependent upon myth as "a unique example of something universal and true which gazes out into infinity,"[29] his own study of the Greeks had exposed myth as the creative act of the Greeks in their response to Being. The modern subject could never divest myth of this subjective grounding, whatever Wagnerian spell was cast. Restoring the aesthetic naïveté of the Greeks was an impossibility, as myth could never again attain a significance that could account for the whole of Being.

In light of this, tragedy was no longer the existential prize within Nietzsche's middle period, and Nietzsche instead came to emphasize the psychology of subjectivity itself as the means for exploring one's relation to Being. This would fall into sharp relief against a further transition into his late-period writings: this, with the close of book 4 of *The Gay Science*, we have the introduction of the "heaviest weight" of eternal recurrence, immediately after which Zarathustra receives his poetic introduction under the auspice of *incipit tragoedia*.[30]

---

26. Balthasar, *Geschichte des eschatologischen Problems*, 45.
27. Nietzsche, *Birth of Tragedy*, 49.
28. Nietzsche, *Birth of Tragedy*, 109.
29. Nietzsche, *Birth of Tragedy*, 83.
30. Nietzsche, *Gay Science* (2001), 195.

Truth and Subject

Tragic affirmation in the late Nietzsche thus transformed into the starker question of how the subject derives and exercises her strength against Being through the creation and destruction of values. In its destructive aspect, Nietzsche philosophized with a hammer: a *Twilight of the Idols* by which the hollowness of nihilistic forms of life could be sounded out and smashed, such as God, Platonism, morality, and metaphysics. As much as an exercise of power in itself, this act facilitates the subject's liberation from the kinds of life denials anathematic to the tragic embrace of existence in its totality. Nietzsche's accompanying creative project then promised a rediscovery of the innocence of Being by resituating the subject within the immediacy and totality of existence freed from illusion. Accordingly, Zarathustra beseeches his audience *"remain faithful to the earth*,"[31] and within his final trio of writings Nietzsche could again promise his reader "a *tragic* age: tragedy, the highest art of saying yes to life."[32]

There persists, though, a sense in which life still requires the mediation of art for its affirmation, and so within this positive project there is always a conception of Being as a haunting void against which art is directed: "The truth is ugly," Nietzsche wrote in an unpublished fragment: "*we have art, lest we perish of the truth.*"[33] Within the shifting semantics of Nietzsche's late-period writings, art is meant to supersede "truth" understood classically by the assertion of its existential priority. So, the opposition of art against truth is intended to transform into the subject's exercise of power in her affirmation of Being, and is her means of flourishing as opposed to her passive reception of meaning as "given."[34]

Incumbent here, though, is Nietzsche's furtherance of Kant's turn to the subject, a model he inherits from Schopenhauer and adapts for his own ends.[35] For Kant, the subject's experience is never simply "given," but mediated through the faculties and categories of the mind, and so epistemology itself shifts from knowing the objects of experience to knowing the transcendental structures of the subject who apprehends the appearances of objects of experience. Nietzsche's transformation of Kant through Schopenhauer was to transpose this model of subjectivity into an existential-axiological plane by which the value of existence itself was mediated by the

---

31. Nietzsche, *Thus Spoke Zarathustra*, 6; emphasis in original.
32. *Ecce Homo*, in Nietzsche, *Anti-Christ*, 110; emphasis in original.
33. *KSA* 13:500 (16[40]); emphasis in original.
34. Nietzsche, *Anti-Christ*, 4.
35. R. Hill, *Nietzsche's Critiques*.

affirming or denying powers of the subject—that is, the will to power. "The world seen from the inside," Nietzsche writes, "would be just this 'will to power' and nothing else."[36] Likewise, seen from the outside: "*This world is the will to power—and nothing besides!* And you yourselves too are this will to power—and nothing besides!"[37]

Balthasar therefore identifies here a continuation of the problematics underling the reconciliation with Being in *The Birth of Tragedy*, again based on a conflict of distance within the subject. On the one hand, the distance between subject and world is eliminated by their inter-mutuality in the will to power, and the recognition of this itself becomes a precondition for the subject's affirmation of existence. Yet, paradoxically, this seems to entail for Nietzsche a tendency toward the self-absolutization of the subject to the degree that her axiology comprises an absolutized affirmation of everything. These tendencies toward self-apotheosis were something taken by Nietzsche in jest, and often regarded as an ironic consequence of the death of God. Yet the absolutized subject, in her embrace of the whole, is led into an increasing solitude, and therefore into a *widening* of the distance between herself and Being. Accordingly, Nietzsche perpetuates an account of distance that betrays the immediacy of experience required for tragic affirmation. Ethically, this manifests in Nietzsche's later distinction between the noble and the common types,[38] and he likewise continued to promote an aesthetics of distance very much in the vein of the Greeks.[39]

Yet what is this ugliness of the "truth" of Being, of which we would perish were it not for art? Without the distance afforded by art, Nietzsche maintains that Being would appear without perspective and would relegate the subject to "nothing but foreground."[40] The ugliness of Being, then, is in fact the inconsequentiality of the subject, which, if recognized explicitly, would entail the inconsequentiality of Being itself. This ugliness is an escalation of that earlier chasm explored by Nietzsche in the tragic age of the Greeks. And considering this anew in his later period, he writes that "even now I stand before this rift with a holy terror."[41] Nietzsche could see that the lie of art was existentially necessary and justified, but that its artifice was premised upon a will to truth that would know Being only in order to overcome it. The

---

36. Nietzsche, *Beyond Good and Evil* (2001), 36.
37. Nietzsche, *Writings from the Late Notebooks*, 39; emphasis in original.
38. Nietzsche, *On the Genealogy of Morality*.
39. Nietzsche, *Gay Science*, 79.
40. Nietzsche, *Gay Science*, 79.
41. *KSA* 13:500.

suicide of Greek tragedy was not itself tragic, as he had once thought:[42] the tragic worldview and its affirmation were *in themselves* nihilistic.

Nietzsche's breakthrough in confronting the ugly truth of Being arises with his affirmation of eternal recurrence as fully disclosive of the nature of existence. In confronting Being as eternally recurring, Nietzsche asks, "Would you not throw yourself down and gnash your teeth and curse the demon who spoke thus," or would you *"long for nothing more fervently* than this ultimate eternal confirmation and seal?"[43] From here on, the rhetorical bravado of Nietzsche's writings on eternal recurrence reveals his derivation of a joyful strength from the contemplation of the ugliness of Being, yet in practice he instead privately harbored a sense of dread. Lou Salomé recollected that "only with a quiet voice and with all signs of deepest horror did he speak [to me] about this secret."[44] Similarly, when Nietzsche disclosed Zarathustra's "secret" to Resa von Schirnhofer, Schirnhofer recounted that "a different Nietzsche was suddenly standing before me and had frightened me."[45] Nietzsche recognized that eternal recurrence was both the sublimation of the finite into the infinite, and a rendering of the infinite as an expression of the finitude of experience. It was both the exultation of one's existence while also a confrontation with the nightmare of Being as a meaningless, repeating abyss of time, in which no sense of purpose was ultimately possible.

This truth of Being is borne out by the figure of Zarathustra, whom Nietzsche anoints as the teacher of eternal recurrence.[46] In many ways, though, Zarathustra functions as an aesthetic mask for Nietzsche, placed over the ugliness of Being in the same way that the infinitude of the mythological image did so for the Greeks. Zarathustra emerges as Nietzsche's literary projection of himself as his means of aestheticizing eternal recurrence into a tragedy of poetic significance—yet, as such, it repeats the simultaneous widening and contracting of distance whereby the subject's reconciliation with Being becomes questionable. Eternal recurrence is the willing embrace of the immanentized whole within the instant of subjective experience, and in this sense the subject is reconciled into an immediacy with Being in which distance is eliminated because her will affirms the full spectrum of joy and suffering. Simultaneously, though, eternal recurrence comprises an axiological feedback loop of power exerted in that embrace of Being that is then concentrated

42. Nietzsche, *Birth of Tragedy*, 54.
43. Nietzsche, *Gay Science*, 195; emphasis in original.
44. Salomé, *Nietzsche*, 130.
45. Gilman, *Conversations with Nietzsche*, 157.
46. Nietzsche, *Thus Spoke Zarathustra*, 177.

back into the subject, and the circumvention by which this avoids devolving into a vicious circle is facilitated by the literary projection of Zarathustra precisely as the distance between Being and the Nietzschean subject. The resulting paradox, then, is that the increasing affirmation of existence leads to an increasing requirement for distance, and so the immediacy of Being is always counteracted by the need for *Einsamkeit*, or solitude. This is the solitude of Zarathustra in his mountain home, a mirroring of Nietzsche in his travels through Sils Maria and Upper-Engadine, and it becomes poetically illustrative of the ethical distance between himself and Being. For, when Nietzsche conceived of the eternal return as the genesis of Zarathustra, he wrote that it was a formula "6,000 feet beyond people and time."[47]

Nietzsche's love of the distant takes on many forms, such as the *Übermensch*, a future age of tragedy, and even in Zarathustra's descent to humankind. But just as those "resplendent, dream-born figures of the Olympians" were, for the Homeric Greek, necessitated only by the "terrors and horrors of existence,"[48] Balthasar detects that Nietzsche's own existential triumphs concealed a profound suffering and need. Here, he proposes that Nietzsche's love of the distant arises from "the ultimate terror of a solitude denuded of God [*entgötterten*]."[49] "Distance," then, is an invention of solitude from within and for its own sake, and Nietzsche, Balthasar notes, is even aware of this: when Zarathustra and the hermit discuss the nature of friendship, the hermit remarks of his solitude that "always one times one—in the long run that makes two!"[50] And the "Aftersong" of *Beyond Good and Evil* concludes with a similar riddle of numbers:

> The friend of noon-time—but—no! don't ask who—
> It was at noon, when one turned into two . . .
>
> Now we can feast, with triumph in the air,
> The fest of all fests:
> Friend Zarathustra came, the guest of all guests!
> The world can laugh, the gruesome curtain tear,
> The wedding day of light and dark was here . . .[51]

For Balthasar, Zarathustra's appearance reads as the bifurcation of Nietzsche himself into a duality expressive of distance. And Zarathustra's counterpart

---

47. *Ecce Homo*, in Nietzsche, *Anti-Christ*, 123.
48. Nietzsche, *Birth of Tragedy*, 23.
49. Balthasar, *Geschichte des eschatologischen Problems*, 45.
50. Nietzsche, *Thus Spoke Zarathustra*, 40.
51. Nietzsche, *Beyond Good and Evil* (2001), 180.

is the incarnate Christ: for just as Christ became flesh as the ecstasis of God from his absolute immanence, so Zarathustra attains to life as an ecstasis of Nietzsche in his own absolutized immanence of eternal recurrence. Balthasar continues,

> Zarathustra, the projection of longing, born of the incest of solitude, becomes an eschatological *Doppelgänger*, a new god, and the solitude with god is solitude with oneself, "the religion of immanence."[52] The god appears messianically adorned, he "has his *hazar*, his kingdom of a thousand years,"[53] he holds the New Supper, he sings the song of the seven seals,[54] but all this is the eschatology of the singular human being, for "in human beings, creature and creator are combined."[55] "In the end, we love our desires and not the thing desired."[56]

Seen thus, Zarathustra is an existential gesture, a soliloquy speaking of eternal recurrence precisely as the means for Nietzsche to performatively affect a distance between himself and the ugliness of Being. Zarathustra is a mask for the solitude of the self-absolutization that accompanies the affirmation of eternal recurrence: an aesthetic expression of Nietzsche's own will to power, which is then reflected back upon himself as the consummation of that very affirmation. Yet this aesthetic double reflection of subjectivity proves a repetition of that play of mirrors in *The Birth of Tragedy*, and so, despite the appearance of affirmation, there is ultimately a neglect of Being owing to the false distancing of the subject in relation to her world. At least the Greek affirmation of life was "dramatic" by virtue of its collectively shared mythological aesthetic, and likewise in the more literal sense of δρᾶμα as "action" and thus as an authentic interchange of meaning. In the later Nietzsche, though, this is supplanted by a pseudo-drama of creative incest within subjectivity itself, whose vacuousness becomes detached from Being. The existential soliloquy of eternal recurrence is rather better characterized by Macbeth's despair at mortal existence as it stretches toward "the last syllable

---

52. Balthasar here references Kierkegaard's *Concluding Unscientific Postscript*. The reference is an example of Balthasar's strategy of placing Nietzsche and Kierkegaard in a dialectical contest by which the philosophical discernment of ultimacy (*die Letzte*) in post-idealist modernity begins. This strategy features in both the *Geschichte des eschatologischen Problems* and the *Apokalypse der deutschen Seele*.

53. *KSA* 11:53.

54. Nietzsche, *Thus Spoke Zarathustra*, 184–85.

55. Nietzsche, *Beyond Good and Evil* (2001), 117.

56. Balthasar, *Geschichte des eschatologischen Problems*, 45; referring to Nietzsche, *Beyond Good and Evil* (2001), 73. Balthasar does not reference the quotations from Nietzsche included within this passage. The citations have been added here for clarity.

of recorded time": by its detachment from Being, the double mirroring of eternal recurrence is ultimately detached from meaning beyond the solitude of the individual and becomes "a tale told by an idiot, full of sound and fury, signifying nothing."[57] Though, as with the Shakespearean drama, could the value of the Nietzschean soliloquy perhaps lie in the fact that its own futility *is* witnessed by his readers? This would render his entire philosophy itself a performance, and the later Nietzsche seems to advocate for such a reading in his later-period writings. But what then?

To witness this soliloquy, Balthasar thinks, is to witness Nietzsche's *Zusammenbruch*—his collapse. Not only in Nietzsche's descent into madness in the first days of 1889, but in the inexorable self-annihilation of Nietzschean subjectivity itself. The *erôs* driving Nietzsche's quest to affirm Being ends in a solipsistic "paean of self-love"[58] with the creation of Zarathustra, which in turn reveals—as cited above—Nietzsche's love of desire rather than of the thing desired. This play of mirrors has Nietzsche transfixed by his own reflection, like Narcissus; and, also like Narcissus, Nietzsche's only recourse thereafter was to self-destruction. Thus, Balthasar writes of Nietzsche,

> And so it is that the steep path of self-sufficiency which Nietzsche treads ends in a frightening and hellish need for self-immolation. The wealth of power and truth that he amasses leads only to the cruel fate of Midas, who, instead of living bread, grasps only immutable gold in his hands. His insatiable desire for truth without lies strays into a wilderness of hopeless appearances, into a hall of mirrors filled with incalculable lies.[59]

No precise textual point signals the turn of Nietzsche's self-mirroring subjectivity back onto him with self-destructive intent, however throughout his final poetry (much neglected in the scholarship, it ought to be noted) Nietzsche bears witness to his and Zarathustra's demise. Indeed, "Amidst Birds of Prey":

> Oh Zarathustra,
> most cruel Nimrod!
> Most recently the hunter of God,
> the trapper's net of all virtue,
> the arrow of evil!
> Now—
> hunted down by yourself,

---

57. *Macbeth* 5.5.21, in Shakespeare, *New Oxford Shakespeare*, 2561.
58. Hans Urs von Balthasar, in Nietzsche, *Anthologien*, 189.
59. Hans Urs von Balthasar, in Nietzsche, *Anthologien*, 288.

your own prey,
withdrawn into yourself . . .

Now—
alone with yourself,
twofold in your own knowledge,
amidst a hundred mirrors
false before yourself,
between a hundred memories
uncertain,
made weary by every wound,
made cold of every frost,
strangled by your own rope,
Self-knower!
Self-hangman![60]

As a whole, this poem portrays an exasperated Nietzsche reckoning with the nihilistic destruction of his own self just as Zarathustra's self-knowledge proves fatal for him. Nietzsche recognizes Zarathustra as a fictional ecstasis born of his own solitude, and that the destruction of his mirroring in Zarathustra will amount to his own existential demise. And here, the phrase "self-hangman" is particularly telling: "the hanged man" (*die Gehenkter*) is a byword Nietzsche reserved to describe Christian nihilism.[61]

A Trinitarian Ontology of Distance

Zarathustra's self-transgression into self-annihilation performs the reductio ad absurdum of the tragic eschaton, but in doing so is simultaneously performative of a theological truth for Balthasar. Precisely because Nietzschean subjectivity shapes itself by the denial of God, its character ends up assuming something of the theological negatively—thus, when it is itself denied into the nothingness of its self-destruction, we do not rest with *ex nihilo nihil fit* but glimpse an apophasis of a specifically Christian metaphysics. If the world for Nietzsche ultimately comprises a kataphasis whose aesthetics are sustained by a mirror play of subjectivity, then its negative shape—the void of its self-destruction—is one comprising an apophasis that points to Being

---

60. *KSA* 6:390.

61. Nietzsche: *Human, All Too Human*, 223; *KSA* 11:327–28; *Thus Spoke Zarathustra*, 203–309 (the first appearance of "The Lament of Ariadne"); *Twilight of the Idols*, in *Anti-Christ*, 182.

as an ontological interplay. In a passage toward the end of the *Apokalypse*, Balthasar revels in the aesthetics of such an interplay:

> The word that simultaneously captures the tremendous magnificence of the swelling surf of the world and the falling emptiness of its hollow foam, that word is: *play*. For "play" imparts that the tragedy of the world, right down to its hells, is yet gripped by a meditating, watchful gaze, that it is a "play before . . ." and thus not an Absolute. "Play" further imparts that the world comprises what Nietzsche saw in it: a weightless balance of forces, a dance of waves which hides a secret desire within every tree, something which leads to dance and foolery in the pathos of its every conduct. And "play" says, ultimately, that it is a secret of communion, of colloquy, and of a round dance into which we are drawn without any possibility of escape.[62]

The unsustainable contradictions of distance that result in the self-negation of Nietzschean subjectivity can be likened to the phenomenon of how opposing mirrors are generative of an infinitude recursion of images, for what is witnessed here is a false infinitude and the proliferation of the recurrence into the infinitesimally small. This captures the fate of tragic subjectivity somewhat, but it fails to impart the terror that led Nietzsche to concede Zarathustra's self-immolation within his late poetry. The metaphor of acoustic feedback is perhaps more apt: it is the sharp, unbearable pitch of what should, for Nietzsche, be music, and it captures the sense of vertigo accompanying the recursion of mirror images but with the acute pain of the infinitesimally small penetrating its listener rather than proceeding into its false landscape. The two metaphors here are in cooperation and reflect Nietzsche's earlier distinction between the Apolline image and Dionysian music, except their complementarity here is not the transfiguration of existence into sublimity, but rather a transmogrification of the self into an eldritch *Unheimlichkeit*.

By contrast, Balthasar's recovery of existence as "play" after the self-annihilation of the tragic subject imbues an innocence to Being by the sense of distance within its "dance and foolery." We can imagine music here, to be sure, but the negation of the Dionysian din of the will to power is rather a kind of quietude and marvel as Being is before us anew. The openness of the subject toward Being positions her to sense a stillness within the "weightless balance of forces" she now intuits of Being. Yet "play" and "stillness" evoke an antagonism akin to that of Nietzsche's Dionysian and Apollonian, and they seem to lack the malleability of their Nietzschean counterparts as they

---

62. Balthasar, *Apokalypse der deutschen Seele*, 3:442.

are denuded of any mythological personification. So, what is it of play that we might find in stillness, and vice versa?

An interpretation here in response to Nietzsche is illuminated within T. S. Eliot's poem "Burnt Norton." Eliot rejects Nietzsche's absolutization of temporality when he prefaces the poem with the couplet "If all time is present / All time is unredeemable." Pure, finite temporality elevated into the infinite as the means for framing Being is fraught; its end excludes any sense of what might have been, and is thus a phenomenology defined by not-Being. Against Nietzsche's privileging of music and the dithyramb as the exclusive aesthetic disclosure of Being—a way in which temporal immanence becomes eternalized—Eliot rebuts that it is only in the ecstatic movement of the in-dwelling stillness of the beauty of Being by which it discloses its completeness:

> Words move, music moves
> Only in time; but that which is only living
> Can only die. Words, after speech, reach
> Into the silence. Only by the form, the pattern,
> Can words or music reach
> The stillness, as a Chinese jar still
> Moves perpetually in its stillness.

By contrast, the Dionysian irruption of time, which drums the beats of satyr's syncopated dance, eventually succumbs to its own frenzy and collapses, much like how a tarantella speeds up the fatal efficacy of the spider venom of nihilism—the very kind that Zarathustra resists.[63] The inversion of the internalizing pathology of the tragic subject with Zarathustra's performative self-destruction thus manifest a release by which the subject is restored to a sobriety of distance, and this enables both a stillness and a movement together. For Balthasar, this captures a theological a priori in the unity of the subject with her other (as opposed to herself) in the reciprocity of their "play." Thus, Dasein—the "existing being" of the subject—"gives itself to play because the experience of being admitted [in Being] is the very first thing which it knows in the realm of Being."[64]

The wordless beauty of form to which Eliot gestures in "Burnt Norton" lends itself well toward grasping the sense of the Trinity that Balthasar envisions as the revelation to which Nietzsche's fate ultimately points. This is grounded by Balthasar's contradiction of Nietzsche's declaration that life first (and ultimately) comprises the "terrors and horrors of existence" intuited by the Greeks; instead, the admission of the subject into Being first

63. Nietzsche, *Thus Spoke Zarathustra*, 76–79.
64. Balthasar, *Glory of the Lord*, 5:616.

discloses the a priori possibility of love as "the selfless communication of what is mine and the selfless welcoming of the other in myself."[65] And while human existence is of course replete with suffering (let alone terrors and horrors), this distance between the self and the other means, for Balthasar, that "there is no 'gravity of life' which would fundamentally surpass this [a priori] beginning."[66]

The Nietzschean affirmation of existence required the subject to apprehend and value Being as her means of exercising her will to power—be that through the Greek tragic drama or one's response to the demon of the eternal return. This seizure of existence is an attitude in response to Being—but one which Balthasar contends is preceded by that initial welcoming of the "I" with its participation in Being: so, "there is no 'taking over control' of existence which might go further than this first experience of miracle and play."[67] Accordingly, the model of subjectivity that Balthasar recovers from Nietzsche's collapse regards both distance and otherness as enabling of the subject's reconciliation with Being and its affirmation. Self and world are not primarily in contest as they are for Nietzsche, since the Kantian vein giving rise to the subject as the will to power is now negated. Nicholas Healy phrases this succinctly: for Balthasar, "otherness is not outside the unity of being because the unity of being is more than just self."[68]

Now, as improbable a leap it is from Zarathustra's self-destruction to Trinitarian revelation, we ought to remember that, for Balthasar, Nietzsche functions as a philosophical *via negativa* that does not so much comprise a divine revelation itself as restore an ontology that displays its openness toward the divine. It is then a matter of theological labor to discern what kind of revelation "fulfils" the absence left in the wake of Nietzsche's tragic ontology. For Balthasar, this theological labor is self-necessitating too. Balthasar's model of the subject and the theological a priori of Being as play implies, as he noted in the *Apokalypse*, a "play before." Thus, the imagination of the subject situated within the play of Being is naturally directed toward intuiting this "before"—the stage of existence itself "poses the problem of Absolute Being."[69] And so it is that Balthasar's study of Nietzsche leads into his later Trinitarian ontology—an account of Being in which the experience of beauty through form corresponds to the immediacy of experience as a gift, and therefore invites a sense of its transcendent bestowal.

65. Balthasar, *Truth of the World*, 123.
66. Balthasar, *Glory of the Lord*, 5:616–17.
67. Balthasar, *Glory of the Lord*, 5:617.
68. Healy, *Eschatology*, 55.
69. Balthasar, "Résumé of My Thought," 1.

There is palpable theological movement and development for Balthasar between the *Apokalypse* and the trilogy, but his mature Trinitarian ontology is latent within his early reading of Nietzsche. And with this reading, "distance" emerges as a theological centerpiece from which the starkest opposite to Nietzschean solitude can emerge: the distance of the cross as the love of God for humankind even by the abandonment of God from God into death. Accordingly, this in turn discloses the simultaneous unity and distance within God himself:

> For only in Christianity does it become comprehensible why love is, in truth, "distance," and must so be—and that love does not so much alleviate distance, but would rather see that it is always affirmed and upheld: for only here will it become apparent that God himself is love *as* the distance within the threefold unity of his nature, and thus the archetype of all true unity, which is not so much a fusion and amalgam, but rather the inner light of reverence and the recognition of the "Thou."[70]

The ontological distances within God himself and between us and God, then, comprise the precondition for the possibility of love at all. It is a grace by which nature itself can be fulfilled in a participation with the perichoretic joy of God, in whom "we live, and move, and have our being" (Acts 17:28 KJV). Our reconciliation with Being is both a stillness and a play; it is the means by which our wonder can enfold us in the mystery of the Trinity and the distance and identity of its persons, and simultaneously our intuition of beauty as divine gift spurs our unlimited ability to regard Being with wonder a priori. It is likewise why Balthasar proposes that given to the modern Christian alone is "the task of performing the act of affirming Being, unperturbed by the darkness and the distortion, in a way that is vicarious and representative for all humanity."[71]

---

70. Hans Urs von Balthasar, in Nietzsche, *Anthologien*, 111; emphasis in original.
71. Balthasar, *Glory of the Lord*, 5:648.

Part Five

Poetics of Reconciliation

13

Christ and the Destabilization of Time

GRAHAM WARD

Christological Time

ONE OF THE MORE dramatic discoveries in modern science concerns the nature of time. There are a number of options proposed. To take only two: time spatializes and warps due to gravity (a familiar proof drawn from the general theory of relativity); or time has no existence at all (a construction of our minds that is embedded in the flows and fluxes of quantum fields). The past is malleable and the future plural. Either way, theoretical physics has enabled us to question the linearity of time in ways that return to us Augustine's reflections in the *Confessions* that the present as such does not exist for us. It is continually folding into and out of memory and anticipation of the future.

In this essay, I wish to develop a christological reading of time, which points to the omnidirectionality of grace and, therefore, also of redemption. I want to explore this, primarily, through examining the portrayal of time in the New Testament, particularly in the writing of Paul and the Gospel of Mark. I will conclude with what I call the twinned "cores" with which the linear gospel narratives conclude: the silence of Holy Saturday and the empty tomb. They are not nihilistic voids. Rather, they are cores of silence, where something is being effected, transacted, and for which we could never have any understanding.[1] They are, nevertheless, operational spaces—like the spaces between words that give individual items grammatical significance. Both of them are occurrences *within* time. Time is not transcended. Yet both occurrences point to a radical revision of linear time, in which time is reconfigured from *within* a temporality that is now recognized as created ex nihilo by an eternal Creator.

The Right Time

In the Gospel of Mark, the deictics of temporality appear under erasure by a Trinitarian dynamic. "Beginning," "end," "then," "now," "immediately" are not annulled. Rather, their content is rendered amphibolous—as protology and eschatology fold into a triune sempiternity and all things are redeemed.[2] The "beginning" (*archē*) that opens Mark's narrative is an aperture into another kind of normal, where life is lived in God. Through this literary portal, John the Baptist strides like a returning ancient patriarch or prophet—making the waters flow with a new grace through the desert. It is an aperture in the wilderness, on the threshold of the promised land. Like Moses, the Baptist will not cross over, until he's handed over—even over to the authorities. And into this flow of grace steps Jesus, who arrives abruptly "without father, without mother, without ancestry [*apatōr, amētōr, agenalogētos*], having neither a beginning of days nor an end of life [*mēte archēn ēmerōn mēte zōēs telos echōn*]" (Heb 7:3).[3] Notice the piling of those alpha-privatives in the first clause that deny human genealogy. These alpha-privatives are then balanced by further negatives in the second clause ("without beginning . . . without end"), which extend the absence of such a human genealogy infinitely, and outwards in all temporal directions.

This is not Mark, but it is speaking about Melchizedek as a figure for Christ. This is Mark:

> And it came to pass in those days [*en ekeinais tais ēmerais*] came Jesus from Nazareth of Galilee and was baptized in [*eis*] the Jordan by John. And immediately rising out of the water [*ek anabainōn udatos*] he saw the heavens being torn open

---

1. I take this phrase from Maggie Ross, *Writing the Icon Heart*, 32–33. Ross is discussing contemplative prayer.

2. For a study of a Jewish reflection on this theme of time and redemption, see Ward, "On Time and Salvation."

3. Throughout this chapter, Scripture translations are the author's own.

[*schizomenous*] and the spirit as a dove coming down [*katabainon*] upon him; and there was a voice out of [*ek*] the heavens: Thou art my Son [*o uios mou*], the Beloved and in you I am well pleased [*en soi eudokēsa*]. . . . [And after John had been handed over] Jesus came into Galilee proclaiming the gospel of God, and saying, "The time has been fulfilled [*peplērōtai o kairos*]." (Mark 1:9–15)

This baptismal epiphany has its recapitulation in the transfiguration, with one major non-identical repetition: in the baptism, only the Son hears the Father speak. In the transfiguration the church in embryo also hears (or overhears). Yet the transfiguration also enables us to look back at that baptismal epiphany and recognize that there is no one here to witness this scene. The narrator and even John who baptizes are effaced. In this scene, the witness, like the drama, is entirely internal to the Trinitarian relations themselves. Here is a moment of Trinitarian intimacy (paternal, filial, pneumatological) that can be located nowhere and authored by no one. We will return to the divine entanglements of that intimacy in a moment. For now, the attention is on the ironies that emerge in the writing when a conversation that is unlocatable and without authorship is fixed into a Palestinian topography: Jesus *from Nazareth of Galilee*, baptized in the *Jordan River*, and the rooting pleonasm of "it came to pass in those days [*en ekeinais tais ēmerais*]" (Mark 1:9).

Hence, time and space are not dissolved in the aperture of the *archē*. Rather they are locked tightly into (the dative locative *en*) particularities. These particularities act like trigger points in a landscape that is radiating with a strange illuminating light. It is a light that distorts perspective, such as that which can often be found in the paintings of Caspar David Friedrich.[4] The historical event in its topographical setting is thus enfolded into a Trinitarian event that is profoundly rhythmic: the *anabasis* of Jesus from the water and the *katabasis* of the Spirit. This rhythmic movement, which reverberates all the way down through the gospel narrative, finds its reversed recapitulation in the descent following the crucifixion and the ascent of the resurrection. And now, in this intra-Trinitarian moment, this figure of "Jesus from Nazareth of Galilee" is given a genealogy: the attesting Father, and the Spirit as a dove (of feminine gender). It is a genealogy and a generation that does not belong to the historical. Rather, time stutters in the movements of *en*, *eis*, and *ek*, in, into, and out of. The verbal tenses play

---

4. For the strange illumination Caspar David Friedrich creates to distorts the viewer's perspective of both the landscape and the objects within it, see Koerner, *Caspar David Friedrich*, 117–46.

out temporal complexities as the perpetual present participles of ascending, descending, and celestial tearing arrive at the first of two pointed culminations: "Thou art [*su ei*]"—followed by an abrupt, almost violent aorist "in you I am well pleased [*en soi eudokēsa*]." Here's the Trinitarian entanglement: the Father's pleasure is *in* the Son. It is not the pleasure of an external observer. If the Son is *in* the Father, as eternally generated by the Father, the Father is *in* the Son. Both fatherhood and sonship are eternal generations in and through the Spirit. And what about that punctuating present active aorist? It marks a point in the present that is, again, unlocatable in chronological time. And so, it punctures history and the historical. The suggestive force of these two grammatical points is that the statement "I am well pleased" is less one about the Father's pleasure in the Son, and more an acclamation of the divine condition of unimaginable Trinitarian satisfaction—like the resolve in Gen 1:31: "So it was; and God saw all that he had made, and it was very good."

If the first culmination is the emphatically present indicative acclamation "thou art [*su ei*]," the second culmination is the temporal knotting involved in "the time has been fulfilled [*peplērōtai o kairos*]." After all the present, active, and aorist tenses when "time" itself is the subject, we have a statement in a perfect passive tense announcing a completion in the recent past.[5] The "when" to which this verbal tense appeals is that of an immemorial past, a history enfolded in a mystery, in which creation is a beneficiary without any possibility of accounting for why. The event it speaks of in the past is outside any historical determination, and yet its fulfillment opens an entirely new possibility for the future of all contingent and temporal events.

In attempting to give expression to how time is redeemed by historical facticity being given its sacred meaning and cosmic location through that which is in and beyond temporality and inhabits time as grace, representation and expression are altogether invested with mythic associations. Hence, when we read a phrase like "the time has been fulfilled [*peplērōtai o kairos*]," it has to be understood as a statement imbued with a mythic sensibility. This sensibility ironizes every understanding that we have of time; calling into question our knowledge of temporality. The fullness, perfection, plenitude (all possible meanings of *plēroma* and *plēroō* in the Pauline corpus) can only lie in the satisfaction of what time longs for—time's own fulfillment, its own telos.

---

5. I would like to acknowledge with gratitude an unnamed delegate at the Sept. 2019 conference "New Trinitarian Ontologies," who called attention to this perfect passive tense.

The word Jesus uses is not *chronos* (time as duration), but rather *kairos* (the chosen time, the right time, and the critical moment). Kairos is what that earlier aorist sense and what that perfect passive sense ("has been") had announced—an immemorial temporality; a time that is not reducible to history and duration. This is, paradoxically, eternal time, aeonic time, and we could translate *peplērōtai* as "has been given plenitudinously." Alternatively, it is some equivalent that is the opposite of "to empty," "to pour out"—for the opposite of *plēroō* in *kenoō*. Hence, *peplērōtai* tells us something about the nature and quality of aeonic time rather than just an action with respect to time. In other words, *peplērōtai* can be understood not just verbally but also adjectivally (you can do this in Greek). What kairos is, then, is time filled in and through the plenitude of grace. And yet *it is a concrete time*, a time that is meaningful because it can be received, experienced, and lived. It is the meaningfulness *of* time. This meaning needs further explication.

The Fullness of Time

In his Letter to the Galatians, Paul famously refers to "the fullness of time" (Gal 4:4). In the context, this phrase refers to the shift from being under the law to being under grace through faith in Jesus Christ. As children, the Jewish people were under the law and "slaves to the elemental spirits of the universe, but when the fullness of time [*to plērōma tou chronou*] came, then God sent forth his son, born of a woman" (Gal 4:4). Paul is speaking here about chronological time, secular time, and the appearance of Christ in history. But this *plērōma* is also part of a rich pneumatology. For in Paul, the mystery of God's gracious and providential operations in the world are those of which we in Christ are stewards. The punctiliar and specifically aorist sense of coming, of Christ, and of born of a woman is not diachronic. Rather, it marks an interruption or a rupture within the chronological, because it is part of an ongoing process of God's spiritual movement in creation. There is an association here between the generation of the Son that announces the Father *as* Father, the "generations of the heavens and the earth" in P's account of divine creation (Gen 2:4) and the generation of Jesus Christ in and through the Virgin Mary. If we leave that analysis hanging for the moment, then what we have in Paul's phrase *to plērōma tou chronou* can be understood as creation becoming conscious of itself as created in and with the coming presence of its Creator. In the words of John's Gospel: God coming to God's own (*ta idia*).[6]

---

6. As we will see later in Rom 11:5, Paul uses the word *kairos*. *Kairos* is also used in Gal 6:10; Eph 5:16; Col 4:5. These are references to a time in Christ for doing good, or

Paul situates Christ with respect to *chronos*. But *chronos* does not accommodate the advent of Christ to chronological time in the way the early Christian historian Eusebius of Caesarea seems to suggest when he proposes that the Pax Romana, established by the accession of Caesar Augustus, provided the historical condition for the coming of Christ:

> In the same year, Caesar—predestined by God for many mysteries—ordered a census of all men in every province of the empire. God made himself seen as a man then, he wanted to be a man then. Christ was born at that time: he was registered shortly after his birth during the Roman census.[7]

Redemption does not wait in the wings for the right historical conditions to pertain for its coming. The coming of Christ at that point in the history of occupied Israel, whether in Luke's Gospel account of the Roman census, or at the point in Mark's Gospel when John was baptizing in the Jordan, is locked into a decisive moment in the Godhead before the foundation of the world—locked in the punctiliar past of that aorist "I was well pleased." Hence, the coming of Christ cannot be dislodged from history and cannot be explained in history. We have no access to divine understanding, foreknowledge, providence, and decision. We have only a fragile understanding that if God is love, then this "decision" was not arbitrary. Perhaps Eusebius's parenthesis about Caesar—"predestined by God for many mysteries"—is attempting to suggest precisely that.[8]

---

for working out what is good. We can understand this use of kairos as the operational time in which the church works with Christ for the redemption of all things. In his book *The Time That Remains*, Agamben understands this as "messianic time"—the time that remains between the coming of Christ and the end of time (defined as apocalyptic time when everything is concluded). He wedges a distinction between messianic time (kairos) and eschatological time. However, I would argue that this is a theological mistake. For with this distinction, the "time that remains" is not redemptive time, and is not the redemption of time. For a sympathetic reading of Agamben's work on time and rhythm for theology, see Eikelboom, *Rhythm*, 90–120.

7. Erik Peterson quotes this text and points to how this is a line of thought is found in John Chrysostom, Prudentius, Ambrose, and Jerome. For Eusebius, history was brought to its predestined completion in Constantine, where, he writes, the "single king on earth corresponds to the single king in Heaven and the single sovereign *nomos* and *Logos*" (*Theologische Traktate*, 50). For a discussion of the importance of this text and others like it for contemporary political theology and the debates between Carl Schmitt and Erik Peterson, see also Agamben, *Kingdom and Glory*, 1–14.

8. In bk. 1 of his *Church History*, Eusebius emphasizes the continuity between the Jewish past and the incarnation of Christ, as he appeals to a "time appointed by the inscrutable council of God" (1:87).

Certainly, that time and that place of Christ's birth in Bethlehem are given a universal, that is, a mythical significance. They are made meaningful in distinctive, symbolic ways. Kairos is graced time, and time as grace, in whose gift historical time is made meaningful. But kairos is, for us, also mythical time. I mean that phrase in two distinct manners: it is mythical time as a mode of representing and narrating something that took place in history, that is, a mode of historiography. It is also mythical time because it is presenting a sensibility beyond (though not outside) our abilities to grasp. In and as representation, this coming appears interruptive—as abrupt as Jesus presenting himself before John the Baptism at the Jordan in Mark's Gospel. But kairos is not simply interruptive. Kairos is not timelessness. It is not the in-breaking of the eternal. If I call kairos aeonic time, it remains a form of time as graced. It is the time of divine operations in creation that redeems chronological time by transposing it into eschatological time. It is the distension of time in both the "now" and "not yet." As such, kairos bears the hallmarks of that which is to come at the end of time, that is, a judgment that fully manifests the truth of things and the depths of our ignorance (and disobedience because of that ignorance); the depths of our difference *from* the divine *in the face of* the divine.[9] As eschatological time, and as time graced, kairos bears also the "not yet," the distensions of waiting, expecting, and stretching out toward a consummation to come. Kairos is not delivery from time and the world, but rather part of the ongoing pedagogy of formation—the ongoing metanoia. Hence, it is time lived to a different beat, as it is transposed by the economy of a divine rhythm. Illuminated by kairos, we cry out the more, we groan the more, for the lostness we see around us, the redemption not yet perfected, and, as Hegel recognized, the histories that have been "slaughter benches." Illuminated by kairos, we are sensitized to the glory that is to come and the presentiments of it now *in* the very abjection that is all too evident. In *chronos* there is no illumination. Temporality is fallen. There is a darkness that cannot comprehend and participate in the operation of its grace. In *chronos* there is only Macbeth's "tomorrow, and tomorrow, and tomorrow."[10]

9. Agamben writes, "The recapitulation of the past is also a summary judgement pronounced upon it" (*Time That Remains*, 78).

10. *Macbeth* 5.5.19, in Shakespeare, *New Oxford Shakespeare*, 2560. Agamben "proposes to interpret messianic time as a paradigm of historical time" (*Time That Remains*, 3). His fascinating *Time That Remains*, an erudite study—erudite to the point of posturing, even self-mockery—is also clearly an act of mourning. For it mourns for a socialism that never could be realized, and for a Roman Catholic Church that has betrayed its messianic calling (*kleitos*). Yet by clarifying this "time that remains," he also opens a nonutopian space for transformative action, which might effect both socialism

The Now Time

In Rom 11:5, Paul defines those caught up in grace as "in the time of the now [*en tō nun kairō*]." To speak in this way of eschatological time as both "now" and "not yet" can give the impression of two distinct times: a realized present; and a future final unfolding of that present. However, this impression is incorrect. For as Augustine has made us aware, there is no pure "now." The "now" is not only mixed up with memory and anticipations of the future, but is itself mediated by an absence—the interval between the eternal and the temporal is marked only in the spaces between the words of a psalm, the beats in a foot, the notes in a bar. Both the "now" and the "not yet" of eschatological time are integral to the processes of temporality, and the processes of change emerging from endless and unfathomable complexities of cause and effect that alert us to how history is never finished and the past is never past. History (in German, *Historie*) makes possible our historical (in German, *geschichtlich*), particular, and located existence in time. A location we cannot overleap because it is the very condition for the eschatological—the condition of time's own fulfillment.[11] And so, while time becomes purposeful and directed to an eschatological telos, the "now" and the "not yet" twist in concrete encounters. Hence, the irony in Mark's Gospel betrays these twists of time, where *chronos* and kairos are interlaced in specific encounters. For example, at the trial before the High Priest, some "stood up and gave false evidence against him to this effect: 'We heard him say, "I will pull down this temple, made with human hands, and in three days I will build another, not made with hands"'" (Mark 14:57–8).[12] The coming of Christ thus inaugurates "the fulfillment of time," and the cross of Christ is the most profound display of this inauguration.

This is the gospel. This is the proclamation. It is not only something that Christ speaks about and announces. It is something that he *is*. He *is peplērōtai o kairos*—the time replete. His coming situates history, *chronos*, within himself. His crucifixion completes that. From the time of the flogging

---

and the church. He cites Benjamin that each instant might be the "small door through which the Messiah enters" (71). Like Derrida, he thus moves beyond false messianisms of endless deferral and operational paralysis.

11. I concur here with Rudolf Bultmann, in his concern for the life of faith as we experience it. He writes: "Human life continues to be 'historic' [*geschichtlich*] even when it is eschatological" ("Reply to the Theses of J. Schniewind," in Bartsch, *Kerygma and Myth*, 1:107).

12. The complex citing and pseudonymity of these verses encapsulates all the anxieties and burdens of authorship that stipple the writing in and of the Gospel of St. Mark.

in the courtyard of the praetorium (Mark 15:16) to the time he pronounces his own godforsakenness (15:35), Jesus loses even his name to history. He is not named. He is rather a pronominal "he" or "him"—abject to the point of anonymity. His own past and person are erased. Now just an object of ridicule, he is consumed by the chronological—or, put another way, by the way of faith. Now in his death, he consumes the chronological. The final irony of kairos and *chronos*, mourning and myth, origin and loss coincide, then lies in the luminous recognition by the gentile centurion that he *was* the Son of God.

History is *in* the aeonic, the transhistorical, the eschatological, just as Christ is in his creation, and creation is a Trinitarian event *in* God. The point is this: kairos does not annul *chronos*. Rather, it works within it, changing the structured relations of chronological time, and is wedded to sin.[13] It is wedded to the sins of the fathers, as it is passed down through the generations, passed down not just to the fourth generation, and to each successive generation, such that fathering continues as a life-giving activity. The operation of grace makes certain chains of action and reaction down the generations inoperative: inoperative in their effect upon history (*Historie*); and inoperative upon the conditions that then prevail within any temporal location (*Geschichte*). In Eph 1:10, Paul picks up the rhythm of this operation, what he calls "the economy of the fulfillment of times [*eis oikonomian tou plērōmatos tōn kairōn*]," in which, he writes, "all things are recapitulated in Christ [*anakephalaiōsasthai . . . en tō christō*], things in heaven and things on earth."[14] In this economy, the spiritual time of grace renders inoperative certain distortions of desire, from which sin issues transfiguring all things. Living in this divine *ikonomia* thus constitutes a pedagogy that governs spiritual and ethical formation *in* Christ *through* the Spirit. In this consists the nurture and sustenance for ethical life. For, in this "fullness of time" we apprehend something of the gravity of our historicity, and our responsibilities as bearers of this very historical locatedness, for the effects of our actions, and for good or ill upon the history to come. Our actions count, and that counting makes our living ethical. In this way, through us and for us, as for the writers of the Gospels and St. Paul, Christ as Logos and mythos is handed on—handed over and lived.

13. Agamben appreciates the transformation, the personal, and the communal, affected by what he calls the "messianic event." He writes: "The messianic vocation is a movement of immanence, of, if one prefers, a zone of absolute indiscernibility between immanence and transcendence, between this world and the future world" (*Time That Remains*, 25).

14. Although I am unsure how to interpret it, there is an interesting use of the plural of "kairos" here.

(Conclusion) Coda[15]

We are beginning to tumble into the christological paradoxes that subvert all logics of merely human invention. These are the enigmas, the paradoxes, and the riddles that appear at the coming of Christ, the Logos and the Mythos. There is, moreover, a final word about time that moves us beyond paradox, and beyond myth, to where the Logos is Logos *for us* most intensely: the tomb. For, in a coda to the foregoing, chronology continues after the crucifixion: after the rending of the temple curtain; and after the last words of Christ, "thirst" (John 19:38), in which, all of a sudden, Jesus withdraws into the dark interiority of the Godhead, sucking out all the poisonous waywardness of humankind. Chronology continues: Friday night, all through Saturday, Sunday morning—each day liturgically framed by the Passover and the Sabbath. The women gather in the dawn of a new era, being human, even as the tomb is empty. *Chronos* continues as the hours and days pass; but what about kairos? What happens to kairos in the tomb?

These are questions that can be asked *because* chronology continues, *because* there is a Good Friday, and *because* there is the Sunday of the resurrection. It makes human sense when the tomb is empty to ask what happened to the body, placed there before the sunset on Friday marking the Sabbath. Yet, although askable, and even inevitable, these questions cannot be easily answered—even speculative approaches to Holy Saturday are attempts to fill this chronological hiatus. Descents into hell and its harrowing continue the association of Logos and Mythos. They can act as representational displacements that veil the hiatus. The emphasis here is on the Mythos: mythos veiling a void. But the silence of Holy Saturday along with the emptiness of the tomb are not voids. Time is not voided, because that would mean a disseverance between *chronos* and kairos—something impossible, because creation itself would cease. And it doesn't. These are, then, the "cores" of divine intensity: cores where only silence can possibly provide some articulation of the profundity of what is occurring—the depths of its hiddenness. For into these core spaces *within* the chronological, all Christian doctrines of the atonement fall. In these core silences, deep in the triune God, everything is accomplished: the reconciliation, the forgiveness, the propitiation, the justification, the satisfaction, and whichever of the New Testament metaphors for atonement we like to emphasize.

The dominions of sin and death are at last brought to an end in an evacuation of representation that Holy Saturday and the tomb render opaque. As always governed by Christ, mediation becomes impossibly opaque *for us*

---

15. This owes much to a conversation with my friend and fellow theologian David Moss.

human creatures. Yet everything that is the ultimate work of salvation goes on here—and then in a time and space that is unaccountable—a time and space upon which everything also depends. It's as if the wounds inflicted upon the body of Christ open deep rents in the fabric of existence, as we have become accustomed to recognize it: one interminable and unquestionable laceration, through which the operations within the Godhead are most intensely *not* seen, not grasped, and yet most apparent. Here, *in* time, time implodes, even as the unnameable and the unthinkable are encountered—or discounted.

14

Repetition and Re-Presentation
Reaching Eternity Through Beauty

ISABELLE MOULIN

Repetition and Re-Presentation:
Reaching Eternity through Beauty

THE DOCTRINE OF THE Trinity constitutes the true originality of the Christian conception of God. Considering the urgency of interreligious dialogue today, it is the most challenging dogma. For, due to the ontological gap of creatures from their Creator it is impossible for a human creature to explain, let alone to logically demonstrate, the essence of their Creator, God, and his Trinitarian nature. In spite of this negative requisite for discourse about God, theologians possess several tools with which to give reasons for the Trinitarian faith. In a certain way, Rémi Brague is right when he says that the doctrine of the Trinity is a way for Christians to *describe* the essence of God without contradicting his unity and unicity.[1] For it implies

---

1. "La Trinité, pour le christianisme, n'est pas une manière d'atténuer la rigueur du monothéisme. Elle est au contraire une façon de la penser jusqu'au bout en disant comment Dieu est un" (For Christians, the Trinity is not a way to mitigate the rigor of

dealing with identity (one God) and difference (three persons). Although the passage from Greek to Latin introduced challenging difficulties,[2] it seemed a natural way, in the history of theology, to interrogate the notion of substance and to create a new vocabulary to apply the imperfect notion of created Being to the non-commensurable God.[3] *Hypostasis*, personae or persons, were conceived to make intelligible this difference, without leading to either Arianism (Christ as not truly divine) or Sabellianism (no true plurality)—let alone polytheism. Another way of resolving the relationship between identity and difference is to study the relations and properties: the distinction of processions and the appropriations of the persons generate a differentiation of origin and of identity of the persons.[4] In this context, Richard of Saint-Victor's *De Trinitate* is of exceptional importance, as Richard proposed a new reading of the relations, conceived not only on the basis of their sole ontological aspects, but essentially on the basis of divine dilection. The third way of differentiation based on temporality (that is the same but different through time) is obviated in advance as it would be applicable only within the created realm. Since, however, God is eternal, the continuity of his Being (identity) through stages (differentiation) cannot be allowed. The Hegelian dialectic of the identity of identity and difference thus appears to be irrelevant, both in its logic and historical aspects.[5] The concept of dialectical sublation (*Aufhebung*) implies a progression that cannot ultimately be appropriate to an immovable Being.[6] Moreover, as Gilles Deleuze shows, *Aufhebung* involves a negative moment, even if it

---

monotheism. On the contrary, it is a way to think seriously about monotheism and to state how God is one) (Brague, *Du Dieu des chrétiens*, 22).

2. See, for instance, Augustine, *Trin.* 5.8.10. There is a lot of literature on the question; see, for instance, Congar, "Unité de foi"; Pépin, "Attitudes d'Augustin"; Housset, *Vocation de la personne*, esp. ch. 2; Libera, *Naissance du sujet*, esp. ch. 1.

3. See for instance, the introduction of the difference between substance and subsistence in Boethius's *De Trinitate*. The main difficulty of Boethius's position lies in his logical conception of Being, which does not sufficiently account for the ontological gap between Creator and creature.

4. See, for instance, Gregory Nazianzen, *Discourses* 31.8-9 (SC 250.290-93); Peter Lombard's notions and the debate at the beginning of the thirteenth century have been studied by Johannes Schneider (*Lehre vom dreieinigen Gott*, 172-80). I am indebted to Gilles Emery's fundamental book for these references: *Théologie trinitaire*, 45-47.

5. The relationship between history and dialectics is problematically articulated in the case of a dialectical thought. See, for instance, John Scottus Eriugena (Moulin, "Philosophie du Verbe").

6. Any dimension of ontological "progression," even dialectical, results in Arianism. I am not dealing with Christology here. As a consequence, I do not study the incarnational event of the divine entering into human history.

occurs within a scheme that is designed to conserve the whole.[7] To interpret incarnation as a negation, the theologian would need not only to enhance the weakness of human nature, but also to introduce a convergence of the whole life of Christ toward his death instead of his resurrection.[8]

In this chapter, I would like to explore another way of considering identity and difference through the concept of repetition, and to analyze its fecundity for the way in which theologians understand the Trinitarian God. For this purpose, one needs to rule out the logical and analytical aspect of repetition. Identity through repetition is not a duplication of being as a mere tautology. The reiterative dimension of repetition, as suggested by the suffix "re-," cannot be reduced to a reposition of the same. Rather, it is of fundamental importance to study this notion within a realm that gives sense to the differentiation. As Bergson has clearly demonstrated, repetition manifests itself through time, and true duration has, for this reason, nothing to do with spatialization, which is the domain of intellectual reasoning. I will then show that repetition is a re-presentation, a "re-instantiation," or, better said, an extension of presence, in a Bergsonian way of speaking, which allows to unite identity and difference and which grants humans to grasp divine eternity. For human nature cannot escape duration, and its proper way of reiteration takes place in time; but repetition, in its similarity with God, opens to an experience of an extended present. Such an experience

---

7. Deleuze, *Différence et répétition*, 76. The role played by the difference considered as negativity is the reason why Deleuze prefers the Nietzschean eternal return as true repetition. In Nietzsche's case, the difference is truly affirmative since "the eternal return is both a product of the repetition from the difference and selection of the difference from repetition" (61). Only the differences that can stand the test of the eternal return will be repeated. The Nietzschean eternal return is then not the cyclical return of identity but the ens commune of the differences, those differences as the fundamental tools of selection ("Seul revient ce qui est extrême, excessif, ce qui passe dans l'autre et devient identique" [61]). It is then a conception of "univocity of Being" (60), considering that the sur-human is the "superior form of all that exists" (60, quoting Nietzsche, *Thus Spoke Zarathustra* §6). Theologically, such a conception is interesting as it unites affirmation and difference, giving consistency to the necessary differences implied by a Trinitarian God. But identity and presentation must be joined with difference, which is not the case for Nietzsche. Moreover, one can wonder if the eternity of the "eternal return" is not merely a perpetuus than an aeternus according to the medieval distinction (see, for instance, the two conceptions of eternity in Albert the Great: *Metaph.* 17.2; *Summa theologiae* 34.1). Whether cyclical as in the Stoics or noncyclical as in Nietzsche, the notion of eternal return implies a "return" which spatializes eternity. Such a conception is not compatible with the true eternity of God.

8. Does kenosis have to be considered as pure negativity and emptiness or the affirmative gift of God? Is the "peak" of incarnation the crucifixion (see Moltmann's conception of the "theology of the cross") or hope of eternal life (see John 12:24)?

occurs within a domain that needs to be both internal and external to the bearer of the experience. The experience of beauty answers to such requirements, though beauty is certainly not the only one.

My contribution will then show how repetition, which articulates identity and difference, accounts for the reappropriation of time by human creatures through the experience of beauty, without, however, appealing to either the Hegelian dialectical or the Nietzschean cyclical conceptions of time. Kierkegaard is the first thinker to unite repetition and aesthetics. I will show that his conception of aesthetics prevents him from understanding the importance of the re-presentation at stake in the experience of beauty. As a counterexample, I will carefully study the French novelist Proust's conception of repetition and beauty that leads to a renewed conception of time. I will then draw some conclusions from a theological point of view and apply them to the relationship between the Trinitarian God and human beings and to some aspects of the religious life, especially in the liturgy and pastoral ministries. For the purposes of this demonstration, I will examine four closely related concepts: repetition, difference, re-presentation (present as duration through repetition), and beauty (as the experience of the correlation of the three other concepts).

I. Repetition and Beauty: The Limits of Kierkegaard's Aesthetics

1.1. Repetition and Re-Presentation in the Experience of Difference

The concept of repetition is central in Søren Kierkegaard's works, especially in his essay "Repetition." As Catherine Pickstock has shown in *Repetition and Identity*, repetition is ontologically and theologically "non-identical,"[9] that is, a milieu where identity (repetition as return) touches difference (non-identical). It is not purely dialectical,[10] as it implies experience and a relation to time. It explains why Kierkegaard gives the paternity of the concept to Leibniz: "The present is big with the future, and he who sees all sees in that which is that which shall be."[11] Since each living monad, different by itself, relates to the whole as its mirror, the *modus legendi* of the harmonious creation of God is a rational whole of its relation of time

---

9. Pickstock, *Repetition and Identity*, xi–xii.

10. "Modern philosophy makes no movement. In general, it merely makes a commotion" (against Hegel's dialectics) (RP 50, §57).

11. Boyer and Forget, *Oeuvres*, 1:1179n3, quoting Leibniz, *Theodicy* §360.

and eternity. Although the Greek concept of reminiscence seems to be the equivalence of repetition,[12] it fails to capture the blissful moment of an instant of time. Both share the notion of "transition,"[13] the combined action of immobility and motion, and of being and nonbeing. Repetition is not the dialectical reconciliation of these two "moments,"[14] but rather the Greek sense of "recollection" (anamnesis) which considers time upside down.[15] The doubling of being in reminiscence implies a remembering of the past idea. Repetition thus occurs backward toward the past, while the true repetition also implies a remembering forward toward the future.[16] Such an act, which could appear as contradictory, is not reduced to mere anticipation, as in the case of hope. It is rather the true enjoyment of the instant.[17] It is defined by life, true joy, and beauty.[18] Repetition is thus a gift of God without which no creation would ever have been possible.[19] To live in the instant is to share some part of divine eternity. The instant is neither instantaneity (the constant iteration of a moment in a pure flowing time) nor pure memory (revival in the present of the being past), but rather the expression of a duration,[20] and the encounter between eternity and the occasion.[21] The repetition occurs first in the experience of a suffering, the event of a crisis, and as the loss of all possessions, such as happiness for Job or the loss of his son for Abraham. This suffering is but the testimony of the irruption of the transcendence,[22] and the sign of the beginning of the repetition. Repeti-

12. "Repetition is a decisive expression for what 'recollection' was for the Greeks" (RP 3, §9). For two different interpretations of Greek recollection in RP, compare Ashbaugh, "Platonism"; and Possen, "Meno." See also Crites, "Blissful Security."

13. RP 19, §25.

14. "One will easily see that precisely this category explains the relation between the Eleatics and Heraclitus, and that repetition is really that which has mistakenly been referred to as mediation" (RP 18, §25). Kierkegaard criticizes here the Hegelian *Aufhebung*.

15. "Repetition and recollection are the same movement, just in opposite directions" (RP 3, §9).

16. In the reminiscence, "what is recollected has already been and is thus repeated backwards, whereas genuine repetition is recollected forwards" (RP 3, §9). See Eriksen, *Kierkegaard's Category of Repetition*.

17. "It has instead the blissful security of the moment" (RP 3, §10).

18. RP 4, §10.

19. RP 4, §11.

20. RP 4–5, §11.

21. "The moment appears precisely in the relation between the eternal resolution and the incommensurable occasion" (PC 101, §232).

22. "A thunderstorm" (RP 69, §80). As Louis Mackey states: Repetition is "the possibility of restoring a personality to integrity after it has been broken by grief and guilt" (*Kierkegaard*, 322n20). See Polk, "Job."

tion by itself is pure happiness, though not as pure as eternity.[23] Job receives everything in double: "Have I not received everything back, only doubled? Have I not myself again, and in such a way that I have a double appreciation of what this means?"[24] Such happiness is a spiritual vision in motion, a renewed instantaneity inhabited by eternity: "There where one ventures one's life every minute, every minute loses it, and then wins it back again."[25] Repetition is, then, a remembering forward, as it is not only a renewal once and for all. Rather the doubling is constantly reiterating itself as long as a human being is open to transcendence. Hence, life is repetition, and repetition takes place in the experience of existence. It is the inescapable milieu of difference, in the experience of unity or duration, through memory, and the constant action of God. Such a human being lives in an "extended present," to use Bergson's definition of duration,[26] where both the past is remembered and the future anticipated. Such a repetition includes difference, without, first, the dialectical negative aspect, as it is *experienced* in the very existence of the self, and as it acquires its true legitimacy by itself, and not as it is indebted to a superior identity of the subject. The negative aspect of the difference is thus endowed with the event of contradiction and suffering, even as it happens in the *res* of the life of the subject, without, second, the spatial dimension of the limitation. For since time conceived as space cannot grant access to the apparently paradoxical situation of "recollected forwards,"[27] it is characteristic of the re-presentation in the act of repetition, without, third, the reduction of the difference to nonbeing, as though difference were thought in terms of opposition. Gilles Deleuze has clearly demonstrated the affirmative aspect of the difference,[28] which cannot be reduced to a "moment" of a greater identity as in the case of representation, or be reduced to nonbeing as in the Parmenidean One.

This conception of difference is of fundamental importance for Trinitarian ontology. For the difference of the divine persons must be more radically affirmed if Christian theologians wish to avoid Sabellianism and

23. "Only Job's children were not returned to him twofold, because a human life does not allow itself to be doubled in this way. Here only a spiritual repetition is possible, even though it cannot be so complete temporally as in eternity where there is true repetition" (RP 75, §88).

24. RP 74, §§87–88.

25. RP 75, §88.

26. Bergson, *Pensée et mouvant* (*Creative Mind*).

27. RP 3, §9.

28. See, for instance, the chapter "La différence en elle-même," in Deleuze, *Différence et répétition*, esp. 71–81.

to properly understand the notion of relation in God.[29] It is also convergent with the eternal dimension of the processions (perichoresis) as the re-presentation is specifically a way for creatures to recapture a sense of eternity and of duration through their timely life condition. Finally, as it is not a mere nonbeing, it is not incompatible with the conception of Trinity itself, as it is not a purely tautological identity.

1.2. Repetition, Aesthetics, and Beauty

According to Kierkegaard, human life has constantly to deal with repetition. Yet true repetition concerns only the religious state. Kierkegaard's conception of the three stages, aesthetical, ethical, and religious, is well known and is developed in his work *Stages on Life's Way* as a series of different monographs, all of which are published via the artifice of the borrowed name of Hilarius Bookbinder. For several reasons, ethics is not the domain of true repetition. For like Job's spouse and friends, it considers that duty and regulation provide happiness, which is not the case. It cannot correlate the individual and the general, because normativity implies generality and morality individuality. It cannot express the exception, and consequently the occasion and event of God in human life. It cannot supply any solution to a transcendent event which appears, at first, totally absurd, as in the divine command of the sacrifice of Isaac. Hence, it is both affirmative and negative, as in the case of self-sacrifice.[30] But aesthetics is no more a good candidate of repetition. For Kierkegaard, it is a state of pleasure, hedonism, and sensuality. Though in the first monograph of the *Stages*, entitled "In vino veritas," aesthetics is not solely concerned with the simple pleasure of the senses, as in the case of art, ideas, or philosophy, it nonetheless refers only to the pleasure of the instant to be considered in its pure instantaneity. The romantic is mostly a poet, but his poetry grants him no access to eternity. The poet lives a life of negativity and constant vanishing.

Aesthetics is not devoid of repetition, but such a repetition is totally sterile. It cannot understand the paradoxical dimension of interiority. If the poet tries to go beyond the seductive dimension of repetition, he experiences the non-repeatability of the experience of beauty, as in the case of a second journey to a well-remembered town.[31] An interesting emblematic figure of aesthetics is the character of Don Juan, in the opera of the same name by Mozart. In his categorization of the different arts, Kierkegaard

---

29. See Milbank, "Second Difference."
30. See Jolivet, *Introduction à Kierkegaard*.
31. RP 20–22, §§26–29.

classifies music as a representative of the implementation of an abstract idea in an abstract medium. Painting is defined as "the medium that is furthest removed from language."[32] An abstract idea is defined as remote from history.[33] Music is then distinguished from architecture (abstract medium but concrete idea) and from poetry (concrete medium and concrete idea). It occurs within the realm of immediacy, whereas language, playing a decisive factor, as the expression of the rational, is reflexive.[34] Repetition occurs when the idea and the medium are the most concrete.[35] Now even if music stands as doubly abstract, it possesses specificity, as it appeals to hearing, which is the most spiritual of the senses.[36] Hence, music belongs specifically to Christianity, as it is defined as "the medium of the immediacy that, qualified by spirit, is qualified in such a way that it is outside the realm of spirit."[37] The spiritual dimension of music is thus tainted with exteriority and immediacy. The opera *Don Juan* is emblematic of the third and final stage of eros,[38] the first one pointing unity by its ideal desire (no true object, Cherubino in *The Marriage of Figaro*), whereas the second stage displays the desire of one object under multiple determinations (Papageno in the *Magic Flute*). But Don Juan's eros desires singularity not as an object but as desire itself.[39] Spiritual love and aesthetical seduction[40] partake of the same relation to desire, even as both are totally in opposition considering their relation to time. For spiritual love is an instant desire for the object, but it is the beginning of a duration, whereas the instantaneity of Don Juan's desire is a whole, and an identity by itself, infinitely repeated.[41] Music is thus the most appropriate medium to show this constantly vanishing and constantly renewed instantaneity. Don Juan's subjectivity has no duration, as it is constituted by an addition of recurring moments,[42] and it is so remote from

32. *EO* 56.

33. *EO* 55.

34. *EO* 70.

35. "The more concrete and thus the richer the idea and likewise the medium, the greater is the probability of a repetition" (*EO* 54).

36. "The ear, in turn, is the most spiritually qualified sense" (*EO* 68).

37. *EO* 71.

38. Or, better said, the stage of the Eros if the previous ones are converging to it, as "metamorphosis" of the final one (*EO* 74).

39. *EO* 85.

40. Aesthetical seduction is to be distinguished from the base notion of seduction, which does not concern Don Juan.

41. *EO* 94.

42. *EO* 95.

reflexion that only music can capture its essence:[43] "Don Juan is absolutely musical."[44] The famous song of the catalog by Leporello exemplifies the devoid unending repetition: 1003 is not only an odd number, as Kierkegaard has remarked,[45] but the beginning of a new thousand series, and Leporello is forced to repeat it within the refrain itself. Don Juan's seduction is thus a repetition of a repetition, miming the desire of desire that is characteristic of his way of life. The unending repetition can be put to a stop only by an ultimate repetitor, the ghost of the Commandor (*revenant*, lit. re-coming), which marks the exit of aesthetics, as Don Juan cannot kill him twice! Ultimate irony is the sign of the passage to the ethical stage.[46]

As exemplified by the musical opera, true repetition fails to occur in the aesthetical stage: in its pure aesthetical state (melancholy of Cherubino); in its ethical dimension (quest for marriage of Papageno);[47] and in its religious dimension (vacuity of Don Juan and repetition incarnated by a ghost).[48] The aesthetical Don Juan is the demonic counterpart of spiritual love.[49] And his instantaneity is the exact opposite of the instant re-presented in the repetition. Aesthetics thus suffers from three radical impediments: it appeals to the senses; it takes place in an instantaneous present; and it escapes true internal subjectivity. Eros as principle, object, or self-love is too external to the subject.[50] Consequently, the arts are ineffective to catch a glimpse of divine eternity. Though they may be useful to help humans understand their own limitation, art and beauty are of no fundamental use for truth. Surely the reader cannot help to notice that Kierkegaard does not make an extended use of the notion of beauty. He is a true representative of the conception of aesthetics based on the senses and pleasure, in which

43. *EO* 101.

44. *EO* 102; repeated on 119.

45. *EO* 93.

46. "Irony is and remains the disciplinarian of the immediate life" (*EO* 121). See also Kierkegaard, *Concept of Irony*.

47. Kierkegaard does not take into account the metaphorical spiritual quest of *The Magic Flute*.

48. One has to keep in mind that the stages are non-dialectical for Kierkegaard. They are more "metamorphosis" than processing steps of a hierarchical ladder. Some states can be momentarily blended, too, but each passage to another stage is existentially lived by the warning of irony (aesthetics) and humor (ethics) and happens as a terrific event. See Gusdorf, *Kierkegaard*, 136.

49. "Demonic" (*EO* 92).

50. See, for instance, Kierkegaard, *Point of View*, esp. §5 where Kierkegaard explains his choice of pseudonyms to grant a certain positivity to aesthetics in order to walk with him on his path of the truth.

art is belittled.[51] Such a "romantic" and reductive conception of art, and indirectly beauty, runs the risk of being detached from the transcendental of Goodness, but also of being precluded from the religious realm—though it is useful in order to dismiss a certain aspect of beauty that would be an obstruction to a real conception of beauty.[52] Yet if one detaches beauty and art from aesthetics, there is also a way to regain the repetition and the re-presentation that Kierkegaard has applied to the religious stage through a metaphysics of beauty. Such a metaphysics can, I suggest, also be extracted from the French novelist Marcel Proust. Of course, not all artists define their work as related to beauty, especially in the twentieth and twenty-first centuries. But he uses the art of writing to show how repetition invites us to reconsider time through the medium of beauty. Repetition and time are two fundamental elements for having a better grasp of a new Trinitarian ontology.

II. The Ontological Experience of Eternity Through Artistic Creation in the Work of Marcel Proust

Repetition and re-presentation are the two central notions in Proust's conception of art. According to Proust, human nature is composed of a series of events, such as gesture, act, and sensation—all piled up in a tridimensional fashion at different levels of depth and height.[53] The richness of these vases exceeds their relation to time. For within the interiority of the subject, they stand as possibly simultaneous through the action of memory.[54] In *Time Regained*, Proust shows how the action of memory drives the inner self to the ultimate grasp of eternity and felicity.[55]

51. Baumgarten, *Aesthetica*.

52. Olivier Boulnois has demonstrated that such a conception of aesthetics is non-applicable in the Middle Ages ("De l'esthétique médiévale").

53. "The gesture, the simplest act remains immured as within a thousand sealed vessels, each one of them filled with things of a colour, a scent, a temperature that are absolutely different one from another; those vessels, moreover, which being disposed over the whole range of our years, during which we have never ceased to change if only of dreams and of thoughts, are situated at quite diverse altitudes, and give us the sensation of particularly varied atmospheres" (*TR* 447; translation modified).

54. "An hour is not merely an hour; it is a vase full of scents and sounds and projects and climates. What we call reality is a certain connection between these immediate sensations and these recollections which simultaneously surround us" (*TR* 467; translation modified).

55. See for instance, Genette, *Figures*, vol. 3; Ricoeur, *Temps et récit* (*Time and Narrative*); Deleuze, *Proust et les signes* (*Proust & Signs*); Descombes, *Proust*.

2.1. The Experience of Repetition and Extra-Temporality

In his *Time Regained*, Marcel Proust expresses three experiences that are emblematic of a sensation of intense blissfulness and extra-temporality: two uneven paving stones,[56] the knocking of a spoon against a plate,[57] the stiffness and starchedness of a napkin,[58] all apparently insignificant experiences that transport the narrator outside time and unveil to him "a being making its appearance only when, through of these identifications of the present with the past, it was to find itself in the one and only medium in which it could live and enjoy the essence of things, that is to say: outside time."[59] They are not experiences of the present, for the senses cannot nourish them. Nor are they strictly speaking experiences of the past, for imagination supplies an absence, and the experiences are vividly present to the mind of the narrator. Such experiences are nonetheless extremely *real* as they provide an "immediate enjoyment" in the life of the self.[60] They are described as "the miracle of an analogy,"[61] a way for the narrator to show the connection between two states, without the differentiation of time. The notion of extra-temporality must not be understood as devoid of time but different than the temporality of the being. Rather, it is called by Proust a "pure time," in which past and present coexist simultaneously in the conscience of the perceiver. It is an experience of concrete being, of the very existence of things in a suspended time, like Boethius's *tota simul*.[62] The concatenation is due to the act of memory, which realizes the coexistence of two faculties in the inner self: sensation and imagination. There is then a process that drives the inner self from pure pleasure to the essence of things through the coexistence of sensation and imagination in pure temporality.

This process can be represented as followed:

Pure Pleasure	Imagination	Past	Pure Time	Experience
	Sensation	Present		of Reality

---

56. *TR* 444.
57. *TR* 445.
58. *TR* 446.
59. *TR* 449; translation modified.
60. *TR* 449.
61. *TR* 449.
62. Boethius, *Consolation of Philosophy*, bk. 5.

The coexistence of past and present that is designated as pure time comes from the co-subsistence of imagination and sensation. Under the action of memory and his two other faculties, the narrator undergoes a process from pleasure to an ontological experience. Even if the text is well known, it is worthwhile to quote this passage in full:

> Only a moment of the past? Very much more, perhaps; something that, common both to the past and to the present, is much more essential than either of them. So often, in the course of my life, reality has disappointed me because at the instant when I was perceiving it, my imagination which was the only organ that I possessed for the enjoyment of beauty, could not apply itself to it, in virtue of that ineluctable law which ordains that we can only imagine what is absent. But here come suddenly that the effect of this harsh law had happened to be neutralised, suspended, by a marvellous expedient of nature which had caused a sensation—the noise of the spoon and of the hammer, same title of a book, etc.—to be mirrored both in the past, so that my imagination was permitted to savour it, and in the present, where the actual shock to my senses of the noise, the touch of linen, etc. had added to the dreams of the imagination the idea of existence, which they usually lack, and through this subterfuge had made possible for my being to secure, to isolate, to immobilise—for the duration of a flash of lightning—, what it never apprehends: a fragment of time in the pure state.[63]

In such an experience, memory has its role to play, even as its involuntary aspect is only the *occasion* to join two "vessels" of the self. As opposed to memory associated with the will, the unconscious act of such a memory does not connect sensation as pure observation of the present, associated with the intelligence that dries out the past, and the will that anticipates future with fragments of the present and of the past chosen for their utility.[64] The will implies facticity and representation. As long as the narrator tries to recapture willingly the past sensation, memory deepens the self into uniformity, as a fake representation of identity.[65] Such a fallacy in the use

---

63. *TR* 449–50; translation modified.

64. "[His being] languishes in the observation of the present, where the senses cannot feed it [with the food of the essence of things], in the consideration of a past desiccated by the intellect, in the anticipation of a future which the will constructs with fragments of the present and the past, whose reality it retrieves still further by preserving of them only what is suitable for an utilitarian, narrowly human purpose for which it intends them" (*TR* 450; translation modified).

65. "As to the fact that there is a vast difference between the true impression which

of memory experienced by the narrator has induced some readers to accentuate in the process the involuntary character of memory. But memory is simply the device that helps to connect sensation and imagination in the experience of an extraneous time. In a text about the style of Flaubert, Marcel Proust warned the reader of a common misconception about his work: involuntary memory is the means used by the narrator to connect one "surface" or "vessel" of the self to another, because memory is purer than fact.[66] The repetitive associative act of the involuntary memory has nothing to do with a true repetition. In the first, the repetition is a doubling in which two sensations are commonly associated. Yet true repetition is the same sensation felt at two distinct periods of time,[67] in such a way that it is not the two-faced sensation that matters, but rather the new aspect of truth that is discovered.[68] The process experienced is not simply the self-pleasure of rediscovery of a past sensation but the delivery of the ontological truth of the essence of things and of the self.[69] The internal experience is not only the

---

we have had of a thing and the artificial impression of it we form for ourselves when we attempt by an act of will to represent it, it did not long detain me . . . I understood too clearly that what the sensation of the uneven paving-stones, the stiffness of the napkin, the taste of the madeleine had re-awakened in me had no relation with what I frequently tried to recall to myself of Venice, Balbec, Combray, with the help of an uniform memory" (*TR* 446–47; translation modified).

66. "Dans *Du côté de chez Swann*, certaines personnes, mêmes très lettrées, méconnaissant la composition rigoureuse bien que voilée . . . crurent que mon roman était une sorte de recueil de souvenirs, s'enchainant selon les lois fortuites de l'association des idées. Elles citèrent à l'appui de cette contre-vérité, des pages où quelques miettes de 'madeleine,' trempées dans une infusion, me rappellent (ou du moins rappellent au narrateur qui dit 'je' et qui n'est pas toujours moi) tout un temps de ma vie, oublié dans la première partie de l'ouvrage. Or, sans parler en ce moment de la valeur que je trouve à ces ressouvenirs inconscients sur lesquels j'assoies, dans le dernier volume—non encore publié—, de mon œuvre, toute ma théorie de l'art, et pour m'en tenir au point de vue de la composition, j'avais simplement pour passer d'un plan à un autre plan, usé non d'un fait, mais de ce que j'avais trouvé plus pur, plus précieux comme jointure, un phénomène de mémoire" (Proust, "'Style' de Flaubert," 328). As Deleuze puts it, involuntary memory is not an association, but the "emergence of the hidden object with a form under which it has never been lived, in its essence or eternity" (*Proust*, 21).

67. "Besides, it was not only an *echo*, a *duplicate* of a past sensation that I was made to feel by the noise of the water in the pipe, it was *that past sensation itself*" (*TR* 452; emphasis added).

68. "Those reminiscences, . . . concealed within them not a sensation dating from an earlier time, but a new truth" (*TR* 456).

69. "But let a noise or a scent, once heard or once smelt, be heard or smelt again *in the present and at the same time in the past, real without being actual, ideal without being abstract, and immediately the permanent and habitually concealed essence of things* is liberated and *our true self*, which seemed, sometimes for a long time, to be dead, but

ecstasy of the self from time, but, through this process, the grasp of reality, as it is mediated by our inner self—which is simply our life.[70]

As far as memory is concerned, the reader needs to avoid two misconceptions of repetition. The first one is the life of the aesthete as described by Søren Kierkegaard. The likeness of the two authors about the vacuity of the aesthetical repetition is striking. A second journey to Venice ("walk once more"/"me repromener") or Balbec ("*return* to"/"*retourner*") provides no pleasure to the narrator of the *Research*, as the Kierkegaardian traveler to Berlin.[71] The names themselves with their false power of attraction upon the imagination are incapable of reaching the true being of the places.[72] The aesthete art lover is lost in a bulimia of artistic events that never nourish him.[73] The willing memory belongs to the art lover. Yet on the other side of the scale, the enjoyment does not come from the pure sensual, aesthetical aspect of the involuntary memory. Such a conception would mix the means and the end. Rather, true repetition is a renewal, a difference then, lived within the coexistence of sensation and imagination, present and past.[74]

2.2 The Novel as Qualitative Difference

The rapturous pleasure experienced by the self is sometimes defined as extraneous temporality or pure time by Proust. Yet its simultaneous character shows that it is an experience of re-presentation, a glimpse of the Boethian *tota simul* of divine eternity and what I have called an "extended present,"

---

was not altogether dead, is awaking, reanimating, as it receives the celestial nourishment that is brought to it. One minute freed from the order of time has re-created in us, to feel it, *the man freed from the order of time*. And this man, one can understand that he should have confidence in his joy, even if the simple taste of a madeleine does not seem to contain *logically* within it the reasons for this joy, one can understand that the word 'death' should have no meaning for him; situated outside time, why should he fear *the future*?" (*TR* 450; translation modified; emphasis added). Note the "at the same time," the indice of a sub specie aeternitatis. For Georges Poulet, "Time is solely truly achieved when it is crowned by eternity" (*Études sur temps humain*, 1:402); see also Ricoeur, *Temps et récit*, 2:213.

70. *TR* 473.
71. *TR* 454; emphasis added.
72. The name in the case of imagination plays the same role as the return to the place in the case of sensation.
73. "And indeed, since they fail to assimilate what is truly nourishing in art, they need artistic pleasures all the time, they are victims of a morbid hunger which is never satisfied" (*TR* 471).
74. "My spiritual renewal" (*TR* 460).

following Bergson's characterization of duration.[75] And it is through such a "duration" that the narrator is able to grasp the essences of external beings through the essence of the self.[76] Such a simultaneity comes through the action of memory from the unity of two faculties, sensation and imagination. Yet what about intelligence? It is first put aside, due to its desiccating action and its interest in utility. Such impressions of the self are, however, lost if they are not formulated and communicated with the help of language. They need to be fixed and expressed. And their beautiful aspect needs the medium of art. Art is even the best medium. Swann, a double of the narrator, unsuccessfully tried to transform it into love instead of artistic creation.[77]

For a novelist, philosophy in the form of the essay is not an option. We know that Proust was tempted by this solution.[78] Yet *Time Regained* significantly closes such an option.[79] Art, and in this case the art of writing, will then stand as the issue of the partly subjective and incommunicability of the impression.[80] Art is thus the *mise en lumière* of truth through the manifestation of the difference. And the intelligence is the light. The subjectivity

---

75. I borrow Bergson's concept but true connection between Proust and Bergson can be challenged; see Megay, *Bergson et Proust*. For Deleuze, Proust's notion of change and Bergson's duration have to be distinguished (*Proust et les signes*, 27). It is true but to a certain extent only, as this analysis tends to show.

76. "The realities of subject and object are, in fact, bound together, but it is the latter that depends on the former for a solid foundation rather than the reverse" (Jordan, "Unconscious," 101).

77. *TR* 455. See Richard Bales's analysis of Swann exhibiting a painting of Boticelli, in lieu of his love, Odette, a debaise of art ("Proust and Fine Arts," 188).

78. In a letter to Jacques Rivière (Feb. 6, 1914), Proust underlines the misconception of the critics after the publication of the first volume of the *Research* and emphasizes the speculative nature of his novel: "J'ai trouvé plus probe et plus délicat comme artiste de ne pas laisser voir, de ne pas annoncer que c'était justement à la recherche de la Vérité que je partais, ni en quoi elle consistait pour moi. . . . Si je cherchais simplement à me souvenir et à faire double emploi par ces souvenirs avec les jours vécus, je ne prendrais pas, malade comme je suis, la peine d'écrire" (*Correspondance*, 13:99). We know that Proust first tried to write an essay entitled "Contre Sainte-Beuve" in 1908. See Descombes: "C'est un roman qui donne la transposition narrative des propositions théoriques d'un essai" (*Proust*, 14). See also Germaine Brée, who underlines that Proust "emptied the novel from its Romanesque essence in benefit of metaphysics, in order to turn it into an essay of concrete metaphysics," which, according to her, is a failure (*Du temps perdu*, 267). Ricoeur has rightly emphasized that Proust's project is double: the narration of the vocation of a writer and a theory about art (*Temps et récit*, 1:199).

79. *TR* 460.

80. See Kandinsky, *Concerning Spiritual in Art*.

of the artist perceives the *qualitative difference*,[81] which has to be the true difference as quantity is the tautological identity of the same. Yet subjectivity needs to be transformed into an intersubjectivity, not only because it has to be communicated, but also because each artist presents an original qualitative difference, multiplying different views of the world. Hence the assumed perspectivist aspect of Proust's novel.

Intelligence has two functions: enlightenment and generalization. It plays the role of a developer, in the photographic sense of the term. It reveals the sense of the lived experience like the black negatives that show their content when exposed to light.[82] Intelligence also opens the way for understanding, and therefore generalization. The qualitative difference of the artistic world is communicable only at that price. Yet it gains from it the perception of laws beyond the singularity of the subjective experience of things and persons. Such a generalization is qualified as "beautiful" by Proust.[83] With the help of intelligence, art transforms the subjective repetition to a repetition, where some differences are lost but some universality is regained. The artist can hear again ("*réentendre*"), understands that the experience can be renewed ("quelque chose de *r*enouvelable") and that it possesses duration. With the help of his intelligence, he chooses the general element to create his artistic work.[84] Duration, writes Proust, needs the general,[85] even if the difference is doubly kept in the artistic process, through the original experience of life and through the vision given by the artist. Art is then the way to escape solipsism, as long as it is considered as an experience.

Such a work of the intelligence needs to use a specific "matter." In literature, this matter is the style, and especially the metaphor. To express the eternal dimension of his "living art," the metaphor has to be chosen, since it is the sole literary device that can "give a sort of eternity to style."[86] I think that the metaphor can be considered the literary equivalent of the notion of

---

81. "It is the revelation ... of the qualitative difference of the fashion in which the world appears to us, a difference which, if there were no art, would remain for ever the secret of each one of us" (*TR* 474; translation modified).

82. See photographic technique in the times of Proust.

83. *TR* 480.

84. "It is the feeling of generality that chooses itself, within the future writer, what is general and can be introduced into the work of art" (*TR* 478; translation modified).

85. *TR* 483.

86. Proust "'Style' de Flaubert," 314. See also "Lettre à Maurice Duplay" (June 1907): "L'image doit avoir sa raison d'être en elle-même sa brusque naissance toute divine" (Proust, *Correspondance*, 7:167).

analogy.[87] Be that as it may, the metaphor is the device that expresses repetition within the realm of eternity.[88]

Marcel Proust opens the path Søren Kierkegaard closed. Repetition can occur within the artistic realm, provided beauty and art not be reduced to their pure aesthetical dimension. Indeed, for Proust as for Kierkegaard, the aesthete is disregarded in the same way and on the same ground of a misconception of repetition: the traveler visiting a town for a second time, the art lover who continually enjoys pieces of art identically. The experience of pure time in a process of repetition appeals to the sense and imagination for Proust. But in that case, it is not reduced to a pure sensual pleasure. Moreover, as it needs intelligence and language to become an intersubjective living experience, it ultimately appeals to all the human faculties.[89] The self in its entirety is summoned.

The concept of repetition is therefore useful to understand the relationship between identity and difference,[90] as long as it is a qualitative rather than a quantitative repetition, taking place in time rather than space, and appealing to all the faculties of the self: senses, imagination, memory, intelligence. Concerning the last point, Proust restricts too much the faculties of human nature in the original experience undergone by the self. For intelligence can follow the whole process of coexistence of past and present, not only as an anticipation of the future, but also together with each of the other faculties. One may, however, need word other than "intelligence" to express such an action—some kind of Bergsonian intuition. Provided one keeps in mind the fundamental gap between the Creator and the creatures, the theologian

---

87. "L'expérience capitale de la mémoire involontaire, dont on sait qu'elle constitue pour Proust le fondement même du recours à la métaphore, en vertu de cette équivalence très simple selon quoi la métaphore est à l'art ce que la réminiscence est à la vie, rapprochement de deux sensations par le 'miracle d'une analogie'" (Genette, *Figures*, 55).

88. Ricoeur has clearly demonstrated that narration allows the coincidence of internal and external time, and, through the use of metaphor, a conscious recognition of eternity: "Si le narrateur appelle vision l'expérience du temps retrouvé, c'est dans la mesure où cet apprentissage est couronné par une reconnaissance qui est la marque même de l'extra-temporel sur le temps perdu" (Ricoeur, *Temps et récit*, 2:279). See also: "Time regained is . . . time lost eternised by the metaphor" (Ricoeur, *Temps et récit*, 1:219); Schattuck, *Proust's Binoculars*.

89. The unity of the faculties is a good criterion for judging the quality of a piece of art. As Ramon Fernandez puts it, artistic creation is the "intern labour of elucidation and aeternisation" (*Proust*, 42).

90. "The Essence revealed in a work of art is a difference" (Deleuze, *Proust et les signes*, 53). Also: "Difference and repetition are the two powers of essence; they are inseparable and correlative" (63).

should further explore the fruitful dimension of the notion of "qualitative repetition" for a better grasp of the Trinitarian God. A qualitative repetition comes from a certain way of considering Being through what we usually improperly call "aesthetics" and which should better be named as "kalology" if I could use such a neologism. The qualitative difference is a way of widening the usual identity and difference distinction on which the doctrine of the Trinity is grounded. The creature reaches eternity through time, through the unity of his or her defected faculties, and through the limitation of his or her nature. Proust's experience teaches us that the self not only reaches some sort of eternity, but also takes pleasure in it. Considering the ontological gap between Creator and creatures, it seems that what are pure goodness and eternity in God are pleasure and re-presentation in human beings, and that creative art allows the human to partake in the creative act of God.

Conclusion

My intent was to explore the use of the concept of repetition for a Trinitarian conception of God. As theologians must face the radical ontological equivocation between the Creator and the creatures, such a concept needs to be explored within the created realm. For God, this repetition of the Trinitarian relation between identity and difference takes place in true eternity. Yet creatures are endowed with temporality. The experience of repetition for creatures needs to take place in time. However, it is noteworthy that their true repetition occurs along with a sense of eternity that can be called duration for Bergson, extended present for Kierkegaard, and extra-temporality or pure time for Proust.

I have called such a sense "re-presentation," which, I believe, is the best way to express both repetitiveness and the timelessness of an eternal presence. There are different ways for creatures to experience true repetition. I have chosen the case of beauty and its application in art. For that purpose, I have deconstructed Kierkegaard's position, in which Kierkegaard forbids us to make any relation between what he calls aesthetic and repetition. I have also found a counterexample of an artist who precisely showed that such a repetition is possible. I chose Marcel Proust, since he offers the best speculative dimension for my purpose. In a certain way, Wassily Kandinsky could have offered similar outcomes.

Two main conclusions can be drawn from what I hope I have succeeded in demonstrating: Beauty is a way to grasp the divine, either in its natural dimension or in its artistic dimension. Art can then be a domain where something that belongs to the divine can be found and also be theologically expressed. Repetition is, as Kierkegaard has rightfully demonstrated, a way for created beings to live in a certain way, the life of God, not simply in its essence, but more decidedly in his Trinitarian dimension, which has to show a specific meaning of ontology. Since there cannot be any univocity between God and the creature, one needs to grasp the difference in many ways. Repetition and re-presentation, which includes the notion of qualitative difference to think it anew, are correlated to qualify being in the case of God. Since negative theology should prevail (God is always beyond our sole experience and language), trying to grasp some specificities of such a being, through some given experiences, especially "philocalic" or "kalological" ones, is necessary. Of course, one can bring the notion of *analogia entis* in the picture. But is it possible to think such an analogy in the very realm of a qualitative being? I do not pretend that the experience of beauty and its communication in art is the sole place where creatures and Creator ontologically meet. Yet I think it could help to better understand the necessary connexion between art and religion, especially in the case of liturgy. I have shown elsewhere the parallelism between the creative act in the arts and the creative act of the Trinity, but also how one needs a different concept of space to penetrate the philocalic dimension.[91] A new conception of a Trinitarian ontology needs new tools to have a better grasp of God, who will always be beyond our cognitive capacities but reveals himself to human beings.

The qualitative repetition deals in a specific way with identity and difference, in which identity and difference are both truly affirmative. Yet it can also help us understand why our religious life is constantly punctuated with repetition: reiteration of most of the sacraments; recurrence of the spiritual life through prayer; acts of charity; rumination of the Scriptures, etc. It affects so much the spiritual life that it is not rare to hear the believer complain. Yet such a complaint has meaning only if the repetition is quantitative. For it is only in the realm of quality that the Eucharist can be constantly repeated in order to reach some part of the living eternity.

---

91. Moulin: "Freedom and Necessity"; "Voir l'invisible."

15

"The Harmonious Silence of Heaven"

Silence, Analogy, and the Incarnate Christ in the Music of Olivier Messiaen and Arvo Pärt

Joel Clarkson

Throughout the twentieth century numerous composers wrote works intended to inculcate an affective reorientation of the human person to the presence of, and participation in, the eternal divine. This approach, taken up in unique ways by composers in both the Christian East and West, involved more than a merely superficial form of symbolism or representation, but was driven by the conviction that music might afford, in the devices unique to it as a medium, a transformative christological encounter. While such musical efforts were not consciously aimed at the metaphysical collapse within twentieth-century philosophy, they nonetheless reflected a prevailing concern with affirming the participation between humans and a divine source of being through their repeated turn to silence, both analogical and literal, as a theme and compositional device. These composers held that within the abyss opened by such music, it is not absence but rather presence that is encountered, the presence of the God who speaks from beyond being, to being in its creaturely experience, through the incarnate Logos.

In dealing with this transcendent subject matter, contrasts in the musical conveyance of this ethos came into play between those interested in engendering contemplation of the incarnate Christ through theological ideas represented by compositional elements in their music, such as Catholic composers Olivier Messiaen and James MacMillan; and those approaching the writing of such music with an almost mystical restraint resistant to such concrete theological statement, such as Orthodox composers Arvo Pärt and John Tavener. This contrast, though not always neatly ordered to Eastern and Western categories of thought, nonetheless is reflective of different ways of explicating Christology, and especially the doctrine of incarnation. MacMillan offers a particularly stark account of this, contrasting his own musical theology, driven by an intention to express the inextricability of the incarnation from the cross through a musical style rooted in "conflict and ambiguity" and "the opposition of extremes finding space within the same space," with the music of Orthodox composers such as Tavener, music that MacMillan suggests "sets out to be iconic" and is thus "mono-dimensional" and concerned with "a deliberate avoidance of conflict."[1] MacMillan insightfully identifies a difference in contemporary sacred concert music between Western styles that pursue a more dialectical approach to composition; and Eastern styles attuned less to theme and development and more to unity and singularity.

This essay is interested in probing the way such contrasting approaches inform different attempts to disclose christological presence in twentieth-century sacred concert music through the integration of actual and analogical silences into music. It does so through examining pieces by two of the above composers, Messiaen and Pärt. I first explicate aspects of Messiaen's *Quartet for the End of Time* and its use of musical analogy to represent theological concepts, so as to communicate to the listener what Messiaen calls the "harmonious silence of heaven."[2] I then turn to Pärt, whose "tintinnabuli" compositional form as represented in his work *Tabula Rasa* is similarly oriented toward silence, but pursues its ends through a stylistic restraint, making use of analogy in a more tacit way. I integrate anecdotal accounts of historical performances of each composer's music and show how these two approaches, one more theologically dialectical and one more mystically singular, affect listeners in a similar way. From these observations, I argue that, at least in regard to the examples I provide, the differences in the respective methods employed by each composer, while not unimportant,

---

1. Interview with MacMillan, quoted in Begbie, *Resounding Truth*, 179. For further explication of MacMillan's interest in the cross, see 180–81.

2. Messiaen, *Quatuor*, "Préface"; as quoted in Burton, *Olivier Messiaen*, 44.

are ultimately second-order features that are both efficacious in their own right by guiding their listeners along different pathways to the same end, an encounter with the event of the incarnation, an event that spans the distance between the time bound and the eternal and generously encompasses both multiplicity and singularity.

Olivier Messiaen and Theological Representations of Silence and Incarnation

Messiaen masterfully navigated between thorny, unconventional compositional styles of twentieth-century concert music and his passionately practiced Catholic faith, which worked itself out in a large corpus of works that focused on various aspects of Christian spirituality. His style was concerned with conveying an experience of the numinous, driven by a fascination with the interplay between time and eternity. Paul Griffiths suggests that Messiaen saw this as finding its impulse in "the meeting of the divine and the human (in the life of Christ, in the continuing presence of Christ in the eucharist, in the celestial life intended for humanity)."[3] Messiaen intended his music to evoke a sense of that transcendent reality through a contemplation of the incarnate Christ.

This engagement can be seen in Messiaen's *Quatuor pour la fin du temps* (Quartet for the end of time), in which he alternates between literal and metaphorical silences to provide a sense of the eternal Christ stepping into time, and of bringing it to a close. While the *quatuor* ultimately focuses on Christ's incarnational mediation of time and eternity, Messiaen approached that more abstract theological concept through the concrete metaphor of birdsong. Birdsong was commonly utilized by Messiaen in his works; he began transcribing it very early on in his musical pursuits and adapted it for many of his compositions, including the *quatuor*. Birds and their capacity for flight made for an ideal expression of earthly reality coming into contact with the divine. As such, birdsong acted as a favorable metaphorical pathway into Messiaen's themes of transcendence and eternity.

Birdsong is representationally figured in various movements of the *quatuor* and is given particular attention in the third movement, "Abîme des oiseaux" (Abyss of birds), which involves a single clarinet breaking out of and back into silence. Messiaen explains, "The abyss is Time, with its weariness and gloom. The birds are the opposite of Time; they represent our longing for light, for stars, for rainbows, and for jubilant song!"[4] Messiaen's

---

3. Griffiths, "Messiaen, Olivier," 16:495.
4. Messiaen, *Quatuor*, "Préface"; as quoted in Burton, *Olivier Messiaen*, 44.

first use of literal silence is to depict this seemingly adverse abyss, in conjunction with the analogy of birdsong. However, Griffiths notes that such a void ought not to be construed entirely as an negative occurrence: "Messiaen's treatment suggests not shame... but rather fear, and from fear it is a short step to awe, and hence to an appreciation of divine glory much more than of the depths from which that glory is being perceived."[5] Thus the abyss of time becomes the very space in which to perceive transcendence. This comprehension of eternity within time is, as Messiaen says himself, made possible through a "Christian cosmology" centered upon the incarnate Christ.[6] For "it is only [Christ's] incarnation in Time that reopens to mankind the entrance to Eternity closed off by sin."[7] In this sense, the analogical images of the abyss of time and birdsong, represented respectively by actual silence and by the solo clarinet that breaks that silence, act as a meaningful theological catalyst for setting the scope of the transcendent content being dealt with in the work.

Ultimately, however, what Messiaen seeks to communicate to the listener through the work is more ambitious, namely, an encounter with, as he calls it, "the harmonious silence of Heaven."[8] This intention is in concert with his larger theological agenda as mediated through analogy, and yet one that, by its nature, cannot be contained in that direct analogy. By seeking to facilitate an interaction with that inexpressible reality through music that uses birdsong as metaphor for earthly human experience crossing the threshold of time into eternity, a paradoxical distance is created between the listener's contemplation of the music's representational elements, which requires an understanding of the properties and relationships of that which is being represented; and the possibility of an actual, encountered eternal silence, which would, by nature, exceed the limits of representation.

This tension, and Messiaen's approach to reconciling it, can especially be seen in the *louange* movements of the work "Louange à l'éternité de Jésus" (Praise to the eternity of Jesus) and "Louange à l'immortalité de Jésus" (Praise to the immortality of Jesus), which associate eternal silence with the person of Christ himself.[9] Messiaen once again describes compositional features of the music as analogies that give theological dimension to what is occurring as a result of the music. In this instance, these are simple repeated pulsations of effervescent piano harmonies and long-held string

---

5. Griffiths, "Messiaen, Olivier," 16:495.
6. Messiaen, *Quatuor*, "Préface"; as quoted in Burton, *Olivier Messiaen*, 58.
7. Messiaen, *Quatuor*, "Préface"; as quoted in Burton, *Olivier Messiaen*, 58.
8. Messiaen, *Quatuor*, "Préface"; as quoted in Burton, *Olivier Messiaen*, 54.
9. Messiaen, *Quatuor*, "Préface"; as quoted in Burton, *Olivier Messiaen*, 54.

lines. Messiaen expressly sees these suspended strings in both movements as, on the one hand, expressions of adoration for the eternal Christ; and on the other, as musically evoking the heavenward movement of that praise. He suggests that the cello in the fifth movement is "inexorably slow, glorifies, with adoration and reverence, the eternity of this mighty yet gentle Word, 'of which the ages never tire.'"[10] Discussing the rising violin line in the eighth movement, he states that "the progressive ascent toward the extremely high register represents the ascension of man toward his Lord, of the son of God toward his Father, of deified Man toward Paradise."[11] The contours of the music act as an analogy of Messiaen's intended christological theology.

While these interpretations are necessary in recognizing what Messiaen sees as the thematic context of the music and its style, they heighten the aporetic contrast between what Messiaen suggests the music is intending to communicate and the ineffable nature of what that musical depiction actually represents. As such, if the music is to be successful in its communication of an "eternal" and an "immortal" incarnate reality, it must necessarily exceed and even negate representation. The stylization in the *louange* movements itself betrays this tension, with its long-held suspensions and continual repetition in the piano set against very gradual thematic development and, ultimately, in the second *louange* movement, upward transposition. The music creates an alluring tension between the evocative, ever-transposing string melodies and the continuity of the pulsating piano chords, which provide a rhythmic and harmonic foundation beneath that thematic movement, even as they shift between registers. The composition thus ebbs and flows between statement and restraint.[12]

Accounts of the first performance of the *quatuor* in 1942 seem to affirm that some sort of silence is indeed engendered by listening to the piece. During the premiere, according to eyewitnesses, the audience listened in rapt attention, maintaining what the premiere's cellist, Etienne Pasquier, called "an almost religious respect."[13] Burton notes that the end of the piece was met with "a total silence that continues for some time after the last note of 'Louange à l'Immortalité de Jésus' has faded into nothingness."[14] Musi-

---

10. Messiaen, *Quatuor*, "Préface"; as quoted in Burton, *Olivier Messiaen*, 62.

11. Messiaen, *Quatuor*, "Préface"; as quoted in Burton, *Olivier Messiaen*, 67.

12. For a more extensive examination of Messiaen's compositional techniques, and their transpositional relationship to concepts of time and transcendence, see Pickstock, "Messiaen and Deleuze," esp. 179–87.

13. Rischin, *For the End of Time*; as quoted in Burton, *Olivier Messiaen*, 70.

14. Burton, *Olivier Messiaen*, 70.

cologist Andrew Shenton corroborates the value of this sort of experience in his discussion of the *quatuor*:

> When listening to Messiaen I am increasingly convinced that at some point we have to put away the musicology and face the music ... we have to listen to what the music says to us on a deep and personal level, freed from Messiaen's verbal accoutrements and from conscious analysis.[15]

Shenton particularly locates this in the two *louange* movements. He suggests that Messiaen's own interpretation of those movements actually might be an "impediment to listening" and that what is more valuable is the music's affective capacities: "For me, the long, ecstatic phrases in the string parts and the regular pulsing of the piano are part of a formal design that transcends the mundane and is in many ways a transformative experience."[16] Thus, for listeners of various sorts, the music of the *quatuor* seems to engender some sort of interior sense of contemplation and, possibly, of inner silence itself.

If such silences are to be identified as the sort of "heavenly" stillness to which Messiaen alludes, then the piece must be understood as a perpetual subversion of itself. The work first frames its intended encounter with eternal quietude by constructing a correspondent musical analogy, which, in tandem with actual silence, provides the contours of a specific theological sensibility. It then supplants that theological framework with a compositional dialectic between repetition and transposition, which transfigures the musical analogy into an invitation to encounter the eternal Christ in his incarnate presence in the world. This contrast in the music discloses that reality to the listener insofar as the depiction itself is ultimately simultaneously infinitely surpassed. If, as Messiaen articulates it, the stillness inculcated by the music is in any way a participation in the ineffable eternity and immortality of Christ, the music itself can be understood as nothing more or less than a perpetually reconstituted aporia, in which the "harmonious silence of heaven" is brought into being by a christological musical analogy that is necessarily both constituted out of and dissolved back into silence.

Arvo Pärt and Embedded Analogy in Silences

Arvo Pärt's music expressed a meditative spirituality in a compositional landscape that was typically void of religious content in the latter half of the

15. Shenton, "Five Quartets," 147.
16. Shenton, "Five Quartets," 160.

twentieth century. Pärt's most known works emerged from a self-imposed silence from 1968 to 1976, in which he abstained from nearly any serious composition. It was as a result of this period that he developed his signature technique, tintinnabuli, which Peter Bouteneff describes as "a new kind of quietude that would now come to characterize the music itself."[17]

The word "tintinnabuli" is taken from the Latin *tintinnabulum*, which roughly translates to "bell" or "little bell." Marguerite Bostonia suggests that this reference cannot be detached from what she calls "the mysteries of Orthodox beliefs in Pärt's life," which she says have "intimate links to tintinnabuli."[18] Bostonia notes the importance that the *zvon*, sets of untuned bells in Russian Orthodox worship, play in Orthodoxy's spiritual life. She describes how these bells take on an iconic nature in Orthodox worship, something that "expresses the joy of the Resurrection, calls the faithful to prayer, and banishes thoughts of sin and weakness."[19] It is this joyful revelation of divine life that Bostonia sees as underpinning Pärt's compositional intention: "The process has become the icon, the quest is aimed towards the Divine, and the 'area' of the search is tintinnabuli."[20] Both the imagery of the *zvon*, with their subliminal evocation of the divine hidden within the warp and woof of daily life, and the notion of that bell imagery as imbued with sort of iconographic sensibility express the way in which Pärt's engagement with silence is embedded deep in the background fabric of his already-constituted world.

Like a bell, whose sounding is summed up not only in the strike that causes the bell to ring but also in the reverberation that continues beyond the strike, there is, in Pärt's tintinnabuli music, an interplay between the postures of expression and reception, between the instant immediacy of a statement and the resulting open and undefined space that surpasses the statement. This can be seen in the method itself, in which, in a way that echoes Messiaen's *louange* movements in the *quatuor*, two musical elements are presented: a melody of long-held notes moving in stepwise motion, placed above or below triadic harmony. The one voice is ever establishing a sense of the always already expressed and expressing, while the other is perpetually arising out of that sound bed and gradually fading back into it again. There is a decided symbiotic unity of purpose in the sound that feels both limitless and, at the same time, imminently present to the moment of encounter. Paul Hillier suggests that such instances "might be described

---

17. Bouteneff, *Arvo Pärt*, 95.
18. Bostonia, "Bells as Inspiration," 129.
19. Bostonia, "Bells as Inspiration," 138.
20. Bostonia, "Bells as Inspiration," 138.

as a single moment spread out in time."²¹ Bouteneff remarks that they are "outside of time, but emphatically Incarnated."²² In statements like these, as with Messiaen, there arises a strange dialectic, which must not be understood, but simply be accepted and experienced. And yet unlike Messiaen, who constructed such contrasting elements intentionally as theological analogy, in tintinnabuli, the paradox is not found in the interplay between representation and experience, but rather as the coincidence of finitude and infinitude in the music itself.

Pärt shies away from the kind of representative language that Messiaen uses to describe compositional features in the *quatuor*, backgrounding instead the way that analogy emerges from and feeds back into his lived encounter with silence:

> Tintinnabulation is an area I sometimes wander into when I am searching for answers.... Here I am alone with silence. I have discovered that it is enough when a single note is beautifully played. This one note, or a silent beat, or a moment of silence, comforts me.²³

In another interview, Pärt addresses the way that silence plays into tintinnabulation and how the experience he discusses above rebuffs the notion of overstating what a given silence means or transmits:

> It has two different wings, so to speak. Silence can be both that which is outside of us and that which is inside a person. The silence of our soul, which isn't even affected by external distractions, is actually more crucial but more difficult to achieve.²⁴

These sorts of statements may suggest that Pärt doesn't so much seek to represent silence theologically as he does to emulate the silence he has encountered and to evoke it in his music for others. In this sense, the analogy that gives scaffolding to that sense of silence, the bell imagery undergirding tintinnabuli, isn't established as a representation of a theological concept, but rather acts, as Bostonia says, like the ever-present bells in Orthodox worship: as an iconic underlay that illuminates the divine life that is already present in the time and space of the listener. In a sense, what tintinnabuli seeks to mediate is already constituted in the fabric of the world.

---

21. Hillier, *Arvo Pärt*, 90.
22. Bouteneff, *Arvo Pärt*, 35.
23. Pärt, program notes, 1984; as quoted in Bostonia, "Bells as Inspiration," 128.
24. Huizenga, "Silence and Awe," para. 11.

Tintinnabuli doesn't create an analogy for the divine in an effort to evoke it. Rather, it acts as a response to something that is already occurring.

One of Pärt's first pieces released after his period of silence that deals implicitly with silence as a theme is his double concerto *Tabula Rasa*, for solo violins, prepared piano, and chamber orchestra. Its second movement, titled "Silentium," is a long mensuration canon that is transposed not directly upward, like Messiaen's final *louange* movement, but rather pressed outward at the seams of sound, with the lower voices descending into the depths and the upper voices ascending into the heights. This polarization of musical lines is cast into multidimensional interspersion with the constant entry and exit of lightly arpeggiated grace notes in the upper voices, and long-held suspensions in the middle and lower strings. The result is that there is ever a sense that each thematic gesture is closely interwoven into the other, no matter its register, as if the transposition of the music is not directional, but rather a perpetual curving of the compositional fabric itself. The counterpoint resists easy correlation, ever emerging into and out of itself in such a way that it becomes difficult to follow its beginnings and endings.

Pärt himself is enigmatic in his discussion of the piece. In recalling *Tabula Rasa*'s first performance, he returns to the theme of oneness: "Something impossible had to be born. And right then what I had been asking for happened: It suffices to play every single note beautifully."[25] Like the music itself, Pärt resists any sense of positive statement, rather letting his description exist in the paradoxical convergence of the way his abundance of shimmering, indeterminate patterns and lines somehow emerges as a singular, consummate whole—a notion most readily affirmable not in analysis but in experience.

As with the *quatuor*, *Tabula Rasa* has its proponents who testify to what the experience of it causes within the listener. The Estonian composer Erkki-Sven Tüür, who was a teenager at the time of the premiere in 1977, recalled his experience: "I was carried beyond. . . . I had the feeling that eternity was touching me through this music." Tüür shared how even long after the piece had finished, "Nobody wanted to start clapping."[26] Manfred Eicher, the founder of Pärt's longtime record label ECM, described his first experience hearing *Tabula Rasa* in similar terms: "It was music you discover that makes you speechless, breathless and thoughtful."[27] The way Tüür's and Eicher's respective listening experiences are articulated are striking in their similarity to Pasquier's comment about the premiere of the *quatuor* and

25. Elste, "Interview," para. 24.
26. Lublow, "Sound of Spirit," para. 33.
27. Huizenga, "Silence and Awe," para. 12.

the instilled quietness that had followed that performance. Not only does the piece in some sense engage with the idea of silence, and with the sense of silence in the openness and simplicity of the music, but it also invokes silence in the listener.

In regard to *Tabula Rasa*, this is especially true for those experiencing illness. In an interview discussing Pärt's music, Russian Orthodox Metropolitan Hilarion Alfeyev notes how he was told of patients dying in hospice who requested the "angelic music" of *Tabula Rasa* to be played as they approached death.[28] Other sources have confirmed a similar phenomenon at play elsewhere.[29] Alfeyev attempts to explain this phenomenon: "It may be that simplicity, harmony and even a certain monotony of Pärt's music correspond to the spiritual search of contemporary man."[30] Clearly in his statement, there is a desire to make sense of a phenomenon that seems to rebuff easy causal lines of connection. Bouteneff observes a similar response in those analyzing Pärt's music who find it surprising that music so devoid of content could readily evoke a profound feeling of substance, music that is "not of this world, but emphatically in it; transcendent but immanent," as Bouteneff says.[31] As in Messiaen there is a sense of dialectic; but in Pärt's music it isn't instantiated by compositional aspects, but somehow arises as a sentiment within the listening experience. Bouteneff notes that this enigma is simply accepted in Eastern religions such as Buddhism and suggests that Christianity is similarly attuned by its incarnational nature.[32]

In this, Bouteneff begins to place his finger on what differentiates Pärt from Messiaen. For Messiaen, an emergent dialectic occurs from the use of christological analogy as a representation of the silent presence of the divine, a sort of fore fronting that ultimately must be constantly deconstructed, even as it arises to describe what the music causes in the experience of listening. Instead, Pärt avoids such representational language, only indicating that the music of tintinnabuli is a response to the mystery of the incarnation itself, which acts, in a sense, as the ground from which music springs. That abstention from statement seems to be born from a deferral to the mystery of the incarnation as constitutive of the world as already given and experienced. As Pärt remarks, all of creation—music, nature, words—emerges from Christ

28. Susanka, "Interview," para. 19.

29. Bouteneff discusses this anecdotally, referencing personal conversations (*Arvo Pärt*, 40–43), and also references Alex Ross's article around this aspect of Pärt's music (A. Ross, "Consolations").

30. Susanka, 'Interview,' para. 19.

31. Bouteneff, *Arvo Pärt*, 37.

32. Bouteneff, *Arvo Pärt*, 37.

as the Logos: "I believe that this concept should not only be conveyed in the text, but in every note of the music as well, in every thought, in every stone. The roots of our skill lie in this thought: 'In the beginning was the Word.'"[33] It is its contemplative emergence from, rather than its theological movement toward, incarnational reality and encounter that gives tintinnabuli its unique expression. Pärt's music is a statement of restraint, of near negation. As Bouteneff says, "It is because the music is pure, honest, and reductive that it manages to induce contemplation and a sense of something greater than ourselves."[34] As an analogy, tintinnabuli isn't meant to be the picture, but rather the frame—a withheld and stripped-back space that cultivates a quiet attention to the suffusion of the incarnate Christ in the whole of the world.

Conclusion

As set out in the introduction of this essay, twentieth-century sacred concert music acts as a generative case study of efforts made beyond of the fields of philosophy and theology to witness to the analogy of being in Christian faith. As I have argued, certain composers of such music made use of analogy to attempt a disclosure of divine encounter through music's unique mediation of the presence of the incarnate Christ. In my analysis, I have considered two composers, Olivier Messiaen and Arvo Pärt, as typifying two diverging approaches to that goal: Messiaen, with his clear-minded representation of christological concepts in musical analogy, sought that end through a more distinctly theological and dialectical means; whereas Pärt, taking up a musical idiom steeped in the waters of restraint, oriented his listeners in a more mystical manner that eschewed propositional discourse and pursued a singularity in sound, oriented around the universal presence of Christ as the Logos of all of creation. While the music examined in each instance has some similarities, it also has key differences that correspond with different theologies at play. One example I outlined is the way Messiaen's upward transposition aligns with a representational sense of movement from earth to heaven; whereas Pärt's multidirectional development of musical lines results in a sense of sonic unity. And yet, despite such differences, I have also shown that the effects their music achieves in their listeners is uncannily similar, namely, a sense of inner silence and tranquility.

There are any number of ways to interpret this result. From a musical perspective, I am sympathetic to recent scholarship by David Brown

33. Restagno et al., *Arvo Pärt in Conversation*, 66.
34. Bouteneff, *Arvo Pärt*, 34–35.

and Gavin Hopps, who argue that music is able to foster divine encounter because it can both give affective context to a spiritual or theological idea, and yet, in its "extravagance," open up resonances that exceed only the mere meaning of that subject and afford the possibility of divine disclosure and participation.[35] In line with this thesis, I would suggest that these particular modes—more dialectical or more singular—seem to operate as second-order features, more important for how they allow the individual composer to approach the subject matter of the incarnation in the manner most appropriate to their tradition than for how capably each respective example mediates transcendent experience. I would argue that Messiaen and Pärt are efficacious in engendering an inner silence in their listeners, not because either implements a "correct" analogical framework, but rather because they both gesture, from their different ecclesial postures, toward the limitless generosity of the mystery of the incarnation and its embrace of both unity and contrast in the reconciliation of human and divine natures in Christ. Indeed, when evaluating these composers and their music, even while acknowledging the import of the different ways they integrate their understanding of faith into their music, equally as valuable is what unifies them: a shared sense of the composer as a type of celebrant. The contrasting modes of analogy that they employ are each intended to serve a greater end of disclosing to the listener the presence of the incarnate Christ.

---

35. Brown and Hopps, *Extravagance of Music*.

16

God He Sees in Mirrors
"Nabokov's Trinity" Revisited

Erik Eklund

The works of Vladimir Nabokov are generally perceived to be indifferent, if not outright inimical, to religion and theology. This attitude has shaped reading practices that may adopt a generalizing and so-called "metaphysical" approach while neglecting specific theological themes and engagement with theological issues in his work. Yet his works reflect a strong and enduring interest in theological themes and issues that have not been properly recognized and examined. This chapter considers some of the (meta)literary issues that *Pale Fire* (1962) raises and examines so as to tease out the theological potency of Nabokov's work for the task of speculating a metaphysics in imitation of God as Trinity.[1] Specifically, this chapter seeks to demonstrate the value and usefulness of Trinitarian ontology for the task of literary criticism by arguing that the ways in which *Pale Fire* suggests that its authorial unity may be conceived of as transcending the conventional dichotomy of identity and difference or unity and multiplicity images the

---

1. All citations from Nabokov, *Pale Fire*, are given in the main text in abbreviated form, as F (foreword), P (poem), C (commentary), and Index, with corresponding page numbers for the foreword; line numbers for the poem and commentary; and entry title (index).

Christian innovation of a Trinitarian metaphysics.

Pale Fire is the fullest expression of the theological aspect of Nabokov's literary performance. It is also a masterpiece of metafiction. Its mimetic gamesmanship points to the aporia of originality in a world where all is repetition, identical or otherwise, offering experiments with questions of identity, difference, and repetition. "The self-conscious activity of *dédoublement* and the self-conscious device of the mirror," writes Robert Alter, "are everywhere in Nabokov's fiction" and "achieve a kind of apotheosis here. Reflections, real and illusory, accurate and distorted, straightforward and magical, are absolutely ubiquitous."[2] "The varieties of mimesis," he adds, "what we suppose to be reality" and "the relation between this world and any imagined world to come" are among the principal concerns of Nabokov's oeuvre, and Nabokov is adamant to tease out their corresponding aesthetic, epistemological, metaphysical, and ontological questions.[3] Nabokov extends these questions in *Pale Fire* to include the religious and the theological through the narrative voice of the queer Christian Charles Kinbote, Nabokov's only openly religious narrator. A shower singer of hymns (C181) and follower of the Anglican Church calendar, Kinbote recites passages from *On the Trinity* by St. Augustine and the *Summa Theologica* of St. Thomas Aquinas from memory and in the same note describes "God's Presence" with such succinctness and beauty that it rivals even the prose of Origen and the Byzantines: "a faint phosphorescence at first, a pale light in the dimness of bodily life, and a dazzling radiance after it" (C549).[4] This is Nabokov, after all. In Kinbote, the varieties of metaliterary and metaphysical experimentation typical of Nabokov's lifelong project fund unexpected religious-philosophical speculations about the varieties of mimesis in art and in life and their relation to a transcendent nonfinite origin. In this transposition, the trope of mirrors and

---

2. Alter, *Nabokov*, 56.

3. Alter, *Nabokov*, 90.

4. Eklund, "Name of God," contextualizes and explicates the significance of St. Thomas Aquinas's and St. Augustine's thought for our appreciation of *Pale Fire*, juxtaposing the practice of apophasis and the question of how God is known in and as distinct from the world with Shade's agnostic protestations. Interestingly, Kinbote offers his fiery gloss on "God's Presence" on St. John's Eve 1959. "Intimately associated with Midsummer throughout European and Slavic countries, St John's Day (otherwise known throughout Slavic countries as Kupala Night or Ivan-Kupala) is often celebrated the night before. The most common form of celebration involves lighting bonfires or torches as an emblem of St John the Baptist, whom Jesus calls 'a burning and shining lamp' (John 5:35 NRSV)" (Eklund, "Name of God," 299–300). Kinbote also explicitly situates the beginning of Shade's writing of canto 2 on the "6th Sunday after Trinity" (C181), rather than, as one might expect, on their shared birthday.

other related mimetic motifs, which Nabokov often utilizes to ask questions of repetition and originality, correspond to questions of the divine.

The Structure of *Pale Fire*[5]

Pale Fire centers on a poem in heroic couplets, titled "Pale Fire," composed, as it were, by John Shade, an American poet and scholar employed at Wordsmith College, in New Wye, Appalachia. Edited and annotated by his colleague and scholar of onomastics, Charles Kinbote, Shade's poem comprises 999 lines and four cantos. According to Kinbote, the thousandth and final line of Shade's poem was to be identical with its first, bringing its fourth and final canto into symmetry with canto 1 (166 lines), while cantos 2 and 3 each consist of 334 lines. A foreword, line-by-line commentary, and index by Kinbote surround Shade's poem.

The basic facts of the plot, D. Barton Johnson observes, are "susceptible to two basic interpretations—each with a number of variants."[6] According to one interpretation, Charles Kinbote is the adopted alias of the incognito Charles Xavier the Beloved (Charles II), the deposed king of Zembla. Haunted by the fear of a stalking regicide, Jakob Gradus, King Charles flees to America, where he lives under the alias of Charles Kinbote, in the residence of one Judge Goldsworth, adjacent to the house of the Shades. The king has cherished Shade's poetry for years. He becomes aware that Shade is writing a poem, which he believes is dedicated to the glories of his recently fallen Zemblan reign. On the day when Shade is to complete his poem, however, Gradus appears on the scene, mistakes Shade for Charles, and fatally shoots him. Having narrowly evaded death, Charles departs New Wye with the manuscript of Shade's poem, which he will edit in his hideout in Cedarn, Utana. But he discovers that the poem has nothing to do with Zembla and everything to do with the premature death of Shade's daughter Hazel and Shade's consequent search for the meaning of death and what comes after it. Charles concludes that the only reasonable explanation for Zembla's absence from Shade's poem is that a group of Shadeans, acting out of jealousy and under the influence of Shade's wife Sybil, have effectively silenced his influence on Shade. After giving himself some time to let the sense of betrayal subside, Charles returns to the poem and discovers a series of cleverly concealed allusions to the story he had been communicating to Shade. Charles then embarks upon setting the record straight by publishing

---

5. This section appears in more or less the same form in Eklund, "Mirror and Icon," 121–23.

6. Johnson, *Worlds in Regression*, 60.

Shade's poem with his notes, without which, he claims in the foreword, "Shade's text simply has no human reality at all" (F28).

This reading of the novel begins to wane as the reader plunges into the note to line 1000 and reads that Gradus resembles one Jack Grey, an "escapee from an asylum, who mistook Shade for the man who sent him there," Judge Goldsworth, whose home Kinbote is renting. The discovery that Gradus is actually Grey cascades into a series of additional hints suggesting not only that Kinbote is critically inept, but that his reading of Shade's poem as being secretly about his native Zembla and an assassin's search for the deposed king are the product of his manic delusions. The regicidal organization to which Gradus belongs, The Shadows, are nothing other than the Shadeans who have tried to prevent Kinbote from editing "Pale Fire," made strange in his broken mind. "None can say how long John Shade planned his poem to be," says one Shadean whom Kinbote quotes in his foreword, "but it is not improbable that what he left represents only a small fraction of the composition he saw in a glass, darkly" (F14). In his note to line 550, Kinbote not only admits that Shade's poem has nothing to do with the Zemblan material that his commentary is otherwise so adamant to argue, but confesses that the variant to line 12 that alone gave license to Kinbote's Zemblan elaborations is not Shade's at all but his own dubious falsification.

Destabilizing and challenging the idea that Shade and Kinbote are responsible for the texts they are said to have authored, impossible incongruities and surreptitious similarities equally suffuse Shade's poem and Kinbote's *apparatus criticus*. The characters of Shade and Kinbote, like Gradus and Grey, may even shed stable identities. This is further suggested by the fact that every character in the novel has a corresponding double across the realms of Appalachia and Zembla. In addition to Gradus and Grey and Kinbote and King Charles, clear instances of doubling include Judge Goldsworth's daughters Alphina, Betty, Candida, and Dee; and Zembla's King Alvin, Queen Blenda, Charles the Beloved, and Queen Disa. Zembla is also home to several doubles, twins, and mirror images that do not seem to correspond to any ostensible reality in Appalachia, such as King Charles's tutor Mr. Campbell and Monsieur Beauchamp; Nodo, the treasonous half-brother of Odon; and the cousin Barons Mandevil, Mirador, and Radomir. Such a proliferation of doubles across the mirrored realms of Zembla and Appalachia obscures the lines that would otherwise distinguish one character from another and has the effect of compelling the reader to ask which characters are invented and by which character they are invented. The reader may even feel compelled to revise the structure of the novel to reflect the authorship of any one (combination) of its characters. In so doing, the reader expresses the conviction that this novel's authorial enigmas are fundamentally concerned with the location of an origin that would explain the play of sameness and difference across poem and commentary.

Against "Who Invented Whom?"

Kinbote's scholarly interest in onomastics—he is "the author of a remarkable book on surnames" published by Oxford University Press in 1956 (C894)—contributes to and complicates the idea that some characters may be the artistic invention of another and the corresponding idea that both meta-texts of *Pale Fire*, the "internal" one ostensibly written by one of its characters and the "external" one written by Nabokov, are each novels parading to be a scholarly edition of a poem. "The name Zembla is a corruption," observes Kinbote, "of Semblerland, a land of reflections, of 'resemblers'" (C894). "'The tongue of the mirror!,' as the great Conmal [Zemblan translator of Shakespeare] had it" (C678). The literal Zemblan meaning of Kinbote's surname is also deeply ironic.

> "Didn't you tell me, Charles, that *kinbote* means regicide in your language?" asked my dear Shade.
> "Yes, a king's destroyer," I said (longing to explain that a king who sinks his identity in the mirror of exile is in a sense just that). (C894)

It is one thing for Kinbote to mirror King Charles; it is another for him to mirror Gradus the regicide and glass-factory worker. Although Gradus's mimetic kinship to Jack Grey is well known, little has been made of the fact that the mirrorly relation that obtains between Kinbote and Gradus grants to Kinbote a further relation to Grey. Complicating matters further, recall that Gradus, who inadvertently shot Shade, intended to kill King Charles (now Kinbote), and that Gradus is a regicide, a king's destroyer, a Zemblan *kinbote*.

Gradus and Shade are also spoken of in eerily similar ways. Gradus is called a "half-man" (C949n2), whereas Shade is "half a shade" (P728). Given that names are often used throughout this novel to suggest relations of identity in difference, it stands to reason that the various instances of synchronicity in this novel may also dramatize the aporia of origins underwriting this novel's authorial enigmas. This is suggested in Kinbote's comment on Gradus's arrival in New York:

> Two silent time zones had now merged to form the standard time of one man's fate; and it is not impossible that the poet in

New Wye and the thug in New York awoke that morning at the same crushed beat of their Timekeeper's stopwatch. (C949n1)

Kinbote's comment that Shade "was his own cancellation" (F26) now takes on a mysterious and particularly alchemic tone in the light of Gradus and Shade's synchronous awakening. The mirror finally shatters on the very day that Shade is murdered by the glass-factory thug Gradus at a fitting age of 61 years and 16 days.

The various ways that each of the novel's principal characters mirror one another complicates the idea that any one of its characters could be responsible for inventing any other character, especially as there is no internal mechanism by which to measure one ostensible author against another. Nor does it clarify anything to point out that Shade, Kinbote, and Gradus were each born on July 5, although Shade is 16 years older than both Kinbote and Gradus. In fact, it makes no narratological difference whether Shade successfully impersonates Kinbote, whether Kinbote impersonates Shade, or whether Vseslav Botkin, "an American scholar of Russian descent" (Index: Botkin, V.), impersonates Kinbote and Shade, since these entities remain separated in the textual performance of the novel.[7]

Yet because each of these distinct literary performances points toward a "higher" or meta-literarily "transcendent" one into which each may be sublimated suggests that in *Pale Fire* one is dealing not with an individual author nor multiple authors, but with an authorial unity that is both one and many. This is suggested by the fact that the expression of the dialectic of origin and variation in Nabokov's works more generally and his English ones especially subverts conventional notions of originality, which conceive of unity and multiplicity as inimical to one another. "The notion of an original text," writes Siggy Frank,

> vanishes in Nabokov's first English works, since the origin of the text itself comes under scrutiny. The formerly rather conservative notion of one original source dissolves in the indeterminacy of collaborative work where questions of authorship and textual property become impossible to decide.[8]

---

7. For a nearly exhaustive analysis of the various theories of *Pale Fire*'s authorship, see Alladaye, *Darker Shades*, 68–111. I offer a broader but updated analysis of the principal theories from the perspective of the problem of repetition and identity in Eklund, "Mirror and Icon," 123–27.

8. Frank, *Nabokov's Theatrical Imagination*, 185.

In *Pale Fire*, this is most clearly expressed in the subtextual presence of William Shakespeare and Thomas Middleton's collaborative effort, *Timon of Athens*, whence Shade receives the title of his poem:

> I'll example you with thievery.
> The sun's a thief, and with his great attraction
> Robs the vast sea. The moon's an arrant thief,
> And her pale fire she snatches from the sun.
> The sea's a thief, whose liquid surge resolves
> The moon into salt tears. The earth's a thief,
> That feeds and breeds by a composture stol'n
> From gen'ral excrement. Each thing's a thief.[9]

In the context of Timon's soliloquy, "pale fire" names the innate violence of mimesis and mediation. Mirrors and the repetition they afford are not iconographic. Ontology, in its turn, is always and irremediably violent. One does not see through mirrors, however darkly, in the Timonian cosmos. Mirrors reflect only the filth of purloined being (*ens*), with all manner of spilled blood and excrement. From this perspective, Kinbote is the thieving moon to Shade's shining sun, the mirror of his commentary eclipsing the serene beauty of Shade's poem. It follows that the most fruitful line of interpretation of this novel's mimetic gamesmanship consists of discerning the true source from its illegitimate copy(s).

But if it is indeed true that the literary self-consciousness that characterizes Nabokov's work renders questions of authorship and textual property, categories that always reinforce the conventional dichotomy between source and copy, unintelligible, then it stands to reason that the maddening ways in which *Pale Fire* parodies the idea of an original text challenge the fitness of categories like source and copy and origin and variation (or, in more literary parlance, text and paratext) to describe the relation between poem and commentary. Indeed, given that the overall effect of the novel is that of being lost in between two mirrors standing at confrontation, each repeating the other from everlasting to everlasting, it may be suggested that the dialectic of identity and difference as it is performed in *Pale Fire* resists the very notion of an author. Roland Barthes's notion of "scriptor" illuminates this approach to *Pale Fire*. "The modern scriptor," says Barthes,

> is born simultaneously with the text, is in no way equipped with a being preceding or exceeding the writing, is not the subject with the book as predicate; there is no other time than that of the enunciation and every text is eternally written *here and now*.

---

9. Shakespeare and Middleton, *Timon of Athens* 14.435–42.

> ... For him, on the contrary, the hand, cut off from any voice, borne by a pure gesture of inscription (and not of expression), traces a field without origin—or which, at least, has no other origin than language itself, language which ceaselessly calls into question all origins.[10]

As the scriptor is no longer an author, the very concept of one authorial origin is seen to be impossible. This is on particularly dazzling display in *Pale Fire*, and it makes sense to see Nabokov as playing at being a scriptor: by calling into question the idea of an authorial origin, Nabokov leaves the text, "remain[s]," in his words, "outside the ambience he suggests."[11] Indeed, Nabokov deconstructs the notion of authorship so much that even the notion of a fictional author becomes impossible.[12]

It follows that this novel's authorial enigmas most fundamentally express the search for what Jean-Luc Marion calls "an origin without original." Transcending the dualities of origin and variation, identity and difference, this nonfinite origin simultaneously "pours itself out or gives itself throughout the infinite depth" of its own creation while its infinitude repudiates all attempts at a finite appearing, representation, or mimesis.[13] In an adaption of Jacques Derrida, we may say that this "origin without original" does truly "*lend itself* to a series of names, but calls for another syntax, and exceeds even the order and the structure of predicative discourse.... It is written completely otherwise."[14] Offering a theological alternative to the ceaseless "call[ing] into question [of] all origins," signified in Barthes's notion of the scriptor and Derrida's mystic X, Marion's notion of "origin without original" aptly describes the problem of authorship in *Pale Fire* and may be further illuminated by John Milbank and Catherine Pickstock's theorization of nonidentical repetition. This alternative way of reading Nabokov's masterpiece leads readers to a new appreciation of the radical reciprocity of sameness and difference that obtains in this novel's authorial unity and offers to theologians a new literary playground for asking after a Trinitarian ontology of non-identical repetition.

---

10. Barthes, "Death of the Author," 146–47; emphasis in original.

11. Nabokov, *Think, Write, Speak*, 279.

12. The irony, of course, is that Nabokov accomplishes this deconstruction so feverishly that his identity as author is forcefully reinforced. See Frank, *Nabokov's Theatrical Imagination*, 8, 194.

13. Marion, *God Without Being*, 20.

14. Derrida, "How to Avoid Speaking," 74; emphasis in original.

Non-identical repetition

Milbank developed the notion of non-identical repetition across multiple works to counter the idea that "ontology as such is complicit with violence," suggesting instead "the possibility of a *different* ontology, which denies that mediation is necessarily violent. Such an ontology alone can support an alternative, peaceable, historical practice."[15] Non-identical repetition therefore accounts for the possibility of a true gift by including "not only the return of an equivalent but different gift, but also a non-exact mimesis (but therefore all the more genuinely exact) of the first gesture in unpredictably different circumstances, at unpredictable times and to unpredictably various recipients."[16] This reciprocal and inexact gift exchange "requires the positing of transcendence," adds Milbank, because the absolutely transcendent or infinite is not inimical to the (vertical) difference that obtains between itself and every series of finite particulars, as the finite "must 'already belong' to infinitude as non-identical repetition." If this were not the case, the mediation required for the confrontation of things (*res*) would be "peaceable" no longer, but complicit with violence.[17] Applied to the Timonian analogy, the moon cannot truly steal the light of the sun, as the sun is not the ontological source of the lunar light, but one of a myriad of "pale fires" of the endlessly refracted divine light transcending the diegesis of creation, as suggested in *The Old English Boethius*, a major subtext of *Pale Fire*.[18] In more Thomistic language, the divine light is in the sun as a solar term and in the moon as a lunar one.

In an important work from 2013, Pickstock engages key literary works that take repetition as (one of) their foremost themes to elaborate upon Milbank's notion of non-identical repetition toward two ends: (1) to offer a theory of the existing thing (*res*), how it is known and, more significantly, why we can trust that it is known; and (2) to throw the whole notion of a finite origin into disarray according to a Trinitarian poetics of non-identical

15. Milbank, *Theology and Social Theory* (2006), 309; emphasis in original.
16. Milbank, "Can a Gift," 125.
17. Milbank, *Theology and Social Theory* (2006), 309.
18. See Meyer, *Find What the Sailor*, 66–69, 74–78. On the challenge that *The Old English Boethius* poses to *Timon of Athens* as determining the "normative" ontology of *Pale Fire*, see Eklund, "Do Not Be Angry." Interestingly, in one of many amplifications to Boethius's text, the author (presumably, King Alfred) anticipates the Shakespearean soliloquy whence comes the title of Shade's poem: "She with her bright splendour dispels the darkness of the swarthy night. So does also the moon with his pale light, which obscures the bright stars in the heaven: and sometimes bereaves the sun of her light, when he is betwixt us and her" (Alfred, *King Alfred's Boethius*, 4).

repetition. Pickstock argues that because the Trinity perfectly embraces the "multiplicity and alterity" that "a finite unity" necessarily refuses, a Trinitarian ontology of non-identical repetition repudiates any definable delineation between identity and difference, origin and copy, within a finite field.

> It is so unthinkably One that it distils, and is in harmony with, all possible variety. There is no outside edge to the divine unity which might constrain and define it. . . . Such a mode of relation overcomes the finite repertoire of the discrete but non-identically repeated *res*, and the chain of repetitions which links things together in a continuous series. God is both one and many, and yet God is neither of these.[19]

This conviction is at the heart of Origen's contention that although "there is no separation in the Trinity," it is "the nature of the Trinity . . . to have nothing that is compound";[20] the Holy Spirit (to take one divine example) must be seen to be "partaken of by each one of the saints" without being "divided into parts" among them.[21] It follows, as Pickstock is right to observe, that "there need be no finite original," as the being (*ens*) of finite things (*res*) simply is "a play of repetitions without origin, where each variation is equally an original because it is equally copy."[22]

Non-identical repetition has clear implications for the doctrine of the incarnation and its adjacent mysteries, which, in their turn, illuminate the authorial enigmas of *Pale Fire*. In much the same way that the second Adam, which is Christ, was the model (source) for the first Adam (as Nicholas Cabasilas [1319/23–92] teaches), the virgin birth of Jesus Christ by the Theotokos mirrors the eternal generation of the Son from the Father, from which it follows, in a surprising paradox—time somersaults to express it—that by taking humanity unto himself, we may say that from eternity God has his mother's eyes.[23] Yet the fact that this Christ is the model for the human project begun in Adam also means that "some feature of the crucified may lurk in every mirror," as Jorge Luis Borges intimates in his parable on Dante's analogy of the Croatian pilgrim who has come to Rome to view the Veronica and asks, "*My Lord Jesus Christ, very God, is this, indeed, Thy likeness in such fashion wrought?*" "A Jew's profile in the subway might be the profile of Christ," muses Borges, "the hands that give us back change at

---

19. Pickstock, *Repetition and Identity*, 195–96.
20. Origen, *On First Principles* 1.3.7, 1.5.3.
21. Origen, *On First Principles* 1.1.3.
22. Pickstock, *Repetition and Identity*, 33.
23. Cabasilas, *Life in Christ* 6.12.

a ticket booth may mirror those that soldiers nailed one day to the cross."[24] This echoes Origen's conviction that "every rational creature needs" and must therefore have "a participation in the Trinity."[25] This participation is made possible by the triunity of God. For because God is triune, God is not inimical to difference and variation, but perfectly embraces these things and must therefore be free to be repeated non-identically in creation. This conviction is perhaps nowhere better expressed than in canto 29 of the *Paradiso*:

> The primal light, whose rays shine out on all,
> is taken up in ways as numerous
> as there are splendours that it couples with.
>   Therefore, since depth of feeling follows act,
> in each of these the sweetness of their love
> seethes differently—and different, too, in warmth.
>   See now the height and all the generous breadth
> of God's eternal worth. These mirrors all
> were made by Him, where He Himself now breaks,
>   one in Himself remaining as before.[26]

Similarly to Kinbote's gloss on "God's Presence" as "a faint phosphorescence at first, a pale light in the dimness of bodily life, and a dazzling radiance after it" (C549), Dante suggests that all are pale fires of the divine flame. It follows, in an extension of Dante's mirrorly analogy, that the notion of a finite origin makes as much sense as seeking an original image within the frame of an infinity mirror. Thus Dante leads us back to Nabokov and, perhaps, to the mystery implicit in the title of his greatest work.

The Patron Saint of *Pale Fire*

Milbank's and Pickstock's theorizations of non-identical repetition provide a clarifying grammar with which to posit an alternative "solution" to the authorial enigmas of *Pale Fire*. As we have seen, the idea of establishing ontological primacy or a hierarchy of being (*ens*) whose final term resides within a finite field is not only impossible but incoherent, as what one discovers in the world is an "unanalyzable compound of the same and the different, in such a way that the same has always become different, and the different

---

24. Borges, "*Paradiso*: XXXI"; emphasis in original.
25. Origen, *On First Principles* 4.4.5.
26. Dante, *Paradiso* 29.136–45.

forever remains in a certain manner the same."[27] This may explain why readers of *Pale Fire* continue to wrestle with the question of who invented whom. Yet the particular form of this question—*Who invented whom?*—presupposes answers that, far from resolving the radical reciprocity of sameness and difference across poem and commentary, actually refuse it. Indeed, many answers to the question of authorship in this novel merely rearrange the fictional data, since the textual entities of "Kinbote" and "Shade" and any other ostensible author remain the same. Whether one chooses to attribute authorship to a single character or to several, the interplay of identity and difference that first gives rise to the question of authorial primacy is blown to bits either by a single authorial unity who has scattered façades of difference throughout *the text* or by a combination of authors whose *texts* (poem and *apparatus criticus*) cannot speak to each other because they have nothing in common. Both lines of interpretation presuppose a stable and singular ontology, when, in fact, *Pale Fire* presents a barrage of questions about what makes for the real and the original as opposed to the irreal and the varied, and we simply cannot know where the line has been crossed. Indeed, it makes little sense to speak of gradations of fictive being (*ens*) when the fiction perpetually calls its own being into question.[28]

The mysterious and critically neglected character of St. Sudarg of Bokay suggests an alternative interpretation. "A mirror maker of genius" and "the patron saint of Bokay in the mountains of Zembla," Sudarg appears in the main text with the short suddenness of Melchizedek, resisting all attempts to identify his beginning and end: "Life span not known" (Index: Sudarg of Bokay).

> He [Charles Xavier the Beloved] awoke to find her [Fleur de Fyler] standing with a comb in her hand before his—or rather, his grandfather's—cheval glass, a triptych of bottomless light, a really fantastic mirror, signed with a diamond by its maker, Sudarg of Bokay. She turned about before it: a secret device of reflection gathered an infinite number of nudes in its depths, garlands of girls in graceful and sorrowful groups, diminishing in the limpid distance, or breaking into individual nymphs, some of whom, she murmured, must resemble her ancestors when they were young—little peasant *garlien* combing their hair in shallow water as far as the eye could reach, and then the wistful mermaid from an old tale, and then nothing. (C80)

27. Pickstock, *Repetition and Identity*, 51.

28. Consensus has yet to be reached even on such a seemingly simple question as the relative reality of Zembla, whether it is as real as Shade's Appalachia or merely a by-product of Kinbote's fabulous delusions.

Sudarg's mirror triptych is unique among *Pale Fire*'s many mirrors in several ways. The work of Nabokov's only named saint, it is also the only infinity mirror in a novel consisting entirely of mirrors and glasswork miracles. As an infinity mirror, Sudarg's gift gives rise to an infinity of reflections, such that each reflection is simultaneously a middle term in an infinite series and a starting point for additional reflections, and arouses within the viewer a gaze that is itself infinite. Moreover, in what is surely a nod to its namesake, Charles Xavier's grandfather Thurgus the Third, the mirror exists precisely as a triune form. These aspects of Sudarg's mirror triptych suggest that his infinity mirror is a metafictional sign of the coincidence of unity (or origin) and multiplicity (or variation), from which it follows, perhaps, that the hall of mirrors that is *Pale Fire* proceeds from a three-piece infinity mirror. All are *kinbotes* in this respect: "a crucial letter g short of king," as Thomas Karshan says of Kinbote, "just kin, subject to family resemblance and analogies."[29] For by refracting and redoubling his autographic trace throughout the multitude of reflections that populate and proceed from his mirror triptych, Sudarg's "triptych of bottomless light" repeats, as sign, the evasive author's power to repeat. As is well known, the name of Sudarg of Bokay is a near-perfect mirror image of the assassin Jakob Gradus, who has traveled from Zembla to Appalachia in search of Zembla's deposed and disguised king, Charles II (the novel mentions no Charles I), whose adopted alias Kinbote means "a king's destroyer" (C894), a regicide—another shade of Gradus refracted and redoubled in Sudarg's fabulous infinity mirror.

Alter has suggested that the mysterious author of *Pale Fire* resides somewhere in the vicinity of this saint with his mirror.[30] This is a compelling interpretation, though a stronger case could be made that the evasive author is iconized, or sacramentally present, in Sudarg's mirror. Coextensive with the world of infinite reflections that it instantiates, the poetics of the mirror triptych adhere to the same logic by which Pickstock concludes that

> God cannot be without his decision to create, or to be remotely repeated . . . by a creation that is, therefore, from the divine perspective . . . itself eternal. . . . In this way, the *pleroma*, comprising God as both God and Creation, eternally and infinitely

---

29. Karshan, *Vladimir Nabokov*, 227.

30. Alter suggests that one "Rippleson," "a famous glass maker who embodied the dapple-and-ringle play and other circular reflections on blue-green sea water in his extraordinary stained glass windows for the Palace" (Index: *Rippleson Caves*), is the closest one comes to an authorial presence in *Pale Fire* (Alter, *Nabokov and the Real World*, 57–58). The index entry for "Tintarron" suggests otherwise: "*Tintarron*, a precious glass stained a deep blue, made in Bokay, a medieval place in the mountains of Zembla . . . see also Sudarg." Rippleson may even be a cipher for Sudarg.

repeats itself, identically and non-identically, as sign, while the sign eternally and infinitely repeats itself, identically and non-identically, as gift.[31]

Similarly, Sudarg's mirror triptych presents to the readerly gaze a kaleidoscopic vision that discovers "inexhaustible variety in 'the same' (or rather the same *as* inexhaustible variety)."[32] This is evident in the literary self-consciousness of Sudarg's mirror. For not only does the triptych repeat the Zemblan image of the naked Fleur de Fyler at mournful dance and the Appalachian one of Hazel Shade drowned in one of the three icy lakes just outside New Wye (see P483–500) (and, more distantly, Shakespeare's Ophelia washed away), but the physical form of Sudarg's "cheval glass" (C80) also repeats the grammatical sign of the those three glassy lakes: Omega, Ozero, Zero—OOO. The secret proportion the entire world of the novel and its complementary parts communicate and cohere, Appalachia and Zembla and poem and commentary, Sudarg's mirror triptych iconizes the mimetic movement by which the evasive author, in more Dionysian parlance, transcendingly transcends the dichotomy of infinity and finitude such that it cannot, or perhaps refuses, to appear within the frame except as the sacramental mimetic movement that makes all things to be "clear and spotless mirrors reflecting the glow of primordial light and indeed of God himself"—"a faint phosphoresce at first, a pale light in the dimness of bodily life, and a dazzling radiance after it" (C80).[33] Mimesis is no longer theft but salvation.

OOO; or, Crystal to Crystal to Crystal

In an age that does not look kindly on Trinitarian analogies, suggesting new or long-forgotten ones is assuredly reckless, just as Gennady Barabtarlo perceived that his suggestion to read Nabokov "also as a mystic could well damage a strong reputation and ruin weaker ones."[34] At the height of his pilgrimage, for instance, Dante describes the Trinity as "three circling spheres, three-coloured, one in span. . . . One, it seemed, was mirrored by the next / twin rainbows, arc to arc. The third seemed fire, / and breathed to first and second equally."[35] Gazing thus upon the "mirrored brilliancy" of the Trinity,

---

31. Pickstock, *Repetition and Identity*, 193, 197.
32. Milbank, "Sublime in Kierkegaard," 307; emphasis in original.
33. Pseudo-Dionysius, "Celestial Hierarchy" 3.2.
34. Barabtarlo, "Nabokov's Trinity," 136.
35. Dante, *Paradiso* 33.117-20.

Dante sees within the infinite depths of the Trinitarian encircling not only the total good that he has sought "gathered up entire in that one light," but also "our ... form" (*nostra effige*).[36] The polysemy of the phrase *nostra effige* may be interpreted to express the notion that what Dante sees buried so deeply in the Trinity is neither himself nor Christ, "the image of the invisible God" (Col 1:15 NRSV), but the ineffable palimpsest of both simultaneously, divine origin and finite image, Christ and himself. And if Dante does indeed see both himself and Christ, in whose image all humankind is made (Gen 1:26–27), then it cannot be that Dante sees merely himself and Christ. Similarly to the way that the mimetic movement of Sudarg's triune mirror iconizes the whole world of *Pale Fire*, as sign (or Borgesian aleph), the revelation of Christ to Dante must involve the whole of creation.[37] In Christ, Dante sees everything—sees, perhaps, himself seeing Christ seeing himself seeing Christ, and so on.

In similar fashion, it may be argued that one compelling analogy for the task of Trinitarian ontologies comes to us via a fictional saint and his "triptych of bottomless light," which accomplishes the paradox of framing and so giving intelligible form to the infinite while simultaneously arousing within the reader a gaze that is also infinite. In this way, the metaliterary gamesmanship of Nabokov's *Pale Fire* may be said to give theo-dramatic form to the arguably Trinitarian mystery at the heart of Nabokov's 1942 poem "Fame":

> Trusting not the enticements of the thoroughfare
>   or such dreams as the ages have hallowed,
> I prefer to stay godless, with fetterless soul
>   in a world that is swimming with godheads.
>
> But one day while disrupting the strata of sense
>   and descending deep down to my wellspring
> I saw mirrored, besides my own self and the world,
>   something else, something else, something else.[38]

---

36. Dante, *Paradiso* 33.128, 33.104, 33.131.

37. In addition to listing Dante (and, rather unexpectedly, the New Testament) among a short list of nine of "the best and most successful works in literature" (Nabokov, *Think, Write, Speak*, 381), Nabokov can also boast of "a burning drop of Italian blood," being himself the descendant of Cangrande della Scala, to whom Dante dedicated the *Paradiso* (424).

38. Nabokov, *Collected Poems*, 112. Link asserts: "Nabokov's image at the end of 'Fame' echoes the conclusion of the *Commedia*—succinctly, of course, but it even includes an evocation of the Trinity in that thrice-uttered 'something else'" (quoted in Eklund et al., "Nabokov and Religion," 10).

The conjunction at the beginning of the poem's final stanza is doing some heavy lifting, to be sure, yet, however obliquely, it forcefully challenges the ostensible secularity or atheism of Nabokov's so-called "mystical" preferences, bearing witness instead to the inexhaustible excess he perceives at the heart of being (*ens*) and which cannot be reduced either to the self or to the world. The ineffable image to which Nabokov's thrice-repeated "something else" refers, moreover, also seems to correspond to the triune form that lends to Sudarg's mirror its unique mimetic movement by which it may be said to iconize the infinite. This movement that constitutes the mirror triptych may be read as suggesting that the author of *Pale Fire* must necessarily reside beyond the text and is therefore incommensurate with any thing (*res*) that falls within the diegetic frame of the novel, though every thing and character therein reflects some aspect of it. Thus the triune form of Sudarg's mirror triptych returns us to a world in which each and every thing is a "pale fire" of the "dazzling radiance" of "God's Presence" (C549), allowing us to "distinguish His sign at every turn of the trail, painted on the boulder and notched in the fir trunk, whe[re] every page in the book of one's personal fate bears His watermark" (C493). God he sees in mirrors.

17

Rivalry, Sacrifice, and the Trinity

Baptism and Inspiration in Florentine Tradition

CATHERINE PICKSTOCK

IN THE FOLLOWING ESSAY, I will explore the curious connections that pertain between the baptistery in the city of Florence and meditations on pride, rivalry, and imitation involved in art, poetry, and invocations of the divine Trinity. I shall show how the depiction on the relief panels of the baptistery doors, of the sacrifice of Isaac, tends to rebuke a dawning "Renaissance" sense of the pride of the artist in Trinitarian terms, before turning to Dante Alighieri's invocation of the baptistery in his *Commedia*, a poetic work much concerned with the complexities of artistic vaunting. I shall show how Trinitarian invocations both sustain the same Christian critique of excessive human pride and rivalry, and yet also integrate this with a Christian humanist dimension that finds room for both a tempered poetic pride and the interplay of human rivalry in virtue.

The Rivalry

In the year 1401, a contest was held between the artists Lorenzo Ghiberti and Filippo Brunelleschi for the commission to execute the design of relief panels for the east door of the Baptistery of Battistero di San Giovanni, located in front of Florence's cathedral or *duomo*, the Basilica di Santa Maria del Fiore.

The baptistery is a Romanesque octagonal edifice with three sets of double bronze doors. The commission for the first set of (east, later moved to the south) doors was awarded to Andrea Pisano (1290–1348) in 1330, and the doors were completed in 1336. In 1452, the doors were moved to their present location on the south side of the building of the Duomo di Firenze.

The competition to design the panels for the north doors in 1401 was announced by the Arte di Calimala, the guild of wool merchants. Both panels were to be made of gilded bronze, and both were to depict the story of the sacrifice of Isaac within the quatrefoil form. The panels were to set the same elements of the story: Abraham, the donkey, the two male companions, the altar with wood and fire, Isaac, the intervening angel, and the ram.

The competition was won by Lorenzo Ghiberti. The runner-up Filippo Brunelleschi was so offended by this decision that he apparently abandoned sculpture for architecture for the rest of his career. But today the panels hang next to each other on the wall of the Museo Nazionale del Bargello, originally the Palazzo del Popolo and later the civic prison.[1] It is as if the competition between Brunelleschi's bloodthirsty Gothic and Ghiberti's more serene classical realism continues to this day, and to present itself for our judgment as to the infinity and proximity of differences and achievements of the two relief artists.[2]

Brunelleschi divided his panel effectively in two, with the main narrative action taking place in the upper half, above the donkey's back. This panel depicts the scene at its most agonizing moment; a disturbingly bloodthirsty Abraham, with protruding veins visible on his arm, is holding his son, Isaac, by the throat with his left hand. Abraham's right hand holds the dagger with which he is about to cut Isaac's throat—indeed, the blade touches its edge. Isaac's mouth is open as if he is about to scream, and his body is twisted awkwardly. The angel reaches out to stay Abraham's hand. The ram stuck in the thicket is just in front of Isaac, while at the bottom of the panel there are two servants and a donkey.

The intensity of Brunelleschi's panel contrasts with the more restrained idiom of Ghiberti's design, which shows Isaac in a classical stance, and

---

1. Particularly good heliographic images of the relief panels are to be found in Shapley and Kennedy, "Brunelleschi in Competition."

2. Shapley and Kennedy, "Brunelleschi in Competition," 32.

Abraham appears sedate; the onlooker might not quite believe that Ghiberti's Abraham could follow through with the sacrifice. The panel is divided on a diagonally vertical axis. On the left-hand side of the slanted mountainside, two servants and the donkey, looking at one another, serve as witnesses of the drama of the main scene. The ram is situated at the top of the mountain, at the same level as the angel, rendering metaphysically explicit that the ram is a substitute sacrifice, seen in the latter's obeisant bearing.

The scene in this panel depicts the moment just before the knife touches Isaac's throat, and prior to the angel's staying of Abraham's arm, leaving open a sense of suspension that allows for a detailed display of this suspended moment in the physical detail of Isaac's torso, not quite submitting the onlooker to the torment and ambiguity of Abraham's ensuing actions. The movement of the angel flying in a foreshortened body above the heads of the two servant figures, the upturned end of the robe that Abraham is wearing, and the turn of Isaac's head contribute to the sense that one is witnessing the force of the events themselves, rather than surveying a static sculpture. The flowing drapery and the conspicuous wool of the ram point to Ghiberti's careful attuning to the interests of the commissioning guild of the competition, and his *Commentaries* indicate his close contact with them during the year in which the competitors worked on their bas-reliefs. Ghiberti urges the viewer to imagine the conclusion, rather than forcing them to confront it; the father lowering his arm, the angel fetching the ram, the child stepping down from the altar to retrieve his clothing.

Poetic Reproach

Scholars have seen the event of this contest as symbolically marking the beginning of the Renaissance and the rise of the cult of the individual artist.[3] Nevertheless, there were several literary and artistic precedents for such a competition in the medieval city-republics, and personal rivalry between competing artificers in the Middle Ages was by no means unknown. Dante Alighieri cites several examples.[4] Panegyric inscriptions of the thirteenth

---

3. Fowler, *Renaissance Realism*; Radke, *Gates of Paradise*; Walker, *Feud*.

4. One can cite the rivalry between Dante Alighieri and classical poets at *Inferno* 25.94–102; artistic rivalry more generally, in the context of reflection of pride and humility at *Purgatorio* 11.79–108; poetic rivalry in relation to Dante's praise style at *Purgatorio* 24.49–62. These examples contrast to *Paradiso* 10–14, the episode of the sun, which shows Dante's presentation of heavenly (Trinitarian) harmony between theologians and theological currents that would have been rivals on earth. At *Paradiso* 25.1–12, Dante imagines returning to the Florence baptistery to be crowned poet, if or when his poetry may cause the political rivalry between himself and the city to

century increasingly imitated the laudatory style of late antiquity. Artists were beginning to be praised for their personal and unique achievements, their unequaled *ingenium*, *dignitas*, *claritas*, and *aptitudo*, and such inscriptions became increasingly competitive in tone, comparing a particular artifex's skill favorably or unfavorably against that of another.

This increasing concern with individual reputation became a source of anxiety, for it presented an infringement of the Christian principle of humility. Such artistic competitions brought together a twofold problem—of *agon* or rivalrous combat, on the one hand, and *fama* or fame, on the other. A Christian anxiety in the face of this double vaunting was at times placated by great works of charity, bequests, or acts of penitence, offered to atone for the personal aggrandizement afforded by winning a competition.

If, however, these aspects of rivalry had begun to inform the commissioning of artistic works, why is that of the baptistery doors especially held to inaugurate the agonistic protocols of early humanism and the Renaissance? The main reason is that a new contrivance and a new criterion here entered the vocabulary of the competition's adjudicators: that of *realism*. The technical reasons that favored the preeminence of Ghiberti's design were that it attained to greater verisimilitude; its perfection lay in its exactness of copying. This innovative standard introduced an even greater agonistic factor, for here was a measurable artistic aptitude or *value*, which ironically deflected attention from the actual scene depicted in its specific mode of execution, to questions of outdoing one's rival's attention to reality. But if the Renaissance is characterized by an intensified sense of personal reputation, it is also known for continued and equally intensified anxiety about this social phenomenon.[5] The increase in rivalry for honor was matched and balanced by an increase in worry about the very custom of honoring. And in the case of the contest between Ghiberti and Brunelleschi, this concern was brought to an extreme pitch. For while earlier artistic competitors had sought to mitigate the problem of fame by means of charitable benefactions, Ghiberti and Brunelleschi effectively found a more complex expiation, which hinged upon their choice of subject matter, namely, Abraham's sacrifice of Isaac.

The content of this story reproaches from the outset the context of the artists' dealings with fame, or concern with reputation in following generations. Abraham's willingness to sacrifice Isaac does not simply threaten

---

cease. At *Purgatorio* 20.40–96, political and ecclesiastical rivalries are configured as a reenactment of Christ's passion; and at *Inferno* 32.124–33.78, these kinds of rivalries are manifested in Hell in the image of cannibalism. With thanks to Robin Kirkpatrick and Vittorio Montemaggi for discussions on this point.

5. See especially the exploration of artistic pride in Dante, *Purgatorio* 11. See also Goffen, *Renaissance Rivals*; Cranston, "Longing for the Lost"; Liebert, "Raphael."

the removal of Abraham's own future lineage; it threatens the dismissal of a whole people, and therefore the possibility of being remembered and celebrated by one's descendants. In consequence, the very condition of possibility for reputation, for fame itself, is put into jeopardy. Isaac represented the future of Israel. In his loins were contained the seed of a whole nation.

If the topic of the competition panels reproached aspiration to fame, so also did the manner of depicting the scene by the competing artists. This occurred in at least three different ways. First, although Ghiberti and Brunelleschi were undoubtedly pursuing realism as part of an individualistic agon, the more realistic their depictions became, the closer their contribution seemed to dissolve into the actuality of a continuing atoning sacrifice, offered by the individual to the city for all to admire, and thereby to advance, without competition, the devotions of all. Second, if a competition nonetheless persists in the rival offering of these works of potential absolution (as in the rival offerings of Cain and Abel, themselves later depicted on the doors), even this is reproached by their own mode of depiction of the scene. Realism is itself negated, together with its accompanying agon, because all that is ever realistically depicted is the not-quite-happening of the sacrifice. Both Ghiberti and Brunelleschi's competition panels capture the scene at or just before the moment of the staying of Abraham's knife.

There is a third reason the story depicted undercuts the battle for ever-greater realism. The architectural context of the doors, the Florentine baptistery, places upon that scene a self-canceling freight. Here, the sacrifice of Isaac fulfills itself as it effaces itself, in pointing as a typological *figura* to Christ's actually fulfilled sacrifice. That this prototypic self-canceling scene is merely transitional—a stage on the way to the consummate christological sacrifice to end all sacrifice—is dramatized by the fact that it is designed for the Janus-faced doors of the baptistery. A two-dimensional relief, which merely gives the illusion of the real, is here shattered or exceeded when one passes three dimensionally through the picture and into the reality of baptism, or initiation into identity with the God-man and his death. Instead of a dubious realism that can be reached only through rivalry, one has a reality that must be lived and cannot be depicted, which can be reached only through self-sacrifice. Instead of mimetic rivalry, one has the living sacrifice of love.

The flat spell of competition and representation is broken when one passes existentially forward into the existential fullness of the new covenant, just as the visible but hidden seal of circumcision, instituted by Abraham, is broken by pointing typologically to the invisible but public mark of baptism. In this passing through the womb of Christ's body, the church, therefore, one passes from the arts of imitation into the "true tragedy," the actual scenes themselves, and no longer their anticipations, shadows, or relief sculptures, although the shadows and reliefs are part of that reality and help us to make sense of it. Representation is achieved in its very cancellation. By passing through the doors, one immediately completes their realism by becoming, in actuality, what they prefigure. By participating in the fulfillment of their typology, one constitutes, as it were, their missing third dimension.

In this way, through real enactment, we redeem the agon of self-expression. For in becoming oneself the work of art, passing beyond art as mimetic realism, one surpasses the potential of rivalry. Performance strives simply to become itself, rather than competitively to become—by copying—something else.[6] We move to a realm where to achieve oneself in and as a work of art is to achieve something incomparably unique and self-remaining. There is room for an infinity of individual excellences, which can scarcely be compared with one another. By passing beyond representative realism as the measure of either art or morality—an exactness of depiction or an exactness of adherence to an ethical norm—we can exceed the idea of a value that is measurable on a scale. Rather, we have recovered a sense of the *good* as something that can only be participated in, in a myriad of different ways. Between these ways can lie a mysterious and resonant echo, rather than the lethal if sotto voce din of social battle and impasse.

To walk into the space of unique personhood in relation with other persons beyond imitative rivalry is to walk into the ontological space of the Trinity. The three dimensionality of liturgy enacted beyond the two-dimensional doors is a figure for this. For since one cannot encompass three dimensions all at once, since there always remains an aspect of a three-dimensional object that is hidden, three dimensionality is inimical to perfect copying. We are here beyond social competition, because there can be many equally valid surmises as to what constitutes the hidden dimension: conjectures as to one's neighbor's hidden depth and the hidden depth of God.

Therefore, by moving through the doors, toward the font, in fulfillment of Abraham's sacrifice, we fulfill the way in which the story in Genesis points toward the Trinity. It does so because Abraham foreshadows God the Father's offering of the Son to the world through the bond of love that passes between them.

We can note that, on his final panel, Ghiberti depicted the scene of Abraham's vision of three angels under the oak at Mamre, traditionally interpreted as a vision of Abraham's worshiping of the triune God. Inversely,

---

6. Bolens, *Style of Gestures*; Chrétien, *Symbolique du corps*; Lakoff and Johnson, *Philosophy in the Flesh*.

the triune God remains the thrice-holy God of Abraham and of the Jewish people. We do not simply advance from error to reality, leaving imperfect conjecture behind, any more than one can on earth abandon one's imperfect struggles to depict mystery and the inevitable contestations that will arise around this, which one must nonetheless seek to temper with love. One must pass through the doors into the inner sanctum of cultic initiation, but the only way to secure a sanctum is to build an edifice around it, and an edifice must first be entered. Even the ambivalent social negotiations and sometimes excessive if well-intended gestures of a still-competitive piety, like that of Abraham, that one must make within fallen time, have somehow been transfigured and lifted up into the Godhead. The fact of the incarnation and the cross reveal that the triune God is eternally and not just for us, but also the God of Abraham, a God from all eternity linked with a strange and specific set of temporal events—a God connected in his inner sanctum of cultic initiation to the cosmic doors of human historical entry.

Trinity, Baptism, and Naming

The most dramatic disclosure of the Trinity in the New Testament is a restaging of the scene of foundation that is the story of Abraham's sacrifice of Isaac. If the latter concerns the foundation of Israel and the institution of the rite of initiation into Israel, namely circumcision, then the disclosure of the Trinity in Mark's account of Christ's baptism by John concerns the foundation of the new Israel, which is the church, and the institution of its new rite of initiation (Mark 1:9–11).

Nevertheless, this new initiation is structured by an economy that undoes and surpasses the protocols of rivalry. Foreshadowed by the prophet Isaiah, who declared that whole nations are accounted mere dust upon the judgment scales (in a final judgment when the criterion will not be who is the best copyist!), while the patient and meek will be renewed and will mount up with wings like eagles, the institution of this rite of renewal and reversal is infused with a protocol of self-sacrificial non-rivalrous yielding: "After me comes he who is mightier than I, the thong of whose sandals I am not worthy to stoop down and untie" (Mark 1:7 NRSV). Far from seeking to hold his own over against him who is to come, John the Baptist announces in advance the yielding of his own watery baptism to the mysterious unknown future baptism of the Holy Spirit. One could say that he stands not just for the old covenant, but for the once-lone God of that covenant, now revealed as the Father, whose truest mark, as with every loving father, is to "make way" for the coming of his Son. Mark's narrative offers a vertical and descending figure of the Trinity, but also a horizontal figure of its earthly imitation through submission to temporal process.

This willingness to decrease for the sake of what lies ahead unravels the lineage of fame and constructs an asymmetrical reciprocity, linked with the nature of baptism. For baptism pertains to the bestowal of names and legacies, establishing an unrepeatable identity that precludes rivalry by rendering it pointless. Such a different and novel citizenship is open to all; there is no privilege or criterion for entry. There is no competition to enter the city, just as this city is not focused on festivals of agonistic rivalry and blood ritual.

Even the universal threefold name of God, within which one receives one's own specific name, is one that must yield and must itself be named. Jesus, who comes to baptize with the Trinitarian baptism of the Holy Spirit, himself undergoes the rite of baptism, in the context of a mysterious cultic hinterland between Israel and the church, which itself enacts the arrival of the historical echo of the eternal Trinitarian process.

It is in this moment of Jesus's obeisance or self-effacement that his identity is disclosed and made receivable by us. This reversal of authority is dramatized when John's paternal naming is a bestowing of grace upon Jesus, in imitation of the eternal "grace" bestowed by the Father on the Son in the Trinity, which is only such because thereby the Father is equally engraced by the Son. The seemingly ironic reversal, whereby the reader knows that it is truly Christ who has come to bestow grace upon John, is not so complete after all: read in terms of Trinitarian *figura*, a mutual bestowing of grace is at work here, just as the baptism of John seems to suggest the reception of Christ himself into a kind of proto-church; almost as it were into a zone of indeterminacy, as between the church and Israel.

This idea of a transition being enacted within a Trinitarian space is confirmed by the circumstance that the moment Christ arose from the waters, the spirit descended from the heavens, and his name was bestowed and exalted all at once: "Thou art my beloved Son; with thee I am well pleased" (Mark 1:11 NRSV).

In this narrative of the first, transitional proto-baptism, we see the significance of the fact that, in being initiated into the name of Jesus, one is initiated into the secret of the three names of Father, Son, and Holy Spirit, always named at the instance of one's personal naming. The name "Jesus" is the name of a perfect yielding to the will of the Father, refusing all rivalry with him. In this yielding, Jesus is identified as unique, precisely because he does not seek to copy the Father, since the Father's being is, of itself, the expression of the Son's absolute specificity. Paradoxically, because the Son does not seek to copy or appropriate the Father, he becomes the perfect likeness or image of God, his stamp of "character," after which Isaiah inquired. Scriptural rejection of idolatry is here consummated in the performed shape of a perfect human life, analogous with the real walking through the doors, and becoming a work of art in one's own life, as opposed to the stasis of a fixed two-dimensional image.

The attainment of unique identity through self-abandonment is, however, not foreclosed within the circle of Father and Son. Their exchange of identity is abandoned to a bestowal beyond themselves. Both the Father and the Son together will into being, in their joint gift of the Holy Spirit, a shared sense of their identity as of itself a third, fully hypostatic, and personal reality, freely interpretive of the import of the Son's image, of its implications without which it could not stand freely as an image beyond the paternal original. For every expression of any reality must always already have entered a third space of reception, if it is not to be pulled back indeterminately into the initial wellspring. A river is other than its source because it flows through a terrain. Similarly, the statue of a person is other than that person because it is erected in a space potentially containing both of them in which it may be encountered, like the baptistery doors.

The Holy Spirit reaches out to and pre-contains all unique created identities that reach their typical acme in spiritual persons, who include human beings. We can assume these identities only in a Trinitarian mode. They do not consist in an identical copying of Jesus, nor are they to be seized as an independent construction, but rather they are received through one's entering into the self-emptying waters of baptism. Here we receive our identities as the gift of the Spirit, the third upshot of non-rivalry between two, in contrast to the reward for the victor of the agon between two competitors, which can be given only to one party. Here the gift of one's identity is the gift of harmony with the identities of others, attained by the blending of differences rather than the monadic imposition of a single point of view.

This pattern is no mere local ecclesial matter. Such calling by name into being characterizes the ontology of creation, just as we recall the stars that are summoned by name into existence in Isaiah. If the bestowal of names, of unique, incommunicable designators, keeps pace with that of being, then is creation not itself a sign of perpetual baptism? Is it not also a sign of the futility of rivalry, since this summoning into existence shows that there is no pristine accomplishment of identity for which one might compete, which is not itself first fractured by anonymity and dereliction? Jesus is recognized as the Logos when he has been plunged into the waters of chaos. His utmost eminence is revealed through abasement and identification with nothingness, just as he is shown to be mightier than John when he has subordinated himself to him. Such a willing submission to this fracturing is the most noble estate to which, along with all of creation, one should aspire: the honor of pointing beyond oneself to that which is the source of one's being and the bestower of one's name.

Dante and the Florentine Baptistery

The metaphysics of baptism was also engaged by Dante Alighieri in his *Commedia*, in connection with the Florence baptistery, as if this were a primal font of human renewal. We can discern a contestation with the dawning themes of the Renaissance.

In *Paradiso* 25, Dante laments his exile from his native city and wonders if his writing of his long poem can restore his reputation and allow him to return. One day, perhaps, he will return to receive the laurel crown in the very baptistery from which he once took his new birth in Christ and simultaneously acquired citizenship—the two being linked in medieval Italy.[7]

What are we to make of this conjunction of Christian grace and revived pagan *fama*? In one sense, Dante makes outrageous claims for his own significance. No longer is his poem a mere *commedia*. It is now a *poema sacro*, of the same genre as David's *teodio*, a divine song, shared by heaven and earth.[8] Through Dante's work, poetry is raised to equivalence with inspired revelation, because he has been granted by God a mission of bringing hope to life. This is achieved through his vision of paradise, since, as he says in this canto, repeating the words of Peter Lombard,[9] hope lies in the certainty of our eventual enjoyment of blessedness.[10] The implicit claim being made is that the plausibility of Dante's vision has itself served to increase this certainty.[11] And it is accompanied by the conceit, here spelled out, that Dante has been uniquely snatched from "Egypt" to "Jerusalem," prematurely transported in this life and in his mortal body to heaven, in order that he might report back to us.[12] Not only this, but he is commissioned by Beatrice to articulate the nature of hope to the three supreme apostles—Peter, James, and John—for whom one might have supposed such an articulation to be redundant.[13]

---

7. Dante, *Paradiso* 25.1–2, 8–9.

8. This construal of his poem picks up on *Paradiso* 23.61–62: "e così, figurarando il paradiso, / convien saltar lo sacrato poema." See Montemaggi, *Reading Dante's "Commedia" as Theology*; Ferzoco, "Changes."

9. Lombard, *Sentences* 3.16.1.

10. Dante, *Paradiso* 25.67–69.

11. Dante, *Paradiso* 25.31–35.

12. Dante, *Paradiso* 25.52–57.

13. Dante, *Paradiso* 25.58–60.

Rather, it is suggested that Dante can appropriately do this because he has lived out the course of hope, from his Florentine baptism onwards, to the point where it now reaches its fruition in paradise.

In one sense, this conveys a bold new humanism for which not only is the individual exalted, but also the individual genius and the ultimate importance of creative imagination for the sustaining of supernatural hope and faith.[14] And yet, at the same time, any mere humanism, in the sense of self-vaunting, is rebuked by Dante, arguably in a refusal of more strident versions of humanist poetics.

This rebuking can be seen in two respects. First of all, Dante's claim to be a successor of David cuts two ways.[15] He claims to be a revealer by virtue of his baptism, his reception of grace, and the fact that he was first "rained on" by earlier sacred singers and witnesses, in such a way that he can in turn "rain" on others, by virtue of an "overflowing."[16] In other words, his self-vaunting stems paradoxically from an initial humility: he has been poetically deified because he first submitted.

Such submission to the free gift of grace is contrasted in canto 19 of *Inferno* with the Simoniacs who seek to purchase sacred office. Their fate is that of an anti-baptism and a naming in shame. Dante describes them as trapped, heads first, within holes that recall for him the font of the Florentine baptistery. And he recalls an event, which there is no reason not to take literally: his rescue of a child from drowning in that very font.[17] Waters, then, can be perilous: we can sink within them, or they can cleanse us. Baptism itself was traditionally seen as in part our divine rescuing from the chaos of sin.

If the attempted purchasers of grace are irredeemable, then this is not true of those who merely lacked sufficient humility when they received it. Their fate is purgatorial, as recounted in cantos 10–12 of *Purgatorio*. Dante is guided through the regions of the prideful by the pagan poet Virgil—a person of supreme natural virtue and ability, whose only fault was a lack of supernatural faith and hope, in such a way that he is now trapped in the numbing but painless darkness of limbo, along with the souls of unbaptized infants. Virgil is forever stuck because he failed to look forward. And yet he is able to teach this virtue to Dante. Not having received grace, he is not guilty of its attempted seizure or confinement. He deciphers the pride of Christians as an attempt to hoard such favor and to remain satisfied with the gift they have been given, as though it were their possession; whereas a gift

14. Dante, *Paradiso* 25.8.
15. See Federici, "Dante's Davidic Journey."
16. Dante, *Paradiso* 76–78.
17. Dante, *Inferno* 19.16–21.

can be received as a gift only if we continue to receive it and receive it again ever anew.[18] Christians are enjoined not to look backwards, and, likewise, Dante himself is reported as not having looked back as the gates clanged behind him at the outset of the canto.[19] If we advance in the faith, we will discover that gravity reverses itself and our steps upwards become lighter and easier than our steps downwards.[20]

On the way upwards, Dante later sees many sculptured depictions of pagan and biblical instances of pride[21] and earlier biblical instances of humility and receptivity: the annunciation and King David's dancing before the ark. These are said to be examples of divine "speech made visible" and have the strange ontological status of being divinely created and so natural mimetic depictions, which accounts for their lifelike perfections—as if they were shadows or mirror images in a lake.[22]

Yet it seems to be suggested that even in this mimesis there lurks a danger: to be prideful is to be frozen, and it is perhaps appropriate that it is visual art that depicts this condition. Even the images of humility will merely remain such if we dwell upon them in a kind of appropriating satisfaction, as if humility were something that could be performed once and for all—or worse, performed *for* us without our need of meritorious appropriation of just this stance. For this reason, it would seem, Dante is warned by Virgil not to let his gaze rest even for an instant on only part of what he has seen. And significantly, he is encouraged to pass from the image of the annunciation *backwards* to the Old Testament scene of the ark, because Christians must return to the old-covenant mode of promise in the face of the eschaton.[23] Even the final revelation in Christ is the revelation of that which is to be shown again, and more fully and universally.

The journey is accompanied by exhortations to remain in the receptive spirit of the Pater Noster.[24] All gifts come from God; he feeds us with abiding glory, and human fame is transient. The shifting fortunes and fashions in painting are mentioned, and it may be significant that it is specifically visual art that is invoked. In an unconscious anticipation of the debate much later occasioned by G. H. Lessing's "Laocoon," Dante would seem

---

18. Dante, *Purgatorio* 10.121–129.
19. Dante, *Purgatorio* 10.1–6.
20. Dante, *Purgatorio* 12.115–126.
21. Dante, *Purgatorio* 12.25–63.
22. Dante, *Purgatorio* 10.34–96.
23. Dante, *Purgatorio* 10.46–69.
24. Dante, *Purgatorio* 11.1–24.

to imply that the invocatory and narrative art of poetry and song is one of passage, transition, and ascent.[25]

For this reason, Dante appears to regard his poetic vocation as one of self-sacrificial commitment. Beginning from a descent into the waters, he merits a name of renown only insofar as he has joined with and celebrated the continual procession of all creatures in a participatory ascent to beatification. To have joined his voice with that of David indeed ranks him above other poets,[26] yet only by paradoxical virtue of his full acceptance of a specifically human and general subordination. At *Paradiso* 25, he is figured as Icarus, but his flying near to the sun is no longer a dangerous self-vaunting, because Beatrice, his guide, is the true Daedalus, who has designed for him wings of pure love. These wings allow such flight to rise even higher, beyond the mere aspirations of power and the desire to know.[27]

The second mode of rebuking of a proto-Renaissance pridefulness is still more paradoxical. It concerns the way in which the three apostles appear to abase themselves before Dante and Beatrice. As we have already seen, Dante is uniquely honored as the new poet-prophet of hope, as though, rather like St. Francis, a claim were being made about his role in salvation history and the opening of a new epoch—indeed, an epoch of a new human confidence in the promise brought to humanity by Christ. Equally, it is remarkable that St. John is said to join the dance of the three apostles, in the way that a modest maiden might join a wedding dance—not to flaunt herself, but rather to glorify the bride.[28] The bride (however much she may stand for Mary as for the church) is immediately identified as Beatrice, with Dante as the implied bridegroom.[29]

How are we to interpret this? The three apostles and their dance may be regarded as a figure of the Trinity. In this case, it is implied that the plenitude of the Godhead included within its dance the creature, and especially the human creature, which by a kenotic reversal now appears to be supreme. It is not that Dante and Beatrice are special, although they are so, but rather that their specialness represents the specialness or exception of each single human being, an epochally new realization and announcement of this specialness. The Trinitarian figure of non-rivalry is a figure of triadic completion that is never in fact complete—its nature is to open toward the fourth term, the term of the creature.

25. See Pickstock, *Repetition and Identity*, 78, 93.
26. Dante, *Paradiso* 20.38.
27. Dante, *Paradiso* 25.49–51.
28. Dante, *Paradiso* 25.103–105.
29. Dante, *Paradiso* 25.110–111.

This reading of the canto is confirmed by its strange climax concerning the question of whether St. John, like Christ and Mary, was immediately assumed into heaven in his earthly body, without waiting for the general resurrection. Dante is depicted as peering to see John's "double clothing," as though at the sun during the eclipse.[30] But he has no need to do so, because John's glorified body is not as yet present. Rather, it is declared to be still upon the earth. We are, it would seem, still "pointing backwards."

Is this after all the gesture of wrongful pride? Are we not supposed to ascend lightly up Mount Purgatory, drawn by the reverse magnetism of the pole of faith? Why is this not a deplorable looking back, including Dante's thoroughly Renaissance hope one day to receive earthly immortality in his native city? But Dante himself is invoking the only humanly valid downcast gaze, which is a recollection of our baptism that must lure us forwards, beyond any progression merely within time.[31] On the other hand, the looking backwards and downwards of the beatified and of God himself is not a matter of ontological nostalgia, but rather the original gesture of creation, and the letting be of the finite cosmos and of finite creatures alongside God himself.

If Dante is ascending toward God, then he is ascending toward a God who does not disdain Florence and who will one day renew the earth as part of the final vision. Dante's arrival in heaven is not therefore incompatible with his hoped-for triumphant return to his native city. They are both the eschaton, since our own humble refusal of rivalry is always trumped by the Trinitarian dance that finds room, after all, also for us, and always for each of us in all our specific human conjoinings and affinities.

Dante and the Invocation of Names

One can see Dante as rebuking the burgeoning Renaissance. He implicitly contrasts the *morta poesi* of pagan self-vaunting, as invoked at *Purgatorio* 7, with a Christian art and poetry that places the valued things of creation in a processual scene, involving their participation in and relative closeness to or distance from the divine. Dante's own words derive from a relative valuing and a constant passing onwards and upwards in an essentially receptive and contemplative spirit.

Moreover, Dante's poetics is one of naming: of a constant identification and judgment, a kind of continuous spiritual baptizing.[32] Every canto is a

---

30. Dante, *Paradiso* 25.88–96.
31. Dante, *Paradiso* 25.37–39.
32. Cervigni, "Beatrice's Act of Naming"; Marks, "Hollowed Names"; Nohrnberg, "Autobiographical Imperative."

kind of litany of names. And as we have seen, *Inferno* 19 describes hell in terms of an anti-baptism, which can be contrasted with the invocation of the Florentine baptistery at *Paradiso* 25. In the latter context, Dante appears to hope that his own art will be accepted as a non-pagan sacrificial activity that will win him acceptance once more into the "sheepfold" of the baptistery, the maternal womb that is transfigured into our enfolding end. And yet we have also seen that Dante makes the boldest possible claims for the significance of his poetry. His creative imagination serves epochally to renew human hope. We can also say that he integrates the dawning Renaissance into his still-medieval purview. As we have already seen, we discover, in Dante's gloss on the Florence baptistery, in his own fontal thoughts, not merely that the invocation of the Trinity rebukes our pride and rivalry, but also that the creative gesture of human craft, and the alternating choreographic gestures of our social intermingling, are not to be simply renounced, any more than Dante's love for Beatrice is to be abandoned in the celestial sphere. These gestures are rooted in the Trinity itself, which is infinite and eminent poetry, as well as circling association. As it turns out, pride is merely tempered by the Trinitarian God, and our proper pride, including the poetic pride of the human creator, is restored in its contributive measure and to its appropriate degree. The teasing rivalry of love is equally restored: the constant displacement of the angelic and human dance, where every place that is graciously forsaken in order to admit the other returns all the more to open one's own place at the next turn of the dance. In our specific finite origin, the going back to heaven is also our beginning again in Florence. So every renunciation is a recirculation of our unique, proper, and personal selfhood.

General Bibliography

Agamben, Giorgio. *The Kingdom and the Glory: For a Theological Genealogy of Economy and Government*. Translated by Lorenzo Chiesa with Matteo Mandarini. Meridian: Crossing Aesthetics. Stanford, CA: Stanford University Press, 2011.

———. *The Time That Remains: A Commentary on the Letter to the Romans*. Translated by Patricia Dailey. Meridian: Crossing Aesthetics. Stanford, CA: Stanford University Press, 2005.

Alarcón, L. F. "Restless Negativity: Blanchot's Hegelianism." *CR: New Centennial Review* 15 (2015) 141–58.

Albert the Great. *Metaphysica*. Edited by B. Geyer. Münster: Aschendorff, 1964.

———. *Summa theologiae, sive De mirabili scientia Dei*. Edited by W. Küble. Münster: Aschendorff, 1978.

Alfred. *King Alfred's Anglo-Saxon Version of Boethius "De consolatione philosophi."* Translated by Samuel Fox. London: John, 1864.

Al-Ghazālī. *The Ninety-Nine Beautiful Names of God*. Translated by David B. Burrell and Nazih Daher. Cambridge: Islamic Texts Society, 1992.

Alladaye, René. *The Darker Shades of Pale Fire: An Investigation into a Literary Mystery*. Paris: Houdiard, 2013.

Alliez, Eric. *De l'impossibilité de la phénoménologie: Sur la philosophie française contemporaine*. Paris: Vrin, 1995.

Alter, Robert. *Nabokov and the Real World: Between Appreciation and Defense*. Princeton: Princeton University Press, 2021.

Anne, David. "The Apocalypse of John and Graeco-Roman Revelatory Magic." *NTS* 33 (1987) 481–501.

Anselm. *"Monologion" and "Proslogion" with the Replies of Gaunilo and Anselm*. Edited and translated by Thomas Williams. Indianapolis: Hackett, 1996.

———. *Proslogium. Monologium. An Appendix in "Behalf of the Fool" by Gaunilo. Cur Deus Homo*. Translated by Sidney Norton Deane. Chicago: Open Court, 1926.

Apostolacus, Katherine. "Althaus-Reid's Deleuzian Theology of Desire." Presentation at the European Academy of Religion annual conference, St. Andrews, Scot., June 2023.

Aquinas, Thomas. *Summa Theologiae*. Translated by Laurence Shapcote. New York: Benziger Bros., 1911.

———. *Summa Theologica*. Translated by Fathers of the English Dominican Province. London: Burns, Oates & Washbourne, 1920–22.

Ashbaugh, Anne Freire. "Platonism: And Essay on Repetition and Recollection." In *Kierkegaard and Great Traditions*, edited by Niels Thulstrup and Marie Mikulová Thulstrup, 1–26. Bibliotheca Kierkegaardiana. Copenhagen: Reitzel, 1981.

Ayres, Lewis. *Nicaea and Its Legacy: An Approach to Fourth-Century Trinitarian Theology*. 10 vols. Oxford: Oxford University Press, 2004.

Baader, Franz von. *Fermenta Cognitionis (1822–1825)*. Edited by Alberto Bonchino. Vol. 3 of *Ausgewählte Werke*. Leiden: Brill Schöning, 2024.

Babich, Babette. *Ein Gottes Glück voller Macht und Liebe: Beiträge zu Nietzsche, Hölderlin, und Heidegger*. Translated by Harald Seubert et al. Weimar: Bauhaus University Press, 2009.

Badiou, Alain. *Being and Event*. Translated by O. Feltham. London: Continuum, 2006.

———. *Briefings on Existence: A Short Treatise on Transitory Ontology*. Edited and translated by Norman Madarasz. Albany: SUNY Press, 2006.

Bales, Richard. "Proust and the Fine Arts." In *The Cambridge Companion to Proust*, edited by Richard Bales, 183–99. Cambridge Companions to Literature. Cambridge: Cambridge University Press, 2001.

Balthasar, Hans Urs von. *Apokalypse der deutschen Seele: Studien zu einer Lehre von Letzten Haltungen*. 3 vols. Einsiedeln, Switz.: Johannes, 1998.

———. *Geschichte des eschatologischen Problems in der modernen deutschen Literatur*. Edited by Alois M. Haas. 2nd ed. Einsiedeln, Switz.: Johannes, 1998.

———. *The Glory of the Lord: A Theological Aesthetics*. Edited by John Riches. Translated by Brian O'Neil and Erasmo Leiva-Merikakis. 7 vols. San Francisco: Ignatius, 1983.

———. *Love Alone Is Credible*. Translated by D. C. Schindler. San Francisco: Ignatius, 2004.

———. *My Work: In Retrospect*. Translated by Brian McNeil. San Francisco: Ignatius, 1993.

———. "A Résumé of My Thought." Translated by Kelly Hamilton. In *Hans Urs von Balthasar: His Life and Work*, edited by David L. Schindler, 1–5. San Francisco: Communio, 1991.

———. *Spirit and Institution*. Vol. 4 of *Explorations in Theology*. San Francisco: Ignatius, 1995.

———. *Theo-Drama*. 5 vols. San Francisco: Ignatius, 1993–98.

———. *Theologie der Geschichte*. Einsiedeln, Switz.: Johannes, 1950.

———. *Truth of the World*. Vol. 1 of *Theo-Logic: Theological Logical Theory*. Translated by Adrian J. Walker. San Francisco: Ignatius, 2001.

Barabtarlo, Gennady. "Nabokov's Trinity (On the Movement of Nabokov's Themes)." In *Nabokov and His Fiction: New Perspectives*, edited by Julian W. Connolly, 109–38. Cambridge Studies in Russian Literature. Cambridge: Cambridge University Press, 2009.

Barad, Karen. "What Flashes Up: Theological-Political-Scientific Fragments." In *Entangled Worlds: Religion, Science, and New Materialisms*, edited by Catherine Keller and Mary-Jane Rubenstein, 21–88. New York: Fordham University Press, 2017.

Barnouw, Jeffrey. "Peirce and Derrida: 'Natural Signs' Empiricism Versus 'Originary Trace' Deconstruction." *Poetics Today* 7 (1986) 73–94. https://doi.org/10.2307/1772089.

Barthes, Roland. "The Death of the Author." In *Image Music Text*, translated by Stephen Heath, 142–48. New York: Hill & Wang, 1977.
Bartsch, Hans-Werner, ed. *Kerygma and Myth: A Theological Debate*. Translated by Reginald H. Fuller. Vols. 1 and 2 combined with enlarged bibliography. London: SPCK, 1972.
Baumgarten, A. G. *Aesthetica*. 2 vols. Frankfurt (Oder): Johann Christian Kleyb, 1750–1758.
Begbie, Jeremy S. *Resounding Truth: Christian Wisdom in the World of Music*. Engaging Culture. Grand Rapids: Baker Academic, 2007.
Benveniste, Émile. *Économie, parente, société*. Vol. 1 of *Le vocabulaire des institutions indo-européennes*. Sens commun. Paris: Minuit, 1969.
Bergson, Henri. *The Creative Mind: An Introduction to Metaphysics*. Translated by M. L. Andison. Mineola, NY: Dover, 2007.
———. *An Introduction to Metaphysics*. Translated by T. E. Hulme. Repr., Indianapolis: Hackett, 1999.
———. *La pensée et le mouvant*. Paris: PUF, 2013.
Berkeley, George. *Philosophical Writings*. Edited by Desmond M. Clarke. Cambridge Texts in the History of Philosophy. Cambridge: Cambridge University Press, 2009.
Bernasconi, Robert. "Poets as Prophets and Painters: Heidegger's Turn to Language and the Hölderlinian Turn in Context." In *Heidegger and Language*, edited by Jeffery Powell, 146–62. Studies in Continental Thought. Bloomington: Indiana University Press, 2013.
Betz, John. "After Heidegger and Marion: The Task of Metaphysics Today." *Modern Theology* 34 (2018) 565–97.
———. *Christ the Logos of Creation: An Essay in Analogical Metaphysics*. Steubenville, OH: Emmaus Academic, 2023.
Blake, William. *Complete Writings, with Variant Readings*. Edited by Geoffrey Keynes. Oxford Standard Authors. Oxford: Oxford University Press, 1988.
Blanchot, Maurice. *The Infinite Conversation*. Translated by Susan Hanson. Minneapolis: University of Minnesota Press, 1993.
———. *The Space of Literature*. Translated by Ann Smock. Lincoln: University of Nebraska Press, 1989.
———. *The Step Not Beyond*. Translated by Lycette Nelson. Intersections: Philosophy and Critical Theory. Albany: SUNY Press, 1992.
———. *Thomas the Obscure*. Translated by Robert Lamberton. New York: Lewis, 1973.
———. *The Work of Fire*. Translated by Charlotte Mandell. Meridian: Crossing Aesthetics. Stanford, CA: Stanford University Press, 1995.
———. *The Writing of the Disaster*. Translated by Ann Smock. Lincoln: University of Nebraska Press, 1995.
Blanchot, Maurice, and Dionys Mascolo. *Maurice Blanchot, passion politique: Lettre-récit de 1984 suivie d'une lettre de Dionys Mascolo*. Edited by Jean Luc Nancy. Paris: Galilée, 2011.
Blondel, Maurice. *Action (1893): Essay on a Critique of Life and a Science of Practice*. Translated by Oliva Blanchette. Notre Dame: University of Notre Dame Press, 2021.
———. *"The Letter on Apologetics" and "History and Dogma."* Edited and translated by Alexander Dru and Illtyd Trethowan. London: Harvill, 1964.
Boehme, Jacob. *Essential Writings*. Edited by Robin Waterfield. London: Crucible, 1989.

Boethius. *The Consolation of Philosophy*. Edited by P. G. Walsh. Oxford World's Classics. Oxford: Oxford University Press, 1999.

Bolens, Guillemette. *The Style of Gestures: Embodiment and Cognition in Literary Narrative*. Rethinking Theory. Baltimore: Johns Hopkins University Press, 2012.

Borges, Jorge Luis. "*Paradiso*: XXXI." In *Collected Fictions*, translated by Andrew Hurley, 108. New York: Penguin, 1999.

Bostonia, Marguerite. "Bells as Inspiration for Tintinnabulation." In *The Cambridge Companion to Arvo Pärt*, edited by Andrew Shenton, 128–39. Cambridge Companions to Music. Cambridge: Cambridge University Press, 2012.

Boulnois, Olivier. "De l'esthétique médiévale, derechef, qu'elle n'existe pas." In *Le beau et la beauté au Moyen Âge*, edited by Oliver Boulnois and Isabelle Moulin, 17–38. Paris: Vrin, 2018.

———. *Être et représentation: Une généalogie de la métaphysique moderne à l'époque de Duns Scot (XIIIe–XIVe siècle)*. Paris: PUF, 1999.

Bouteneff, Peter. *Arvo Pärt: Out of Silence*. Yonkers: St. Vladimir's Seminary Press, 2015.

Bowie, Andrew. *Schelling and Modern European Philosophy: An Introduction*. London: Routledge, 2002.

Boyer, Régis, and Michel Forget, eds. and trans. *Oeuvres complètes de Søren Kierkegaard*. By Søren Kierkegaard. 2 vols. Paris: NRF Gallimard, 2018.

Brague, Rémi. *Du Dieu des chrétiens et d'un ou deux autres*. Champs essais 945. Paris: Flammarion, 2008.

Brée, Germaine. *Du temps perdu au temps retrouvé: Introduction à l'oeuvre de Marcel Proust*. Études françaises 44. Paris: Belles Lettres, 1950.

Brown, David, and Gavin Hopps. *The Extravagance of Music*. London: Palgrave Macmillan, 2018.

Bryant, Levi, et al., eds. *The Speculative Turn: Continental Materialism and Realism*. Anamnesis. Melbourne: Re.press, 2011.

Buffo, Raul, et al. *Lessico di ontologia trinitaria*. Rome: Istituto Universitario Sophia, Città Nuova, 2023.

Bulgakov, Sergei. *The Wisdom of God: A Brief Summary of Sophiology*. Translated by Patrick Thompson et al. Hudson, NY: Lindisfarne, 1993.

Bulgakov, Sergii. *Philosophy of the Name*. Edited and translated by Thomas Allan Smith. NIU Series in Orthodox Christian Studies. Ithaca, NY: Cornell University Press, 2022.

Bulgakov, Sergij. *The Tragedy of Philosophy (Philosophy & Dogma)*. Translated by Stephen Churchyard. New York: Angelico, 2020.

Bulgakov, Sergius. *The Comforter*. Translated by Boris Jakim. Grand Rapids: Eerdmans, 2004.

———. *The Lamb of God*. Translated by Boris Jakim. Grand Rapids: Eerdmans, 2008.

———. *Sophiology of Death: Essays on Eschatology: Personal, Political, Universal*. Translated by Roberto J. De La Noval. Eugene, OR: Cascade, 2021.

———. *Spiritual Diary*. Translated by Mark Roosien and Roberto J. De La Noval. New York: Angelico, 2022.

Burton, Richard D. E. *Olivier Messiaen: Texts, Contexts, & Intertexts (1937–1948)*. Edited by Roger Nichols. New York: Oxford University Press, 2016.

Cabasilas, Nicholas. *The Life in Christ*. Translated by Carmino J. De Catanzaro. Crestwood, NY: St. Vladimir's Seminary Press, 1974.

Canguilhem, Georges. *Le normal et le pathologique* [The normal and the pathological]. 4th ed. Quadrige. Paris: PUF, 1979.
Catren, Gabriel. *Pleromatica, or Elsinore's Trance*. Translated by Thomas Murphy. London: Urbanomic, 2023.
Causse, Guilehm. "Temporalité de la reconnaissance." *Revue d'Éthique et de Théologie Morale HS* 281 (2014) 23–35.
Cervigni, Dino S. "Beatrice's Act of Naming." *Lectura Dantis* 8 (1991) 85–99.
Chrétien, Jean-Louis. "La limite de la métaphysique selon Malebranche." In *La voix nue: Phénomenologie de la promesse*, 295–315. Philosophie. Paris: Minuit, 1990.
———. *Symbolique du corps: La tradition chrétienne du Cantique des cantiques*. Paris: PUF, 2005.
———. "Thomas Traherne et l'Eden retrouvé." In *La joie spacieuse: Essai sur la dilatation*, 163–204. Paris: Minuit, 2007.
Clarke, W. Norris. *Explorations in Metaphysics: Being, God, Person*. Notre Dame: University of Notre Dame Press, 1994.
———. *The One and the Many: A Contemporary Thomistic Metaphysics*. Notre Dame: University of Notre Dame Press, 2001.
Clemenzia, Alessandro, and Valentina Gaudiano. *Sulla soglia tra filosofia e teologia*. Rome: Città Nuova, 2019.
Clemenzia, Alessandro, and Julie Tremblay, eds. *Un pensiero per abitare la frontiera*. Rome: Città Nuova, 2016.
Coakley, Sarah. *God, Sexuality, and the Self: An Essay "On the Trinity."* Cambridge: Cambridge University Press, 2013.
———. "'Persons' in the 'Social' Doctrine of the Trinity: Current Analytic Discussion and 'Cappadocian' Theology." In *Powers and Submissions: Spirituality, Philosophy and Gender*, 109–29. Challenges in Contemporary Theology. Oxford: Blackwell, 2002.
Coda, Piero. *From the Trinity: The Coming of God in Revelation and Theology*. Edited by William Neu. Washington, DC: Catholic University of America Press, 2020.
———. "Ontologia trinitaria." In *Dictionnaire critique de théologie*, edited by Jean-Yves Lacoste, 1412–15. Rome: Città Nuova, 2005.
———. "L'ontologia trinitaria, che cos'è?" *Sophia* 2 (2012) 159–70.
———. *Para una ontología trinitaria: Si la forma es relación*. Translated by Raul Buffo. Buenos Aires: Agape, 2018.
———. *Un pensiero per abitare la frontiera*. Rome: Istituto Universitario Sophia, Città Nuova, 2016.
———. *Per una lettura trinitaria del prologo di Giovanni*. Milan: Bompiani, 2007.
Coda, Piero, and Andreas Tapken, eds. *La Trinità e il pensare: Figure, percorsi, prospettive*. Roma: Città Nuova, 1997.
Coda, Piero, et al. "Dizionario dinamico di ontologia trinitaria." In *Manifesto: Per una ri-forma del pensare*, 1:296–340. Dynamic Dictionary of Trinitarian Ontology 1. Rome: Città Nuova, 2021.
———. *Manifesto: Per una ri-forma del pensare*. Dynamic Dictionary of Trinitarian Ontology 1. Rome: Città Nuova, 2021.
Colacicco, Giancarlo. "Trinitarian Ontology of and Early Jesuit Metaphysics: The Case of Francisco Suárez Between Principles and Causes." *Quaestio* 23 (2023) 383–404.
Congar, Yves. "Unité de foi, diversité de formulation théologique entre Grecs et Latins dans l'appréciation des Docteurs occidentaux." *RevScRel* 54 (1980) 21–31.

Conrad-Martinud, Hedwig. *Das Sein*. Munich: Kösel, 1957.
Courtine, Jean-François. *Suarez et le système de la métaphysique*. Paris: PUF, 1990.
Cranston, Jodi. "Longing for the Lost: Ekphrasis, Rivalry, and the Figuration of Notional Artworks in Italian Renaissance Painting." *Word & Image* 27 (2011) 212–19.
Crites, Steven. "The Blissful Security of the Moment: Recollection, Repetition, and Eternal Recurrence." In *"Fear and Trembling" and "Repetition,"* edited by Robert L. Perkins, 225–46. International Kierkegaard Commentary 6. Macon: Mercer University Press, 1993.
Curi, Maria Benedetta. *Pensare dall'unità: Franz Rosenzweig e Klaus Hemmerle*. Rome: Città Nuova, 2017.
Cusa, Nicholas. "De Docta Ignorantia." In *Nicholas of Cusa: Selected Spiritual Writings*, translated by H. L. Bond, 85–206. Mahwah, NJ: Paulist, 1997.
———. "De Visione Dei." In *Nicholas of Cusa: Selected Spiritual Writings*, translated by H. L. Bond, 233–90. Mahwah, NJ: Paulist, 1997.
Dallmayr, Fred. "Heidegger, Hölderlin, and Politics." In *Heidegger Studies* 2 (1986) 81–95.
Daniélou, Jean. *God and the Ways of Knowing*. Translated by Walter Roberts. San Francisco: Ignatius, 2003.
———. *The Lord of History: Reflections on the Inner Meaning of History*. Translated by Nigel Abercrombie. London: Longmans, Green and Co., 1958.
———. "La notion de personne chez les Pères grecs." *Bulletin des Amis du Card. Danièlou* 19 (1983) 3–10.
———. *La Trinité et le mystère de l'existence*. Paris: Desclée, De Brouwer, 1968.
Dante. *The Divine Comedy: Inferno, Purgatorio, Paradiso*. Edited and translated by Robin Kirkpatrick. Penguin Classics. London: Penguin, 2012.
———. *Le Opera di Dante*. Edited by F. Brambilla Ageno et al. Revised by D. De Robertis and G. Breschi. Società Dantesca Italiana. Florence: Polistampa, 2012.
Deleuze, Gilles. *Différence et répétition*. Epiméthée. Paris: PUF, 1968.
———. *The Logic of Sense*. Translated by Mark Lester. London: Athlone, 1990.
———. *Proust & Signs: The Complete Text*. Translated by Richard Howard. Minneapolis: Minnesota University Press, 2003.
———. *Proust et les signes*. Edited by Philippe Garcin. A la pensée. Paris: PUF, 1996.
Deleuze, Gilles, and Félix Guattari. *Anti-Oedipus: Capitalism and Schizophrenia*. Translated by Robert Hurley et al. London: Continuum, 2005.
Derrida, Jacques. "Discussion Between Jacques Derrida, Philippe Lacoue-Labarthe, and Jean-Luc Nancy (2004)." In *For Strasbourg: Conversations of Friendship and Philosophy*, edited by Pascale-Anne Brault and Michael Naas, 17–30. New York: Fordham University Press, 2014. https://doi.org/10.1515/9780823256525-003.
———. *Geschlecht III: Sex, Race, Nation, Humanity*. Edited by Geoffrey Bennington et al. Translated by Katie Chenoweth and Rodrigo Therezo. Chicago: University of Chicago Press, 2020.
———. "How to Avoid Speaking: Denials." In *Derrida and Negative Theology*, edited by Harold Coward and Toby Foshay, translated by Ken Frieden, 73–142. New York: SUNY Press, 1992.
———. *Of Spirit: Heidegger and the Question*. Translated by Geoffrey Bennington and Rachel Bowlby. Chicago: University of Chicago Press, 1991.

Descombes, Vincent. *Proust: Philosophie du roman*. Collection "Critique." Paris: Minuit, 1987.
———. *Proust: Philosophy of the Novel*. Translated by Catherine Chance Macksey. Stanford CA: Stanford University Press, 1992.
Desmond, William. *Being and the Between*. SUNY Series in Philosophy. Albany: SUNY Press, 1995.
———. *Ethics and the Between*. SUNY Series in Philosophy. Albany: SUNY Press, 2003.
———. *God and the Between*. Oxford: Blackwell, 2008.
———. *Hegel's God: Counterfeit Double?* Ashgate Studies in the History of Philosophical Theology. London: Routledge, 2003.
———. "Hegel's God, Transcendence, and the Counterfeit Double: A Figure of Dialectical Equivocity?" *Owl of Minerva* 36 (2005) 91–110.
———. *Perplexity and Ultimacy: Metaphysical Thoughts from the Middle*. Albany: SUNY Press, 1995.
———. "Response to Stephen Houlgate." *Owl of Minerva* 36 (2005) 175–88.
———. *The Voiding of Being: The Doing and Undoing of Metaphysics in Modernity*. Studies in Philosophy and the History of Philosophy. Washington, DC: Catholic University of America Press, 2019.
———. "Wording Time: On Augustine's *Confessions* XI; Transcriptions, Variations, Improvisations." *Maynooth Philosophical Papers* 10 (2020) 57–95.
Difrisco, James. "Merleau-Ponty's Ontology of Life." *Pli* 23 (2012) 50–71.
Duns Scotus, John. *The Ordinatio of Blessed Duns Scotus*. Edited by Christian B. Wagner. Translated by Peter L. P. Simpson. N.p.: N.p., 2022.
Echaurren, Alejandra Novoa, and Noemi Sanches. "'Being Rooted in Love': The Trinitarian Ontological Perspective of Simone Weil's Notion of Rootedness." *Religions* 14 (2023) 1033. https://doi.org/10.3390/rel14081033.
Edwards, Mark. *Aristotle and Early Christian Thought*. Studies in Philosophy and Theology in Late Antiquity. London: Routledge, 2019.
Eikelboom, Lexi. *Rhythm: A Theological Category*. Oxford Theology & Religion Monographs. Oxford: Oxford University Press, 2018.
Eikrem, Asle. "On the Possibility of a Metaphysical Theology After Onto-Theology." In *Groundless Gods: The Theological Prospects of Post-Metaphysical Thought*, edited by Eric E. Hall and Hartmut von Sass, 255–70. Eugene, OR: Pickwick, 2008.
Eklund, Erik. "Do Not Be Angry at the Moon: *Pale Fire* and *The Old English Boethius*." *Nabokovian* 83 (2022) 1–13.
———. "The Mirror and the Icon: An Alternative Reading of Nabokov's *Pale Fire*." *Partial Answers* 22 (2024) 117–40.
———. "'The Name of God Has Priority': 'God' and the Apophatic Element in Vladimir Nabokov's *Pale Fire*." *Literature and Theology* 36 (2022) 298–315.
Eklund, Erik, et al. "Nabokov and Religion: Forum, Part Two." *Nabokov Online Journal* 17 (2023) 1–24.
Eliot, T. S. "Burnt Norton." In *Collected Poems, 1909–1962*, 175–81. London: Faber & Faber, 2002.
Elste, Martin. "An Interview with Arvo Pärt." *Arvo Pärt*, Mar.–Apr. 1998. https://www.arvopart.ee/en/arvo-part/article/an-interview-with-arvo-part/.
Emery, Gilles. *La théologie trinitaire de saint Thomas d'Aquin*. Paris: Cerf, 2004.
Eriksen, Niels Nymann. *Kierkegaard's Category of Repetition: A Reconstruction*. Kierkegaard Studies: Monograph Series 5. Berlin: De Gruyter, 2000.

Eriugena, Johannes Scottus. *Periphyseon: The Division of Nature.* Edited by John J. O'Meara. Translated by I. P. Sheldon-Williams. Washington, DC: Dumbarton Oaks, 2020.

Eriugena, Johannes Scottus. *See also* John the Scot.

Escrivá, Josemaría. *The Way: The Essential Classic of Opus Dei's Founder.* New York: Doubleday, 1992.

Esposito, Constantino. "Die Geschichte des letzten Gottes in Heideggers *Beiträge zur Philosophie.*" *Heidegger Studies* 11 (1995) 33–61.

Eusebius. *Church History.* In *NPNF2*, translated by Arthur Cushman McGiffert, 1:73–387.

Falque, Emmanuel. "Blaise Pascal and the Anxiety of Faith." *Louvain Studies* 42 (2019) 151–74. https://doi.org/10.2143/LS.42.2.3286593.

———. *Crossing the Rubicon: The Borderlands of Philosophy and Theology.* Translated by Reuben Shank. Perspectives in Continental Philosophy. New York: Fordham University Press, 2016.

———. *Dieu, la chair et l'autre: D'Irénée à Duns Scot.* Epiméthée. Paris: PUF, 2015.

———. *God, the Flesh, and the Other: From Irenaeus to Duns Scotus.* Translated by William Christian Hackett. Evanston, IL: Northwestern University Press, 2015.

———. *Métamorphose de la finitude: Essai philosophique sur la naissance et la résurrection.* Paris: Cerf, 2004.

———. *The Metamorphosis of Finitude: An Essay on Birth and Resurrection.* Translated by George Hughes. Perspectives in Continental Philosophy. New York: Fordham University Press, 2012.

———. *Les noces de l'Agneau: Essai philosophique sur le corps et l'eucharistie.* Paris: Cerf, 2011.

———. *Passer le Rubicon: Philosophie et théologie; Essai sur les frontières.* Philosophie LeXio. Brussels: Lessius, 2013.

———. "Saint Thomas and the Entrance of God into Philosophy." In *Saint Bonaventure and the Entrance of God into Theology,* translated by Brian Lapsa and Sarah Horton, 219–57. St. Bonaventure, NY: Franciscan Institute, 2018.

———. "Seul un Dieu peut encore nous sauver." *Transversalités* 131 (2014) 151–75.

———. "Toward an Ethics of the Spread Body." In *Somatic Desire: Recovering Corporeality in Contemporary Thought,* edited by Sarah Horton et al., 91–116. Lexington, MA: Lexington, 2019.

———. *Triduum philosophique: Le passeur de Gethsémani. Métamorphose de la finitude. Les noces de l'Agneau.* Rev. ed. Paris: Cerf, 2015.

———. *The Wedding Feast of the Lamb: Eros, the Body, and the Eucharist.* Translated by George Hughes. Perspectives in Continental Philosophy. New York: Fordham University Press, 2016.

Falque, Emmanuel, and Sabine Fos-Falque. *Éthique du corps épandu* [Falque]. *Une chair épandue sur le divan* [Fos-Falque]. Paris: Cerf, 2018.

Federici, Theresa. "Dante's Davidic Journey: From Sinner to God's Scribe." In *Dante's "Commedia": Theology as Poetry,* edited by Vittorio Montemaggi and Matthew Treherne, 180–209. William and Katherine Devers Series in Dante and Medieval Italian Literature. Notre Dame, IN: University of Notre Dame Press, 2010.

Fell, Matthew. "Wisdom Within, Wisdom Without: Rediscovering the Apocalyptic Paradox of the Augustinian Soul." Presentation at the European Academy of Religion annual conference, St. Andrews, Scot., June 2023.

Fernandez, Ramon. *Proust; ou, La généalogie du roman moderne*. Paris: Nouvelle Revue Critique, 1943.
Ferzoco, George. "Changes." In *Vertical Readings in Dante's "Comedy,"* edited by Heather Webb and George Corbett, 3:51–70. Cambridge: OpenBook, 2017. https://books.openbookpublishers.com/10.11647/obp.0119/.
Feuerbach, Ludwig Andreas. *The Essence of Christianity*. Translated by George Eliot. Dover Philosophical Classics. Mineola, NY: Dover, 2008.
Fiedler, Eduard. "Klaus Hemmerle on the Trinitarian Ontology of the Human Person." *Acta Universitatis Carolinae Theologica* 2 (2021) 59–75.
Fornari, Giuseppe. *A God Torn to Pieces: The Nietzsche Case*. Translated by Keith Buck with Giuseppe Fornari. Studies in Violence, Mimesis & Culture. East Lansing: Michigan State University Press, 2013.
Fowler, Alastair. *Renaissance Realism: Narrative Images in Literature and Art*. Oxford: Oxford University Press, 2003.
Francis of Assisi. "Salutation of Blessed Virgin." Sacred Texts, 1905. From *The Writings of St. Francis of Assisi*, translated by Paschal Robinson. https://sacred-texts.com/chr/wosf/wosf19.htm.
Frank, Siggy. *Nabokov's Theatrical Imagination*. Cambridge: Cambridge University Press, 2012.
Friedman, Russell L. *Medieval Trinitarian Thought from Aquinas to Ockham*. Cambridge: Cambridge University Press, 2010.
Gabellieri, Emmanuel, and Simone Kotva. "From Self to World." In *The Oxford Handbook of Apophaticism*, edited by John Betz. Oxford: Oxford University Press, forthcoming.
Gadamer, Hans Georg. *Truth and Method*. Translated by Joe Weinsheimer and Donald G. Marshall. New York: Crossroad, 1960.
Gallaher, Brandon. "Antinomism, Trinity and the Challenge of Solov̈evan Pantheism in the Theology of Sergij Bulgakov." *Studies in East European Thought* 64 (2012) 205–25.
Gasché, Rodolphe. *The Tain of the Mirror: Derrida and the Philosophy of Reflection*. Cambridge: Harvard University Press, 1986.
Genette, Gérard. *Figures*. Vol. 3 of 5. Collection poétique. Paris: Seuil, 1972.
———. *Figures of Literary Discourse*. Translated by Alan Sheridan. Vol. 3 of 5. New York: Columbia University Press, 1982.
Gilman, Sander L., ed. *Conversations with Nietzsche: A Life in the Words of His Contemporaries*. Translated by David J. Parent. Oxford: Oxford University Press, 1987.
Gilson, Étienne. *John Duns Scotus: Introduction to His Fundamental Positions*. Translated by James Colbert. Illuminating Modernity. London: T&T Clark, 2019.
Girard, René. *Battling to the End: Conversations with Benoît Chantre*. Studies in Violence, Mimesis & Culture. East Lansing: Michigan State University Press, 2009.
Gnilka, Christian. *Der Begriff des "rechten Gebrauchs."* Vol. 1 of *Chrêsis: Die Methode der Kirchenväter im Umgang mit der antiken Kultur*. Basel: Schwabe, 2012.
Goffen, Rona. *Renaissance Rivals: Michelangelo, Leonardo, Raphael, Titian*. New Haven: Yale University Press, 2002.
Gordillo, M. "La virginidad trascendente de María Madre de Dios en S. Gregorio de Nisa y en la antigua tradición de la Iglesia." *Estudios Marianos* 21 (1960) 117–55.

Gramont, Jérôme de. "Le nom le plus commun et le nom propre par excellence." *Transversalités* 148 (2019) 9–18. http://dx.doi.org/10.3917/trans.148.0007.

Granier, Jean. "Perspectivism and Interpretation." In *The New Nietzsche*, edited and translated by D. B. Allison, 190–200. Cambridge, MA: MIT Press, 1985.

Grant, Euan A. "An Eschatological Critique of Catherine Pickstock's Liturgical Theology." *New Blackfriars* 100 (2019) 493–508.

Griffiths, Paul. "Messiaen, Olivier (Eugène Prosper Charles)." In *The New Grove Dictionary of Music and Musicians*, edited by Stanley Sadie and John Tyrrell, 16:491–504. London: Macmillan, 2001.

———. *Modern Music and After*. 3rd ed. Oxford: Oxford University Press, 2010.

Grossmann, Andrea. "The Myth of Poetry: On Heidegger's Hölderlin." *Comparatist* 28 (2004) 29–38.

Gschwandtner, Christina M. "Martin Heidegger and Onto-theo-logy." In *Postmodern Apologetics? Arguments for God in Contemporary Philosophy*, 19–38. Perspectives in Continental Philosophy. New York: Fordham University Press, 2013.

Gunton, Colin E. *The One, the Three, and the Many: God, Creation, and the Culture of Modernity*. New York: Cambridge University Press, 1993.

Gusdorf, Georges. *Kierkegaard*. Paris: CNRS, 2011.

Haar, Michael, and Regina Lilly. "Heidegger and the God of Hölderlin." *Research in Phenomenology* 19 (1989) 89–100.

Haecker, Ryan. "Gothic Fireflies: The Trinitarian Grammar of Analogy in Pseudo-Dionysius the Areopagite." *Analogia* 16 (2023) 33–99.

———. "The Light of Christian Gnosis: Logic, Dialectic, and the Divine Intellect in Origen of Alexandria." In *Human and Divine Nous from Ancient to Byzantine and Renaissance Philosophy and Religion: Key Themes, Intersections, and Developments*, edited by Ilaria Ramelli. Leiden: Brill, forthcoming.

———. "The Light of the Leaf: A Theological Critique of Timothy Morton's 'Dark Ecology.'" In "Literature and Eco-Theology," edited by Alison Milbank, special issue, *Religions* 12 (2021) 755–67.

———. "Restoring Reason: Origen's Theology of Logic." PhD diss., University of Cambridge, 2021.

———. *Restoring Reason: Origen's Theology of Logic*. Baden-Baden, Germ.: Alber, forthcoming.

———. "Sacramental Engines: The Trinitarian Ontology of Computers in Charles Babbage's Analytical Engine." *Religions* 13 (2022) 757–82. https://doi.org/10.3390/rel13080757.

———. "The Silicon Bough: A Report on Hyperdigital Magic." In "Magic and Mischief: Philosophy, Theology, and the Sciences," edited by Khegan Delport and Annette Potgieter, special issue, *R&T* 30 (2023) 266–92. https://doi.org/10.1163/15743012-bja10065.

———. "Triadic Circles: On The Trinity as the Structure of the System in Origen's *On First Principles*." In *Papers Presented at the Eighteenth International Conference on Patristic Studies held in Oxford 2019: Vol. 8: Origen*, edited by Markus Vinzent, 91–100. StPatr 111. Leuven: Peeters, 2021.

———. "Via Digitalis: From the Postdigital to the Hyperdigital." *Postdigital Science and Education* 5 (2023) 823–50. https://doi.org/10.1007/s42438-023-00413-9.

Hamann, Johann Georg. "Metacritique of the Purism of Reason." In *Writings on Philosophy and Language*, edited by Kenneth Haynes, 205–19. Cambridge Texts in the History of Philosophy. Cambridge: Cambridge University Press, 2007.

Han-Pile, Béatrice. "'The Doing Is Everything': A Middle-Voice Reading of Agency in Nietzsche." *Inquiry* 63 (2019) 42–64. https://doi.org/10.1080/0020174X.2019.1669977/.

Haraway, Donna J. *Staying with the Trouble: Making Kin in the Chthulucene*. Durham: Duke University Press, 2016.

Harnack, Adolf. *Die Entstehung des Kirchlichen Dogmas*. Vol. 1 of *Lehrbuch der Dogmengeschichte*. 2nd ed. Freiburg: Mohr Siebeck, 1888.

Hart, David Bentley. *The Beauty of the Infinite: The Aesthetics of Christian Truth*. Grand Rapids: Eerdmans, 2003.

———. *The Experience of God: Being, Consciousness, Bliss*. New Haven: Yale University Press, 2013.

———. "Masks, Chimaeras, and Portmanteaux: Sergii Bulgakov and the Metaphysics of the Person." In *Building the House of Wisdom: Sergii Bulgakov and Contemporary Theology: New Approaches and Interpretations*. Edited by Barbara Hallensleben et al., 43–62. Epiphania 19. Münster: Aschendorff, 2024.

———. *The New Testament: A Translation*. 2nd ed. New Haven: Yale University Press, 2023.

Healy, Nicholas J. *The Eschatology of Hans Urs von Balthasar: Being as Communion*. Oxford Theology and Religion Monographs. Oxford: Oxford University Press, 2005.

Heath, Joshua. "Bulgakov's Linguistic Trinity." *Modern Theology* 37 (2021) 888–912.

Hegel, Georg Wilhelm Friedrich. *Hegel's "Science of Logic."* Translated by A. V. Miller. New York: Humanities, 1969.

———. *Lectures on the Philosophy of Religion: The Lectures of 1827*. Edited by Peter C. Hodgson. Translated by R. F. Brown et al. Voices Revived. Berkeley: University of California Press, 1987.

———. *Die objektive Logik*. Part 1 of *Wissenschaft der Logik*. Edited by Eva Moldenhauer and Karl Markus Michel. Vol. 5 of *Werke in zwanzig Bänden*. Frankfurt am Main: Suhrkamp, 1969.

———. *The Phenomenology of Spirit*. Edited and translated by Terry P. Pinkard and Michael Baur. Cambridge Hegel Translations. New York: Cambridge University Press, 2018.

———. *Science of Logic*. Edited by Klaus Brinkmann and Daniel O. Dahlstrom. Part 1 of *Encyclopedia of the Philosophical Sciences in Basic Outline*. Cambridge Hegel Translations. Cambridge: Cambridge University Press, 2010.

———. *The Science of Logic*. Translated by George di Giovanni. Cambridge Hegel Translations. Cambridge: Cambridge University Press, 2010.

Heidegger, Martin. *Being and Time*. Translated by John Macquarrie and Edward Robinson. New York: Harper & Row, 1927.

———. *Being and Time*. Translated by Joan Stambaugh. Revised by Dennis J. Schmidt. SUNY Series in Contemporary Continental Philosophy. New York: SUNY Press, 2010.

———. *Bremen and Freiburg Lectures: "Insight into That Which Is" and "Basic Principles of Thinking."* Translated by Andrew J. Mitchell. Studies in Continental Thought. Bloomington: Indiana University Press, 2012.

———. *Contributions to Philosophy (Of the Event)*. Translated by Richard Rojcewicz and Daniela Vallega-Neu. Studies in Continental Thought. Bloomington: Indiana University Press, 2012.

———. *Early Greek Thinking*. Translated by David Farrell Krell and Frank A. Capuzzi. San Francisco: Harper & Row, 1984.

———. "The End of Philosophy and the Task of Thinking." In *Basic Writings*, edited by David Farrell Krell, 427–50. New York: Harper & Collins, 1964.

———. *The Essence of Truth: On Plato's Cave Allegory and Theaetetus*. Translated by Ted Sadler. Athlone Contemporary European Thinkers. London: Athlone, 2002.

———. *Existence and Being*. Translated by Werner Brock. New Haven, CT: Gateway, 1953.

———. *Hölderlins Hymne "Andenken."* Edited by Curd Ochwadt. Vol. 52 of *Gesamtausgabe*. 2nd ed. Frankfurt am Main: Klostermann, 1992.

———. *Hölderlins Hymnen "Germanien" und "Der Rhein."* Edited by Susanne Ziegler. Vol. 39 of *Gesamtausgabe*. 4th ed. Frankfurt am Main: Klostermann, 2022.

———. *Identity and Difference*. Translated by Joan Stambaugh. Chicago: Harper & Collins, 1957.

———. *Introduction to Metaphysics*. Translated by Gregory Fried and Richard Polt. 2nd ed. New Haven: Yale University Press, 2014.

———. *Introduction to Philosophy—Thinking and Poetizing*. Translated by Phillip Jacques Braunstein. Bloomington: Indiana University Press, 2011.

———. *Kant and the Problem of Metaphysics*. Translated by Richard Taft. 5th ed. Studies in Continental Thought. Bloomington: Indiana University Press, 1997.

———. "Kant's Thesis About Being." In *Pathmarks*, edited and translated by William McNeill, 337–65. Cambridge: Cambridge University Press, 1998.

———. *The Metaphysical Foundations of Logic*. Translated by Michael Heim. Bloomington: Indiana University Press, 1984.

———. *Mindfulness*. Translated by Parvis Emad and Thomas Kalary. Athlone Contemporary European Thinkers. London: Continuum, 2006.

———. *Nietzsches Metaphysik. Einleitung in die Philosophie Denken und Dichten*. Edited by Curd Ochwadt. Vol. 50 of *Gesamtausgabe*. 2nd ed. Frankfurt am Main: Klostermann, 2005.

———. *On the Way to Language*. Translated by Peter D. Hertz. New York: Harper & Row, 1971.

———. "The Origin of the Work of Art." In *Basic Writings*, edited by David Farrell Krell, 139–213. New York: Harper & Collins, 1935.

———. "Plato's Doctrine of Truth." In *Pathmarks*, edited and translated by William McNeill, 155–83. Cambridge: Cambridge University Press, 1998.

———. ". . . Poetically Man Dwells . . ." In *Poetry, Language, Thought*, translated by Alfred Hofstadter, 209–27. Harper Perennial Modern Thought. New York: Perennial Classics, 2001.

———. *The Principle of Reason*. Translated by Reginald Lilly. Studies in Continental Thought. Bloomington: Indiana University Press, 1991.

———. "The Provenance of Art and the Destination of Thought (1967)." *Journal of the British Society for Phenomenology* 44 (2013) 119–28.

———. "The Question Concerning Technology." In *Basic Writings*, edited by David Farrell Krell, 307–43. New York: Harper & Collins, 1954.

———. *Seminare, 1951–1973*. Edited by Curd Ochwadt. Vol. 15 of *Gesamtausgabe*. 2nd ed. Frankfurt am Main: Klostermann, 2005.

———. "What Is Called Thinking." In *Basic Writings*, edited by David Farrell Krell, 365–93. New York: Harper & Collins, 1952.

———. "What Is Metaphysics?" In *Basic Writings*, edited by David Farrell Krell, 93–114. New York: Harper & Collins, 1929.

Hemmerle, Klaus. *Leben aus der Einheit: Eine theologische Herausforderung*. Edited by Peter Blättler. Freiburg: Herder, 1995.

———. "L'ontologia del *Paradiso '49*." *Sophia* 6 (2014) 127–37.

———. *Un pensare ri-conoscente: Scritti sulla relazione tra filosofia e teologia*. Edited by Valentina Gaudiano. Rome: Città Nuova, 2018.

———. *Thesen zu einer trinitarischen Ontologie: Deutsch und Englisch*. Edited by Wilfried Hagemann. Translated by Thomas J. Norris. Würzburg: Echt, 2020.

———. *Theses Towards a Trinitarian Ontology*. Translated by Stephen Churchyard. Brooklyn, NY: Angelico, 2020.

Herder, Johann Gottfried. *Philosophical Writings*. Edited by Michael N. Forster. Cambridge Texts in the History of Philosophy. Cambridge: Cambridge University Press, 2002.

———. *Schriften zur Litteratur und Philosophie 1780–1800*. Edited by H. D. Irmscher. Vol. 13 of *Werke*. Frankfurt am Main: Deutsche Klassik, 1998.

Higgins, Michael Joseph. "Being as Communion in Aquinas's Trinitarian Theology." *New Blackfriars* 104 (2023) 428–47. https://doi.org/10.1111/nbfr.12810.

Hilbert, David, and Stephen Cohn-Vossen. *Geometry and the Imagination*. Translated by P. Nemenyi. 2nd ed. Providence: AMS Chelsea, 1999.

Hill, Geoffrey. "Poetry as Menace and Atonement." In *Collected Critical Writings*, edited by Kenneth Haynes, 3–20. Oxford: Oxford University Press, 2008.

Hill, Leslie. *Maurice Blanchot and Fragmentary Writing: A Change of Epoch*. New York: Bloomsbury, 2012.

Hill, R. Kevin. *Nietzsche's Critiques: The Kantian Foundations of His Thought*. Oxford: Clarendon, 2003.

Hillier, Paul. *Arvo Pärt*. Oxford Studies of Composers. Oxford: Clarendon, 1997.

Hölderlin, Friedrich. *Selected Poems and Fragments*. Edited by Jeremy Adler. Translated by Michael Hamburger. Penguin Classics. London: Penguin, 1998.

Hölderlin, Johann Christian Friedrich. *Essays and Letters*. Edited and translated by Jeremy Adler and Charlie Louth. Penguin Modern Classics. London: Penguin, 2009.

Honnefelder, Ludger. "Metaphysics as a Discipline: From 'The Transcendental Philosophy of the Ancients' to Kant's Notion of Transcendental Philosophy." In *The Medieval Heritage in Early Modern Metaphysics and Modal Theory 1400–1700*, edited by Russell L. Friedman and Lauge O. Nielsen, translated by Jörn Müller with Russell L. Friedman, 53–74. New Synthese Historical Library 53. Dordrecht: Kluwer, 2003.

———. "Raison et metaphysique: Les trois étapes de la constitution de son objet chez Duns Scotus et Kant." Translated by Jacob Schmutz. *Philosophie* 70 (2001) 30–50.

———. *Scientia transcendens: Die formale Bestimmung der Seiendheit und Realität in der Metaphysik des Mittelalters und der Neuzeit (Duns Scotus, Suárez, Wolff, Kant, Peirce)*. Hamburg: Meiner, 1990.

Houellebecq, Michel. *The Map and the Territory*. Translated by Gavin Bowd. Vintage International. London: Vintage, 2012.

Houlgate, Stephen. "Hegel, Desmond, and the Problem of God's Transcendence." *Owl of Minerva* 36 (2005) 131–52.

Housset, Emmanuel. *La vocation de la personne: L'histoire du concept de personne de sa naissance augustinienne à sa redécouverte phénoménologique*. Epiméthée. Paris: PUF, 2007.

Huizenga, Tom. "The Silence and Awe of Arvo Pärt." *Deceptive Cadence*, June 2, 2014. https://www.npr.org/sections/deceptivecadence/2014/06/02/316322238/the-silence-and-awe-of-arvo-p-rt.

Hume, David. *A Treatise of Human Nature*. Edited by David Fate Norton and Mary J. Norton. Oxford Philosophical Texts. Oxford: Clarendon, 2007.

Hunt, Anne. *The Trinity: Insights from the Mystics*. Collegeville, MN: Liturgical, 2010.

Husserl, Edmund. *Cartesian Meditations*. Translated by Dorion Cairns. The Hague: Nijhoff, 1960.

———. *On the Phenomenology of the Consciousness of Internal Time (1893–1917)*. Translated by John Barnett Brough. Vol. 4 of *Husserliana: Edmund Husserl—Collected Works*. Dordrecht: Kluwer Academic, 1991.

Ignatius of Loyola. *Ignatius of Loyola: The Spiritual Exercises and Selected Works*. Classics of Western Spirituality. Edited by George E. Ganss, SJ. New York: Paulist, 1991.

Jacobi, Friedrich Heinrich. *Main Philosophical Writings and the Novel "Allwill."* Edited and translated by George di Giovanni. McGill-Queen's Studies in the History of Ideas Series 18. Montreal: McGill-Queen's University Press, 1994.

Janicaud, Dominique. *Phenomenology and the "Theological Turn": The French Debate*. Translated by Bernard G. Prusak. New York: Fordham University Press, 2000.

John XXII, Pope Saint. "Opening Address to the Council." Catholic Culture, Oct. 11, 1962. From *The Encyclicals and Other Messages of John XXIII* (Washington, DC: TPS, 1964). https://www.catholicculture.org/culture/library/view.cfm?recnum=3233.

John the Scot. *Periphyseon: On the Division of Nature*. Translated by Myra L. Uhlfelder. Eugene, OR: Wipf and Stock, 2011.

John the Scot. See also Eriugena, Johannes Scottus.

Johnson, Donald Barton. *Worlds in Regression*. Ann Arbor: Ardis, 1985.

Johnston, Sarah Iles. *Hekate Soteira: A Study of Hekate's Roles in the Chaldean Oracle and Related Literature*. American Classical Studies 21. Atlanta: Scholars, 1990.

Jolivet, Régis. *Introduction à Kierkegaard*. Paris: Fontelle, 1946.

Jonas, Hans. "The Concept of God After Auschwitz." In *Mortality and Morality: A Search for Good After Auschwitz*, edited by Lawrence Vogel, 131–43. Studies in Phenomenology and Existential Philosophy. Evanston, IL: Northwestern University Press, 1996.

Jordan, Jack. "The Unconscious." In *The Cambridge Companion to Proust*, edited by Richard Bales, 100–116. Cambridge Companions to Literature. Cambridge: Cambridge University Press, 2001.

Kandinsky, Wassily. *Concerning the Spiritual in Art*. Translated by M. T. H. Sadler. New York: Dover, 1977.

Kant, Immanuel. *Critique of Pure Reason*. Edited and translated by Paul Guyer and Allen W. Wood. Cambridge Edition of the Works of Immanuel Kant. Cambridge: Cambridge University Press, 1998.

———. "Idea for a Universal History with a Cosmopolitan Aim." In *Anthropology, History, and Education*, edited and translated by Robert B. Louden and Günter Zöller, 107–20. Cambridge Edition of the Works of Immanuel Kant. Cambridge: Cambridge University Press, 2007.

Karshan, Thomas. *Vladimir Nabokov and the Art of Play*. Oxford English Monographs. Oxford: Oxford University Press, 2011.

Keller, Catherine. *Cloud of the Impossible: Negative Theology and Planetary Entanglement*. New York: Columbia University Press, 2014.

———. *Political Theology of the Earth: Our Planetary Emergency and the Struggle for a New Public*. New York: Columbia University Press, 2018.

Keller, Catherine, and Mary-Jane Rubenstein, eds. *Entangled Worlds: Religion, Science, and New Materialisms*. Transdisciplinary Theological Colloquia. New York: Fordham University Press, 2017.

Kierkegaard, Søren. *The Concept of Irony: With Continual Reference to Socrates. Notes of Schelling's Berlin Lectures*. Edited and translated by Howard V. Hong and Edna H. Hong. Kierkegaard's Writings. Princeton, NJ: Princeton University Press, 1990.

———. *The Point of View for My Work as an Author: A Report to History, and Related Writings*. Edited by Benjamin Nelson. Translated by Walter Lowrie. Cloister Library. New York: Harper Torchbooks, 1962.

———. *Stages on Life's Way*. Edited and translated by Howard V. Hong and Edna H. Hong. Kierkegaard's Writings. Princeton: Princeton University Press, 1988.

Kilbey, Karen. *God, Evil and the Limits of Theology*. London: Bloomsbury, 2020.

Klossowski, Pierre. *Nietzsche and the Vicious Circle*. Translated by Daniel W. Smith. London: Athlone, 1997.

Koerner, Joseph Leo. *Caspar David Friedrich and the Subject of Landscape*. 2nd ed. London: Reaktion, 2014.

Kofman, Sarah. *Nietzsche and Metaphor*. Translated by Duncan Large. London: Athlone, 1993.

Lacoste, Jean-Yves. *The Appearing of God*. Translated by Oliver O'Donovan. Oxford: Oxford University Press, 2018.

Lacoue-Labarthe, Philippe. "Bye Bye Farewell." *L'Animal* 19–20 (2008) 191–98.

———. *Ending and Unending Agony: On Maurice Blanchot*. Translated by Hannes Opelz. Lit Z. Fordham, NY: Fordham University Press, 2015.

———. *Heidegger, Art and Politics: The Fiction of the Political*. Translated by Chris Turner. Oxford: Blackwell, 1990.

———. *Typography: Mimesis, Philosophy, Politics*. Translated by Christopher Fynsk. Stanford, CA: Stanford University Press, 1998.

Lakoff, George, and Mark Johnson. *Philosophy in the Flesh: The Embodied Mind and Its Challenge to Western Thought*. New York: Basic, 1999.

Land, Nick. *Fanged Noumena: Collected Writings, 1987–2007*. London: Urbanomic, 2012.

———. *Thirst for Annihilation: Georges Bataille and Virulent Nihilism*. London: Routledge, 1996.

Law, David R. "Negative Theology in Heidegger's *Beiträge zur Philosophie*." *International Journal for Philosophy of Religion* 48 (2000) 139–56.

Leung, King-Ho. "Ontology and Anti-Platonism: Reconsidering Colin Gunton's Trinitarian Theology." *Neue Zeitschrift für Systematische Theologie und Religionsphilosophie* 62 (2020) 419–40. https://doi.org/10.1515/nzsth-2020-0022.

———. "Transcendentality and the Gift: On Gunton, Milbank, and Trinitarian Metaphysics." *Modern Theology* 38 (2022) 81–99.

Leung, King-Ho, and John Milbank. "Postmodern Philosophy and Theology." *St Andrews Encyclopaedia of Theology*, Aug. 24, 2022. Edited by Brendan N. Wolfe et al. https://www.saet.ac.uk/Christianity/PostmodernPhilosophyandTheology.

Leibniz, G. W. *Theodicy: Essays on the Goodness of God, the Freedom of Man, and the Origin of Evil*. Edited by Austin Farrar. Translated by E. M. Huggard. La Salle, IL: Open Court, 1952.

Levinas, Emmanuel. "Ideology and Idealism." In *Of God Who Comes To Mind*, translated by Bettina Bergo, 3–14. Meridian: Crossing Aesthetics. Stanford, CA: Stanford University Press, 1998.

———. "Philosophy and Transcendence." In *Alterity and Transcendence*, translated by Michael B. Smith, 6–10. London: Athlone, 1999.

———. *Time and the Other (and Additional Essays)*. Translated by Richard A. Cohen. Pittsburgh: Duquesne University Press, 1990.

Libera, Alain de. *Naissance du sujet*. Vol. 1 of *Archéologie du sujet*. Paris: Vrin, 2016.

Liebert, Robert S. "Raphael, Michelangelo, Sebastiano: High Renaissance Rivalry." *Notes in the History of Art* 3 (1984) 60–68. https://doi.org/10.1086/sou.3.2.23207820.

Louth, Andrew. "Sergii Bulgakov and the Task of Theology." *Irish Theological Quarterly* 74 (2009) 243–57.

Lublow, Arthur. "The Sound of Spirit." *New York Times Magazine*, Oct. 15, 2010. https://www.nytimes.com/2010/10/17/magazine/17part-t.html.

Lyonhart, J. D. *The Journey of God: Christianity in Six Movements*. Lisle, IL: IVP Academic, 2025.

———. *MonoThreeism: An Absurdly Arrogant Attempt to Answer All the Problems of the Last 2000 Years in One Night at a Pub*. Eugene, OR: Cascade, 2021.

MacDonald, George. *Alec Forbes of Howglen*. 3 vols. Liepzig: Tauchnitz, 1865.

Macek, Petr. "'The Golden Thread of Freedom': Impulses for Considerations on the Relations Between the Trinitarian Ontology and Social Reality in the Work of D. C. Schindler." *Acta Universitatis Carolinae Theologica* 11 (2021) 145–63.

MacIntyre, Alasdair. *Three Rival Versions of Moral Enquiry: Encyclopaedia, Genealogy, and Tradition*. Notre Dame: University of Notre Dame Press, 1990.

Mackey, Louis. *Kierkegaard: A Kind of Poet*. Anniversary Collection. Philadelphia: University of Pennsylvania Press, 1972.

Margolis, Joseph. *Reinventing Pragmatism: American Philosophy at the End of the Twentieth Century*. Ithaca, NY: Cornell University Press, 2018.

Marks, Herbert. "Hollowed Names: Vox and Vanitas in the *Purgatorio*." *Dante Studies* 110 (1992) 135–78.

Marion, Jean-Luc. *The Erotic Phenomenon*. Translated by Stephen E. Lewis. Chicago: University of Chicago Press, 2008.

———. *Givenness & Hermeneutics*. Translated by Jean-Pierre Lafouge. Père Marquette Lecture in Theology 2013. Milwaukee: Marquette University Press, 2013.

———. *God Without Being: Hors-Texte*. Translated by Thomas A. Carlson. 2nd ed. Chicago: University of Chicago Press, 2012.

Mascolo, Dionys. *Le communisme: Révolution et communication, ou, La dialectique des valeurs et des besoins*. Fécamp, Fr.: Lignes, 2018.

Maspero, Giulio. *The Cappadocian Reshaping of Metaphysics: Relational Being*. Cambridge: Cambridge University Press, 2023.

———. *Dio trino perché vivo: Lo Spirito di Dio e lo spirito dell'uomo nella patristica greca*. Letteratura cristiana antica. Brescia: Morcelliana, 2018.

———. *Essere e relazione: L'ontologia trinitaria di Gregorio di Nissa*. Teologia. Rome: Città Nuova, 2013.

———. "El misterio de la Virgen toda limpia en Gregorio de Nisa." *Scripta de Maria* 2 (2004) 183–205.

———. "Patristic Trinitarian Ontology." In *Rethinking Trinitarian Theology: Disputed Questions and Contemporary Issues in Trinitarian Theology*, edited by Robert J. Wozniak and Giulio Maspero, 211–29. London: T&T Clark, 2012.

———. *Uno perché trino: Breve introduzione al trattato su Dio*. Fuori collana. Siena: Cantagalli, 2011.

———. "Ratzinger's Trinitarian Ontology and Its Patristic Roots: The Breakthrough of Introduction to Christianity." *Wrocławski Przegląd Teologiczny* 31 (2023) 5–33.

———. *Rethinking the Filioque with the Greek Fathers*. Grand Rapids: Eerdmans, 2023.

———. "Trinitarian Ontology and Interdisciplinary Research." In *Social Science, Philosophy and Theology in Dialogue: A Relational Perspective*, edited by Pierpaolo Donati et al., 74–93. New York: Routledge, 2019.

Mateo-Seco, L. F. "La mariología de San Gregorio de Nisa." *ScrTh* 10 (1978) 409–66.

Mazzer, Stefano. *Lì amò fino alla fine: Il nulla-tutto dell'amore, tra filosofia, mistica e teologia*. Rome: Città Nuova, 2014.

McFarland, Ian. *From Nothing: A Theology of Creation*. Louisville: Westminster John Knox, 2014.

McGrath, Alister E. "The Doctrine of the Trinity: Intellectual Construct or Ontological Reality? Reflections from the Philosophy of Science." *International Journal of Systematic Theology* 26 (2024) 70–90. https://doi.org/10.1111/ijst.12612.

Megay, Joyce N. *Bergson et Proust: Essai de mise au point de la question de l'influence de Bergson sur Proust*. Essais d'art et de philosophie. Paris: Vrin, 1976.

Merleau-Ponty, Maurice. *The Structure of Behavior*. Translated by Alden L. Fisher. Pittsburgh: Duquesne University Press, 1983.

———. *The Visible and the Invisible*. Edited by Claude Lefort. Translated by Alphonso Lingis. Studies in Phenomenology and Existential Philosophy. Evanston, IL: Northwestern University Press, 1968.

Messiaen, Olivier. "Préface." In *Quatuor pour la fin du temps*, unnumbered pages. Paris: Durand, 1942.

Meyer, Priscilla. *Find What the Sailor Has Hidden: Vladimir Nabokov's "Pale Fire."* Middletown, CT: Wesleyan University Press, 1988.

Milbank, John. *Being Reconciled: Ontology and Pardon*. Routledge Radical Orthodoxy. London: Routledge, 2003.

———. *Beyond Secular Order: The Representation of Being and the Representation of the People*. Illuminations: Theory & Religion. Oxford: Blackwell, 2014.

———. "Can a Gift be Given? Prolegomena to a Future Trinitarian Metaphysics." *Modern Theology* 11 (1995) 119–61.

———. "The Dissolution of Divine Government: Gilson and the 'Scotus Story.'" In *John Duns Scotus: Introduction to His Fundamental Positions*, by Étienne Gilson, 538–

76. Translated by James G. Colbert. Illuminating Modernity. London: Bloomsbury, 2019.

———. Foreword to *The Tragedy of Philosophy*, by Sergij Bulgakov. Translated by Stephen Churchyard. New York: Angelico, 2020.

———. "Genealogies of Truth: Theology, Philosophy and History." *Modern Theology* 39 (2023) 708–72.

———. "Hume Versus Kant: Faith, Reason and Feeling." *Modern Theology* 27 (2011) 276–97.

———. "Knowledge: The Theological Critique of Philosophy in Hamann and Jacobi." In *Radical Orthodoxy: A New Theology*, edited by John Milbank et al., 21–37. Routledge Radical Orthodoxy. London: Routledge, 1999.

———. "Materialism and Transcendence." In *Theology and the Political*, edited by Creston Davis et al., 393–426. Durham: Duke University Press, 2005.

———. "Number and the Between." In *William Desmond's Philosophy Between Metaphysics, Religion, Ethics and Aesthetics: Thinking Metaxologically*, edited by Dennis Vanden Auweele, 15–44. London: Palgrave-MacMillan, 2018.

———. "One in Three and Two in One: The Double Coincidence of Opposites in Nicholas of Cusa." In *Why We Need Cusanus/Warum wir Cusanus brauchen*, edited by Enrico Peroli and Marco Moschini, 43–89. Münster: Aschendorff, 2022.

———. "Orthodoxy, Knowledge, and Freedom." In *Exorcising Philosophical Modernity: Cyril O'Regan and Christian Discourse After Modernity*, edited by Philip John Paul Gonzalez, 229–53. Veritas. Eugene OR: Wipf and Stock, 2020.

———. "Postmodern Critical Augustinianism: A Short *Summa* in Forty-Two Responses to Unasked Questions." *Modern Theology* 7 (1991) 225–37.

———. "Problematizing the Secular: The Post-Postmodern Problematic." In *Shadow of Spirit: Postmodernism and Religion*, edited by Philippa Berry and Andrew Wernick, 30–44. London: Routledge, 1993.

———. "Sacred Triads: Augustine and the Indo-European Soul." *Modern Theology* 13 (1997) 451–74.

———. "The Second Difference: For a Trinitarianism Without Reserve." *Modern Theology* 2 (1986) 213–34.

———. "Sophia and Theurgy." In *Encounter Between Eastern Orthodoxy and Radical Orthodoxy: Transfiguring the World Through the Word*, edited by Adrian Pabst and Christoph Schneider, 45–73. Abingdon-on-Thames, UK: Taylor & Francis, 2009.

———. "The Sublime in Kierkegaard." *Heythrop Journal* 37 (1996) 298–321.

———. *The Suspended Middle: Henri De Lubac and the Debate Concerning the Supernatural*. 2nd ed. Grand Rapids: Eerdmans, 2014.

———. *Theology and Social Theory: Beyond Secular Reason*. Oxford: Blackwell, 1991.

———. *Theology and Social Theory: Beyond Secular Reason*. 2nd ed. Oxford: Blackwell, 2006.

———. "Trinitarian Ontology and the Division of Being: A Rosminian Reflection." *Sophia* 3 (2021) 189–231.

———. *The Word Made Strange: Theology, Language, Culture*. Oxford: Blackwell, 1997.

Milbank, John, et al., eds. *Radical Orthodoxy: A New Theology*. Routledge Radical Orthodoxy. London: Routledge, 1999.

Mitchell, Andrew J. *The Fourfold: Reading the Late Heidegger*. Edited by Anthony J. Steinbock. Studies in Phenomenology and Existential Philosophy. Evanston, IL: Northwestern University Press, 2015.

Moltmann, Jürgen. *The Trinity and the Kingdom: The Doctrine of God*. Translated by M. Kohl. London: SCM, 1981.

Montemaggi, Vittorio. *Reading Dante's "Commedia" as Theology: Divinity Realized in Human Encounter*. Oxford: Oxford University Press, 2016.

Moran, Dermot. "'Officina Omnium' or 'Notio Quaedam Intellectualis in Mente Divina Aeternaliter Facta.'" In *L'homme et son univers au moyen âge: Actes du septième Congrès International de Philosophie Médiévale (30 août–4 septembre 1982)*, edited by Christian Wenin, 195–204. Philosophes médiévaux. Louvain-la-Neuve, Belg.: Éditions de l'Institut Supérieur de Philosophie, 1986.

Morrison, Elise. "The Re-Enchantment of the Gift: Exchange in Dante's Paradiso as a Response to Derrida's Account of Unilateral Donation." Presentation at the European Academy of Religion annual conference, St Andrews, Scot., June 2023.

Morton, Timothy. *Being Ecological*. London: Pelican, 2018.

Moulin, Isabelle. "Freedom and Necessity of the Creative Act: The Cosmological Aspect of Kandinsky's Principle of Inner Necessity." *Modern Theology* 40 (2024) 82–96.

———. "La philosophie du Verbe: L'union de la christologie et de la dialectique chez Jean Scot Erigène." *RThom* 109 (2009) 385–411.

———. "Voir l'invisible: L'expérience métaphysique de la vérité dans l'art; Le cas de l'espace." In *Kandinsky: Expérience artistique et culture du spirituel*, edited by Isabelle Moulin and Phillipe Sers, 53–71. Mesnil-Saint-Loup, Fr.: Quatre Vivants, 2023.

Murphy, Francesca Aran. "The Influence of Maurice Blondel." In *T&T Clark Companion to Henri de Lubac*, edited by Jordan Hillebert, 57–92. Bloomsbury Companions. London: T&T Clark, 2017.

Nabokov, Vladimir. *Collected Poems*. Edited by Thomas Karshan. Translated by Dmitri Nabokov. Penguin Classics. London: Penguin, 2012.

———. *Pale Fire*. New York: Vintage, 1989.

———. *Think, Write, Speak: Uncollected Essays, Reviews, Interviews and Letters to the Editor*. Edited by Brian Boyd and Anastasia Tolstoy. London: Penguin, 2019.

Nadler, Steven M. "Arnauld, Descartes, and Transubstantiation: Reconciling Cartesian Metaphysics and Real Presence." *Journal of the History of Ideas* 49 (1988) 229–46.

Negarestani, Reza. *Intelligence and Spirit*. London: Urbanomic, 2018.

Nietzsche, Friedrich Wilhelm. *Anthologien: Vom vornehmen Menschen. Vergeblichkeit. Von Gut und Böse*. Edited by Hans Urs von Balthasar. Revised by Alois M. Haas. Studienausgabe der frühen Schriften Hans Urs von Balthasar 5. Einsiedeln, Switz.: Johannes, 2000.

———. *"The Anti-Christ," "Ecce Homo," "Twilight of the Idols," and Other Writings*. Edited by Aaron Ridley and Judith Norman. Cambridge Texts in the History of Philosophy. Cambridge: Cambridge University Press, 2005.

———. *Beyond Good and Evil*. Translated by R. J. Hollingdale. Penguin Classics. Middlesex: Penguin, 1973.

———. *Beyond Good and Evil: Prelude to a Philosophy of the Future*. Edited by Rolf-Peter Horstmann and Judith Norman. Cambridge Texts in the History of Philosophy. Cambridge: Cambridge University Press, 2001.

———. *"The Birth of Tragedy" and Other Writings*. Edited by Raymond Geuss and Ronald Speirs. Cambridge Texts in the History of Philosophy. Cambridge: Cambridge University Press, 1999.

———. *The Birth of Tragedy: Out of the Spirit of Music*. Edited by Michael Tanner. Translated by Shaun Whiteside. Penguin Classics. London: Penguin, 1993.

———. *The Gay Science: With a Prelude in German Rhymes and an Appendix of Songs*. Edited and translated by Walter Kaufman. New York: Vintage, 1974.

———. *The Gay Science: With a Prelude in German Rhymes and an Appendix of Songs*. Edited by Bernard Williams. Translated by Josefine Nauckhoff and Adrian Del Caro. Cambridge Texts in the History of Philosophy. Cambridge: Cambridge University Press, 2001.

———. *Human, All Too Human: A Book for Free Spirits*. Translated by R. J. Hollingdale. Cambridge Texts in the History of Philosophy. Cambridge: Cambridge University Press, 1996.

———. *"On the Genealogy of Morality" and Other Writings*. Edited by Keith Ansell-Pearson. Translated by Carol Diethe. Rev. ed. Cambridge Texts in the History of Political Thought. Cambridge: Cambridge University Press, 2006.

———. "On Truth and Lying in a Non-Moral Sense." In *"The Birth of Tragedy" and Other Writings*, edited by Raymond Geuss and Ronald Speirs, 139–53. Cambridge Texts in the History of Philosophy. Cambridge: Cambridge University Press, 2007.

———. *Philosophy in the Tragic Age of the Greeks*. Translated by Marianne Cowan. Washington DC: Regnery, 2012.

———. *Sämtliche Werke: Kritische Studienausgabe*. Edited by Giorgio Colli and Mazzino Montinari. 15 vols. Berin: De Gruyter, 1980.

———. *Thus Spoke Zarathustra*. Edited by Adrian Del Caro and Robert Pippin. Cambridge Texts in the History of Philosophy. Cambridge: Cambridge University Press, 2006.

———. *Writings from the Early Notebooks*. Edited by Raymond Geuss and Alexander Nehamas. Cambridge Texts in the History of Philosophy. Cambridge: Cambridge University Press, 2009.

———. *Writings from the Late Notebooks*. Edited by Rüdiger Bittner. Translated by Kate Sturge. Cambridge Texts in the History of Philosophy. Cambridge: Cambridge University Press, 2023.

Nohrnberg, James. "The Autobiographical Imperative and the Necessity of 'Dante': *Purgatorio* 30.55." *Modern Philology* 101 (2003) 1–47.

Obrigewitsch, Alex. "Between Narcissus and Echo: The Agony of the Subject." *Bollettino Filosofico* 36 (2021) 287–98.

———. "How Is Translation Possible? The Secret of Maurice Blanchot." *Journal of Comparative Literature & Aesthetics* 45 (2022) 40–49.

———. "Tragic Agony & the Mortality of Thought: Rethinking the Relation Between Philosophy and Literature." PhD diss., University of Sussex, 2024.

Oltvai, Kristóf. "The Sign of Jonah: Divine Abandonment as Human Freedom in Karl Barth's Mature Trinitarian Ontology." *Journal for Continental Philosophy of Religion* 6 (2023) 189–223. https://doi.org/10.1163/25889613-bja10054.

Origen of Alexandria. *Commentary on the Gospel According to John, Books 1–10*. Translated by Ronald E. Heine. Fathers of the Church: A New Translation. Washington, DC: Catholic University of America Press, 1989.

———. *Commentary on the Gospel According to John, Books 13–32*. Translated by Ronald E. Heine. Fathers of the Church: A New Translation. Washington, DC: Catholic University of America Press, 1993.

———. *Homilies on Genesis and Exodus*. Translated by Ronald E. Heine. Fathers of the Church: A New Translation. Washington, DC: Catholic University of America Press, 1981.

———. *On First Principles*. Edited and translated by John Behr. 2 vols. Oxford Early Christian Texts. Oxford: Oxford University Press, 2017.

O'Regan, Cyril. *The Anatomy of Misremembering: Von Balthasar's Response to Philosophical Modernity*. 2 vols. Chestnut Ridge, NY: Crossroad, 2014.

Pascal, Blaise. "Pascal's Memorial." College of St. Benedict/Saint John's University, 1999. Translated by Elizabeth T. Knuth. http://www.users.csbsju.edu/~eknuth/pascal.html.

———. *Pensées*. Translated by A. J. Krailsheimer. Penguin Classics. London: Penguin, 1995.

Pazzini, Domenico. *In principio era il Logos: Origene e il prologo del Vangelo di Giovanni*. Brescia: Paideia, 1983.

———. "L'interpretazione del Prologo di Giovanni in Origene e nella patristica greca." *Annali di Storia dell'Esegesi* 11 (1994) 45–56.

Peirce, Charles S. *Philosophical Writings of Peirce*. Edited by Justus Buchler. New York: Dover, 2011.

Pelster, Franz. "Roger Marston O.F.M. (f 1303), ein englischer Vertreter des Augustinismus." *Scholastik* 3 (1928) 526–56. https://doi.org/10.71742/sch.v3i4.83526.

Pépin, J. "Attitudes d'Augustin devant le vocabulaire philosophique grec." In *La langue latine, langue de la philosophie: Actes du colloque de Rome (17-19 mai 1990)*, 277–307. Collections de l'École Française de Rome 161. Rome: École Française de Rome Press, 1992.

Pérez de Laborda, Miguel. "La preesistenza delle perfezioni in Dio: L'apofatismo di san Tommaso." *AT* 21 (2007) 279–98.

Peterson, Erik. *Theologische Traktate*. Vol. 1 of *Ausgewählte Schriften*. Würzburg: Echter, 1994.

Pfau, Thomas. *Minding the Modern: Human Agency, Intellectual Traditions, and Responsible Knowledge*. Notre Dame: Notre Dame University Press, 2013.

Pickstock, Catherine. *After Writing: On the Liturgical Consummation of Philosophy*. Oxford: Blackwell, 1998.

———. *Aspects of Truth: A New Religious Metaphysics*. Cambridge: Cambridge University Press, 2020.

———. "The Cosmic Poetics of Jean-Louis Chrétien." In *Fragility and Transcendence: Essays on the Thought of Jean-Louis Chrétien*, edited by Jeffrey Bloechl, 131–72. Reframing Continental Philosophy of Religion. Lanham, MD: Rowman & Littlefield, 2023.

———. "Duns Scotus: His Historical and Contemporary Significance." *Modern Theology* 21 (2005) 543–74.

———. "The Late Arrival of Language: Word, Nature, and the Divine in Plato's *Cratylus*." *Modern Theology* 27 (2011) 238–62.

———. "Messiaen and Deleuze: The Musico-Theological Critique of Modernism and Postmodernism." *Theory, Culture & Society* 25 (2008) 173–91.

———. *Repetition and Identity*. Literary Agenda. Oxford: Oxford University Press, 2013.

Pili, Emanuele. "L'ontologia trinitaria: Che cosa 'non' è?" *Sophia* 9 (2017) 47–57.

Plato. *The Collected Dialogues of Plato, Including the Letters*. Edited by Edith Hamilton and Huntington Cairns. Translated by Paul Shorey. Bollingen 71. Princeton: Princeton University Press, 1961.

Pöggeler, Otto. *Der Denkweg Martin Heideggers*. Pfullingen, Germ.: Neske, 1963.

Polk, Timothy H. "Job: Edification Against Theodicy." In *The Old Testament*, edited by Lee C. Barrett and Jon Stewart, 115–43. Vol. 1 of *Kierkegaard and the Bible*. Kierkegaard Research: Sources, Reception and Resources 1. London: Routledge, 2016.

Possen, David D. "Meno: Kierkegaard and the Doctrine of Recollection." In *Socrates and Plato*, edited by Jon Stewart and Katalin Nun, 27–44. Vol. 1 of *Kierkegaard and the Greek World*. Kierkegaard Research: Sources, Reception and Resources 2. London: Routledge, 2016.

Poulet, Georges. *Études sur le temps humain*. 4 vols. Paris: Plon, 1952.

Priest, Graham. *One: Being an Investigation into the Unity of Reality and of Its Parts, Including the Singular Object Which Is Nothingness*. Oxford: Oxford University Press, 2014.

Proust, Marcel. "A propos du 'style' de Flaubert." In *Écrits sur l'art*, edited by Jérôme Picon, 314–29. Paris: Flammarion, 1999.

———. *Correspondance*. Edited by Philip Kolb. 21 vols. Paris: Plon, 1985.

Prudhomme, Jeff Owen. "The Passing-By of the Ultimate God: The Theological Assessment of Modernity in Heidegger's *Beiträge zur Philosophie*." *JAAR* 61 (1993) 443–54.

Przywara, Erich. *Analogia Entis: Metaphysics; Original Structure and Universal Rhythm*. Translated by John R. Betz and David Bentley Hart. Ressourcement: Retrieval and Renewal in Catholic Thought. Grand Rapids: Eerdmans, 2014.

Pseudo-Dionysius. "The Celestial Hierarchy." In *Pseudo-Dionysius: The Complete Works*, translated by Colm Luibheid, 143–91. Notes and translation collaboration by Paul Rorem. Classics of Western Spirituality. Mahwah, NJ: Paulist, 1987.

———. "The Mystical Theology." In *Pseudo-Dionysius: The Complete Works*, translated by Colm Luibheid, 133–42. Notes and translation collaboration by Paul Rorem. Classics of Western Spirituality. Mahwah, NJ: Paulist, 1987.

Purslow, Alfred. *Poesis and the Inner Experience of God: On the Poetry of Charles Péguy and Zorica Latcu Teodosi*. Presentation at the European Academy of Religion annual conference, St. Andrews, Scot., June 2023.

Radke, Gary M., ed. *The Gates of Paradise: Lorenzo Ghiberti's Renaissance Masterpiece*. High Museum of Art. New Haven: Yale University Press, 2007.

Rahner, Karl. *Hearer of the Word: Laying the Foundation for a Philosophy of Religion*. Edited by Andrew Tallon. Translated by Joseph Donceel. New York: Continuum, 1997.

———. *Spirit in the World*. Translated by William Dych. New York: Continuum, 1994.

Ramelli, Ilaria L. E. "Origen's Anti-Subordinationism and Its Heritage in the Nicene and Cappadocian Line." *VC* 65 (2011) 21–49.

Reale, Giovanni. *Toward a New Interpretation of Plato*. Edited and Translated by John R. Catan and Richard Davies. Washington, DC: Catholic University of America Press, 1984.

Renczes, Ph. G. "La patristica e la metafisica nel secolo XX." *Gregorianum* 90 (2009) 76–85.

Restagno, Enzo, et al. *Arvo Pärt in Conversation*. Translated by Robert J. Crow. Estonian Literature. Champaign, IL: Dalkey Archive, 2012.

Richard of St. Victor. *On the Trinity: English Translation and Commentary*. Translated by Ruben Angelici. Illustrated ed. Eugene, OR: Cascade, 2011.

Ricoeur, Paul. *Temps et récit*. Edited by François Wahl. 3 vols. Ordre philosophique. Paris: Seuil, 1984.

———. *Time and Narrative*. Translated by Kathleen McLaughlin [Blamey] and David Pellauer. 3 vols. Chicago: University of Chicago Press, 1984–88.

Rischin, Rebecca. *For the End of Time: The Story of the Messiaen Quartet*. Ithaca, NY: Cornell University Press, 2003.

Robinette, Brian D. *The Difference Nothing Makes: Creation, Christ, Contemplation*. Notre Dame: University of Notre Dame Press, 2023.

Rockmore, Tom. *On Heidegger's Nazism and Philosophy*. Berkeley: University of California Press, 1992.

Rorty, Richard. *Philosophy and the Mirror of Nature*. Princeton Classics. Princeton: Princeton University Press, 1980.

Rose, Gillian. *Hegel Contra Sociology*. London: Verso, 1995.

———. *Love's Work: A Reckoning with Life*. New York: New York Review, 1995.

Rosmini, Antonio. *Teosofia*. 5 vols. Torino: Società Editrice di Libri di Filosofia, 1893.

Ross, Alex. "Consolations: The Uncanny Voice of Arvo Pärt." *New Yorker*, Dec. 2, 2002. https://www.newyorker.com/magazine/2002/12/02/consolations.

Ross, Maggie. *Writing the Icon Heart: In Silence Beholding*. Abingdon, UK: Bible Reading Fellowship, 2011.

Ruether, Rosemary Radford. *Gaia & God: An Ecofeminist Theology of Earth Healing*. San Francisco: Harper & Row, 1992.

Sallis, John. "Dionysus—In Excess of Metaphysics." In *Exceedingly Nietzsche: Aspects of Contemporary Nietzsche-Interpretation*, edited by David Farrell Krell and David Wood, 3–12. Warwick Studies in Philosophy and Literature. London: Routledge, 1988.

Salomé, Lou. *Nietzsche*. Edited and translated by Siegfried Mandel. Chicago: University of Illinois Press, 2001.

Sandner, Wolfgang. "Program Notes." *Tabula Rasa*. Translated by Anne Cattaneo. ECM New Series 1275, 1984, compact disc.

Schelling, F. W. J. "On the Possibility of a Form of All Philosophy." In *The Unconditioned in Human Knowledge: Four Early Essays (1794–1796)*, translated by Fritz Marti, 38–55. Cranbury, NJ: Associated University Presses, 1980.

———. "'Presentation of My System of Philosophy' and 'Further Presentations from the System of Philosophy.'" In *The Philosophical Rupture Between Fichte and Schelling: Selected Texts and Correspondence (1800–1802)*, by J. G. Fichte and F. W. J. Schelling, edited and translated by Michael G. Vater and David W. Wood, 141–226. SUNY Series in Contemporary Continental Philosophy. Albany: SUNY Press, 2012.

Schluga, Hans. *Heidegger's Crisis: Philosophy and Politics in Nazi Germany*. Cambridge: Harvard University Press, 1993.

Schmaus, Michael. *Die trinitarischen Lehrdifferenzen*. Part 2 of *Der Liber propugnatorius des Thomas Anglicus und die Lehrunterschiede zwischen Thomas von Aquin und Duns Scotus*. Beiträge zur Geschichte der Philosophie des Mittelalters: Texte und Untersuchungen 29. Münster: Aschendorff, 1930.

Schneider, Johannes. *Die Lehre vom dreieinigen Gott in der Schule des Petrus Lombardus.* Munich: Hueber, 1961.

Schürmann, Reiner. "In the Name of the One." In *Broken Hegemonies*, translated by Reginald Lilly, 48–188. Studies in Continental Thought. Bloomington: Indiana University Press, 2003.

Sciacca, Michele Frederico. *Ontologia triadica e trinitaria: Discorso metafisico teologico.* Edited by N. Incardona. Palermo: L'Epos, 1990.

Shakespeare, William. *The New Oxford Shakespeare: The Complete Works.* Edited by Gary Taylor et al. Modern Critical Edition. Oxford: Oxford University Press, 2016.

Shakespeare, William, and Thomas Middleton. *The Life of Timon of Athens.* Edited by John Jowett. Oxford Shakespeare. Oxford: Oxford University Press, 2004.

Shapley, Fern Rusk, and Clarence Kennedy. "Brunelleschi in Competition with Ghiberti." *Art Bulletin* 5 (1922) 31–34.

Schattuck, Roger. *Proust's Binoculars: A Study of Memory, Time, and Recognition in "À la recherche du temps perdu."* New York: Random House, 1963.

Shaw, Gregory. *Theurgy and the Soul: The Neoplatonism of Iamblichus.* 2nd ed. New York: Angelico, 2014.

Shenton, Andrew. "Five Quartets: The Search for the Still Point of the Turning World in the War Quartets of T. S. Eliot and Olivier Messiaen." In *Messiaen the Theologian*, edited by Andrew Shenton, 145–62. New York: Taylor & Francis, 2016.

———. "Introduction: The Essential and Phenomenal Arvo Pärt." In *The Cambridge Companion to Arvo Pärt*, edited by Andrew Shenton, 1–9. Cambridge Companions to Music. Cambridge: Cambridge University Press, 2012.

Smith, K. F. "Hekate's Suppers." In *The Goddess Hekate*, edited by Stephen Ronan, 57–64. Studies in Ancient Pagan and Christian Religion & Philosophy. Hastings, Eng.: Chthonios, 1992.

Solovyov, Vladimir. *Lectures on the Divine Humanity.* Translated by Boris Jakim. Library of Russian Philosophy. New York: Lindisfarne, 1995.

Soskice, Janet. *Naming God: Addressing the Divine in Philosophy, Theology and Scripture.* Cambridge: Cambridge University Press, 2023.

Souriau, Étienne. *"The Different Modes of Existence," followed by "On the Work to Be Made."* Translated by Erik Beranek and Tim Howles. Univocal. Minneapolis: University of Minnesota Press, 2015.

Spacehog. "In the Meantime." Track 1 on *Resident Alien*. Elektra Entertainment, 1995, compact disc.

Spinoza, Baruch. *Ethics.* Translated by W. H. White and A. K. Stirling. St. Ives, Eng.: Wordsworth, 2001.

Staley, Kevin M. "Towards a Trinitarian Ontology: Roscelin, Anselm, and Rahner on Overcoming Mere Monotheism." *Saint Anselm Journal* 17 (2022) 47–85.

Starhawk [Miriam Simos]. *Dreaming the Dark: Magic, Sex and Politics.* Boston: Beacon, 1982.

Stein, Edith [Teresa Benedicta of the Cross]. *Der Aufbau der menschlichen Person: Vorlesung zur philosophischen Anthropologie.* Edited by Beate Beckmann-Zöller. Edith Stein Gesamtausgabe 14. Freiburg: Herder, 2004.

———. *Endliches und Ewiges Sein: Versuch eines Aufstieges zum Sinn des Seins.* Edited by Andreas Uwe Müller. Edith Stein Gesamtausgabe 11. Freiburg: Herder, 2006.

———. *Finite and Eternal Being: An Attempt at an Ascent to the Meaning of Being.* Edited by L. Gelber and Romaeus Leuven. Translated by Kurt F. Reinhardt. Collected Works of Edith Stein 9. Washington, DC: Institute for Carmelite Studies, 2002.

———. *The Hidden Life: Essays, Meditations, Spiritual Texts.* Edited by L. Gelber and Michael Linssen. Translated by Waltraut Stein. Collected Works of Edith Stein 4. Washington, DC: Institute for Carmelite Studies, 1992.

———. *The Science of the Cross.* Edited by L. Gelber and Romaeus Leuven. Translated by Josephine Koeppel. Collected Works of Edith Stein 6. Washington, DC: Institute for Carmelite Studies, 2003.

Susanka, Joseph. "An Interview with Metropolitan Hilarion Alfeyev." *Crisis Magazine.* Feb. 28, 2012. https://www.crisismagazine.com/2012/an-interview-with-metropolitan-hilarion-alfeyev.

Tanner, Kathryn. *Jesus, Humanity, and the Trinity: A Systematic Theology in Brief.* Minneapolis: Fortress, 2001.

Tertullian of Carthage. "On the Flesh of Christ." In *The Ante-Nicene Fathers,* edited by Alexander Roberts et al., 3:521–43. Repr., Edinburgh: T&T Clark, 1993.

Thayer, H. S., ed. *Pragmatism: The Classic Writings.* Indianapolis: Dover, 1982.

Thompson, Iain. "The End of Onto-Theology: Understanding Heidegger's Turn, Method, and Politics." PhD diss., University of California San Diego, 1999.

Tonstad, Linn Marie. *God and Difference: The Trinity, Sexuality, and the Transformation of Finitude.* Gender, Theology and Spirituality. New York: Routledge, 2015.

Tritten, Tyler. *Beyond Presence: The Late F. W. J. Schelling's Criticism of Metaphysics.* Quellen und Studien zur Philosophie 111. Berlin: De Gruyter, 2012.

Ulrich, Ferdinand. *Homo Abyssus: The Drama of the Question of Being.* Translated by D. C. Schindler. Washington, DC: Humanum Academic, 2018.

Vahanian, Noëlle. *The Rebellious No: Variations on a Secular Theology of Language.* Perspectives in Continental Philosophy. New York: Fordham University Press, 2014.

Vigorelli, Ilaria. "Ontology and Existence: *Schésis* of the Soul in Gregory of Nyssa's *In Canticum Canticorum.*" In *Gregory of Nyssa: "In Canticum Canticorum"; Analytical and Supporting Studies; Proceedings of the 13th International Colloquium on Gregory of Nyssa (Rome, 17–20 September 2014),* edited by Giulio Maspero et al., 527–38. VCSupp 150. Leiden: Brill, 2018. https://doi.org/10.1163/9789004382046_030.

Vioulac, Jean. *Apocalypse of Truth: Heideggerian Meditations.* Translated by Matthew J. Peterson. Chicago: University of Chicago Press, 2021.

Volek, Peter. "Relations in Ramon Llull's Trinitarian Ontology." *Religions* 14 (2023) 909. https://doi.org/10.3390/rel14070909.

Walker, Paul Robert. *The Feud That Sparked the Renaissance: How Brunelleschi and Ghiberti Changed the Art World.* New York: Morrow, 2002.

Ward, Graham. "On Time and Salvation: The Eschatology of Emmanuel Levinas." In *Facing the Other: The Ethics of Emmanuel Levinas,* edited by Seán Hand, 153–72. Routledge Jewish Philosophy. Richmond, UK: Curzon, 1996.

Weil, Simone. *Oppression and Liberty.* Translated by Arthur Wills and John Petrie. London: Routledge, 1958.

Weinandy, Thomas. *The Father's Spirit of Sonship: Reconceiving the Trinity.* Eugene, OR: Wipf and Stock, 1995.

Wikipedia. "English Versions of the Nicene Creed." Wikipedia, last edited Sept. 14, 2025. https://en.wikipedia.org/wiki/English_versions_of_the_Nicene_Creed.

William of Ockham. *Opera Philosophica*. Edited by Juvenal Lalor et al. 7 vols. St. Bonaventure, NY: Franciscan Institute, 1974–88.

———. *Opera Theologiae*. Edited by R. F. Brown et al. 10 vols. St. Bonaventure, NY: Franciscan Institute, 1967–79.

Williams, Rowan. "Deflection of Desire: Negative Theology in Trinitarian Discourse." In *Silence and the Word: Negative Theology and Incarnation*, edited by Oliver Davies and Denys Turner, 115–35. Cambridge: Cambridge University Press, 2002.

———. Foreword to *Theses Towards a Trinitarian Ontology*, by Klaus Hemmerle. Translated by Stephen Churchyard. Brooklyn, NY: Angelico, 2020.

———. "A True Otherness." *Political Theology* 22 (2021) 393–97. https://doi.org/10.1080/1462317X.2021.1955574.

Wolfe, Judith. "Eschatology and Human Knowledge of God." In *Within the Love of God: Essays on the Doctrine of God in Honour of Paul S. Fiddes*, edited by Anthony Clarke and Andrew Moore, 157–65. Oxford: Oxford University Press, 2014.

———. *Heidegger and Theology*. Philosophy and Theology. London: Bloomsbury, 2014.

———. *Heidegger's Eschatology: Theological Horizons in Martin Heidegger's Early Thought*. Oxford Theology and Religion Monographs. Oxford: Oxford University Press, 2013.

———. *The Theological Imagination: Perception and Interpretation in Life, Art, and Faith*. Current Issues in Theology. Cambridge: Cambridge University Press, 2023.

Wood, Jordan Daniel. *The Whole Mystery of Christ: Creation as Incarnation in Maximus Confessor*. Notre Dame: University of Notre Dame Press, 2022.

Wu, Abraham. "'Looking Again at the Tangled Web': The Dynamics of Interiority and Its Moral Significance in St. Augustine and Iris Murdoch." Presentation at the European Academy of Religion annual conference, St. Andrews, Scot., June 2023.

Zagzebski, Linda Trinkaus. *Epistemic Authority: A Theory of Trust, Authority, and Autonomy in Belief*. Oxford: Oxford University Press, 2012.

Žak, Lubomir. "Unità di Dio: Quaestio princeps dell'ontologia trinitaria." *PATH* 11 (2012) 439–64.

———. "Verso una ontologia trinitaria." In *Abitando la Trinità: Per un rinnovamento dell'ontologia*, edited by Piero Coda and Lubomir Žak, 5–25. Rome: Città Nuova, 1998.

Žižek, Slavoj. *The Sublime Object of Ideology*. Essential Žižek. London: Verso, 1989.

Zizioulas, John D. *Being as Communion: Studies in Personhood and the Church*. Contemporary Greek Theologians Series 4. Crestwood, NY: St. Vladimir's Seminary Press, 1985.

———. *Communion & Otherness: Further Studies in Personhood and the Church*. Edited by Paul McPartlan. T&T Clark: London, 2006.

Index

Adam, 10, 34, 123, 296
aesthetics, 15, 83, 125, 159, 166, 216, 225–38, 259–65, 273, 288
analogy, 11, 17, 75–77, 79, 81, 87–88, 164–65, 181, 189, 266, 272, 274–76, 278–80, 282–86, 295–97
analogy of being, 11, 75–76, 81, 83, 85–88, 137, 176, 274, 285
anamnesis, 16, 205, 260
Anselm of Canterbury, 7, 26, 44, 170, 196
apophatic theology (negative theology), 15, 42–43, 45, 54, 74, 76, 83, 188, 190, 198, 219–20, 222, 228, 237, 274, 288
Aquinas, Thomas, 5, 7, 26, 41, 43–47, 53, 63, 76–77, 84, 99, 103, 180, 194–95, 205, 207–8, 288
　Summa Theologica, 44–46, 103, 194–95, 207–8, 258, 288
　Thomism, 43–46, 48, 74, 76, 79, 83, 85–86, 166, 295
Aristotle, 7, 9, 26, 35–36, 40, 43, 45, 65, 74, 83, 99, 109–10, 112, 143, 159, 164, 208, 213–14
Athanasius of Alexandria, 38–39, 57
Augustine of Hippo, 7, 9, 25, 45, 67, 79, 120, 149, 168, 178, 205, 245, 252, 257, 288

Badiou, Alain, 7, 82, 96, 131–32, 138, 141, 148, 177
Balthasar, Hans Urs von, 7–8, 15, 27–28, 48–51, 54, 88, 95, 195, 224–25, 228–30, 232, 234–41
Beauty, 16, 25, 59, 84, 168, 225–26, 228–29, 239–40, 256, 259–60, 262, 264–65, 267, 272–74, 288, 293
Bergson, Henri, 7, 97, 147, 157, 258, 261, 270, 272–73
Bonaventure, 5, 7, 26, 205
Bouteneff, Peter, 281–85
Bulgakov, Sergii, 7, 13, 28, 125, 133–34, 140–47, 150, 156–58, 163, 168, 172, 179

Christ, 4, 8, 12, 13, 16, 24, 26–32, 34, 42–44, 50–51, 54, 55–61, 63, 66, 87–91, 95–104, 123–24, 126, 144, 168–73, 177–79, 183, 192, 194, 196–97, 199, 207–8, 235, 245–46, 249–58, 261, 275–76, 277–80, 284–86, 296, 301, 306–7, 309–10, 312–16
Coda, Piero, 10, 21, 33, 42, 56

Daniélou, Jean, 46, 48–50, 54
Dante Alighieri, 26, 120, 296–97, 300–301, 303, 305–6, 312–17
De Lubac, Henri, 5, 28, 204, 206

deconstruction, 3, 6, 146–47, 210, 294
Deleuze, Gilles, 82, 92, 141, 148, 152, 155, 167, 174, 257–58, 261, 265, 268, 270, 272, 279
Derrida, Jacques, 4, 7, 92, 147, 153–54, 166, 174, 176, 252, 294
Desmond, William, 11–13, 67, 107, 115, 117, 120–23, 137, 158–62, 171–72, 198
    metaxological, 11–12, 67, 107–17, 120–23, 158–62
dialectic, 6, 16, 17, 27, 34, 36–37, 44, 48–50, 52, 75, 81, 107–8, 113–17, 120–22, 128, 130, 136, 138, 140, 159, 162, 164, 176, 178, 235, 257–61, 264, 276, 280–86, 282, 284, 292–93
Dionysius the Areopagite (Pseudo-Dionysius), 7, 25, 74, 76, 81, 142, 158, 164, 166, 189

ecstasy, 11, 73, 77, 89, 90, 226–28, 269
ecology, 9, 13, 23, 123, 187–92
eschatology, 14, 82, 121, 203, 207–8, 235, 240, 246

faith, 1–3, 8–9, 11, 14, 18, 26–28, 52, 57–58, 65, 77, 80, 83, 93–94, 97, 104–5, 128, 136, 141, 146, 148, 193–98, 249, 252–53, 256, 277, 285–86, 313–14
Falque, Emmanuel, 11–12, 92–93, 98–104, 127

gift, 4, 6–11, 13, 15–18, 22–23, 25, 27, 29–32, 42, 44, 50, 56–57, 59, 75–77, 84, 87, 90, 94, 97, 114, 118–19, 144, 170, 175, 183, 196–99, 203, 206, 228, 240–41, 251, 258, 260, 295, 299–300, 311, 313–14

Hegel, G. W. F., 6, 8, 12–13, 16, 26, 48, 63, 67, 77–78, 81–82, 84, 108–13, 115–22, 127, 129–30, 132–33, 135, 137–39, 140, 143, 152, 176, 178, 180, 181, 204, 212, 251, 257, 259–60

Heidegger, Martin, 4, 6, 7–8, 11–12, 14–15, 27, 35, 49, 73–77, 82–85, 90, 130–32, 137–39, 141, 143–45, 148, 151, 153–56, 160, 167, 174, 178, 203–4, 207, 209–24,
    kehre, 6, 15, 75, 85, 209–11, 215, 218–19, 222
Hemmerle, Klaus, 8, 29, 31–32, 93–95, 105
Hölderlin, Friedrich, 15, 143, 179, 209–10, 215–19, 221–22
Husserl, Edmund, 6, 8, 12, 75, 82, 100, 102, 132

immanence, 5, 27, 39–42, 48, 50–51, 54–56, 76, 78, 82, 85, 90, 108–9, 113, 115, 117, 122, 128, 140, 203, 225, 227, 229, 235, 253
incarnation, 12, 17–18, 24, 27, 38, 45, 50, 57, 59, 60–61, 63, 65, 101–2, 123, 135, 142, 150–51, 162, 171–72, 175, 179, 250, 257–58, 276–78, 284–86, 296, 303
Irenaeus of Lyons, 25, 102

kairos, 16, 50, 247–54
Kant, Immanuel, 5–6, 8, 27, 79–80, 97, 125, 127, 130–31, 136, 149, 152, 156–57, 174, 181, 203–4, 211–12, 227, 229, 231, 240
kenosis, 24, 76, 84, 92, 94–95, 258
Kierkegaard, Søren, 7, 16, 27, 82, 203, 235, 259–60, 262, 264–65, 269, 272–74, 300

liturgy, 13, 97, 149, 158, 163, 183, 206–7, 254, 259, 274, 308
logic, 1–3, 5–7, 12, 27, 29, 49, 78, 81, 83, 108, 110, 112–14, 116, 118–19, 130, 133, 135–37, 140, 142, 146–48, 152, 158–59, 164–65, 169, 171–74, 179, 181–82, 194, 206, 212, 226, 257, 299
logos, 3–4, 10, 24, 35–44, 54, 61, 63, 77, 82, 86, 88–89, 91, 109, 116–17, 123, 137, 144, 171–73, 182, 195, 216, 250, 253–54, 275, 285, 311

Love, 2, 10, 12–13, 16, 25, 31–32, 37, 51, 55, 57–59, 61, 66–69, 77, 84, 89–91, 98–99, 105, 116–23, 135, 145–46, 164, 168, 173, 177, 179, 182–83, 188–89, 195–99, 207–8, 234–36, 241, 247, 250, 263–64, 269–70, 272, 289, 297, 307–10, 315, 317
   agapeic, 12, 113–23, 159, 161
   erotic 116, 118, 123, 161, 236, 263–64

Marion, Jean-Luc, 73, 89, 96–97, 104, 127, 199, 205, 294
Maspero, Giulio, 10–11, 21, 33, 36, 41–43, 54
Maximus the Confessor, 7, 25, 63–64, 91
Messiaen, Olivier, 17, 275–86
metaphysics, 1, 2, 5, 57, 73, 107, 125 187
Milbank, John, 10–12, 17, 57–58, 61–62, 64, 66–67, 126–28, 130, 136, 139–40, 142, 145, 148–49, 155, 158, 163–65, 168–72, 175, 178, 180, 183, 206, 262, 294–95, 297, 300
modernity, 15, 25, 26–27, 48, 52, 87, 110, 129–31, 146, 153–54, 210, 224, 230, 235
   postmodernity 2–3, 8, 29, 52, 54, 56, 87, 146, 151, 153, 163, 168–70, 180
monism, 115, 120, 177
Moulin, Isabelle, 16, 256–57, 274
mystical theology, 7, 164, 188–89, 191

Nabokov, Vladimir, 17, 287–302
new materialism, 7
Nietzsche, Friedrich, 5, 15, 27, 48, 52, 85, 90, 96–98, 101, 131, 139, 143, 145, 149, 153–54, 178, 211, 218, 222, 224–41, 258
nihilism, 3, 6–7, 11–12, 27–28, 69, 90, 97, 154, 225–27, 229–31, 233, 237, 239, 246
non-identical repetition 4, 17, 172, 174, 182, 247, 259, 294–97, 300

ontotheology, 1–2, 6, 14–15, 73–74, 125, 209–11, 213–16
Origen of Alexandria, 4, 7, 38–39, 288, 296–97

participation (methexis), 2, 14–15, 18, 30, 32, 37, 55, 67, 69, 144, 157, 167, 172, 193–99, 203, 206–8, 240–41, 275, 280, 286, 297, 316
Paul of Tarsus (Saint Paul), 4, 7, 58–59, 60, 67, 97–98, 141, 158, 161, 179, 208, 245, 248–49, 250, 252–53
perichoresis, 25, 32, 68, 120, 158, 181, 196, 241, 262
phenomenology, 6, 9, 11, 22, 92–105, 127, 129–30, 132, 138, 150, 162, 167, 203–7, 239
philosophy, 1–6, 9, 21, 33, 57, 73, 92, 107, 125, 187, 193, 203, 209, 224, 245, 256, 275, 287, 303, 319
Pickstock, Catherine, 10, 16–17, 128, 140, 145, 149, 153, 156–57, 162–63, 165–68, 170, 176, 179–81, 195–96, 198–99, 206, 259, 279, 294–300, 315
Plato, 2–3, 8, 26, 31, 35–39, 74, 83–85, 110, 128–32, 141, 144–45, 148, 153, 161, 174, 199, 213–14, 231, 260
Plotinus, 4, 26, 41, 64, 110, 139
poetics, 1, 5–6, 9, 13, 16–17, 128, 131, 134, 139, 145, 148–49, 151–52, 159, 164, 170, 172, 174, 178, 181–82, 209, 215–16, 218–19, 222–23, 230, 233–34, 295, 299, 303, 305, 313, 315–17.
Proust, Marcel, 259, 265–66, 268–73
Przywara, Erich, 28, 76, 78, 81–83, 85–86, 88, 128, 137, 158, 176
Pärt, Arvo, 17, 275–76, 280–286

Radical Orthodoxy, 8, 15, 125, 128, 140, 162, 167, 174, 179, 206
Rahner, Karl, 27–28, 51, 76, 95, 204–5

relational ontology, 11, 33, 47, 50, 52–54
ressourcement, 15, 34, 126, 206
Rorty, Richard, 7, 140
Rosmini, Antonio, 7, 29, 47–48, 67

Schelling, F. W. J., 6, 26–27, 62, 67, 78–79, 110, 116, 133, 143, 152, 154, 175
schesis (relation), 8, 40
Scotus, John Duns, 7, 26, 127–28, 140, 149–50, 160, 174
Sophia (Divine Wisdom), 21, 64, 142, 147, 157–58, 163–64, 166, 168–69, 172, 178–79, 181–82

theology, 1–9, 11–18, 21–22, 26–30, 33–34, 38 -39, 42–54, 56, 62, 73–78, 80–85, 87, 89–90, 97, 99, 101–5, 107–8, 112, 116, 119, 126, 128, 133–37, 139–41, 148–53, 155–56, 164, 166, 168–72, 178, 183, 187–92, 194–95, 197–99, 204–5, 207–16, 220, 222–25, 228, 237–41, 250, 256–59, 272–74, 276–80, 282, 282, 285–88, 294–95, 305, 312
theosophy, 29, 47, 60
tragedy, 15, 22, 28, 141–43, 145, 157, 217, 225–35, 237–40, 307

Trinity, 1–14, 16, 18 21, 24–60, 62–69, 73, 77–78, 82–84, 89–90, 92–93, 95–96, 102, 104–5, 107–10, 112–23, 125–26, 133–35, 140–46, 148–51, 153, 156, 158, 162–64, 168, 170–83, 187–96, 198–99, 206–7, 209, 213, 222–25, 237, 239–41, 247–48, 253, 256–59, 261–62, 265, 273–74, 287–88, 294–97, 300–301, 303, 305, 308–11, 315–17
  immanent and economic Trinity, 12, 115, 120–21, 123
Trinitarian Ontology, 1–12, 15, 17, 21, 29–31, 33–34, 36, 38, 41, 43, 45–47, 49, 51–52, 54, 56, 64–65, 67, 82–84, 89–90, 93–95, 102, 104–5, 108, 125, 140, 192, 207, 209, 222–25, 237, 240–41, 248, 261, 265, 274, 287, 294, 296, 301

univocity, 5, 11, 15, 75, 77, 79, 81–82, 87, 107–8, 110, 113–17, 121, 128, 159–60, 165, 206, 258, 274

Ward, Graham, 16
Wittgenstein, Ludwig, 6, 139
Wolfe, Judith, 14, 82, 207

www.ingramcontent.com/pod-product-compliance
Lightning Source LLC
Chambersburg PA
CBHW032013300426
44117CB00008B/1008

9 781666 768114